THE CAMBRIDGE COMPANION TO
THE BOOK OF ISAIAH

Few writings have shaped the world as much as the book of Isaiah. Its lyricism, imagery, theology, and ethics are all deeply ingrained into us, and into Jewish and Christian culture more generally. It has been a cultural touchstone from the time when it was formed, and it influenced later biblical authors as well. The book of Isaiah is also a complex work of literature, dense with poetry, rhetoric, and theology, and richly intertwined with ancient history. For all these reasons, it is a challenge to read well. *The Cambridge Companion to Isaiah* serves as an up-to-date and reliable guide to this biblical book. Including diverse perspectives from leading scholars all over the world, it approaches Isaiah from a wide range of methodological approaches. It also introduces the worlds in which the book was produced, the way it was formed, and the impacts it has had on contemporary and later audiences in an accessible way.

Christopher B. Hays is the D. Wilson Moore Professor of Old Testament and Ancient Near Eastern Studies at Fuller Theological Seminary and a research associate of the University of Pretoria (South Africa). He is the author of *The Origins of Isaiah 24–27* (Cambridge University Press, 2019) and *Death in the Iron Age II and in First Isaiah* (2011), and coauthor of *Isaiah: A Paradigmatic Prophet and His Interpreters* (2022). He co-translated Isaiah for the Common English Bible.

Frontispiece A seal impression from 2009 excavations in the
Jerusalem Ophel. Source: Reese Zoellner/Armstrong Institute
of Biblical Archaeology

The impression, or bulla, shown in the frontispiece is incomplete, but it bears
the given name Isaiah (ישׁעיה[ו]) in the top register; the second register was understood by the excavator Eilat Mazar to read [נב[יא, "prophet."[1] Because the bulla can
be dated both stratigraphically and epigraphically to the end of the eighth century,
it was interpreted as being an impression of the seal of Isaiah ben Amoz himself.
It was found just a few feet from a bulla of Hezekiah, with whom the prophet is
closely linked in 2 Kgs 19–20||Isa 37–39, and Isaiah is quoted as saying, "Bind up
the testimony, seal the teaching among my disciples" (8:16), which implies the
use of just such a seal.

Although the find was part of a scientific excavation, and its authenticity is
not in question, doubts have been raised about its interpretation. The restoration of the word "prophet" can be questioned, and there are some uncommon
features in the form and content of the proposed seal. Some of these concerns
have already begun to be addressed as the conversation has unfolded,[2] but it is

[1]   Eilat Mazar, *The Ophel Excavations to the South of the Temple Mount, 2009–2013: Final
      Reports 1* (Jerusalem: Shoham Academic Research and Publication, 2015), 175–186.
[2]   William Schniedewind, "The Isaiah Bulla, Jeremiah the Priest/Prophet, and
      Reinterpreting the Prophet (Nbyʾ) in the Persian Scribal Community," in *Jewish
      Culture and Creativity: Essays in Honor of Michael Fishbane on the Occasion of His
      Eightieth Birthday*, ed. Eitan P. Fishbane and Elisha Russ-Fishbane. Boston: Academic
      Studies Press, 2023), 36–52.

possible that not even the discovery of a complete bulla or the seal itself would fully resolve the matter.[3]

In the end, I have selected this image not because its significance is certain, but because it is evocative of the origins of the tradition that became the book of Isaiah.

3 Christopher A. Rollston, "The Yeša'yah[û] ("Isaiah") Bulla and the Putative Connection with the Biblical Prophet: A Case Study in Propospography and the Necessity of Methodological Caution," in Christopher A. Rollston, Susanna Garfein, and Neal H. Walls, eds., *Biblical and Ancient Near Eastern Studies in Honor of P. Kyle McCarter Jr.*, ANEM 27 (Atlanta: SBL Press, 2022), 409–426.

(continued after index)

THE CAMBRIDGE COMPANION TO

THE BOOK OF ISAIAH

Edited by

Christopher B. Hays
Fuller Theological Seminary

CAMBRIDGE
UNIVERSITY PRESS

Shaftesbury Road, Cambridge CB2 8EA, United Kingdom

One Liberty Plaza, 20th Floor, New York, NY 10006, USA

477 Williamstown Road, Port Melbourne, VIC 3207, Australia

314–321, 3rd Floor, Plot 3, Splendor Forum, Jasola District Centre,
New Delhi – 110025, India

103 Penang Road, #05–06/07, Visioncrest Commercial, Singapore 238467

Cambridge University Press is part of Cambridge University Press & Assessment,
a department of the University of Cambridge.

We share the University's mission to contribute to society through the pursuit of
education, learning and research at the highest international levels of excellence.

www.cambridge.org
Information on this title: www.cambridge.org/9781108471862

DOI: 10.1017/9781108692809

First published 2024

A catalogue record for this publication is available from the British Library

Library of Congress Cataloging-in-Publication Data
NAMES: Hays, Christopher Baird, 1973– author.
TITLE: The Cambridge companion to the book of Isaiah / edited by Christopher
Baird Hays, Fuller Theological Seminary, California.
DESCRIPTION: Cambridge ; New York, NY, USA : Cambridge University Press,
2024. | Series: Cambridge companions to religion | Includes bibliographical
references and index.
IDENTIFIERS: LCCN 2023039450 | ISBN 9781108471862 (Hardback) |
ISBN 9781108456784 (Paperback) | ISBN 9781108692809 (ebook)
SUBJECTS: LCSH: Bible. Isaiah – Study and teaching. | Bible. Isaiah – Criticism,
interpretation, etc.
CLASSIFICATION: LCC BS1515.52 .H389 2024 | DDC 224/.106–dc23/
eng/20231206
LC record available at https://lccn.loc.gov/2023039450

ISBN 978-1-108-47186-2 Hardback
ISBN 978-1-108-45678-4 Paperback

Contents

Notes on Contributors

Shawn Zelig Aster is Associate Professor in the Martin (Szusz) Department of Land of Israel Studies and Archaeology at Bar-Ilan University. He recently published *Reflections of Empire in Isaiah 1–39: Responses to Assyrian Ideology* (2017); and with Avraham Faust he co-edited *The Southern Levant Under Assyrian Domination* (2018).

Brennan Breed is Associate Professor of Old Testament at Columbia Theological Seminary and Theologian-in-Residence at First Presbyterian Church of Marietta, Georgia. He is author of *Nomadic Text: A Theory of Biblical Reception History* (2014) and provided reception-historical studies for Carol Newsom's Daniel commentary (2014).

Joshua Ezra Burns is Associate Professor in the Department of Theology at Marquette University and Associate Dean of Academic Affairs for the Klingler College of Arts and Sciences. He is the author of *The Christian Schism in Jewish History and Jewish Memory* (Cambridge University Press, 2016).

M. Daniel Carroll R. (Rodas) is Scripture Press Ministries Professor of Biblical Studies and Pedagogy at Wheaton College and Graduate School. He has written extensively on Old Testament ethics and immigration. He wrote the commentary on Amos for the New International Commentary on the Old Testament series (2020) and his latest book is *The Lord Roars: Recovering the Prophetic Voice for Today* (2022).

Michael J. Chan is the Executive Director for Faith and Learning at Concordia College. Prior to that, he was Associate Professor of Old Testament at Luther Seminary in St. Paul, Minnesota, and a postdoctoral researcher at the University of Helsinki. He is the author of *The Wealth of Nations: A Tradition-Historical Study* (2017) and numerous articles on Isaiah in its ancient Near Eastern environments.

J. Blake Couey is Professor of Religion at Gustavus Adolphus College in St. Peter, Minnesota. He is the author of *Reading the Poetry of First Isaiah: The Most Perfect Model of the Prophetic Poetry* (2015) and coeditor of *Biblical Poetry and the Art of Close Reading* (Cambridge University Press, 2018). His current research focuses on Isaiah and animal studies.

C. L. Crouch is Professor of Hebrew Bible/Old Testament and Ancient Judaism and Chair of the Department of Textual, Historical and Systematic Studies of

Judaism and Christianity at Radboud University (Nijmegen, Netherlands). She is also a research associate of the University of Pretoria (South Africa) and the coauthor of *Isaiah: A Paradigmatic Prophet and His Interpreters* (2022), as well as numerous other books and articles about the Hebrew prophets.

Christopher B. Hays is D. Wilson Moore Professor of Old Testament and Ancient Near Eastern Studies at Fuller Theological Seminary and a research associate of the University of Pretoria. He is the author of *The Origins of Isaiah 24–27* (Cambridge University Press, 2019) and *Death in the Iron Age II and in First Isaiah* (2011), and coauthor of *Isaiah: A Paradigmatic Prophet and His Interpreters* (2022). He co-translated Isaiah for the Common English Bible.

J. Todd Hibbard is Professor and Chair of the Department of Religious Studies at the University of Detroit Mercy. He is the author of *Intertextuality in Isaiah 24–27: The Reuse and Evocation of Earlier Texts and Traditions* (2006). With Jacob Stromberg, he coedited *The History of Isaiah* (2022) and is currently working on a commentary on Isaiah.

Jesper Høgenhaven is Professor of the Old Testament at the University of Copenhagen. He wrote his doctoral thesis on the book of Isaiah (*Gott und Volk bei Jesaja*, 1988) and has published extensively on a number of Old Testament topics, including prophetic writings and wisdom literature, and, in particular, the Dead Sea Scrolls and apocalypticism. His most recent monograph is *The Cave 3 Copper Scroll: A Symbolic Journey* (2020).

Hyun Chul Paul Kim is Harold B. Williams Professor of Hebrew Bible at the Methodist Theological School in Ohio. His publications include *Reading Isaiah: A Literary and Theological Commentary* (2016); *You Are My People: An Introduction to Prophetic Literature* (coauthored with Louis Stulman; 2010); *Second Wave Intertextuality and the Hebrew Bible* (coedited with Marianne Grohmann; 2019); and *Formation and Intertextuality in Isaiah 24–27* (coedited with J. Todd Hibbard; 2013).

Hanne Løland Levinson is Associate Professor in the Department of Classical and Near Eastern Religions and Cultures at the University of Minnesota. Her first book, *Silent or Salient Gender?: The Interpretation of Gendered God-Language in the Hebrew Bible* (2008), received the John Templeton Award for Theological Promise. She is also the author of *The Death Wish in the Hebrew Bible* (Cambridge University Press, 2021). She is currently working on the use of the Bible in contemporary dystopian novels. She cofounded the SBL program unit on metaphor theory and the Hebrew Bible.

David W. Pao is Academic Dean and Professor of New Testament at Trinity Evangelical Divinity School. Among his publications are *Acts and the Isaianic New Exodus* (2000), *Thanksgiving: An Investigation of a Pauline Theme* (2002), *Commentary on Colossians and Philemon* (2012), and *1–2 Timothy, Titus*. Brill Exegetical Commentary Series (2023).

Matthew R. Schlimm is Professor of Old Testament at the University of Dubuque Theological Seminary. His work includes *This Strange and Sacred Scripture: Wrestling with the Old Testament and Its Oddities* (Baker Academic, 2015). His expertise is in the areas of biblical theology, ethics, and emotion.

Lucas L. Schulte is the author of *My Shepherd, Though You Do Not Know Me: The Persian Royal Propaganda Model in the Nehemiah Memoir* (2016). He is a research fellow of the Harris Center for Judaic Studies at the University of Nebraska and Program Associate for the Tri-Faith Initiative in Omaha, Nebraska. He cofounded and cochaired Claremont's annual Religions in Conversation Conference and has excavated at Ramat Rahel and Tel Akko. He has taught at the University of Nebraska–Lincoln, Claremont School of Theology, and Pomona College, among others.

Jonathan Stökl is Assistant Professor in Hebrew and Aramaic at Leiden University's Institute for Area Studies and was formerly Reader in Hebrew Bible/Old Testament at King's College London. He is the author of *Prophecy in the Ancient Near East: A Philological and Sociological Comparison* (2012) and coeditor of *Prophets Male and Female: Gender and Prophecy in the Hebrew Bible, the Eastern Mediterranean, and the Ancient Near East* (2013). His research focuses on the language and culture of ancient Israel and Judah in the context of the Middle East in antiquity, with special attention to religious institutions such as the priesthood and prophecy.

Marvin A. Sweeney is Professor of Hebrew Bible at Claremont School of Theology and serves on the faculty of Religion at Claremont Graduate University. His books include *Isaiah 1–39* and *Isaiah 40–66* in the Forms of the Old Testament Literature series (1996 and 2016); *Reading Prophetic Books* (FAT 89; 2014); *The Prophetic Literature: Interpreting Biblical Texts* (2005); and *Isaiah 1–4 and the Post-Exilic Understanding of the Isaianic Tradition* (BZAW 171; 1988).

Lena-Sofia Tiemeyer is Professor of Old Testament Exegesis at Örebro School of Theology, Sweden, and Research Associate at the Department of Old Testament and Hebrew Scriptures, Faculty of Theology and Religion, University of Pretoria. She has worked extensively on biblical prophecy, with two monographs on Isaiah: *Priestly Rites and Prophetic Rage: Post-Exilic Prophetic Critique of the Priesthood* (2006) and *For the Comfort of Zion: The Geographical and Theological Location of Isaiah 40–55* (2011). She also edited the *Oxford Handbook of Isaiah* (2020).

Ronald L. Troxel is Professor Emeritus at the University of Wisconsin–Madison, where he taught courses in the Hebrew Bible, Hellenistic Judaism, and early Christian literature. Many of his publications addressed issues in textual criticism, especially *LXX-Isaiah as Translation and Interpretation* (2008) and *A Commentary on the Old Greek and Peshiṭta of Isaiah 1–25* (2021).

Acknowledgments

The planning for this volume began in 2018. Not long after, the COVID-19 pandemic hit, and many people's lives (including their publication plans) were thrown into disarray. Nevertheless, every one of the contributors came through, and I am deeply grateful to them. For all of us who have been anticipating this volume, the wait was well worth it.

Special thanks are due to Timothy Graham for his timely editing of the manuscript, to A. J. Fletcher for compiling the indices, and to Beatrice Rehl, Nicola Maclean, Santhamurthy Ramamoorthy, and all those associated with Cambridge University Press who supported us all throughout the process.

Timeline of Events Related to the Book of Isaiah

At the end of the Late Bronze Age, the great powers that had dominated the Near East – notably the Hittite Empire in the north and the Egyptian New Kingdom in the south – had collapsed or largely withdrawn from the western shores of the Mediterranean Sea. Thus in the early first millennium (1000–800 BCE), the Levant was a collection of small kingdoms still emerging within a complex matrix of cultural connections. These included Israel, Judah, Moab, Aram, and Philistia. Without the burden of an imperial overlord or tribute payments, many of these experienced a period of relative prosperity, especially in the eighth century.

Isaiah ben Amoz began to prophesy in the second half of the eighth century, when Mesopotamian imperialism began to make itself felt: The Neo-Assyrian Empire, which would go on to conquer the entire region, was already on the rise to the northeast. The superscript of the book (Isa 1:1) dates the prophet's career to the reigns of four kings of Judah: Uzziah (r. 783–742), Jotham (r. 742–735), Ahaz (r. 735–715), and Hezekiah (r. 715–687). The book's formation continued, however, notably under Josiah (r. 640–609) and into the Persian Period after the Babylonian Exile; it even names Cyrus the Great, one of the architects of the Achaemenid Empire (44:28; 45:1). Still later layers of the book attest the building of the Second Temple (56:5; 66:6, 20). The earliest surviving witnesses to the text of Isaiah are from the second century BCE.

750 BCE

745: Tiglath-pileser III becomes king in Assyria and begins westward expansion.

734–731: The "Syro-Ephraimite Crisis": The northern kingdom of Israel and its Syrian allies try to force Judah to join a coalition against Assyria, but Judah resists and sides with the empire (Isa 7, etc.).

722: Israel rebels against Assyria, prompting the Assyrians to besiege Samaria. The city is defeated and much of its population deported. Israel is broken up into Assyrian provinces. Deportees are sent from elsewhere in the empire are to repopulate the region (2 Kgs 17).

714–712: Assyrian conquest of Ashdod (Isa 20).

705: Sargon II of Assyria dies and Judah rebels, led by King Hezekiah (2 Kgs 18:7).

701: The new Assyrian king, Sennacherib, attacks Judah and gains its resubmission, but does not destroy Jerusalem (2 Kgs 18:13–16; Isa 36–37, etc.).

700 BCE

First half of the seventh century: Judah, under Hezekiah and Manasseh, is a client state of the Assyrian empire.

650 BCE

631(?): Aššurbanipal of Assyria dies; a series of short reigns follow.

620s: Assyrian power begins to weaken; rebellions break out across the empire. Josiah begins to assert greater religio-political independence in Judah.

612: Babylonia succeeds Assyria as the dominant power in Mesopotamia. Babylonia and Egypt fight for control of the Levant; Judah vacillates between the two (2 Kgs 24).

609: Josiah killed by Pharaoh Necho in Megiddo (2 Kgs 23:29).

600 BCE

597: Judah rebels while a Babylonia vassal; Nebuchadnezzar lays siege to Jerusalem and defeats it, deporting the royal family and the king (Jehoiachin) to Babylon and installing Zedekiah as king (2 Kgs 24:13–17).

587: Judah rebels again; Nebuchadnezzar besieges Jerusalem for a second time, destroys the city, and orders further deportations (2 Kgs 24:18–25:21).

550 BCE

500 BCE

200 BCE

586–536: Many Judean elites taken to exile in Babylonia; part of the population remains in Judah; Jerusalem and the Temple are not rebuilt.

539: The Persians, led by Cyrus, defeat the Babylonians and take over and expand their empire (Isa 44–45).
536: The Edict of Cyrus allows Judeans and their descendants to return to their homelands; Judah is part of a Persian province (Ezra 1).
515(?): Rebuilding of the temple in Jerusalem, perhaps with Persian support.

Mid-fifth century: Missions of Ezra and Nehemiah from Babylonia to Jerusalem; regular correspondence between Jerusalem temple leadership and Egyptian diaspora communities such as Elephantine; increasing evidence of sectarian disputes within the community.

Early second century: Copying of the Great Isaiah Scroll from Qumran (1QIsa^a).
Ca. 135: Septuagint translation of Isaiah into Greek.

Abbreviations

AB	Anchor Bible
ABS	*Archaeology and Biblical Studies*
ANEM	Ancient Near East Monographs
AO	*Der Alte Orient*
ARM	Archives Royales de Mari
BAR	*Biblical Archaeology Review*
BBC	Blackwell Bible Commentaries
BBRSup	*Bulletin for Biblical Research*, Supplements
BETL	Bibliotheca Ephemeridum Theologicarum Lovaniensium
BHS	*Biblia Hebraica Stuttgartensia*, edited by Karl Elliger and Wilhelm Rudolph. Stuttgart: Deutsche Bibelgesellschaft, 1983
Bib	*Biblica*
BibleInt	The Bible and its Interpretation
BIOSCS	*Bulletin of the International Organization for Septuagint and Cognate Studies*
BLS	Bible and Literature Series
BWA(N)T	Beiträge zur Wissenschaft vom Alten (und Neuen) Testament
BZABR	Beihefte zur Zeitschrift für altorientalische und biblische Rechtsgeschichte
BZAW	Beihefte zur Zeitschrift für die alttestamentliche Wissenschaft
CAD	*The Assyrian Dictionary of the Oriental Institute of the University of Chicago.* Chicago: The Oriental Institute of the University of Chicago, 1956–2006.
CBET	Contributions to Biblical Exegesis and Theology
CBQ	*Catholic Biblical Quarterly*
CD	Cairo Damascus Document
CEB	Common English Bible

ConBOT	Coniectanea Biblica: Old Testament Series
COS	*The Context of Scripture.* Edited by William W. Hallo. 3 vols. Leiden: Brill, 1997–2002.
CurTM	*Currents in Theology and Mission*
DSD	Dead Sea Discoveries
EB	Echter Bibel
EBR	*Encyclopedia of the Bible and Its Reception.* Berlin: Walter de Gruyter, 2009–
ETL	*Ephemerides Theologicae Lovanienses*
FAT	Forschungen zum Alten Testament
FLP	Museum siglum, Free Library of Philadelphia
FM	Florilegium Marianum
FOTL	Forms of the Old Testament Literature
FRLANT	Forschungen zur Religion und Literatur des Alten und Neuen Testaments
HBAI	*Hebrew Bible and Ancient Israel*
HBM	Hebrew Bible Monographs
HBT	*Horizons in Biblical Theology*
HCOT	Historical Commentary on the Old Testament
HSM	Harvard Semitic Monographs
HThKAT	Herders Theologischer Kommentar zum Alten Testament
HTR	*Harvard Theological Review*
HUCA	*Hebrew Union College Annual*
ICC	International Critical Commentary
Int	*Interpretation*
IOS	*Israel Oriental Studies*
JAOS	*Journal of the American Oriental Society*
JBL	*Journal of Biblical Literature*
JJS	*Journal of Jewish Studies*
JSJSupp	*Journal for the Study of Judaism in the Persian, Hellenistic and Roman Period,* Supplements
JSNT	*Journal for the Study of the New Testament*
JSOT	*Journal for the Study of the Old Testament*
JSOTSup	Journal for the Study of the Old Testament, Supplement Series
JSS	*Journal of Semitic Studies*
KAI	*Kanaanäische und aramäische Inschriften.* Herbert Donner and Wolfgang Röllig. 2nd ed. Wiesbaden: Harrassowitz, 1966–1969.
KD	*Kerygma und Dogma*

KTU³	M. Dietrich et al. (eds.), *The Cuneiform Alphabetic Texts from Ugarit, Ras Ibn Hani and Other Places* (Abhandlungen zur Literatur Alt-Syrien-Palästinas, 8; Münster: Ugarit-Verlag, 3rd ed., 2013)
LHBOTS	The Library of Hebrew Bible/Old Testament Studies
LNTS	Library of New Testament Studies
NJPS	New Jewish Publication Society
NovTSup	Novum Testament, Supplements
NRSV	New Revised Standard Version
NTDH	Neukirchener Theologische Dissertationen und Habilitationen, Neukirchen-Vluyn
OBT	*Overtures to Biblical Theology*
OTE	*Old Testament Essays*
OTL	Old Testament Library
OTRM	Oxford Theology and Religion Monographs
RA	*Revue d'assyriologie et d'archéologie orientale*
RC	*Religion Compass*
RevQ	*Revue de Qumran*
RevScRel	*Revue des sciences religieuses*
RIMA	The Royal Inscriptions of Mesopotamia, Assyrian Periods
RIME	The Royal Inscriptions of Mesopotamia, Early Periods
RINAP	Royal Inscriptions of the Neo-Assyrian Period
ROT	Reading the Old Testament
RS	Ras Shamra
SAAS	State Archives of Assyria
SBL	Society of Biblical Literature
SBLAIL	Society of Biblical Literature Ancient Israel and its Literature
SBLANEM	Society of Biblical Literature Ancient Near East Monographs
SBLDS	Society of Biblical Literature Dissertation Series
SBLSym	Society of Biblical Literature Symposium Series
SBS	Stuttgarter Bibelstudien
SemeiaSt	Semeia Studies
SHANE	Studies in the History of the Ancient Near East
SNTSMS	Society for New Testament Studies Monograph Series
SOTS	Society for Old Testament Study
SOTSMS	Society for Old Testament Study Monograph Series
STDJ	Studies on the Texts of the Desert of Judah

TDOT	G. J. Botterweck and H. Ringgren (eds.), *Theological Dictionary of the Old Testament.* Translated by J. T. Willis; 14 vols. Grand Rapids, MI: Eerdmans, 1974–1993
Them	*Themelios*
TSAJ	Texte und Studien zum antiken Judentum
UNHCR	United Nations High Commissioner for Refugees
VT	*Vetus Testamentum*
VTSup	Vetus Testamentum, Supplements
WMANT	Wissenschaftliche Monographien zum Alten und Neuen Testament
WO	*Die Welt des Orients*
WUNT	Wissenschaftliche Untersuchungen zum Neuen Testament
ZAW	*Zeitschrift für die alttestamentliche Wissenschaft*

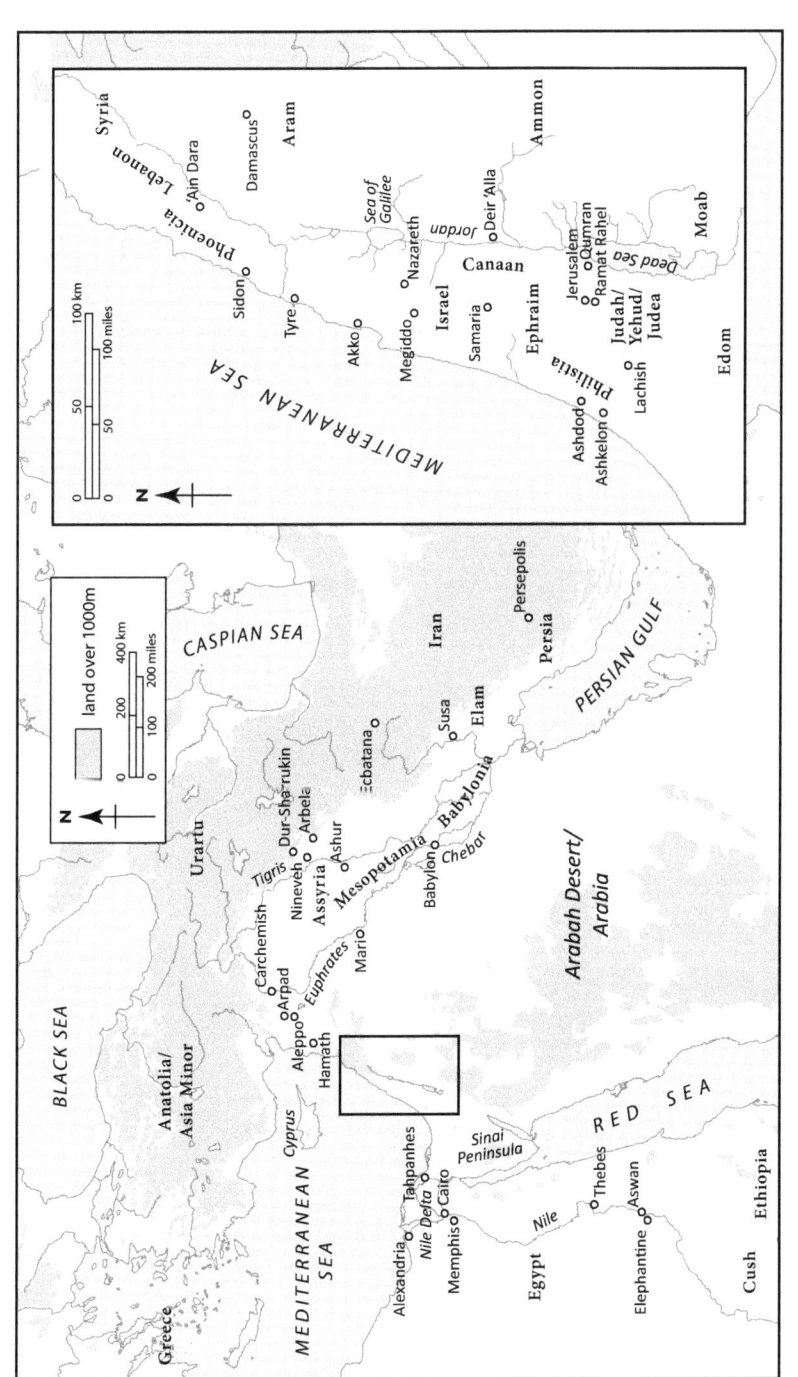

Figure 0.1 The Ancient Near East. Map by David McCutcheon FBCart.S www.dvdmaps.co.uk.

1 Introduction

CHRISTOPHER B. HAYS

Few writings have shaped the world as much as the book of Isaiah has – its lyricism, imagery, theology, and ethics are all deeply ingrained into us, and into our culture. From this standpoint, perhaps it needs no introduction.

The prophet Isaiah and the book in his name became paradigms in the biblical tradition relatively quickly. Other prophetic books were modeled on it in their processes of formation. In Jewish tradition, the Babylonian Talmud called Isaiah a lawgiver on the level of Moses (b. Mak. 24a), and about half the haftaroth readings in Jewish synagogue liturgy are drawn from Isaiah. In more recent times, the book has been considered one of the greatest works of literature ever produced, the founding document of widespread monotheism, and a taproot of the Christian Gospels. It merits ongoing attention for the impact it continues to have, and for the enduring mysteries it still contains.

Isaiah can also be overwhelming. It has connections to a huge span of history and intertextual links to a wide array of literature from across the ancient world, as well as much of the biblical canon. As such, reading it well demands knowledge of the history of the Bible itself and the numerous methods and approaches involved in studying it. Thus, from a different standpoint, Isaiah desperately needs introduction – a set of starting points from which one can begin to explore.

ABOUT THIS VOLUME

With any book, one should ask why it needs to exist: What is its purpose? Some would say that the genre of Companion or Handbook is a tired one. Often these are enormous compendia of essays from every imaginable angle, and are presumably most at home in reference libraries. There is much to be said for this approach – not least, the editor has the chance to employ all his or her friends and make some new ones. Part of me would have liked to produce such a volume, and is even jealous of those who have. From the start, however, I decided on a more concise approach to this volume, based on three motivations.

First, it seems to me that a Companion should be an introductory work – albeit an introduction intended for relatively engaged advanced readers. This Companion is built to accompany the student who is beginning to explore Isaiah more deeply, perhaps a student in a first exegesis course, or a scholar in an adjacent field. And so I exhorted the contributors to write for that audience, and not for the few dozen specialized scholars who have strong enough opinions about Isaiah to disagree on certain details. There are certainly fresh and creative ideas and perspectives represented here, but we have tried above all to keep the writing clean and clear, and the footnotes to a minimum.

Second, I teach the book of Isaiah, and I wanted a book that would be useful in my teaching. We work in a digital age in which even books nominally bound between two covers are regularly sliced up, sold, and read piecemeal. Access is easier than it ever was, and diverse readings can be pulled from numerous sources and posted on course websites. The goal of "comprehensiveness" in a handbook seemed less important when most professors and teachers prefer to assign readings from various sources anyway. This book is meant to serve as a basic and cost-effective foundation for whatever an instructor wants to add to it.

Third, I've grown wary of assigning commentaries. Partly this is because of the commentary genre itself and the current state of humanities education: Too often students do not know how to engage with a commentary critically, and so quote it as the absolute truth. In other cases, they find commentaries alienating, so they ignore them rather than disagreeing with them. And, of course, every biblical commentary is a monument to a certain time and place, and to the background of the scholar who wrote it. For all the erudition and interesting conversation among commentaries, I have not found one that serves my students especially well here and now. Admittedly, I'm preparing a commentary of my own so that I can join that dusty pantheon, but perhaps a more diverse group of voices will serve better in the classroom. This volume is designed to provide students with the basic information that interpreters can begin from: information about history, literature, themes, and theologies. Hopefully, it equips its readers to join the conversation.

Variety of perspective is valuable in itself, but in addition, every chapter of this volume is written by a scholar who would be recognized by anyone in the field of biblical studies as a leading expert in the area. They are also experienced teachers of the material. One could imagine the end product of their labors as an opportunity to attend a symposium on Isaiah by the very best team of lecturers imaginable.

ABOUT THE CHAPTERS

The opening section of the book is on the historical contexts of the book of Isaiah and its formation over time. The earliest texts in Isaiah were written more than 2,700 years ago, in the eighth century BCE, and other texts that make up the book continued to be written for approximately three centuries. The earliest *extant* manuscripts and translations of the book are centuries later still; they begin to be attested around the beginning of the second century BCE. No informed interpretation of the book can afford to ignore these data; they tell us when the book began to be written and the point by which it must have been completed. Investigations of the historical contexts of the composition and formation of the book have thus been one of the major interests of critical scholars.

In the early days of modern scholarship, there was a particular fascination with the prophets as historical figures – their personalities and the words they actually spoke. Whether this was based on a belief in direct verbal inspiration by God or because of a sense that they were religious geniuses, this orientation toward prophetic personalities often led to a sharp distinction between "authentic" utterances and everything else. This sometimes led to an impoverished appreciation of the multilayered nature of the book of Isaiah. Then again, in other corners of the field, scholars demonstrated excessive confidence in their ability to identify numerous stages of editing within single passages. Based on their presuppositions, they divided up texts into many redactional layers, without empirical models of the way scribes functioned in the ancient world. Therefore, while critical scholars generally agree on the broad contours of the book's formation, there is little consensus on various finer points.

A realistic historical approach to a prophetic book's formation takes account of both the possible complexity of the prophet's thought and also the realities of scribal production in the ancient world. An eighth-century BCE prophet such as Isaiah was not a writer – he may have occasionally scratched out a single phrase (8:1), but more generally he would have relied on the scribal skills of followers to record and transmit his messages (8:16); those early records, in turn, would have been recopied and recompiled in later periods. We can see this process concretely, albeit over a very short period of a few years, in contemporaneous Neo-Assyrian texts in which prophecies delivered in one historical situation were taken up again and applied to a new one.

In the case of Isaiah, it is clear that the process of formation continued over centuries. Not only are there explicit references to events and figures of the Persian Period in the book, but the later writings also look back on the Babylonian Exile, and are distinguishable from pre-exilic texts given the use of late features in their Hebrew language. In order to introduce all this, the volume begins with chapters on each of the major periods of Isaiah's formation.

In **"The Book of Isaiah in the Neo-Assyrian Period"** (Chapter 2), **Michael J. Chan** offers an overview of the centuries of Assyrian dominance in the Levant, and he takes five exegetical case studies, spanning the eighth and seventh centuries BCE, that demonstrate the historical and literary impact of that Mesopotamian power on the rest of the ancient Near East, as reflected in the writings of Isaiah and his successors. In particular, he observes how Assyrian imperial propaganda was subverted by the prophets in various ways.

Lena-Sofia Tiemeyer (**"The Book of Isaiah and the Neo-Babylonian Period,"** Chapter 3) investigates the "black hole" in the book that is the Babylonian Exile. She examines texts from all sections of the book and notes how the experience of suffering under Babylonian rule casts a shadow over them. At the same time, very little material in the book of Isaiah was composed during the Neo-Babylonian period, and nothing necessitates the conclusion that any of its authors and audience lived in Babylon.

Lucas L. Schulte takes on a large task in **"The Book of Isaiah in the Persian Period"** (Chapter 4), since this was a crucial time in the book's overall development. He shows how Persian emperors were able to enlist scribal elites in various subject nations and win their support. The well-known Cyrus Cylinder from Babylon may be the most prominent example, but Isa 40–66 also reflects its own interpretation of this international Persian Royal Propaganda Model. This chapter also shows how the later parts of the book of Isaiah interacted with religious and sociopolitical issues in the postexilic Persian province, comparing and contrasting it with the viewpoints of Ezra and Nehemiah in particular.

The textual transmission of the book of Isaiah was relatively stable. The structure of the book in the Hebrew Masoretic Text, based on Jewish manuscripts from about 1000 CE, is common to all the major ancient witnesses and translations. This is a very different situation from other prophetic books, such as Jeremiah, which is much shorter and arranged differently in the Greek Septuagint and the Hebrew text; or Ezekiel, which had at least three variant editions in circulation in the Hellenistic and Roman periods. Isaiah's form was apparently fixed earlier than that of other prophetic books; this may reflect something about its perceived authority and date of "canonization." Despite the lack of variant editions, the earliest manuscripts of Isaiah and the translated Versions still preserve numerous readings that diverge from the Masoretic Text, some of them certainly older. These other textual witnesses are the subject of the next two chapters.

Jesper Høgenhaven ("The Book of Isaiah at Qumran," Chapter 5) offers a concise overview of the texts related to Isaiah that were discovered among the Dead Sea Scrolls. The book's importance for the Qumran community is attested not only by the large number of copies that survived, but also by various other genres of sectarian literature that drew from and reflected on the book, including the pesher commentaries and even the Community Rule (1QS). The Great Isaiah Scroll (1QIsa^a) is the longest biblical scroll found at Qumran. It is both an important witness for reconstructing the oldest text of the book and subtly reflects some of the earliest interpretive decisions about it.

In **"Early Versions of Isaiah as Translations and Interpretations"** (Chapter 6), **Ronald L. Troxel** analyzes the Greek and Syriac translations that are among the earliest witnesses to the book. He shows that the translators didn't just offer equivalents to Hebrew words, but sometimes shaped their versions to accord with their faith communities' interpretations of the book. Such interpretive renderings can make it difficult to reconstruct the Hebrew text. The challenge facing textual critics is to discern whether the differences were the translators' own interpretation, or if they arose from different Hebrew words in the translator's manuscript. Troxel's chapter cites examples of these conundrums, and illustrates how scholars attempt to reason about their origins.

With these overviews of the history of the book and its textual traditions as background, **Marvin A. Sweeney ("The Formation of the Book of Isaiah,"** Chapter 7) analyzes the history of scholarship about the editorial processes that gave rise to the Hebrew text as we have it. As scholars have long done, he takes Bernhard Duhm's nineteenth-century commentary as a starting point, but then shows the myriad ways in which more recent scholars have challenged his presuppositions and greatly improved on his findings. In the process, he identifies many of the themes and features in the book that have led him and other interpreters to perceive a redactional shaping of the book in four major phases – broadly one per century in the eighth through fifth centuries BCE. Sweeney's most significant contributions to the study of Isaiah, reflected here, have been his demonstration of the Davidic covenant in the final form of the book and his refinement of our understanding of the Josianic layer from the late seventh century BCE.

Part II shifts to various approaches to understanding the book of Isaiah in its historical, cultural, and religious contexts. Isaiah reflects the surrounding world in many ways, and it also testifies to the ways its authors helped to shape that world.

Hebrew prophets such as Isaiah were not the only ones speaking words on behalf of the gods in the ancient Near East, nor was spoken prophecy the only form of divination practiced. **Jonathan Stökl ("Ancient Near Eastern Prophecy and the Study of Isaiah,"** Chapter 8) locates the book of Isaiah within this larger world of ancient prophecy and divination. Texts and accounts of prophecy from Syria and Mesopotamia shed light on the likely balance between oracles of comfort and judgment in the prophet's actual career and on the role of gender in prophecy. Stökl also scrutinizes the theory that collections of Assyrian prophecy provide empirical examples of how the earliest layers of the book might have been compiled from reports of Isaiah's own oracles.

Like religious leaders in any period, the prophets functioned within a religious world that was broader and more diverse than a surface reading might suggest. My own contribution (**"The Book of Isaiah in the History of Israelite Religion,"** Chapter 9) analyzes various religiohistorical aspects of the book, such as the role of writing and symbolic action; the supernatural images of the divine throne room; the book's role in developing ideas about death and afterlife; its central role in the formulation of biblical monotheism, including its polemics against idols; and its relationship to the Jerusalem Temple and its priests.

Religion and politics were thoroughly interwoven in the ancient world, and in **"Isaiah and Empire"** (Chapter 10), **Shawn Zelig Aster** considers how the authors of the book reacted to and against imperial propaganda. Focusing on the well-attested rhetoric of Neo-Assyrian kings, he shows through various specific case studies how their claims were contested in the early prophecies of the book. Isaiah is, in a very real sense, some of the earliest resistance literature in world history: The prophet and his tradents consistently sought to reorient the thinking of their audiences, to relativize and undermine the absolutizing boasts of the Neo-Assyrian Empire.

The book of Isaiah reflects many of the population movements that took place in the period of its formation. Much biblical scholarship focuses on *"the* (Babylonian) Exile," but as **C. L. Crouch ("Migration in the Book of Isaiah,"** Chapter 11) points out, mass population movements were carried out in the sphere of Israel and Judah by the Assyrians long before the Babylonians overthrew Jerusalem. She also calls attention to the migrations experienced by other nations, and to forces of displacement other than deportation, such as warfare, famine, and natural disasters. She analyzes the literary reception of these numerous involuntary migrations, and the ways in which the prophet and his audiences made sense of them.

Part III of the book turns to considering the book of Isaiah as literature. From the beating of swords into plowshares in chapter 2 to the soaring eagles' wings of chapter 40 to the new Jerusalem of chapter 65, Isaiah has been a touchstone for authors and artists ever since. The great literary critic and poet Matthew Arnold famously professed to have received more "delight and stimulus" from Isaiah than from the greatest authors of his own native English such as Shakespeare and Milton.

J. Blake Couey ("Isaiah as Poetry," Chapter 12) begins with the basic fact that nearly all of the book is written as poetry, and encourages readers to approach it as such. He surveys its erudite vocabulary, its creative use of sound, and its parallelism and larger strophic structures. He closes with an extended appreciation of the "imaginative worlds" evoked in the book through the use of imagery and metaphors. He observes of its poetic vision that "its scope is nearly boundless."

One of the poetic features of Isaiah is its intertextuality. Previous chapters noted its incorporation of rhetoric and texts from the surrounding world. It is also well established that the authors of the later portions of the book worked with attention to the existing Isaianic texts, so that the book as a whole is woven together by common themes and vocabulary. Furthermore, the book is full of allusions to other biblical books, and was itself eventually a touchstone for later biblical authors. (Sometimes it is even uncertain which text came first!) **Hyun Chul Paul Kim ("Isaiah in Intertextual Perspective,"** Chapter 13) analyzes the book at each of these levels, and then looks forward to "points of intersectionality" between Isaiah and the modern world.

As the foregoing chapters indicate, there are essentially endless ways to look at Isaiah from a literary standpoint, but this section closes with two in-depth case studies. **Hanne Løland Levinson's "Gendered Imagery in Isaiah"** (Chapter 14) looks at one of the most significant and striking features of Isaiah: its repeated use of feminine imagery for God.

She begins with an advanced yet accessible discussion of how metaphors work, then goes on to analyze how the use of imagery comparing God to a pregnant woman, a midwife, and a breastfeeding mother – alongside more widespread masculine imagery – combines to challenge and transform the ways in which readers perceive God. In conclusion, she points out the importance of female god-language in a world in which gender continues to be a basis for inequality and exclusion.

J. Todd Hibbard's "Divine and Human Plans in the Book of Isaiah" (Chapter 15) follows the occurrences of a Hebrew root that means "to plan, advise, counsel" through the whole book, bringing to light one of its central themes. He shows how Isaiah's theological rhetoric begins with a plan against Judah that involves foreign nations, but eventually undermines the plans of those nations as well. As with feminine imagery in the book, it is possible to identify a kind of episodic narrative running through the book in relation to certain themes in a way that holds the book together despite the historical ground that it covers. The divine plans for Judah and nations eventually come together and culminate with the summoning of Cyrus as messiah.

The introduction began by noting the enduring impact of Isaiah. As one of the greatest and most widely read religious and literary texts produced in antiquity, it has been the subject of ongoing reflection ever since. Without any pretense to comprehensiveness, **Part IV** looks at the book's legacy from various angles.

With its many voices that are joined together, Isaiah is akin to a massive choir or symphony, and it sometimes strikes dissonant notes. **Matthew R. Schlimm's "Theological Tensions in the Book of Isaiah"** (Chapter 16) looks at a number of different themes on which the book contains contrasting testimonies: God is portrayed as both a loving savior and a wrathful punisher; God is said to be a mighty sovereign, and yet humans frequently do not act according to his will; God is universal and transcendent, and yet also portrayed as intimate with his people, particularly Zion; humans are sometimes seen as pervasively sinful, but are exhorted to do good; the creation, too, is sometimes good and blessed, and yet elsewhere seen as corrupted; and the same leaders and empires are alternately condemned and used as divine agents. Schlimm reflects on the way in which these complexities press readers beyond simple answers.

One of Isaiah's most forceful messages concerns justice, and the sociopolitical conditions necessary to support it. In **"The Ethical and Political Vision of Isaiah"** (Chapter 17), **M. Daniel Carroll R.** looks at the fundamental themes and vocabulary of the book's moral vision and surveys approaches that seek to better understand the socioeconomic injustice and politics it condemns. These sins include the greed and malfeasance of governing elites in ancient Judahite society, systemic socioeconomic abuses of agricultural and trade systems, and decisions leading to catastrophic war. At the same time, this prophetic text looks forward to a messianic age of justice and peace under a Spirit-filled king/servant. In closing, Carroll looks at how Isaiah's ethical messages have been received (and resisted) in the pursuit of justice, peace, and ecology.

Isaiah was also arguably the most influential book of the Hebrew Bible for the authors of the New Testament. It was the most frequently quoted book, apart from the lengthier book of Psalms, but as **David W. Pao** points out in **"Isaiah in the New Testament"** (Chapter 18), it also supplied language and structural models for significant theological themes of early Christianity. He analyzes the role of Isaiah in New Testament themes such as eschatology, Christology, obduracy, and universalism. Then he looks at the way in which whole New Testament writings were shaped by Isaianic influence, including all four Gospels, Acts, Romans, and Revelation. All this illustrates why Isaiah has been called "The Fifth Gospel."

Joshua Ezra Burns' "Impressions of Isaiah in Classical Rabbinic Literature" (Chapter 19) turns to the reception of the book in postbiblical Jewish tradition. He notes that, like other classical interpreters, the sages did not feel constrained by the historical horizons of the text, but found in it words that spoke to later situations as well. The sages did not systematically idealize Isaiah, however, for example criticizing him for being overeager to be called by God (Isa 6:8). Some were fascinated by the prophet's role in Hezekiah's court and elaborated on the limited details found in Isa 36–39. In other cases they took his promises of restoration to apply to the Second Temple after its destruction by the Romans. Finally, Burns looks at the diverse ways in which the book of Isaiah did (and did not) figure in the Jewish messianic interpretations.

The final chapter, **Brennan Breed's "The Reception History of Isaiah"** (Chapter 20), takes a single theme attested in just a few verses (Isa 8:16; 29:11; and 30:8) and shows how it has been reinterpreted by readers ceaselessly across the centuries, all the way from later biblical authors to modern times, in response to everything from sectarian divisions to African-American slavery to the trauma of the Holocaust. These verses refer to the words of the prophet being sealed, especially to those who are ignorant, until the time comes for their meaning to be revealed. This theme brings into focus the ways in which Isaiah has been used polemically, but it also points to the texts' power as a seemingly inexhaustible well of meaning.

Breed's essay is a fitting note on which to end this introduction, in that the many arcs of interpretation that it identifies extend into our own times and will continue into future generations. These many threads are profoundly interwoven through the cultural tapestries of the past, to the point that history is less comprehensible without an awareness of them. The book of Isaiah stands at the center of various biblical traditions that continue to shape a great percentage of the world's inhabitants. We will continue to understand Isaiah better in the future; and in light of the ethical, social, and historical perspectives explored in this book, it will continue to help us understand ourselves. Like all of the world's greatest works of literature, it serves as a particular mirror on humanity.

Part I

The Book of Isaiah Through History

2 The Book of Isaiah in the Neo-Assyrian Period

MICHAEL J. CHAN

The book of Isaiah's historical notice (Isa 1:1) locates the prophet within the reigns of the Judahite kings Uzziah (r. 783–742), Jotham (r. 742–735), Ahaz (r. 735–715), and Hezekiah (r. 715–687). Taken as such, the book of Isaiah presents itself as a product of the Neo-Assyrian Period (c. 1000–609) and of the Southern Kingdom of Judah. But these dates are only a starting point. As SWEENEY shows in "The Formation of the Book of Isaiah: Foundations and Current Issues," (Chapter 7 in this volume), the book of Isaiah is the work of many generations. The texts that can be dated to the Neo-Assyrian Period are all located in Chapters 1–39, and even those chapters contain ample evidence of editorial activity that extends far beyond the life of the historical Isaiah, meaning that one must distinguish Isaiah the prophet from Isaiah the book.

Judah's long-standing and complicated relations with Assyria profoundly shaped the first thirty-nine chapters of Isaiah. This chapter explores the nature of that impact by examining several Isaianic responses to Assyria's presence, actions, and policies in Judah's geographical neighborhood. Some Isaianic texts deliberately engage Assyrian imperial ideology. Others respond to and interpret historical events in which Assyria was somehow involved. And still others – written and/or edited long after the Neo-Assyrian Empire had fallen – represent responses to the historical *memory* of Assyria. Given the long and complicated compositional history associated with the book of Isaiah, these distinctions cannot be drawn too sharply. Nevertheless, it helps to recognize that Assyria's influence on the composition of Isa 1–39 did not end when the Assyrian empire was destroyed at the end of the seventh century (all dates are BCE unless otherwise noted). This was part of the biblical literature's broader reflection on Assyria long after the empire's demise (see, e.g., Jonah, Tobit, and Judith). Clearly, the Neo-Assyrian period left a lasting mark on Isa 1–39.

Rather than aspiring to comprehensiveness, this chapter seeks to crack open a door of inquiry and invite readers to explore the book of

Isaiah with a particular set of questions in mind: How did the texts within Isa 1–39 respond to Assyria's presence, policies, and actions in the region? How did the memory of Assyria shape the theology of Isa 1–39? How did Judah's encounter with Assyria shape the particular texts? How did Judah's experiences with Assyria impact readers and editors of Isa 1–39? These questions will be explored exegetically, through an examination of five texts: Isa 7:1–8:18; 10:5–15; 20; 24–27; 36–37.

ASSYRIA AND THE LEVANT IN THE NINTH TO SEVENTH CENTURIES

It will be helpful to ground our discussion in a brief review of Assyrian history in the first millennium. Particular attention will be paid to Assyria's relations with the Levant, including especially the Northern Kingdom of Israel and the Southern Kingdom of Judah.

The ninth to seventh centuries were deeply consequential for Assyria's relationship to Levantine powers such as Israel and Judah (YOUNGER 2018; YOUNGER 2003). While there had been incursions into the west by earlier kings, the intensity of Assyria's efforts increased significantly in the nineth century under Aššurnaṣirpal II (r. 883–859) and his more expansionistic son Shalmaneser III (r. 859–824). The former campaigned once in the Levant, whereas the latter campaigned nineteen times. Expansionism was an important element in Assyrian royal ideology, as in the royal title, *šar kibrāt erbetti* ("king of the four regions"), suggesting domination of the entire world (ASTER: 13).[1]

The death of Shalmaneser III resulted in a period of withdrawal owing to both internal and external forces, but Assyria still took a strong interest in Levantine affairs. For example, when the kingdom of Damascus – a powerful Aramean city-state – rallied an alliance to attack Zakkur at Hadrak, the Assyrian king Adad-nerari III (r. 810–783) came to Zakkur's aid. The Assyrians not only defeated Damascus and reduced its territory, but also compelled it to offer a crippling amount of tribute. Under the reign of Joash/Jehoash, Israel also paid tribute to Adad-nerari III in 796.[2]

---

[1] Alasdair Livingstone, "New Dimensions in the Study of Assyrian Religion," in *Assyria 1995: Proceedings of the Tenth Anniversary Symposium of the Neo-Assyrian Text Corpus Project*, ed. Simo Parpola and R. M. Whiting (Helsinki: Neo-Assyrian Text Corpus Project, 1997), 165–77; M. J. Seux, "Les titres royaux šar kiššati et šar kibrāt arba'i," *RA* 59 (1965): 1–18.

[2] See Shuichi Hasegawa, *Aram and Israel During the Jehuite Dynasty*, BZAW 434 (Berlin: De Gruyter, 2012), 119.

Assyria stirred again after a revolt in 746 led to the enthronement of Tiglath-pileser III (r. 744–727). His reign marked a peak of Assyrian power in the late eighth and early seventh centuries, with dramatic consequences for both Israel and Judah. Tiglath-pileser III was an enthusiastic warrior – campaigning, securing tribute, and putting down revolts. Eventually, he wore the crowns of both Assyria and Babylonia.[3] He also innovatively implemented a system of provinces, whereby outlying regions were integrated into Assyria itself, resulting in a more direct form of Assyrian rule.

Isa 6:1 recounts a call story dated to "the year that King Uzziah died," perhaps 742. The regnal dates of these eighth-century kings are somewhat disputed, but Isaiah's prophetic career would certainly have begun during the reign of Tiglath-pileser III, and it spanned this crucial period in the late eighth century during which the northern kingdom fell to Assyria and Judah was under constant imperial pressure as well.

As Assyria exerted its power in the Levant, weaker states had a limited number of political options. Many simply paid tribute (see, e.g., 2 Kgs 17:1–4), thereby avoiding military conflict and perhaps even deportation and provincialization. Others formed alliances to try to fight off the "yoke" of Assyrian domination (an agricultural metaphor that the Assyrians used themselves; see Isa 14:25, etc.).

Both of these strategies were at work when Rezin, another king of Damascus, formed an anti-Assyrian coalition, which also included Tyre, Gaza, Ashkelon, Arab groups, and the Northern Kingdom of Israel (see, e.g., 2 Kgs 15:37–16:9; Isa 7:1–8:22). Coalition members had hoped to recruit Ahaz, the king of Judah, to their cause. When that failed, Rezin, the king of Damascus, and Pekah, the king of Israel, together besieged Jerusalem in order to replace Ahaz with a more malleable partner (Isa 7:6). This event is often called the "Syro-Ephraimitic Crisis." Ahaz, however, appealed to Tiglath-pileser III, paid tribute, and pledged loyalty (2 Kgs 16:7). In retaliation, Tiglath-pileser III eventually defeated Rezin and turned Damascus into a provincial capital. He put Hoshea on the throne in the Northern Kingdom's capital, Samaria, and annexed other portions of it.

A few years later, however, even Hoshea rebelled against Assyria by seeking to form an alliance with Egypt, so Shalmaneser V (r. 727–722) arrested him and eventually, in 722, claimed to have conquered Samaria after several years of siege warfare. Sargon II (r. 722–705) made the same claim, so – allowing for the exaggeration of ancient royal rhetoric – it

3   J. A. Brinkman, *A Political History of Post-Kassite Babylonia, 1158–722 B.C.*, AO 43 (Rome: Pontificium Institutum Biblicum, 1968), 240–42.

is possible that the completion of the conquest spanned both reigns. In any case, Sargon turned the northern kingdom into a province called Samerina, deported some of its population, and repopulated it with foreigners (2 Kgs 17) (YOUNGER 2018: 27).[4] Deportees from Israel, in fact, seem to have been involved in the construction of Sargon's new Assyrian capital at Dur-Sharrukin, modern Khorsabad (YOUNGER 2018: 27).

Upon Sargon's death, revolts broke out both in Babylon and in the Levant, demanding the attention of the newly crowned Sennacherib (r. 705–681), but Assyria's momentum continued. The Babylonian revolts were led by Marduk-apla-iddina II, who sent envoys to Hezekiah, perhaps with the intention "to coordinate the resistance to Assyria" he is called Merodach-baladan in the Bible; see Isa 39; 2 Kgs 20:12–21) (YOUNGER 2018: 28).

In 701, Sennacherib dedicated his forces to dealing with rebellious western powers. This is undoubtedly his best-known campaign, attested in multiple biblical and cuneiform accounts, and in Assyrian reliefs. An entire room of Sennacherib's Southwest Palace at Nineveh is dedicated to the king's conquest of the Judahite city of Lachish, where visitors can still see the remains of a huge siege ramp. Lengthy narratives are dedicated to this campaign in the book of Isaiah (see Isa 36–37; cf. 2 Kgs 18–19; 2 Chr 32). Despite its rebellion, Jerusalem was not destroyed, and Hezekiah managed to stay on the throne, although he was forced to pay enormous tribute as a penalty. The city's survival was viewed as a miracle and became a touchstone for "Royal Zion" theology, which held that Yhwh would always protect his holy city (e.g., Isa 31:4–5). The various biblical and cuneiform sources about the campaign have provocative similarities, such as the amount of gold paid by Hezekiah to Sennacherib. However, they also disagree on other details, complicating attempts to reconstruct the underlying historical events.

Sennacherib ruled until 681, and although gaps in the cuneiform records make it difficult to be sure, there is no indication that he ever found it necessary to march on Judah again. He was murdered by one of his sons (Urdu-Mullissu) in 681 and ultimately succeeded by another son, Esarhaddon (r. 680–669). The reference to these events in Isa 37:38. the historically "telescoped," i.e., it makes it sound like they happened

---

4   The historical details around the fall of Samaria are fraught with complications. See K. Lawson Younger, Jr., "The Fall of Samaria in Light of Recent Research," *CBQ* 61 (1999): 461–82; K. Lawson Younger, Jr., "The Repopulation of Samaria (2 Kgs 17:24, 27–31) in Light of Recent Study," in *The Future of Biblical Archaeology*, ed. James K. Hoffmeier and Alan R. Millard (Grand Rapids, MI: Eerdmans, 2004), 242–68; Lester Grabbe, *Ancient Israel: What Do We Know and How Do We Know It?* (London: Bloomsbury, 2017), 159–209.

immediately afterwards. However, the long gap in mind reflects that the tradition about Jerusalem's salvation from the Assyrians in 701 continued to be valued and developed.

Esarhaddon was succeeded by his son Aššurbanipal (r. 669–631), during whose reign the empire reached its pinnacle and widest extent, reaching even into Egypt. Esarhaddon's and Aššurbanipal's major campaigns did not involve Judah, because the area had been effectively pacified as an Assyrian client state by Sennacherib. During their dominance of the region, the Assyrians established military bases in various locations in Judah that offered administrative footholds, vantage points for surveillance, and control over important trade routes.

These three Assyrian kings (Sennacherib, Esarhaddon, and Aššurbanipal) overlapped chronologically with the lengthy reign of Manasseh (r. 687–642). Manasseh is depicted very negatively in the biblical historical books, and is even blamed in 2 Kgs 21 for the Babylonian conquest of Judah, which took place long after his death. From Assyria's standpoint, however, he was a faithful vassal subject, and his relations with Assyria seem to have been amicable. Indeed, Manasseh's accommodating disposition toward the Assyrians may have contributed to 2 Kgs's roundly negative depiction of the monarch.[5] The tradition in 2 Chr 33 of Manasseh's deportation to Babylon at the hands of the Assyrian military followed by his subsequent repentance seems to be legendary in nature.

The Neo-Assyrian empire declined after the death of Aššurbanipal, which probably took place in 631.[6] The empire seems to have been overextended, so that it was vulnerable to attacks closer to home. These came from the neighboring Babylonians and Medes in the 620s and 610s. The Assyrian capital, Nineveh, fell in 612, and the empire's forces had crumbled completely by 609. Sometime during this crisis, the Assyrian troops and administrators would have had to leave Judah. The beneficiary of these events was Josiah (r. 640–609), who ruled over Judah during this period of increasing independence and both economic and military power. The optimism of Josiah's reign is thus reflected in the book of Isaiah, as elsewhere in the Bible. However, Josiah did not, in the end, successfully navigate the rough political waters of the end of

---

[5]   J. Maxwell Miller and John H. Hayes, *A History of Ancient Israel and Judah*, 2nd ed. (Louisville, KY: Westminster John Knox, 2006), 434.

[6]   Certain details of the end of the Neo-Assyrian empire are difficult to reconstruct precisely, owing to gaps in the cuneiform sources. Aššurbanipal is not attested after 631, though later sources claim for him a forty-two-year reign, which would have extended until 627.

the eighth century, as he was killed by the Pharaoh Necho at Megiddo
(2 Kgs 23:29–30). The reasons for this are not explained in any text, but
it appears he may have tried to reassert Judah's control over that important northern city.

EXEGETICAL EXPLORATION #1: ISA 7:1–8:18

These chapters are related to the aforementioned "Syro-Ephraimitic
Crisis," which took place during the reigns of Ahaz of Judah, Pekah
of Israel, and Tiglath-pileser III of Assyria. An anti-Assyrian coalition,
formed by Rezin, king of Damascus, and joined by Pekah, attempted to
replace Ahaz with a ruler friendlier to their cause. Members of the coalition had formerly paid tribute to Assyria, but now found it expedient
to rebel against the empire. Despite their focus on a particular event,
the compositional history of Isa 7:1–8:18 is obscure and complicated.[7]
Reference will be made to compositional and redactional issues as they
emerge in interpretation.

In keeping with the old adage that "the enemy of my enemy is my
friend," Ahaz called for assistance from the Assyrian king, Tiglath-
pileser III. Help came at the price of submission, however. According to
2 Kgs 16:7–9, the events unfolded as follows:

> Ahaz sent messengers to King Tiglath-pileser of Assyria, saying,
> "I am your servant and your son. Come up, and rescue me from the
> hand of the king of Aram and from the hand of the king of Israel,
> who are attacking me." Ahaz also took the silver and gold found
> in the house of Yhwh and in the treasures of the king's house, and
> sent a present to the king of Assyria.[8] The king of Assyria listened
> to him; the king of Assyria marched up against Damascus, and took
> it, carrying its people captive to Kir; then he killed Rezin.

The Isaianic telling of the story pays greater attention to the terror
caused by the attack: "When the house of David heard that Aram had
allied itself with Ephraim, the heart of Ahaz and the heart of his people
shook as the trees of the forest shake before the wind" (Isa 7:2). This is
an important literary point that foreshadows the prophet's oracle in 7:4,

---

[7] For a helpful review of the issues, see H. G. M. Williamson, *Isaiah 6–12*, ICC (London:
    Bloomsbury/T&T Clark, 2018), 102–11.
[8] The term "present" used here has the specific connotation of a bribe; see, for example,
    Ex 23:8; Deut 16:19; 1 Sam 8:3; Isa 1:23; 5:23. (Unless otherwise indicated, all transla-
    tions are from the NRSV.)

which urges Ahaz, "Take heed, be quiet, do not fear, and do not let your heart be faint because of these two smoldering stumps of firebrands, because of the fierce anger of Rezin and Aram and the son of Remaliah." The central issue in Isa 7:1–8:18 is trust. Will Ahaz trust in Yhwh's words given through Isaiah?

The precise nature of Isaiah's political advice is not entirely clear, however. Is Ahaz being urged to remain neutral in the alliance's conflict with Assyria? This makes no sense, since the text is clear that Rezin and Pekah are attacking Jerusalem in order to depose Ahaz, not to convince him to join (Isa 7:6). His reign and life are at stake, not simply his political stance on the alliance. Is Isaiah telling Ahaz not to call upon the aid of Assyria? This interpretation is problematic because it requires one to use 2 Kgs 16 to fill in contextual details for Isa 7, since Isa 7 never mentions an appeal to Assyria. There is no evidence in Isa 7:1–8:18 that Isaiah is trying to dissuade Ahaz from reaching out to the king of Assyria. Rather, Isaiah is exhorting Ahaz to trust in divine help. Whether this means that Ahaz is simply to sit back passively and wait for miraculous intervention or that Ahaz is called to take up arms himself, trusting in a victory, is unclear.[9] In either case, Isaiah urges Ahaz to trust in the downfall of his enemies (vv. 8–9). Such "oracles of well-being" were commonly delivered by ancient Near Eastern prophets.

Isaiah offers to Ahaz a sign "as deep as Sheol or as high as heaven," but the king refuses (vv. 10–12). His refusal to seek and trust Yhwh's words marks a rhetorical shift from comforting the king to threatening judgment, signaled by Isaiah's retort in v. 13: "Hear then, O house of David! Is it too little for you to weary mortals, that you weary my God also?" Yhwh then offers a sign of his own choosing: the well-known promise of a son called "Immanuel" (v. 14). This came to be interpreted as a messianic promise (see Pao, "Isaiah in the New Testament," Chapter 18 in this volume) but in its original context its meaning was simpler: It was a promise that God would overthrow the powers that threatened Judah in the 730s within a couple of years (7:16: "before the child knows how to refuse the evil and choose the good").

The alternative to trust in Isaiah's words is alluded to in 7:17: "Yhwh will bring on you and on your people and on your ancestral house such days as have not come since the day that Ephraim departed from Judah – the king of Assyria." This is consistent with the various examples already discussed of Assyria's power to make and break kings and kingdoms.

9 For a more detailed treatment of these arguments, see Williamson, *Isaiah 6–12*, 124–25.

Verses 18–25 clearly mark the beginning of a new unit, which was likely added to develop the theme of Assyrian judgment in v. 17. Verse 20 describes the judgment as follows: "On that day Yhwh will shave with a razor hired beyond the River – with the king of Assyria – the head and the hair of the feet, and it will take off the beard as well." The imagery suggests not only humiliation but emasculation (ASTER: 104–6). Official Assyrian literature and imagery depicts the king – as exemplar of militaristic masculinity – with a full and long beard (WINTER: 1:3–70).[10] The unnamed victim in v. 20 will be the opposite of this, being deprived of all external masculine markers.

A remnant will remain in the land, even though it is afflicted by desertification – transformed into a barren landscape in which expensive vines are replaced with briers and thorns (vv. 21–23).

Chapter 8 introduces a new oracle that reinforces the previous one: Assyria will plunder Damascus and Samaria (8:4). But Judah will also suffer judgment because of Ahaz's unwillingness to trust Yhwh:

> Because this people has refused the waters of Shiloah that flow gently, and melt in fear before Rezin and the son of Remaliah; therefore, Yhwh is bringing up against it the mighty flood waters of the River, the king of Assyria and all his glory; it will rise above all its channels and overflow all its banks; it will sweep on into Judah as a flood, and, pouring over, it will reach up to the neck; and its outspread wings will fill the breadth of your land, O Immanuel. (8:6–8)

The use of flood imagery to describe the Assyrian king and military echoes similar motifs found in official Assyrian propaganda, including that of Tiglath-pileser III (MACHINIST 1983: 726–7; ASTER: 106–7). The text contrasts the peaceful waters of "Shiloah" with the destructive torrents of the Assyrian king.[11] But the flood does not kill; it only reaches "up to the neck" – an important but subtle detail. The judgment brought upon Judah by Assyria would damage but not annihilate. Limits would be placed upon Assyria's imperial violence – a point made elsewhere in Isaiah (see later on Isa 10:5–7).

---

[10]   This full and long beard is especially prominent in Neo-Assyrian imperial art, which frequently features the king.

[11]   It is unclear to what the "waters of Shiloah" refer. As Williamson notes, however, the most likely suggestion is that they "were a channel by which the water of the Gihon was directed down along the east side of the city towards the south, and this has usually been identified with what has come to be known as Channel (or Canal) I; it is partly open and partly covered, and it has various openings that apparently allowed it to be used for the irrigation of the Kidron Valley." Williamson, *Isaiah 6–12*, 243.

In stark contrast to the account in 2 Kgs 16, Ahaz does not call upon Assyria for help in 7:1–8:18. Ahaz's only ally is Yhwh, who approaches the king through the prophet Isaiah. But the king rejects that help, thereby inviting judgment upon Judah. The agent of that judgment is Assyria, which is represented as a powerful and violent agent of judgment, sometimes using themes and imagery found also in Assyrian royal sources. This more complicated perspective on Assyria is a result of the ongoing formation of these chapters during and after the Assyrian campaign again in Judah thirty years later, in 701.

EXEGETICAL EXPLORATION #2: ISA 10:5–15

Isa 10:5–15 is a woe oracle directed specifically at Assyria.[12] It begins with a description of Assyria's divinely granted assignment:

Ah, Assyria, the rod of my [Yhwh's] anger—
  the club in their hands is my fury!
Against a godless nation I send him,
and against the people of my wrath I command him,
to take spoil and seize plunder,
and to tread them down like the mire of the streets.

Echoing themes in Isa 7:1–8:18, Assyria is depicted as a tool of judgment in the hand of an angry God. The book of Isaiah interprets Assyrian violence theologically, and not simply in terms of actions taken on an historical stage. And like Isa 8:6–8, these verses draw on imagery found in Assyrian royal sources.

It is common in Assyrian inscriptions to claim that the kings were chosen and commissioned by Aššur and other deities. For example, Ashurnasirpal II is called "strong king, king of the universe ... beloved of the gods Anu and Dagan, destructive weapon [kašūš] of the great gods." (CHAN: 722–26).[13] Similarly, Isa 10:5–6 understands Assyria to be a divine weapon. However, this passage rhetorically dethrones Aššur and replaces him with Yhwh, God of Israel. Yhwh invades Aššur's mythical space and hijacks the cosmic throne normally occupied by the Assyrian royal deities.

A second example is the claim that Yhwh is the deity who provides the divine weapons, not the gods of Assyria. Verse 10:5b understands

---

[12] This section is adapted from CHAN.

[13] Ninurta Temple Inscription, obv. line i11 (RIMA 2:194). In line i21 of the same text, the same phrase is used: "designate of the warrior god Ninurta, destructive weapon [kašūš] of the great gods."

the king to be the bearer of divine weaponry: "[T]he club in their hands is my fury!" (Isa 10:5b). Similar imagery is very well represented in the inscriptional evidence of the Assyrian monarchs. Šamšī-Adad V records, for instance, that "[t]hey [the Medes] took fright in the face of the angry weapons of Aššur."[14] Or, from Shalmaneser III's annals at Fort Shalmaneser: "When Aššur, the great lord, chose me in his steadfast heart ... named me for the shepherdship of Assyria, he put in my grasp a strong weapon which fells the rebel."[15]

The text abruptly changes focus, shifting away from God's intentions to the contrary intentions of Assyria:

> But this is not what he [the Assyrian] intends,
>   nor does he have this in mind;
> but it is in his heart to destroy,
>   and to cut off nations not a few.

For he says:

> "Are not my commanders all kings?
> Is not Calno like Carchemish?
>   Is not Hamath like Arpad?
>   Is not Samaria like Damascus?
> As my hand has reached to the kingdoms of the idols
>   whose images were greater than those of Jerusalem and Samaria,
> shall I not do to Jerusalem and her idols
>   what I have done to Samaria and her images?" (Isa 10:7–11)

Yhwh intends for Assyria to be a tool of judgment in his hands. But out of arrogance and pride, the empire plans to go beyond that mandate and to "destroy" and "cut off." This conflict of intentions ultimately leads to the agent of judgment becoming the object of judgment: "When Yhwh has finished all his work on Mount Zion and on Jerusalem, he will punish the arrogant boasting of the king of Assyria and his haughty pride" (Isa 10:12). The oracle also contains a series of boastful statements from the Assyrian king, which emphasize his own strength and deeds (vv. 13–14). Verse 15 concludes the section, however, with a damning statement from Yhwh about the absurdity of a tool protesting against its user.

Isa 10:5–15 is a fascinating example of an Isaianic response to Assyria. Like Isa 7:1–8:18, the text seems to draw intentionally upon imagery and language found in Assyrian sources. That imagery is then

---

[14]   Calah Stele, obv. lines 28 (RIMA 3:185).
[15]   Fort Shalmaneser Stone Slab, obv. lines 11–13 (RIMA 3:8).

employed to depict Assyria as a powerful nation that Yhwh will use to judge his people. But Isa 10:5–15 also differs from Isa 7:1–8:18 in a significant way: Assyria's ambitions take it well beyond its divine mandate. As a result, Assyria will be judged alongside Judah (cf. Isa 14:24–27).

EXEGETICAL EXPLORATION #3: ISA 20

Isa 20 contains a brief sign-act report in which Isaiah warns Judah against trusting in Egypt's protection and joining a revolt against Assyria. Sign-act reports describe actions taken by the prophet to embody their prophetic messages dramatically.[16]

Verse 1 sets the scene "in the year that the commander-in-chief, who was sent by King Sargon of Assyria, came to Ashdod and fought against it and took it." That was 714–712, during the reign of Hezekiah. At that time, the Philistine city of Ashdod rebelled against Assyria, removed their pro-Assyrian ruler and replaced him with a certain Yamani. According to Sargon's Nineveh Prism, Ashdod was one of a number of Levantine states that plotted against Assyria and sought out an alliance with Egypt.

In that period, Egypt was ruled by the Twenty-Fifth Dynasty, which is often called "Kushite" based on the Semitic name, but also rendered as "Ethiopian" or "Nubian." When Assyria campaigned to Ashdod to quell the rebellion, Yamani fled to Egypt, thinking to find asylum at the Kushite court. But they extradited him to Assyria instead. This would have reinforced Isaiah's sense that the Egyptians were not trustworthy allies.

Isaiah's symbolic actions in Isa 20 portended desolation, defeat, and exile for "Egypt and Kush" at the hands of Assyria. More specifically, Isaiah says that Yhwh commanded him to "go, and loose the sackcloth from your loins and take your sandals off your feet," and he had done so, "walking naked and barefoot" (v. 2). The interpretation of the symbolic action follows:

> Just as my servant Isaiah has walked naked and barefoot for three years as a sign and a portent against Egypt and Ethiopia, so shall the king of Assyria lead away the Egyptians as captives and the Ethiopians as exiles, both the young and the old, naked and barefoot, with buttocks uncovered, to the shame of Egypt. And they shall be dismayed and confounded because of Ethiopia their hope and of Egypt their boast. (20:3–5)

---

[16] Other notable symbolic reports include 1 Kgs 22; Jer 13:1–11; Ezek 4:1–3; 5:1–4.

Yhwh strongly warns against seeking the help of Egypt and Ethiopia, noting that these potential allies are in fact weak before the Assyrian army.

The final verse of the passage (20:6) is a statement from the "inhabitants of this coastland" indicating that trust in an alliance with Egypt/Ethiopia is ultimately misplaced: "See, this is what has happened to those in whom we hoped and to whom we fled for help and deliverance from the king of Assyria! And we, how shall we escape?" The text does not specifically call upon Isaiah's audience to trust in Yhwh. As a warning, Isa 20's objective is primarily negative: to prevent Judah from entering an alliance of convenience that would ultimately end in humiliating defeat. Implied in the critique of this alliance is the assumption that Yhwh alone should be Judah's "hope" and "boast" (20:5). This is part of a running theme in Isaiah in which the prophet condemns alliances with Egypt (cf. 19:1–15; 30:1–5).

EXEGETICAL EXPLORATION #4: ISA 24–27

The book of Isaiah has deep connections also to the reign of King Josiah – a monarch who witnessed the Assyrian empire both at its zenith and at its nadir.[17] One passage in which this is perceptible is Isa 24–27, although it presents formidable interpretive challenges for the modern reader. These chapters have often been described as an "apocalypse," because they begin with a crisis. However, they have almost none of the formal features of apocalypses, a genre that only developed later; instead, they are similar to ancient Near Eastern royal-propagandistic literature from Egypt, Mesopotamia, and the Levant, and across many periods.[18]

The crisis in 24–27 is the state of the land of Judah near the end of the Assyrian Empire, but it is progressively resolved. Descriptions of the demise of a once-lofty city recur in the passage (Isa 24:10–12; 25:2; 26:5; 27:10). Christopher B. Hays has demonstrated that chapters

---

[17]   See, for example, SWEENEY, "The Composition of the Book of Isaiah: Foundations and Current Issues," Chapter 7 in this volume, along with Christopher B. Hays, *The Origins of Isaiah 24–27: Josiah's Festival Scroll for the Fall of Assyria* (Cambridge: Cambridge University Press, 2019); Hermann Barth, *Die Jesaja-Worte in der Josiazeit*, WMANT 48 (Neukirchen-Vlyun: Neukirchener Verlag, 1977). For a contrary view, see H. G. M. Williamson, "The Theory of a Josianic Edition of the First Part of the Book of Isaiah: A Critical Examination," in *Studies in Isaiah: History, Theology, and Reception*, ed. T. Wasserman, G. Andersson, and D. Willgren (London: Bloomsbury/T&T Clark, 2017), 3–21.

[18]   See Christopher B. Hays, "From Propaganda to Apocalypse: An Empirical Model for the Formation of Isaiah 24–27," *HBAI* 6 (2017): 120–44.

were originally composed as the Assyrian Empire was collapsing during Josiah's reign, and that the fallen city refers to the Assyrian palaces in and around Ramat Raḥel, located 4 km outside Jerusalem.[19] According to this interpretation, the passage as a whole reflects the Assyrians' abandonment of the site under great pressure, Judah's delight over their downfall (Isa 24:14–15), and Josiah's appeal to members of the previously conquered Northern Kingdom to "make peace" with Jerusalem and return to Davidic rule (Isa 27:2–6).

The authors (presumably heirs of the "disciples" mentioned in 8:16) attributed the fall of the city to divine aid:

> O Yhwh, you are my God;
>> I will exalt you, I will praise your name;
> for you have done wonderful things,
>> plans formed of old, faithful and sure.
> For you have made the city a heap,
>> the fortified city a ruin;
> the palace of aliens is a city no more,
>> it will never be rebuilt (Isa 25:1–2)
>
> …
>
> For he has brought low
>> the inhabitants of the height;
>> the lofty city he lays low.
> He lays it low to the ground,
>> casts it to the dust (26:5)
>
> …
>
> For the fortified city is solitary,
>> a habitation deserted and forsaken, like the wilderness;
> the calves graze there,
>> there they lie down, and strip its branches. (Isa 27:10)

The city itself is never explicitly named. Gathering all of the verses together, however, the following description of the city and its fate emerges: The city is derogatorily called a "city of chaos" (24:10); domestic life comes to a standstill (24:10); joy and gladness are banished

---

[19] Hays, *The Origins of Isaiah 24–27*, 95–126. The chapters' remarkable parallels to Zephaniah also support this thesis. See also Christopher B. Hays, "Isa 24–27 and Zephaniah Amid the Terrors and Hopes of the Seventh Century: An Intertextual Analysis," in *Isaiah and the Twelve/Jesaja und die Zwölf: Parallels, Similarities and Differences*, ed. Richard Bautch, Joachim Eck, and Burkard M. Zapff, BZAW 527 (Berlin: De Gruyter, 2020), 131–56. This is not to say that Isa 24–27 did not undergo later editing and development, only that a core of material can be traced back to the time of Josiah.

(24:11); the only thing remaining in the city is desolation, set behind battered gates (24:12); the city is a heap and a ruin (25:2); it is no longer a "palace of aliens" or "palace of foreigners," presumably because it has been abandoned; Yhwh lays low the "lofty city," even to the ground (26:5). With a tone of derision and *schadenfreude* (comparable to that found in Nahum), these texts celebrate the dramatic downfall of Ramat Raḥel and its subsequent abandonment by its foreign population. As an architectural symbol of Assyria's domination of Judah, the fall of this once-great citadel was likely met with widespread celebration and relief.

In keeping with the larger theological themes of Isaiah, Yhwh is the ultimate agent behind the destruction of the city. His decision to lay low Ramat Raḥel is in keeping with a previously established divine plan (see Isa 25:1–2; cf. 37:26–28), emphasizing again who the ultimate mover of history is, as in Isa 10. The unnamed city in Isa 24–27 is also similar to other Isaianic symbols of Assyrian domination in that the city needed to be brought low, humbled, and desolate (cf. Isa 2:11–13; 10:33–34).

EXEGETICAL EXPLORATION #5: ISA 36–37

This lengthy narrative describes an encounter between the armies of the Assyrian king Sennacherib, who is represented by the Rabshakeh, and the Judean king Hezekiah, who is represented by several court officials. Alternative versions of the story are also told in 2 Kgs 18:13–19:37 and 2 Chr 32:1–23. Sennacherib's western campaign, which included his siege of Jerusalem, is also well attested in cuneiform sources. When both biblical and extrabiblical historical sources are considered, this is the most widely attested event in the Hebrew Bible (YOUNGER 2003: 236).[20]

Even a cursory reading of the three accounts (2 Kgs 18:13–19:37; Isa 36–37; 2 Chr 32:1–23) reveals significant differences among them. Not unlike the Gospels, these texts purport to tell a common narrative but do so in such distinct ways that a complex compositional history spanning generations is all but certain (KAHN). Something of the historical Isaiah's voice and actions may remain, but his unnamed successors certainly also played a significant role, not just in shaping the narrative but doing so in a way that made the story ring with relevance in the ears

---

[20]   For a helpful summary of the biblical and nonbiblical sources, see Christopher B. Hays, *Hidden Riches: A Sourcebook for the Comparative Study of the Hebrew Bible and Ancient Near East* (Louisville, KY: Westminster John Knox, 2014), 221–34.

of subsequent readers. The preservation and updating of Isa 36–37 demonstrates how profoundly Assyria's actions and policies impacted the book of Isaiah, both in the Neo-Assyrian period and beyond.

A coherent story nevertheless emerges. In the midst of a larger campaign against Judah, Sennacherib sends his Rabshakeh (a military leader) from Lachish to Jerusalem (Isa 36:1–3). Standing "by the conduit of the upper pool on the highway to the Fuller's Field" (v. 2, cf. Isa 7:3), the Rabshakeh offers a blistering public speech to Hezekiah's officials, hoping to secure submission without actual military conflict. To that end, the speech makes the following claims intended to erode Hezekiah's confidence: (1) Egypt is a weak and unreliable ally (Isa 36:5–6, 8–9); (2) Judah's God, Yhwh, cannot be trusted to help (Isa 36:7); and in fact (3) Yhwh himself has commissioned the Assyrians to attack Judah (Isa 36:10).

The themes of trust and reliance are shared with 7:1–8:18, and also pervasive in Assyrian inscriptions to describe the misplaced reliance of Assyria's enemies (COHEN: 32–48; ASTER: 254). While proof is not possible, it seems likely that the text is drawing on known Assyrian motifs, as Isa 10:5–15 did. The preponderance of speeches, oracles, and prayers in Isa 36–37 emphasizes that this narrative is about a war of words. In particular, the conflict is over whose words Hezekiah will ultimately trust – Yhwh's through the prophet Isaiah, or Sennacherib's through his messenger the Rabshakeh.

The three Jerusalemite officials present (Eliakim, Shebna, and Joah) ask the Rabshakeh to communicate in Aramaic (the diplomatic language of the day), but instead continues mocking Jerusalem's inhabitants in Hebrew (Isa 36:11–20). Once again, the Rabshakeh chips away at their trust in Yhwh, urging them to disregard Hezekiah's words and rely on his own (ASTER: 256).[21] He makes them what looks like an offer of peace that is really just an invitation to forced deportation, a fate previously suffered by the Northern Kingdom under Tiglath-pileser III (see 2 Kgs 17): "Make your peace with me and come out to me; then every one of you will eat from your own vine and your own fig tree and drink water from your own cistern, until I come and take you away to a land like your own land, a land of grain and wine, a land of bread and vineyards" (36:16–17). As Shawn Zelig Aster has noted, "This speech is a classic Isaianic re-interpretation of Assyrian imperial propaganda: when the Assyrians spoke of their universal sovereignty, Isaiah heard an attack on the universal sovereignty of YHWH" (ASTER: 257).

---

[21] Isa 36:20 contains the phrase "the god of the lands" (Heb. ʾĕlōhê hāʾărāṣôt), which seems to be a direct translation of ilāni mātāti.

After remaining silent throughout the Rabshakeh's speech, the three aforementioned officials approach Hezekiah and communicate the Assyrian message (Isa 36:21–22). Upon hearing it, Hezekiah tears his clothing, covers himself in sackcloth, enters the temple, and orders his officials to inform Isaiah (37:1–2). The prophet issues a short, straightforward oracle: "Do not be afraid because of the words that you have heard, with which the servants of the king of Assyria have reviled me. I myself will put a spirit in him, so that he shall hear a rumor, and return to his own land; I will cause him to fall by the sword in his own land" (Isa 37:6–7). This prophecy is fulfilled in Isa 37:37–38. As in Isa 10:5–15 and 14:24–27, Yhwh is set in opposition to Assyria, undermining the Rabshakeh's claim to be acting at Yhwh's command (Isa 36:10).

Verses 8–9 transition to a new section that seems to stem from a parallel source (ROBERTS 2015).[22] This secondary section contains another message in the form of a letter from the Assyrians that is again meant to erode trust in Yhwh (Isa 37:10–13), followed by a prayer from Hezekiah (vv. 14–20) and additional oracles and signs from Isaiah (vv. 21–35). In his prayer, Hezekiah appeals to the God who is master of "all the kingdoms of the earth" (37:16). But the prayer also acknowledges the realities of the Assyrian threat, and finally concludes with a petition for divine intervention (37:18–20).

In response to Hezekiah's prayer, Isaiah offers a lengthy message of his own, in stark contrast to that offered by the Rabshakeh. Isaiah's oracle begins by noting Assyria's scorn against Zion (37:22). But for Isaiah, Assyria's scorn is not in fact directed against the city, but rather against Yhwh, the "Holy One of Israel" (37:23). As in Isa 10:5–15, the oracle also contains quoted speech from the Assyrians:

> By your servants you have mocked Yhwh,
>   and you have said, "With my many chariots
> I have gone up the heights of the mountains,
>   to the far recesses of Lebanon;
> I felled its tallest cedars, its choicest cypresses;
>   I came to its remotest height, its densest forest.

[22] For a discussion of composition-historical matters, see especially Kahn 2020; William R. Gallagher, *Sennacherib's Campaign to Judah: New Studies*, Studies in the History and Culture of the Ancient Near East 18 (Leiden and Boston: Brill, 1999), 143–262 and the appropriate sections in Joseph Blenkinsopp, *Isaiah 1–39*, AB 19 (New York: Doubleday, 2000); see also ROBERTS and Marvin A. Sweeney, *Isaiah 1–39*, FOTL 16 (Grand Rapids, MI: Eerdmans, 1996).

I dug wells and drank waters,
> I dried up with the sole of my foot all the streams of
> Egypt." (37:24–25)

The imagery of the king felling trees and ascending mountains is another common theme in Neo-Assyrian royal sources (CHAN: 730–3; ASTER: 264–9). The image is grounded in the well-known Assyrian royal practice of traveling to the western mountain ranges (e.g., the Amanus range, Lebanon) for the sake of felling their prized trees (such as cedars and junipers) and bringing them back to Assyria for use in royal building projects. In this case, the theme is used to bolster the arrogant depiction of the Assyrian king.

What the king does not realize, Isaiah says, is that Yhwh had planned all of this far in advance (37:26–27). The king's greatness is not his own. Assyria's decision to "rage" against Yhwh (37:28–29) places it squarely in the crosshairs of divine judgment:

> I will put my hook in your nose and my bit in your mouth;
> I will turn you back on the way by which you came. (37:29)

Depicting Assyria as a bull in need of taming is a poignant image that reinforces the king's place in the cosmos as a servant of Yhwh, the true universal sovereign. It also reverses the aforementioned yoke imagery, so that now Assyria rather than Judah is the bovine.

For several reasons, Isa 36–37 is one of the most fascinating responses to Assyria's presence and policies in Judah. To begin with, Hezekiah's response to Assyria's threat contrast starkly to Ahaz's response in Isaiah. H. G. M. Williamson has compiled a helpful list of similarities, demonstrating that the two narratives were likely edited with an eye toward the other:

> in both passages the king is confronted with an invading army which is threatening Jerusalem (7.1; 36.2), he is reduced to near panic (7.2; 37.1), and Isaiah offers him a reassuring "fear not" oracle (7.4; 37.6–7), backed up in each case by the offer of a "sign" (7.11; 37.30; see too 38.7, 22). Although in both narratives the king and city are spared, this is followed by a prediction that a worse disaster will follow in the future (7.15–17; 39.6–7). A significant element of detail is that both feature the otherwise unknown location "the channel of the upper pool by the highway leading to the Fuller's Field" (7.3; 36.2; and it may also be of relevance that the expression "the zeal of Yhwh of hosts will do this" occurs at both 9.6 and 37.32).[23]

---

[23] Williamson, *Isaiah 6–12*, 103–4.

These similarities are used by the book's authors to draw attention to the contrasting reactions of the two kings: Ahaz distrusts Yhwh's words through Isaiah, but Hezekiah trusts them, proving himself to be the more worthy king, worthy of miraculous deliverance.

Comparing these two stories indicates that in Isa 1–39, the Assyrian presence was interpreted not only as a geopolitical threat, but also as a cosmic contest between Yhwh and the Assyrians. In that contest, Yhwh protects Zion/Jerusalem, making both accounts important contributions to the multifaceted and complex "Zion" tradition.[24]

CONCLUSIONS

The imprint of Assyria on Isa 1–39 is strong. It contains several texts that directly and forcefully engage propagandistic and ideological material found in official Assyrian sources. In many cases, the propaganda is undermined and set in stark contrast with theological claims about Yhwh. How Isaianic scribes came into contact with Assyrian sources remains an unresolved matter (for more on that question, see ASTER, "Isaiah and Empire," Chapter 10 in this volume). The prevalence of linguistic and thematic connections between Isaianic texts and Assyrian sources, however, suggests that the Isaianic scribes had high levels of familiarity with these materials, and exploited that knowledge in their prophetic oracles. Many texts in Isa 1–39 were forged in the polemical interplay between Israelite religion and Assyrian imperial domination.

A number of significant and consistent theological assumptions emerge. To begin with, Yhwh is himself a great king who rules over creation, including even powerful empires such as Assyria. In response to Israel's or Judah's sins, Yhwh deploys empires such as Assyria as agents of judgment; they are like tools in his hands (Isa 10:15). This remarkable and potentially disturbing claim closely associates the activity and will of Yhwh with the ambitions and activities of brutal imperial rulers.[25] But those agents of judgment can also act against Yhwh's will, exceeding their divine mandate and inviting divine wrath and judgment.

Another key theme emerging from these polemical exchanges is that victory over powerful adversaries comes from trust in Yhwh.

---

[24] For a discussion of the Zion tradition and further literature, see Michael J. Chan, *Wealth of Nations: A Tradition-Historical Study*, FAT 93 (Tübingen: Mohr Siebeck, 2017), 23–32.

[25] Terence Fretheim has explored the significant theological implications of Yhwh's use of divine agents. See, especially, Terence Fretheim, "'I Was Only a Little Angry': Divine Violence in the Prophets," *Int* 58 (2004): 365–75.

Ahaz and Hezekiah were tested in this regard. Ahaz brushed aside Isaiah's words of assurance and sought safety elsewhere (see Isa 7–8). Hezekiah, however, trusted Isaiah's words and thus experienced Yhwh's deliverance when he faced Sennacherib's armies (Isa 36–37). These stories of Ahaz and Hezekiah in particular narratively embody the Isaianic conviction that trust in Yhwh, the true king, brings deliverance. The later authors responsible for Isa 24–27 make a similar point:

> Those of steadfast mind you keep in peace—
>   in peace because they trust in you.
> Trust in Yhwh forever,
>   for in Yah, the LORD[26]
>   you have an everlasting rock. (Isa 26:3–4)

The injunction to "trust" in Yhwh is immediately followed by a stark contrast between Yhwh and the Assyrian citadel: Yhwh, the "everlasting rock," will bring the impermanent "lofty city" to the ground (26:5). Victory over imperial Assyria – seen here as the abandonment and destruction of Ramat Raḥel – belongs to Yhwh.

Isa 1–39 contains a rich array of texts that respond to Assyria's presence, policy, and actions. For the student of the Hebrew Bible, these texts can be more fully appreciated when read in conversation with adjacent disciplines such as Assyriology, archaeology, and history. In doing so, one quickly recognizes that the texts many call "Scripture" are profoundly shaped by common human realities such as fear, hope, and the will to survive.

FURTHER READING

Aster, Shawn Zelig. *Reflections of Empire in Isaiah 1–39: Responses to Assyrian Ideology.* ANEM 19. Atlanta, GA: SBL Press, 2017.

Ben-Zvi, Ehud. "Who Wrote the Speech of the Rab-Shakeh and When." *JBL* 109 (1990): 79–92.

Beuken, Wim. "'Lebanon with Its Majesty Shall Fall. A Shoot Shall Come Forth from the Stump of Jesse' (Isa 10:34–11:1): Interfacing the Story of Assyria and the Image of Israel's Future in Isa 10–11." In F. Postma, K. Spronk, and E. Talstra, eds., *The New Things: Eschatology in Old Testament Prophecy* (Festschrift for Henk Leene). Leuven: Katholieke Universiteit, 2002, 17–34.

Chan, Michael J. "Rhetorical Reversal and Usurpation: Isaiah 10:5–34 and the Use of Neo-Assyrian Royal Idiom in the Construction of an Anti-Assyrian Theology." *JBL* 128:4 (2009): 717–33.

[26]   The Hebrew reads, literally, 'Yah, Yhwh.'

Cohen, Chaim. "Neo-Assyrian Elements in the First Speech of the Biblical Rab-Shaqe." *IOS* 9 (1979): 32–48.

De Jong, Matthijs J. *Isaiah Among the Ancient Near Eastern Prophets: A Comparative Study of the Isaiah Tradition and the Neo Assyrian Prophecies.* VTSup 117. Leiden: Brill, 2007.

Dubovský, Peter. "Tiglath-pileser III's Campaigns in 734–732 BC: Historical Background of Isa 7; 2 Kgs 15–16 and 2 Chr 27–28." *Biblica* 87 (2006): 153–70.

Irvine, Stuart A. *Isaiah, Ahaz, and the Syro-Ephraimitic Crisis.* SBLDS 123. Atlanta, GA: Society of Biblical Literature, 1990.

Kahn, Dan'el. *Sennacherib's Campaign against Judah: A Source Analysis of Isaiah 36–37.* Cambridge: Cambridge University Press, 2020.

Machinist, Peter. "Assyria and Its Image in the First Isaiah," *Journal of the American Oriental Society* 103 (1983): 719–37.

Machinist, Peter. "Ah Assyria … (Isaiah 10:5ff) Isaiah's Assyrian Polemic Revisited," in *Not Only History: Proceedings of the Conference Held in Honor of Mario Liverani*, Sapienza University of Rome, Department of Sciences of Antiquity, April 20–21, 2009, ed. Gilda Bartoloni and Maria Giovanna Biga in collaboration with Armando Bramanti. Winona Lake, IN: Eisenbrauns, 2016, 183–218.

Roberts, J. J. M. *First Isaiah.* Hermeneia. Minneapolis, MN: Fortress, 2015.

Winter, Irene J. "Art in Empire: The Royal Image and the Visual Dimensions of Assyrian Ideology." In *On Art in the Ancient Near East.* 2 vols., Vol. 1. Culture and History of the Ancient Near East. Leiden: Brill, 2010, 3–70.

Young, Robb A. *Hezekiah in History and Tradition.* Leiden: Brill, 2012.

Younger Jr., Lawson. "Assyria's Expansion West of the Euphrates (ca. 870–701 BCE)." In Zev I. Farber and Jacob L. Wright, eds., *Archaeology and History of Eighth-Century Judah.* ANEM 23. Atlanta, GA: SBL Press, 2018, 17–34.

Younger Jr., Lawson. "Assyrian Involvement in the Southern Levant at the End of the Eighth Century B.C.E.," In Andrew G. Vaughn and Ann E. Killebrew, eds., *Jerusalem in Bible and Archaeology: The First Temple Period.* Atlanta, GA: Society of Biblical Literature, 2003, 235–63.

3 The Book of Isaiah and the Neo-Babylonian Period

LENA-SOFIA TIEMEYER

INTRODUCTION

Babylon was one of the mightiest cities in the ancient world. It first rose to power at the beginning of the second millennium BCE as an independent city state, but gradually became the capital of the area of southern Mesopotamia normally referred to as Babylonia.

During the next 1,200 years, its influence over Mesopotamia waxed and waned. After having been subdued for nearly 300 years by the Neo-Assyrians, another political superpower, Babylon rose to political dominance one last time under Nabopolassar (r. 626–605 BCE). This so-called Neo-Babylonian Empire reached its zenith under Nebuchadnezzar II (r. 605–562 BCE), when it ruled an area reaching from the Mediterranean to the Persian Gulf. It played a central role in the history of Judah. The Neo-Babylonians curtailed Judah's political freedom during its last 50 years, culminating in Jerusalem's destruction in 586 BCE and a series of forced migrations.

The Neo-Babylonian Empire came to an end during Nabonidus's reign (r. 556–539 BCE) at the hands of the Persian king Cyrus II. As a result of the Neo-Babylonian hegemony during this crucial part of Judah's history, the Neo-Babylonian Empire, or Babylon for short, is a key topic throughout much of the Hebrew Bible.

Despite this, no text in the book of Isaiah stems from the Neo-Babylonian period. This is a rather drastic statement and appears, for all practical purposes, to render this chapter redundant. However, as it sets out to show, the *memory* of Babylon cast a long shadow. A reference to Babylon is an ambiguous indicator of the date and geographical origin of a given text. Babylon became a symbol of destruction, exile, and diaspora at quite an early date, so references to it are best understood as part of the Bible's discourse on empire.

This chapter seeks to accomplish three things. First, it analyzes how the book of Isaiah conceptualizes Babylon. We are dealing with what is often called cultural memory: What function do the images of Babylon play within Isaiah, and how did the Isaianic authors construe their own identity and religion when faced with this empire?

Second, it explores the dating of those texts in Isaiah that are traditionally assigned to the Neo-Babylonian period owing to their polemic against Babylon and clear support of Cyrus. This endeavor is mainly text-historical in character: What criteria do scholars use for dating the composition of the pertinent material (Isa 13–14; 21; and 40–55) to this period, and how well do they stand up to scrutiny?

Third, it examines the issue of geographical provenance of these same chapters. Do references to Babylonia demand an author based in Babylon? That is, do these chapter reveal an insider's familiarity of Babylonian matters, or do they reflect the kind of general knowledge that many people living within the realm of the Empire would be expected to have?

BABYLON IN THE BOOK OF ISAIAH

The Neo-Babylonian Empire is deeply woven into the fabric of Isaiah. We shall here look at two key images of Babylon that appear in the book. Both images reflect on Babylon's transience, by contrast stressing the endurance of the God of Israel and his eternal care for his people.

"Fallen is Babylon"

One prevailing image of Babylon emphasizes its defeat. In Isa 13–23, Babylon is treated as Israel's (and Yhwh's) archenemy; it is an evil force that will be defeated. Throughout Isa 13, Babylon's fall is conceptualized as an event of cosmic proportions. The global scope and the mythological language of Isa 14 likewise emphasize the far-reaching consequences of Babylon's fall. Finally, the magnitude of Babylon's fall is epitomized in Isa 21:9 through its harrowing statement "fallen is Babylon."

The fall of Babylon is also the key message of Isa 47. This oracle places Babylon in the center of attention as it addresses "Virgin Babylon" in direct speech. Its style is reminiscent of that of Mesopotamian city laments (FRANKE: 416–17). There is an affinity between Isa 47 and Isa 13–14. First, all three oracles fall into the typical category of the so-called Oracles Against the Nations (OAN). As such, their main purpose was to inform *the people of Israel* about Yhwh's power in comparison with that of the deities of the foreign nations. Second, all three oracles are given a prominent position in their wider literary context. Isa 47 forms the pivotal oracle in Isa 40–55, and chapters 13–14 constitute the opening oracles of Isa 13–23.

The fall of Babylon in Isa 47 is conceptualized as a "reversal of fortunes." This notion is emphasized in two ways. First, within Isa 40–55 itself, Isa 47 ends the description of downtrodden Israel that has been the main theme of Isa 40–6 and commences the series of descriptions of the elevation and rejoicing of Zion-Jerusalem in 48–55. Second, there is significant overlap between the depiction of Babylon in Isa 47 and that of Daughter Zion in Lamentations:

1. Both the opening line in Isa 47:1a and the command to sit in silence in Isa 47:5 are modelled after Lam 2:10;
2. Babylon's nakedness in Isa 47:3 echoes the similar state of Zion in Lam 1:8;
3. Babylon's thoughtless arrogance described in Isa 47:7b alludes to the description of Zion in Lam 1:9;
4. The description of God's anger in Isa 47:6aα is reminiscent of that in Lam 5:22;
5. God pollutes Babylon in Isa 47:6aβ and his heritage in Lam 2:2b and 5:2;
6. The plight of the elderly in Isa 47:6bβ brings Lam 1:19aβ and 2:21 to mind;
7. The imagery of Babylon (not) sitting as a widow in Isa 47:8bα is modeled after Lam 1:1a.

In sum, Isa 47 depicts the downfall of Babylon in the same terms as those used by the people of Judah for remembering the downfall of Jerusalem. Jerusalem and Babylon thus change places and become each other's mirror images. Yhwh allowed Babylon to destroy Jerusalem, but now Yhwh is restoring Jerusalem to her former glory while Babylon will pay the price for its actions against Yhwh's city.

THE POWERLESSNESS OF BABYLON'S GODS

Yhwh's power over Babylon includes his power over its gods. Isa 21:9 brings the message home succinctly, as it depicts the images of the Babylonian gods lying shattered on the ground. Isa 44:24–5 and 47:12–15 likewise extol Yhwh's supremacy as he makes a fool of Babylonian divination practices. All three passages accentuate that the Babylonian gods and their human interlocutors have no power when set up against the God of Israel.

This message is expanded in Isa 46:1–4. In its polemic against Bel (Marduk) and Nebo (Nabu), the chief deities of Babylon, Yhwh declares that he is mightier and more dependable than they, and therefore better suited to care for Jacob-Israel. Verses 3–4 repeat the vocabulary of verses 1–2 to underline this message: The Babylonian deities are worthless compared with Yhwh's omnipotence and reliability.

The imagery of verses 1–2 has been understood to portray one of three different scenarios: (1) the *akītu* festival, (2) the Babylonians bringing their idols to safety, or (3) the Babylonian idols being carried into captivity (TIEMEYER: 118–23). The first option, namely that Isa 46:1–2 contains an eyewitness account and/or a parody of the part of the *akītu* festival that featured the statues of Marduk and Nabu being carried in a procession through Babylon, is ultimately unpersuasive.

The starting point of exegesis must be the literary presentation of Isa 46:1–4 as a whole. In the biblical text, the imagery of deities being carried by animals is a sign of their lowliness and powerlessness, in contrast with Yhwh's ability to carry those in his care. The second interpretation is likewise not compelling, as it does not fit well with the reference in verse 2b to the statues being taken into exile. Instead, Isa 46:1–2 is most likely a depiction of how Babylon's enemies carried away the statues of Marduk and Nabu as trophies. This interpretation harmonizes well with the general message of Isa 46:1–2 that the idols themselves are unable to deliver a burden (v. 2ab); instead they themselves must be carried (v. 2b). It also sets the scene for the contrasting imagery in verse 3 where God carries his people Israel.

THE (NON-)NEO-BABYLONIAN DATING OF ISAIAH

The dating of biblical texts is a vexed issue. Many factors, such as content, language, and ideology, play a role, but the outcome is seldom certain. On the one hand, texts tend to address issues relevant to their contemporary times. It is natural to regard Isaianic texts dealing with Babylon as stemming from the Neo-Babylonian period, but texts may also make such references retrospectively. A text about Babylon may thus reflect in hindsight on the Neo-Babylonian Empire. It may also be ideological in nature – that is, it may depict Babylon in a way that corresponds only partly to historical reality.

One recurring issue in the dating debate is the Isaianic depictions of the fall of Babylon. The available historical records, the Babylonian

Chronicles,[1] the Cyrus Cylinder,[2] and the Verse Account of the reign of Nabonidus,[3] indicate that the fall of the Neo-Babylonian Empire to Persia in October 539 BCE was relatively peaceful. The Persian forces defeated the Babylonians at the battle of Opis in June. Later the same year, the Persian king Cyrus II entered Babylon without destroying the city. The Babylonians' lack of military resistance to the takeover can in part be explained by their dissatisfaction with the rule of their monarch Nabonidus and his preference for the moon god Sîn over Marduk. In contrast to these Persian sources, however, the book of Isaiah envisages the downfall of Babylon as a violent incident. This discrepancy provides a data point when dating the relevant Isaianic material: Is it *earlier* than 539 BCE and describing the hoped-for (but never realized) future destruction of Babylon, or is it a *later* ideological reflection of what happened (symbolically) to the city?

Another matter of frequent debate is how to account for the negative portrayal of Babylon in Isaiah. On the one hand, one might assume that this type of material must postdate 539 BCE, given the presumed danger of writing such polemic texts during the regime itself. Their outspoken declaration of Babylon's demise, and equally clear propaganda in favor of Cyrus, would presumably have constituted high treason. On the other hand, one might instead posit that these Hebrew oracles were of no great concern of Neo-Babylonian officials. They probably could not read them anyway, so the oracles would have been of little interest as long as they were not uttered as part of inflammatory speeches on the streets of the cities in the empire.

Finally, the scholarly tendency to assign the creation and redaction of multiple texts to the single decade leading up to 539 BCE needs to be evaluated. Accepting that this was a time of political instability, this setting may either have prompted or hindered text production. We also need to consider to what extent the (relatively peaceful) Persian takeover of Babylon actually constituted a substantial change for the Jews living in either Babylonia or Judah sufficient enough to justify this presumed scribal frenzy.

---

[1] For an English translation of the relevant section, see Alan Millar, "The Babylonian Chronicle," in *COS* 1.137:467–8.

[2] For an English translation, see Mordechai Cogan, "Cyrus Cylinder," in *COS* 2.124:314–16.

[3] For an English translation, see "Nabonidus and the Clergy of Babylon," trans. A. Leo Oppenheim (*ANET*, 312–5). For online access, see www.livius.org/sources/content/anet/verse-account-of-nabonidus/

BABYLON IN THE ORACLES AGAINST THE NATIONS (ISAIAH 13–23)

In light of these observations and questions, we shall look at three key texts among the OAN that feature Babylon (Isa 13:1–22; 14:3–23; 21:1–10). In each case, the arguments for and against a dating within the Neo-Babylonian period 626–539 BCE are evaluated.

The theme "Babylon" opens both sets of five "burdens" against the nations. This prominence has often been understood to support a Babylonian setting for and/or redaction of the OAN. Williamson, for example, dates the current form of Isa 13–14 shortly before the fall of Babylon owing to its similarity with Isa 40–55 (WILLIAMSON: 156–75; LEE: 180). Yet this affinity may point toward either a late Neo-Babylonian or an early Persian date, depending on how one dates Isa 40–55. Other scholars see the final form of chapters 13–14 as the product of the Persian period. Berges, for instance, speaks of a Persian-period "Babylonization" of the earlier preexilic collection of the OAN (BERGES: 125–8, 137–41).

Isaiah 13:1–22

Isa 13:1–22 depicts the "fall of Babylon" as an event of cosmic proportions. The lack of identifiable historical events makes dating the chapter difficult; rather it reads like an ahistorical end-time vision. This notion of universal judgment, together with the twofold references to the "Day of Yhwh" (vv. 6, 9), point to a Persian or even later dating.

Given that Babylon is the explicitly stated focal point of the oracle (v. 1), a date prior to the rise of the Neo-Babylonian Empire during the reign of Nabopolassar is unlikely, following the aforementioned rationale that prophets address issues of contemporary relevance. In parallel, the inexact and at times factually erroneous description of Babylon's fall may point to a date prior to the conquest of Babylon of Cyrus the Great in 539 BCE (BLENKINSOPP).

For two reasons, however, this reasoning is not watertight. First, Babylon was a major city throughout the second and first millennia BCE. It was sacked twice, first by Sennacherib in 689 BCE and later by Xerxes in 482 BCE. It is therefore not strictly necessary to see Isa 13:1 as a reflection on the (non)destruction in 539 BCE (BERGES: 140–1). Second, the final stanza in verses 16–22 invites a retrospective interpretation. Verse 17 mentions the *Medes*. Although the Medes, an ancient Iranian people, were known since the end of the second millennium, the various tribes rose to prominence as they formed a coalition between

678 and 549 BCE. A reference to the Medes therefore appears to suggest a date contemporary with the Neo-Babylonian period, yet the term "Medes" is confused with "Persians" in later texts, such as Dan 9:1.

To sum up, Isa 13:1–22 could be an oracle composed prior to 539 BCE in which the envisaged destruction of the superpower forms an exercise in wishful thinking, but in my view it appears to be a Persian-period discussion of the fall of an Empire, couched in stereotypical language of destruction (cf. Isa 34:5–17), in which the term "Babylon" has become a symbol of an "evil empire."

Isaiah 14:3–23

The final form of Isa 14:3–23 about the "king of Babylon" (v. 4a) is probably also Persian rather than Neo-Babylonian in origin. This *māšāl* (a literary genre often translated as "proverb," but also as "parable," "satire," or even "dirge") envisages the king's "fall." This text contains few concrete references to the historical Neo-Babylonian Empire; the scope is global and the language mythic. This latter feature explains the later traditions that interpret this chapter as speaking about the fall of Satan (e.g., Luke 10:18). The "king of Babylon" can thus be (and has been) identified with many Mesopotamian kings, and no consensus view is in sight.

Given this lack of specific historical details, the composition is extremely difficult to date. The fact that the king is described as already dead suggests a past monarch. Scholarly views range from those who identify an earlier kernel directed toward a Neo-Assyrian monarch (Isa 14:4b–21) and a later framework that transformed the material to speak against a Neo-Babylonian king (LEE: 179), to those who see the entire chapters as a later addition to the OAN composed during the Persian era (BERGES: 140–1). The strong parallels between Isa 14 and Ezek 28:11–19 and Ps 82:6–7, as well as its affinity with the material about Babylon in Isa 47:8, 10, may provide a relative textual chronology. Yet even though it is likely that some of the texts depend on the other ones, it is nonetheless difficult to determine their dates. First, it is notoriously difficult to identify which text is the source text and which one is the alluding text. Second, the uncertain dates of all the texts involved, including the composition of Isa 40–55, hinder us from reaching an unequivocal verdict.

Isaiah 21:1–10

The "fall of Babylon" is also the focus of Isa 21:1–10, as indicated by verse 9b: "fallen, fallen, is Babylon." As in the previously mentioned cases, the question is whether this section, either in part or as a whole, is a text from the Neo-Babylonian period that visualizes the hoped-for yet still future fall of the Empire, a retrospective elaboration of the historical demise of the Neo-Babylonian Empire in 539 BCE, or an ahistorical and symbolic rendering of the fall of the mighty. As in the case of Isa 13:17, much pivots around the "Medes" in 21:2: Taken at face-value, Isa 21 probably predates the Persian defeat of the Neo-Babylonian Empire; taken as a code word for "Persians," a post-539 BCE dating gains credence. Much likewise depends on our estimation of the final part of verse 9, namely that "all the images of her gods are shattered to the ground." As this vision stands in utter contrast to Cyrus's expressed wish, attested in the Cyrus Cylinder, to honor Babylon's deities, it is once again difficult to determine whether Isa 21 predicts a "wrong" future or describes retrospectively the demise of Babylon on a more symbolic level. Finally, the similar grammatical structure of Isa 21:9 with material in Isa 40–55 (40:1; 51:9, 12, 17; 52:1, 11) (WILLIAMSON: 157; BERGES: 134–5) may tip the balance either way, depending on whether the material in Isa 40:1–11 and Isa 51–2 is Neo-Babylonian or Persian in origin.

Conclusion

The three texts in Isa 13–23 that focus on Babylon – Isa 13, 14, and 21 – may either stem from the very last years of the Neo-Babylonian Period or, in my view more likely, from the Persian period. In both cases, the questions arise as to "why" and "for what audience"? Are they political "anti-Babylonian" pieces of propaganda (BLENKINSOPP) that seek to undermine the ruling colonial powers? Are they retrospective gloating of the reversal of fate experienced by their former oppressors? Are they later theological reflections of the fall of proud empires? These three options are not all mutually exclusive. Each in their own way, they emphasize the symbolic value of "Babylon" and how the city gradually came to represent God's (and Israel's) antitype (e.g., Rev 17:5).

BABYLON IN ISAIAH 39

The narrative in Isa 39 is set during the latter part of Hezekiah's reign (r. 715–687 BCE), more than 60 years prior to Nabopolassar's ascent to the Babylonian throne. At this point, Babylon was fighting for independence from the Neo-Assyrian Empire. The Babylonian king Merodach-Baladan, mentioned in Isa 39:1||2 Kgs 20:12 as having sent an embassy with a letter and a gift to Hezekiah, is an historical character (Marduk-apla-iddinna II). He wrested Babylon from Assyria in 722 BCE and reigned independently until 710 BCE, when Sargon II expelled him from Babylon. He later recaptured the Babylonian throne, which he held for a year (703–702 BCE), until he was defeated by the Assyrians. The reason for the letter and present Marduk-apla-iddinna II sent to Jerusalem was, according to Isa 39:1, to congratulate Hezekiah on having recovered from his illness. The same embassy is presumably mentioned in 2 Chr 32:31, where the reason for the inquiry relates to the "miraculous signs" that have occurred in the land. Discussing the possible historicity behind the narrative, Blenkinsopp suggests that the Babylonian ruler sent his embassy to explore the option of enrolling Hezekiah in an anti-Assyrian scheme (BLENKINSOPP).

Isa 39 concludes with a divine oracle about the destruction of Jerusalem and the Babylonian exile (vv. 6–8||2 Kings 20:17–19). In its current literary setting in the Neo-Assyrian period, this oracle appears out of place. It is therefore likely that it constitutes a later addition that forms a *vaticinium ex eventu*, a prophecy after the fact (BEUKEN: 450–1). This reference to the Neo-Babylonian destruction of Jerusalem and the ensuing exile of the upper echelons of the Judean population thus effectively pushes the composition of the passage well into the Neo-Babylonian or Persian period. More specifically, this reference serves to connect the material in Isa 1–39 with the following material in Isa 40 and onwards: It foreshadows the rebuilding of Jerusalem and the exiles' return to the city that together form the focal point of Isa 40–48 (STROMBERG: 218–19, 250). Given this function as a transition text, Isa 39:6–8 is probably later than Isa 40–8, and therefore probably composed in the Persian rather than the Neo-Babylonian period.

ISAIAH 40–66

The same uncertainty faces us when seeking to date the material in Isa 40–66. Again, a few passages might have been composed during the last few years of Neo-Babylonian hegemony in the ancient Near East, but it is overall more likely that most, if not all, of Isa 40–66 was written *after* 539 BCE.

Isaiah 40–8

There is a marked thematic distinction between Isa 40–8 and Isa 49–55: Whereas the former speaks about Babylon, the latter speaks about Zion. Many scholars therefore argue for a break, either in terms of authorship, date, or geographical setting, after chapter 48. It is common, especially among continental European scholars, to view Isa 40–55 as a gradually grown textual corpus that comprises at least three chronologically distinct textual layers written by different authors of differing geographical origins. The earliest core composition, to be found in (parts of) Isa 40–8 (BERGES: 385–6) or (parts of) Isa 40–52 (HERMISSON: 303–4), is thought to stem from an individual or a group of people in the exilic community in Babylon. Later, upon their arrival in Judah, either these same people or their disciples reworked the original core text by adding significant amounts of material.

The identified core layer is often understood to stem from before 539 BCE, whereas the later redactional material originated in the Persian period from around 520 BCE and later. A smaller number of scholars doubt that *any* part of Isa 40–55 stems from the Neo-Babylonian period. Kratz, for example, identifies five developmental stages of Isa 40–55, yet dates even his Babylonian core collection, containing most of Isa 40:1–48:21* and 52:7–10, to a time soon after 539 BCE (KRATZ: 148–9, 170, 217 [table]).

The dating of Isa 40–8 pivots around the references to Babylon and Cyrus in the text. The same issue as earlier persists: Do these references *predict* or *presuppose* Babylon's downfall? And do they predict Cyrus's *future* ascent to the throne of Babylon, or reflect his already *past* defeat of Babylon?

Cyrus in Isaiah 40–8

Cyrus is mentioned explicitly in Isa 44:24–45:7. Isa 41:2–3, 25; 43:14; 46:11; and 48:14–15 most likely also allude to him. According to these passages, Cyrus is Yhwh's shepherd who fulfils his will (44:28; 46:11), he is Yhwh's anointed who will subdue the nations (54:1), he will walk before Yhwh and destroy all obstacles (45:2), and Yhwh will strengthen him (45:4). Cyrus will further bring destruction to Babylon (43:14) and carry out Yhwh's purpose against it (48:14–15). These references together suggest a date of composition after 559 BCE when Cyrus became King of Anshar, after his overthrow of the Median kingdom in 547 BCE, and probably also after his conquest of Elam in 540 BCE. In short, the Cyrus texts in Isa 40–8 were likely inspired by Cyrus's military prowess and thus unlikely to predate his defeat of the Neo-Babylonian Empire in 539 BCE by many years.

The strong possibility remains, though, that these oracles may, in fact, postdate 539 BCE. These texts are polemic in character insofar as they emphasize that Yhwh, rather than Cyrus, is the main benefactor of Cyrus's work. Cyrus is Yhwh's military tool who does his bidding, and the result of Cyrus's activity is that everybody will know Yhwh (45:5) and the nations will be handed over to Yhwh (41:2–3, 25). The message of Isa 40–8 about Cyrus is thus less about his rise to power; rather it is a reflection of the anticipated global faith in Yhwh that will result from Cyrus's conquest of Babylon. In this discussion, there is compelling evidence that shows the depiction of Cyrus in Isa 40–8 serves as a cipher for later rulers (cf. David) (WILSON). That is to say, the Isaianic language of messianic expectations that Cyrus inspired was applied to other rulers (and hoped-for rulers) for centuries afterwards.

There is a certain similarity between the descriptions of Cyrus in Isa 40–8 and that in the Cyrus Cylinder. In both texts, the representatives of the local deities (Marduk in Babylon, and Yhwh in Jerusalem) explain that Cyrus is the god's chosen king and savior. Even certain phraseology, such as "taking the hand" are common to both texts (Isa 42:6). Several scholars have consequently explained this similarity as a matter of direct influence (ANTHONIOZ: 32). These parallels are probably not extensive enough to indicate direct literary influence of the Cyrus Cylinder on Isa 40–8 (TIEMEYER: 96–8). It is more likely that each text was independently motivated by similar Persian policies and propaganda. Since the cylinder dates from shortly after the fall of Babylon in 539, the similarities to Isaiah would again suggest a post-Neo-Babylonian date for the latter, in any case.

Babylon in Isaiah 47

Along with the elevation of Cyrus and the restoration of Jerusalem, Isa 40–8 speaks of the destruction of Babylon. On the one hand, the descriptions of Babylon's fate in Isa 47 convey a sense of future: These things are *anticipated* to befall Babylon (e.g., 48:14: "he shall perform his purpose on Babylon"). Furthermore, this description of the utter shaming of Babylon and its gods disagrees with historical reality: Cyrus honored Babylon's deities and spared the city.

On the other hand, the portrayal of a defeated and humiliated Babylon is clearly ideological in character as it aims to contrast that of Zion's suffering and rehabilitation: Whereas Babylon is to "go down" and "sit in the dust" (Isa 47:1), Zion is to "shake off [her] dust" and "rise up" (52:2); whereas Babylon's nakedness will be exposed (Isa 47:2–3), Zion is invited to put on fine garments (52:1); whereas Babylon is widowed and childless (47:8–9), Zion will have many children (Isa 49:20–1; 54:1–4; cf. 60:4, 8–9; 66:7–9) (TIEMEYER: 124). Therefore even in their original composition, these passages were seemingly not meant as journalistic reports about Cyrus's conquest of Babylon, but instead form part of a broader discourse about Yhwh's power over the rise and fall of nations.

Conclusion: "Mind the Gap"

To conclude the discussion of dating, it is unlikely that the book of Isaiah contains material composed during the Neo-Babylonian period, yet the possibility cannot be ruled out. The references to Babylon could be future-oriented expressions of wishful thinking about the downfall of Israel's archenemy, but they are more likely to form retrospective reflections of its fate, where Babylon's ultimate defeat at the hands of Cyrus is contrasted with Yhwh's care for his people Israel and his city Jerusalem.

Pausing for a bit, we just observed that the texts in Isaiah about Babylon either predict its future fall or reflect on its past fall. What is missing are texts about Babylon's actions against Judah. There is nothing about Nebuchadnezzar's defeat of Jerusalem in 586 BCE. Compared with the other prophetic books (Jeremiah, Ezekiel, the Book of the Twelve), this absence is glaring. The reader "jumps" from the prediction of destruction and exile in Isa 39 (set more than a century before it happened) to God's promise to comfort his city in Isa 40:1. In between, we have a gap or, in the words of Poulsen, a "black hole" where the exile would be (POULSEN). This black hole forms the true center of the book of Isaiah, and it is here that we find the real Neo-Babylonian Empire and its destructive actions against Jerusalem and the people of God.

A BABYLONIAN SETTING FOR ISAIAH 40–55?

In the previous section, we sought to ascertain *when* the texts in Isa 40–55 were composed. In this final section, we address the related question of *where* they were composed. Most biblical scholars conclude that Isa 40–55 is the product of the exilic Jewish community – first in Babylon, and then in Judah after their return. The issue here is whether those Isaianic texts that speak about Babylon necessitate that their authors lived in Babylon. I argue that they testify instead to the pervasive Neo-Babylonian imperial influence over the general culture of the ancient Near East. The two views are, of course, not mutually exclusive; yet a text that speaks about Babylon does not automatically indicate a Babylonian origin.

The question of *where* blurs the line between the Neo-Babylonian and Persian periods insofar as it challenges the significance of 539 BCE: To what extent did the change of political regime in Babylon make a palpable difference for the Judeans, regardless of their whereabouts? Although Cyrus's ascent to the Babylonian throne effectively ended the Neo-Babylonian period, the city of Babylon, the larger region of

Babylonia, and its cultural dominance survived the political shift. The Cyrus Cylinder is a case in point: Although it was written in the Persian period, it is modeled after Neo-Babylonian inscriptions in terms of language, style, and outer appearance.

As background, it is important to note that Isa 40–55, as we read it, is very much concerned with Jerusalem and Judah; its people and land are a primary focus. Texts such as 40:2–9 ("Speak tenderly to Jerusalem ... say to the cities of Judah...") and 44:26–8 ("who says of Jerusalem ... and of the cities of Judah ... and of the temple...") are addressed to or about the land of Judah. Indeed, Babylon disappears entirely from the book after chapter 47. Chapter 48 is addressed to a seemingly reconstituted people of "Israel," and by chapter 49, the people of God are being summoned "from far away ... from the north and from the west, and ... from the land of Syene [i.e., Aswan, in the south]." All this strongly suggests that the author is writing from the perspective of the homeland of Judah.

Neo-Babylonian Imperialism

There is no doubt that the Neo-Assyrian and the subsequent Neo-Babylonian empires exerted cultural and religious dominance over the surrounding nations. Imperial ideas and institutions were exported to the areas under their control, and both resistance to and familiarity with these ideas naturally developed among the conquered peoples (see CHAN, "The Book of Isaiah in the Neo-Assyrian Period," Chapter 2 in this volume). A relatively large degree of Mesopotamian influence over the intellectual life of Israel and Judah is thus to be expected. Although the degree of knowledge of the Akkadian language and its literature among the biblical authors is uncertain, and although some of this cultural familiarity may have been filtered through Aramaic, we may nonetheless assume that the people in Judah during the ascent of Neo-Babylonian power had some familiarity with Mesopotamian religious customs and beliefs (TIEMEYER: 79–83). A Judahite setting of the composition of Isa 40–55 thus does not in itself imply lack of exposure to Babylonian literary culture.

Turning the issue upside down, only very limited evidence suggests that cultural exchange took place between the exiles in Babylon and the surrounding Babylonian literary world. As demonstrated by Waerzeggers, the extant cuneiform records, which preserve the activities of the Jewish exiles, suggest that the only interface where cultural exchange took place was in the mercantile world, where some Babylonian traders with literate background may have served as "cultural brokers" (WAERZEGGERS: 131–46). A Babylonian setting of the composition of Isa 40–55 thus does not in itself imply access to Babylonian literary culture.

Neo-Babylonian Influence on Isaiah 40–55

Scholars have commonly appealed to three sets of texts in Isa 40–55 to support a Babylonian provenance of the authors behind Isa 40–55, yet none offers unequivocal support for this claim. Instead, they anchor the message of Isa 40–55 within the imperial Neo-Babylonian religious and cultural sphere.

The first set includes the references to idol-making in 42:9–20, and to astrology, divination, and magic in Isa 44:24–5 and 47:12–15; but these are exactly the kinds of things that people *throughout* the ancient world would have associated with Babylon. They do not indicate specific local knowledge. Second, the description of the downfall of Marduk and Nabû in Isa 46:1–4 likewise does not demand an author residing in Babylon. A prophet in either Babylon or Judah would have been able to envisage the fall of Babylon along the lines of the well-known ancient Near Eastern ideology of deportation of statues. The focus on Marduk and Nabû in Isa 46:1–4 in fact reveals a *lack* of in-depth knowledge of the religious situation during Nabonidus's reign. His unpopular proclivity for the moon god Sîn was presumably a well-known fact among Babylon's inhabitants (HÄGGLUND: 153). This unfamiliarity, in turn, invites the conclusion that the author of Isa 46:1–4 lived at some distance from Babylon. Third and finally, the OAN in Isa 47 shows no awareness of local customs, but instead seeks to ensure the Judeans, regardless of their whereabouts, of Yhwh's supremacy over Babylon. The abovementioned similarities between Isa 47 and Lamentations point in the same directions: This oracle aimed to bring comfort to the Judeans by emphasizing Babylon's ephemerality and Yhwh's perpetuity (TIEMEYER: 123–6).

Summing up, none of these texts contains anything amounting to local knowledge of Babylon. Instead, they reveal superficial knowledge of Mesopotamian culture and religious practices – fully in line with what would be expected of any author living in the shadow of the Neo-Babylonian Empire. What we have in Isa 40–55 is thus nothing more and nothing less than the result of Babylonian cultural and religious hegemony in the sixth century BCE (TIEMEYER: 116–17).

CONCLUSION

We have looked at the influence of the Neo-Babylonian Empire upon the book of Isaiah. On the one hand, it is unlikely that any Isaianic text was composed during the Neo-Babylonian period. In a few cases, it may be possible to isolate a core text from the Neo-Babylonian era, yet their final form is a product of the Persian period.

On the other hand, the Neo-Babylonian Empire cast a long shadow over the book. The oracles reflecting on its downfall in Isa 13, 14, 21, and 47 together emphasize Babylon's impact on the people of Judah in terms of both culture and military power. Likewise, the material about Babylon in Isa 39, forming a bridge to the oracles of comfort beginning in Isa 40, emphasizes the destructive repercussions of the Neo-Babylonian Empire for Jerusalem and its inhabitants. Ultimately, however, the Isaianic authors sought to underscore Babylon's weakness and transitory existence, and to assert that its demise was the result of Yhwh's supremacy over Babylon's own deities. Although the data about Babylon included in Isaiah (e.g., its diviners, its chief deities) have suggested to some readers that its authors lived in Babylon, a Judean setting is fully in line with the wide-ranging influence of the Neo-Babylonian Empire.

FURTHER READING

Anthonioz, Stéphanie. "La polémique contre l'idolâtrie (Is. 40–48) à la lumière du cylindre de Cyrus." *Revue des Sciences Religieuses* 84 (2010): 19–42.

Berges, Ulrich. *The Book of Isaiah: Its Composition and Final Form*. Translated by Millard C. Lind. HBM 46. Sheffield: Phoenix Press, 2012.

Beuken, Willem A. M. *Jesaja 28–39*. Translated by Andrea Spans. HThKAT. Freiburg: Herder, 2010.

Blenkinsopp, Joseph. "Isaiah and the Neo-Babylonian Background." Pages 159–75 in *The Oxford Handbook of Isaiah*. Edited by Lena-Sofia Tiemeyer. Oxford: Oxford University Press, 2020.

Franke, Chris A. "The Function of the Satiric Lament over Babylon in Second Isaiah (xlvii)." *VT* 41 (1991): 408–18.

Hägglund, Fredrik. *Isaiah 53 in the Light of Homecoming after Exile*. FAT II/31. Tübingen: Mohr Siebeck, 2008.

Hermisson, Hans-Jürgen. "Einheit und Komplexität Deuterojesajas: Probleme der Redaktionsgeschichte von Jes 40–55." Pages 287–312 in *The Book of Isaiah / Le livre d'Isaïe: Les oracles et leurs relectures unité et complexité de l'ouvrage*. BETL 81. Edited by Jacques Vermeylen. Leuven: Leuven University Press, 1989.

Kratz, Reinhard G. *Kyros im Deuterojesaja-Buch: Redaktionsgeschichtliche Untersuchungen zu Entstehung und Theologie von Jes 40–55*. FAT 1. Tübingen: Mohr Siebeck, 1991.

Lee, Jongkyung. *A Redactional Study of the Book of Isaiah 13–23*. OTRM. Oxford: Oxford University Press, 2018.

Poulsen, Frederik. *The Black Hole in Isaiah: A Study of Exile as a Literary Theme*. FAT 125. Tübingen: Mohr Siebeck, 2019.

Stromberg, Jacob. *Isaiah After Exile: The Author of Third Isaiah as Reader and Redactor*. OTM. Oxford: Oxford University Press, 2011.

Tiemeyer, Lena-Sofia. *For the Comfort of Zion: The Geographical and Theological Location of Isaiah 40–55*. VTSup 139. Leiden: Brill, 2011.

Waerzeggers, Caroline. "Locating Contact in the Babylonian Exile: Some Reflections on Tracing Judean-Babylonian Encounters in Cuneiform Texts." Pages 131–46 in *Encounters by the Rivers of Babylon: Scholarly Conversations between Jews, Iranians and Babylonians in Antiquity*. TSAJ 160. Edited by Uri Gabbay and Shai Secunda. Tübingen: Mohr Siebeck, 2014.

Williamson, H. G. M. *The Book Called Isaiah: Deutero-Isaiah's Role in Composition and Redaction*. Oxford: Clarendon Press, 1994.

Wilson, Ian Douglas. "Yahweh's Anointed: Cyrus, Deuteronomy's Law of the King, and Yehudite Identity." Pages 325–61 in *Political Memory in and after the Persian Empire*. ANEM 13. Edited by Jason M. Silverman and Caroline Waerzeggers. Atlanta, GA: SBL, 2015.

4 The Book of Isaiah in the Persian Period

LUCAS L. SCHULTE

The Persian Period permeates the book of Isaiah. From explicit references to the Persian emperor Cyrus and his conquests, to Isaiah's concepts of universalism paralleling that of the pluralistic ideals of the Persian Empire, to allusions to the social and theological currents of the Restoration period in Judah, to more subtle editorial activity that reshaped and reframed the entire book, the Persian Period provides invaluable perspective.

A BRIEF HISTORY OF THE FIRST PERSIAN EMPIRE

The first Persian Empire is usually dated from approximately 550 to 330 (all dates are BCE unless otherwise noted), and is sometimes referred to as the Achaemenid Empire to distinguish it from later Persian empires.[1] "Achaemenid" comes from the name of Achaemenes, whom Darius I, the third Persian emperor, claimed was an ancestor he had in common with the first and second Persian emperors (Cyrus II and Cambyses II). There is some doubt as to whether Achaemenes was a real historical figure or a fictional invention of Darius created to fortify his claim to rule, given that he was not descended from Cyrus the Great.[2]

The Persian Empire began with the rise of its first emperor, Cyrus II "the Great." This is the Cyrus mentioned by name in the book of Isaiah. The prophet who authored Isa 40–55 (often called "Deutero-Isaiah" or "Second Isaiah") would have been his contemporary. In around 559,

---

[1] For example, the Parthian/Arsacid Persian Empire (i.e. the second Persian Empire, c. 247 BCE–224 CE) and the Sasanian Persian Empire (i.e. the third Persian Empire, c. 224–651 CE)

[2] The Behistun inscription of Darius I (ii.1) and Herodotus (Hist. 7.11; cf. also 3.75) both report that Achaemenes was the father of Teispes, ancestor of Cyrus II and Darius I. However, Cyrus II does not mention Achaemenes at all in his own detailed genealogy in the Cyrus Cylinder. The possibly mythical nature of Achaemenes is underscored by Plato's comment in Alcibiades 1 (Plat. Alc. 1 120e) that Achaemenes was descended from Zeus. Inscriptions from Pasargadae (CMa and CMc) call Cyrus II an Achaemenid as well, but these may have been composed under Darius I.

Cyrus ascended the throne of the small kingdom of Persia, located in southwestern Iran and centered on the region of Fars, in close contact with the Elamites and the Medes. After defeating the Median army in 550 and conquering Lydia and much of western Anatolia, Cyrus reached the pinnacle of his imperial campaigns with the successful conquest of Babylon in 539.

In addition to his military prowess, Cyrus seems to have had a special gift for "public relations." A Babylonian inscription known as the Cyrus Cylinder describes how he conquered Babylon peacefully with the aid of the Babylonian god Marduk. The cylinder goes on to describe Cyrus as "King of Babylon," and attributes to him benevolent deeds such as freeing the Babylonian people, returning other peoples and their gods to their homes, and rebuilding the dilapidated sanctuaries of the Babylonian gods. Another Babylonian inscription known as the Nabonidus Chronicle claims that during Cyrus' siege of Babylon, his troops made sure not to interrupt any religious services or festivals at the Babylonian temples. Whether or not Cyrus and the Persian army did all of these things exactly as described, we can say these texts present him as supporting and being supported by certain Babylonian religious elements – particularly those of the Babylonian chief god Marduk. During further campaigns in central Asia, Cyrus apparently died in August 530.

Cyrus' son Cambyses II succeeded him, and also assumed the title "King of Babylon." A fragmentary portion of the Nabonidus Chronicle mentions Cambyses and many elements of the *akitu*, the Babylonian New Year festival. It appears that Cambyses "took the hand" of the god Nabu in that festival, a role traditionally performed only by Babylonian kings (SCHULTE 2016b: 47–48).

After using Persian financial resources to acquire a powerful navy, Cambyses successfully invaded Egypt in about 525, subsuming that great power into the Persian empire. Although classical authors describe Cambyses as hostile to Egyptian religion,[3] there is no evidence of this in Egyptian sources. Rather, just as Cyrus was presented in Babylonian texts as "King of Babylon," who supported Babylonian religious institutions and was supported by a Babylonian god, Cambyses was presented as a pharaoh in Egyptian texts. The Egyptian inscription on the Statue of Udjahorresnet as well as an inscription on an Apis Bull stele portray Cambyses as being supported by the Egyptian goddess Neith, receiving traditional titles of an Egyptian pharaoh (including "Son of Re," another

---

[3]   See Herodotus, *Hist.* 3.27–29; Strabo, *Geography* 17.

Egyptian god), and perhaps even participating in Egyptian religious roles of pharaoh for the goddess Neith and the Apis Bull's funeral. Cambyses died in 522 along the way to Syria from Egypt – possibly as the result of an assassination plot instigated by his successor, Darius I.

The accession of Darius I "the Great" to the Persian throne occurred in the midst of confusion surrounding Cambyses' death. A person claiming to be Cambyses' brother Bardiya attempted to claim the throne. In the monumental Behistun Inscription (carved into a mountainside near modern Bisotun, Iran), Darius claimed Bardiya had already been killed by Cambyses and that this impostor was actually a Magian named Gaumata. At the same time, Darius also claimed to be from another branch of the larger Achaemenid royal dynasty from which Cyrus and Cambyses supposedly descended, therefore making Darius the rightful heir to the Persian throne. The supposedly close physical resemblance of "Gaumata" to Bardiya, as well as the numerous and geographically extensive rebellions that arose throughout the empire following "Gaumata's" death, may point to a very different interpretation: that Darius had Cambyses killed and usurped the throne from Cambyses' brother Bardiya, the legitimate heir. Darius' prolific inscriptions and iconography, including the Behistun inscription, may protest too much in repeatedly stating that Darius did not lie about his accession to the throne, and thus reflect the disputed nature of the claim.

The Persian Empire reached its greatest extent during the reign of Darius I, stretching from the Indus River in the east to Thrace and even the Danube River in the west. Darius also held the title "King of Babylon" and perhaps even took part in the traditional religious role of the King of Babylon for the Babylonian New Year's festival. Several Egyptian inscriptions, including the Statue of Udjahorresnet, the Statue of Darius I, the Apis Stele of Year 4 of Darius I, and the Canal Stelae of Darius I, also give Darius the traditional titles of an Egyptian pharaoh and portray him as supported by Egyptian gods. In addition to these accomplishments, Darius initiated massive building and public-works projects during his reign. Examples include the completion of the Egyptian canal linking the Red Sea to the Mediterranean, the construction of the new capital of Persepolis, and the foundation of new palaces in Susa and Ecbatana. At the time of his death from an illness in November 486, Darius was preparing both to campaign against Greece and to put down an Egyptian insurrection.

Following Darius I's death, his son and heir Xerxes acceded to the Persian throne. Xerxes' reign, like that of Darius, began amid insurrection – albeit insurrection that was not as geographically wide-spread. Xerxes had to suppress a rebellion in Egypt that had begun shortly before the death of Darius. In addition, Babylonia revolted in the fifth year of Xerxes' reign. Yet Xerxes successfully met these challenges. The Egyptian rebellion was put down within a year of his ascension to the throne, and after successfully suppressing Babylon's revolt, he subdivided the province of Babylon into two parts. Xerxes also accomplished several building projects at Persepolis, including the completion of the Palace of Darius, the north staircase of the Apadana, the Gate and Stairs of All Nations, the Palace of Xerxes, the Harem and Southern Buildings, and the Tripylon.

Xerxes is perhaps best known for his campaigns against the Greeks. This is surely owing to the fact that the classical Greek sources describe that war in depth whereas his activities in other parts of his empire are not as copiously documented. The Persian armies of Xerxes had some initial victories against the Greeks, particularly at Thermopylae, and managed to enter central Greece as well as to assert Persian authority from Thebes and Thessaly. In 480, however, the Greeks turned the tables by winning an important naval battle against the Persians at the straits of Salamis. Ultimately the Greeks defeated the Persian army at the battle of Plataea in 479.

The Greek sources present a rather negative view of Xerxes, which has led many scholars to assume that he was less tolerant of non-Persian religions than his predecessors. However, some anti-Persian bias seems to have been at work in these sources. Babylonian texts continued to use the title "King of Babylon" for Xerxes throughout his reign. Likewise, Egyptian sources continue to bestow upon him the titles of Egyptian pharaohs, including "Son of Re." Even Greek sources state that Xerxes offered sacrifices at Greek religious centers such as the Acropolis and assigned Athenians serving in the Persian forces to some of these religious centers.

King Xerxes and his son and heir (another Darius) were murdered in a court intrigue in August 465. Following the assassination of Xerxes and the crown prince Darius, one of Xerxes' younger sons became King Artaxerxes I in 465. The real nature of the death of Artaxerxes I and the crown prince was likely obscured by the new king, Artaxerxes I, who may have been complicit. In the midst of the turmoil surrounding the assassination of Xerxes and the battle for the throne that ensued, a Libyan named Inarus led a revolt of Egyptians within the Nile Delta against the Persians in order to win back the Egyptians' freedom. With support from the Athenians, this Egyptian revolt lasted from c. 464–454.

However, the Achaemenid general Megabyzus led the Persian army and navy to defeat these Egyptian rebels and their Athenian allies, executing Inarus and allowing some of the Athenians to return to Greece via the Libyan Desert. The Athenians later attempted a campaign against Persian forces in Cyprus, but ultimately failed in this endeavor.

Like his Persian royal predecessors, Artaxerxes I continued to hold traditional titles and roles in his main subject nations. Babylonian sources continue to apply the title "King of Babylon" to Artaxerxes until at least the 24th year of his reign, and the Babylonian temples and other religious institutions appear to have continued uninterrupted. Egyptian sources, too, continued to apply the traditional religious titles of Egyptian pharaohs to Artaxerxes I. He also completed several building projects in Persepolis and elsewhere. The mission of Nehemiah to rebuild the walls of Jerusalem almost certainly occurred during the rule of this builder king (Neh 2:1; 5:14). Although the book of Nehemiah does not specify which Artaxerxes he served as cup-bearer, the general scholarly consensus places him in the reign of Artaxerxes I, between 445 and 433. Artaxerxes and his wife died in Babylonia during the winter, c. 424. After a struggle between the sole legitimate son Xerxes II and several of Artaxerxes' illegitimate sons, the throne was eventually assumed c. early 423 by Artaxerxes' illegitimate son, Ochus, who took the name Darius II. Fewer sources have survived for the reigns of the later Persian kings, and since they had little discernible impact on the book of Isaiah, the remainder of the history of the Persian empire until its conquest by Alexander the Great can be passed over.

It is important to observe that the Persian policies that allowed for the rebuilding of Jerusalem's walls and temple, and that offered ongoing support to Jerusalem's leaders, were probably made and carried out with political purposes in mind. The Persian Empire continued to struggle for control of the far corners of its territory, from Egypt to Greece to Asia Minor. Under these conditions, it was important to have peace in the intermediary regions. Persian kings discovered what the Assyrians and Babylonians seem never to have figured out: It was both easier and more cost-effective to inspire allegiance through benevolence than through terror.

THE CYRUS CYLINDER: TEMPLATE FOR PERSIAN PROPAGANDA

One of the most important texts for understanding the Persian-period context of the book of Isaiah is the Cyrus Cylinder – the earliest and clearest example of Persian royal propaganda.[4] It was written by native Babylonian priestly scribes who were worshippers of Marduk. It appears that they were infuriated by the decision of the Babylonian king, Nabonidus, to favor the moon-god Sîn for many years. Because of his neglect of Marduk's cult, they seem to have supported Cyrus as a "King of Babylon," and to have thrown the theological support of Marduk behind him. (They may also have thrown open the city to him, which would explain how Cyrus took it without a fight.)

The Cylinder lists Marduk's divine attributes and describes the formerly miserable situation under the reign of the Babylonian king Nabonidus, and it takes great pains to specify that Cyrus' reign over Babylon is the result of Marduk's magnanimous divine will. The text portrays a benevolent Marduk as searching far and wide among kings of the earth, and finally choosing Cyrus owing to his similarly benevolent rule. Marduk then personally accompanies Cyrus on his march to Babylon, peacefully admits him into the city, and hands over King Nabonidus to him. Cyrus manifests the will of Marduk, and the text at times may even blur the two together owing to their synergistic wills. The first half of the text concludes with the rejoicing of the people verifying the wisdom of Marduk's choice of Cyrus.

The second half of the text lists all sorts of magnanimous deeds that Cyrus did on behalf of the people: He sought Babylon's safety, soothed the weariness of the Babylonians and freed them, returned foreign peoples to their settlements and their native gods to their sanctuaries, and even worked to strengthen the defenses of the wall of Babylon. The text explicitly states that Marduk bestowed his benevolence upon Cyrus, while every day Cyrus sought out Marduk in awe. The Cyrus Cylinder emphasizes the following reciprocal relationships: 1) Marduk's care for the Babylonian people and their worship of Marduk, 2) Marduk's care for Cyrus and Cyrus' praise of Marduk, and 3) Cyrus' care for the Babylonian people and the Babylonians' rejoicing for Cyrus' rule. This ideological propaganda in which the Persian imperial dominion is depicted as a benevolent one supported by their subjects' deities is crucial background for understanding the character of the Persian Period more generally and the nature of the Persian rule in Yehud (the Persian province of Judea) more particularly.

---

[4] A translation of the Cyrus Cylinder can be found at www.britishmuseum.org/collection/object/W_1880-0617-1941.

ISAIAH IN PERSIAN-PERIOD BABYLON

One only needs to look at the tectonic changes wrought by the new Persian Empire to see how the authors of Isa 40–48 could interpret Cyrus as an agent of Yhwh intervening for the exilic community in Babylon, and for Judah and Jerusalem.

As a preliminary matter, it is important to stress that not all Jewish exiles in Babylonia shared similar experiences. Some elites were taken in Babylon, where they were likely to integrate. At the end of the book of Kings, we are told that the former king of Judah, Jehoiachin, was released from prison, given a seat at the Babylonian king's table and an allowance to support him (2 Kgs 25:27–30); and remarkably, cuneiform ration records have survived that confirm this account.[5] Another indication of assimilation comes from the prophet Jeremiah's exhortation to the exiles:

> Build houses and live in them; plant gardens and eat what they produce. Take wives and have sons and daughters; take wives for your sons, and give your daughters in marriage, that they may bear sons and daughters; multiply there, and do not decrease. But seek the welfare of the city where I have sent you into exile, and pray to Yhwh on its behalf, for in its welfare you will find your welfare. (Jer 29:5–7)

In contrast to this, other exiles from Judah were settled outside the capital. The Babylonian practice was to settle deportees in communities according to their place of origin. Judean exiles were thus grouped in locations in need of rebuilding or development. Ezekiel describes settlements near Nippur at Tel Abib on the river Chebar (Ezek. 1:3, 3:15), as well as Tel Melah and Tel Harsha. The element "tel" in these names usually refers to a "ruin mound," which may indicate the condition of the sites. Cuneiform texts from the year 498 also make mention of "the city (of) Judah/Yahudu" (*URU ya-a-hu-du*), apparently located near Sippar, where some Judeans deported from Jerusalem may also have been settled.[6]

Levels of Jewish assimilation to Babylonian culture also varied (ALSTOLA). Judeans owned seals with divine symbols and images other than Yhwh, such as symbols and images of the Babylonian deities Marduk, Ishtar, and Sin, as well as the Persian deity Ahura Mazda (ALSTOLA: 220–222, 267, 275–276). Similarly, Judean marriage

---

5 The so-called "Jehoiachin Rations Tablet," Babylon 28178=VAT 16378, Pergamon Museum, Berlin. See ANET 308.

6 Joannès, F., and André Lemaire. "Trois tablettes cunéiformes a onomastique ouest-sémitique (collection Sh. Moussaieff) (Pls. I–II)," *Transeuphrates*, 17 (1996): 17–27.

agreements in Babylonia call upon Babylonian deities to punish the vio-
lators of the agreements. Furthermore, it is noteworthy that the majority of Judean exiles living in the area of Yahudu bore names referencing
Yhwh, while only a few chose Akkadian and non-Yahwistic names.
Naming practices may not be clear indications of actual religious practices, but this contrasted with the practice of Judean merchants in the
Sippar area of Babylonia, who mostly took on Akkadian names for their
children and may have assimilated more to Babylonian culture. In any
case, the descendants of the Judean exiles would continue to grow and
thrive over the next millennium, eventually producing major Jewish
documents such as the Babylonian Talmud.

In exile, devotion to Yhwh endured alongside assimilation. Practices
of ritual purity, Sabbath observance, circumcision, and even sacrifice
continued even far from the homeland. There were Yahwistic temples
throughout Egypt, in locations such as Elephantine and Leontopolis, and
this was probably the case in Babylonia as well (Ezra 8:15–20 records a
request to send Levites or other temple functionaries from Casiphia in
Babylonia; and Ezekiel 11:16 also may refer to "a small sanctuary" in
the land of exile), it is also possible and perhaps even likely that Judean
priests and elders may have gathered in homes such as Ezekiel's for
consultation of prophets and priests. Perhaps these homes, public areas
in Judean villages, or even shrines and small temples in places such as
Yahudu and Casiphia may have been places for the composition and
liturgical performances of religious texts such as that of Deutero-Isaiah
(Sweeney: 34–35).

When Cyrus' Persia conquered the Neo-Babylonian Empire, a
new hope arose among many in Babylon – including the descendants
of the Judean exiles. The rhetorical weight of Isa 40–55 – particularly
Isa 40 – is clearer in the context of the Persian offer to return home.
With tender intimacy reminiscent of a husband speaking to his wife,
Yhwh speaks of reconciliation with Yhwh's bride, Jerusalem, and her
people in exile in Babylon. Isa 40 is the turning of the tide of Yhwh's
judgment against Jerusalem (and the descendants of her exiled leaders).
The prophet makes clear that the exiles have reached the fullness of
time for returning to Jerusalem, and all obstacles to their return are to
be removed – even leveling mountains and valleys. Israel's paradigmatic
and defining moment of the Exodus and journey through the wilderness
out of enslavement in Egypt are not only recalled but also reemployed
for a new exodus from Babylon.

The rhetorical firepower of Isa 40, however, also reflects the challenge of convincing at least some of the former exiles and their families
to undertake the arduous journey home to a shattered Jerusalem and a

now somewhat foreign homeland. Nehemiah 11:1–2 reports that "the people cast lots to bring one out of ten to live in the holy city Jerusalem, while nine-tenths remained in the other towns; and the people blessed all those who willingly offered to live in Jerusalem." In other words, the unlucky people who were determined by a throw of the dice had to do the rest of the population a favor by working to restore a Jerusalem that was thoroughly destroyed and left unpopulated (LIPSCHITS). And there were conflicts between those who returned from exile and those who had remained in Judah, over who had the right to the land (Ezek 33:23–31; Ezra 4). Given that many Jews seem to have achieved a sort of middle-class life in Babylonia, it may have been difficult to convince many of them to return.

Part of the challenge was theological. Perhaps rebutting the perception that the gods of Babylon had defeated Yhwh, Isa 40–55 proclaims Yhwh the sole god and creator the entire universe – while the Babylonian deities are instead "created" as the crafted idols of humankind – and that he has achieved salvation for exiles through an even more powerful human agency: the Persian Empire.

Isa 40–55 is therefore similar in purpose and message to the Cyrus Cylinder. We have seen how the Persian kings had themselves portrayed in various ways as legitimate rulers "adopted" into the royal titles and local kingships of various subject peoples. They are said to be favored by the local gods (e.g., Marduk in Babylon, Neith in Egypt) and even participating in the traditional religious roles of the local kings, such as Cyrus and Cambyses participating in the Babylonian New Year (akītu) Festival, or Cambyses and Darius providing for the elaborate funerals of the Egyptian Apis bulls. I have termed this systematic portrayal of Persian kings taking on local titles and the support of local gods as the Persian Royal Propaganda Model (SCHULTE 2016b).

The anonymous author of Isa 40–55 likely encountered this concept of Cyrus as King of Babylon, chosen by Marduk, in multiple forms of expression. While the Cyrus Cylinder itself was likely buried within the structure or walls of a temple, copies of its text have been found in flat fragments of conventional tablets. This likely indicates that at least portions of the Cyrus Cylinder text were promulgated far and wide – not only in Babylonia but also perhaps throughout the territories of the Persian Empire.[7] The literary prophet who authored Isa 40–55 was himself almost certainly part of an intelligentsia that would have spent

---

[7] Irving Finkel, "The Cyrus Cylinder: the Babylonian Perspective," in *The Cyrus Cylinder: The King of Persia's Proclamation from Ancient Babylon* (New York: I. B. Tauris, 2013), 18–21.

time in Babylon and encountered these copies of the Cyrus Cylinder texts. Marvin A. Sweeney has even proposed that Isa 46 is based on the prophet's eyewitness account of Cyrus being proclaimed King of Babylon at the *akītu* festival of 539 (SWEENEY: 33–35).

The prophet both adopts and transforms the Persian Royal Propaganda Model: Instead of a "King of Babylon" chosen by Marduk as described in the Cyrus Cylinder, Isa 45 declares Cyrus as Yhwh's "Anointed One," a term used to describe both priests and kings (particularly Davidic kings) of Israel and Judah. One of the best examples in the Hebrew Bible of anointing a king to rule by Yhwh's favor is 1 Samuel 16:1–13, where Yhwh directs the prophet Samuel to anoint David, the youngest son of Jesse, with oil, rather than his older brothers. After Samuel anoints David with oil, the passage then describes the spirit of Yhwh remaining strongly with David from that day onward. The author of Deutero-Isaiah likewise explicitly links Yhwh's favor and presence with Cyrus, who is Yhwh's "Shepherd" (44:28) and "Anointed" (45:1), and whom Yhwh will "grasp by his right hand" (45:1) and "I will embrace you though you do not know me" (45:5). Isa 45's reference to Yhwh grasping the hand of Cyrus seems to allude to the key concept of the king of Babylon taking the hand of Marduk and leading the statue of Marduk out into the city during the Babylonian New Year (*akītu*) festival, as we have seen in the cases of Cyrus and Cambyses. The prophet may also be rebutting the role of Marduk in the *akitu* festival – that it is Yhwh, not Marduk, who is taking Cyrus by the hand.

The prophet not only invokes the theme of divinely guided reign by an anointed king but also the theme of Yhwh as creator and re-creator. Deutero-Isaiah emphasizes Yhwh's creation of the universe. The Persian Empire ruled the known universe – and for Deutero-Isaiah the Persian emperor, Cyrus, manifested the favor of Yhwh. Yhwh's guidance of the emperor of the known universe is an extension of Yhwh's role as creator and ruler of the universe. Through Yhwh's agent, Cyrus, the children of Israel in Babylon could then partake of a new exodus: a new act of creation to once again conquer the primordial forces of chaos manifested in the Exile and restore the created rule of Yhwh by returning to the Promised Land and restoring the Temple.

Much of this language of restoring Yhwh's created order would have dovetailed nicely with elements of Zoroastrianism found in the Persian Empire. While the initial paradisical garden created by Ahura Mazda (the Persian god) may have been spoiled by the foul spirit known as Angra Mainyu, each human being is called upon to choose to follow *arta* (Old Persian for "Truth/Order") instead of *druj* (Old Persian for

"The Lie/Chaos") and help return the world to its garden state. Our English word "paradise" even ultimately comes from the Old Persian word for "garden" (*pairidaēza*; cf. Hebrew *pardes*). It appears that Cyrus' actions described in the Cyrus Cylinder of allowing exiles to return to their homes, for gods to be returned to their temples and shrines, and for those shrines to be rebuilt, may all have had a Persian religious component of helping restore the world to its garden state – Darius I had himself portrayed in the Behistun Inscription as Ahura Mazda's agent of Truth/Order against the Lie/Chaos. This Persian ideology of tending the "garden" of the world was even manifest in the Persian-period garden of the administrative center at Ramat Raḥel, just outside Jerusalem, where impressive waterworks supported a garden with plants from the far corners of the Persian Empire: citron from India, Persian walnut, cedar of Lebanon, birch from Anatolia, and more – something that is attested by pollen samples (LIPSCHITS ET AL. 2017).

The Persians populated their gardens with diverse plants from all over their empire, and their military with troops from the many nations. In keeping with this, much of Persian iconography (such as the monumental reliefs of the Persian royal tombs at Naqsh-e-Rostam and Persepolis, as well as the Egyptian Statue of Darius I and the Suez Canal Stelae of Darius I), highlights the diversity of peoples under Persian rule through differentiating their physiognomy, costume, and hairstyle – while portraying them all unified in adulation of the Persian kings. A similar universalistic perspective is found in the book of Isaiah, in which all peoples from the world will stream to Yhwh's temple in Jerusalem (see particularly Isa 2; 56; 60; and 66); this is explored in the next section.

ISAIAH IN PERSIAN-PERIOD JUDAH (YEHUD)

Although Babylon and its culture were among the primary concerns of Isa 40–8, Babylon disappears from the book thereafter, and Isa 40–55 as a whole has been reshaped to address the concerns of an audience in Jerusalem and Judah. The goals of the Persian-Period Jewish officials there included inviting diaspora Jews home, and also correcting their theology and worship, as shown by the "Passover Papyrus" and other letters sent from Jerusalem to the Yahwistic community in Elephantine, Egypt.[8] In this period, according to Jeremiah, Jews lived all

---

[8] Bezalel Porten, *The Elephantine Papyri in English: Three Millennia of Cross-Cultural Continuity and Change*, DMOA 22 (Leiden: Brill, 1996), 77–84, 125–126.

up and down the Nile – in Migdol, Tahpanhes, Memphis, and "the land of Pathros" (Jer 44:1; 46:14). Deutero-Isaiah's employment of the Exodus motif would have resonated for Jews there, and polemic against the idea that Yhwh is a Hidden God, that he speaks in secrecy and darkness (Isa 45:15–19), was most plausibly a polemic against Amun, the chief Egyptian deity whose name meant "Hidden One." The anti-Egyptian claims also would have supported the plans of the Persian kings to conquer Egypt (45:1–3).[9]

The last portion of the book of Isaiah, consisting of chapters 56–66, consists of writings that assume an audience now living in Yehud, the Persian province located in the heart of what was formerly known as Judah. Our main sources of information about Yehud are archaeology and biblical books that may give some indications of life within Yehud. Some biblical texts present the land as empty during the period of the Babylonian exile. For example, 2 Kgs 24:14 asserts that "[Nebuchadnezzar] carried away all Jerusalem, all the officials, all the warriors, ten thousand captives, all the artisans and the smiths; no one remained except the poorest people of the land" (see also 2 Chr 36:20–21). However, the land was never empty of people (LIPSCHITS). More likely, the later traditions describing the land as empty rationalized the precedence of the descendants of the Babylonian exiles over the descendants of those Judeans not exiled to Babylon.[10]

There was, however, a large decline in population during this period: Whereas the population of Judah at the end of the Iron Age (which ended with the Babylonian conquest of Judah) was estimated as 108,000 people, the estimated population of Yehud during the Persian Period was only 30,125 people (LIPSCHITS: 270). Most of these lived in small communities, the majority of the population living in the region of Benjamin, secondarily in the North Judean Hills, thirdly in the Shephelah, and about 10 percent of the population in the area of Jerusalem (LIPSCHITS: 270–271). The ongoing vitality of life in Judah is also attested by biblical traditions such as Jeremiah 40–43 and 2 Kgs 25:22–26, which describe lots of activity among a governor, nobles, soldiers, priests, prophets, and others after the Babylonian capture of Jerusalem in 586.

The biblical books set in Persian-period Judah containing material from Persian Period include Ezra, Nehemiah, Haggai, Zechariah,

---

[9] Christopher B. Hays, "A Hidden God: Isaiah 45's Amun Polemic and Message to Egypt," *VT* 72 (2022): 1–17.

[10] J. Maxwell Miller and John H. Hayes, *A History of Ancient Israel and Judah*, 2nd ed. (Louisville, KY: Westminster John Knox, 2006), 521.

and Malachi, in addition to parts of Isaiah. These do not paint a complete picture of Jews, Judaism, or Judah during the reigns of Cyrus, Cambyses, Darius, and Xerxes, but they do tell us something about the tensions among various groups; despite the reduced population, the land seems not to have been big enough for its inhabitants to live in peace.

In addition to struggles over rights to the land, a particular crux of these tensions was the Temple. The efforts to rebuild it are mentioned or alluded to in various texts crediting various figures: Ezra 1 and 5:6–17 (Sheshbazzar "the prince of Judah"); Ezra 3 and 6:19–22 (Zerubbabel and Jeshua, a priestly leader) for the restoration; and the books of Haggai 1–2 and Zechariah 3:1–10, 6:11 credit Zerubbabel and Joshua (=Jeshua), with support from the prophets themselves. The process took at least a couple of decades after the return of the first exiles from Babylon (the date of 515 has often been assigned), and there appear to have been struggles for authority over the Temple.

The complex development of Isa 40–66 is demonstrated by its mixed messages about the Temple: 64:11 looks back on the destruction of the Temple with lament: "Our holy and beautiful house,/ where our ancestors praised you,/ has been burned by fire." And initially, in 44:28, Yhwh says of the temple: "Your foundation shall be laid." These texts reflect the importance of the Temple to the postexilic community. Once the Temple is rebuilt, however, there was clearly sectarian conflict over it. Isa 56–57 includes a forceful critique of religious leaders ("Israel's sentinels are blind,/ they are all without knowledge"; 56:10; also 66:3–4), and these appear to have been affiliated with the temple, since 57:13 says that the unrighteous will be blown away, while "whoever takes refuge in me [Yhwh] shall possess the land/ and inherit my holy mountain." It is clear that the authors of the latest book of Isaiah continued to believe in the importance of the Temple: For example, in 60:7, Yhwh promises, "I will glorify my glorious house," but they increasingly think that its leadership is corrupt, and that it needs to be cleansed; in 66:6, the prophet announces that he has heard "a voice from the temple – / The voice of Yhwh,/ dealing retribution to his enemies!" And indeed 66:1–2 even suggests that Yhwh does not require the Temple.

In some respects, then, Isa 40–66 is in harmony with Ezra and Nehemiah, who were among the key political agents of the Restoration. In all of these books, the building and purity of the Temple are of concern. And Ezra similarly imagined the people's return to Jerusalem from Babylonian exile through the desert as a kind of new Exodus from slavery

and a re-entry into Canaan.[11] Furthermore, the reform programs of Ezra
and Nehemiah are consistent with certain themes in Isa 56–66. Both
emphasize the keeping of the Sabbath: In Nehemiah 13, those working
on the Sabbath are condemned, and orders are given to close the doors
and gates to keep merchants and sellers outside the walls of Jerusalem
until after the Sabbath (cf. Isa 56:4, 6). Furthermore, both Isaiah and
Ezra-Nehemiah link temple ritual and moral observance: Isa 58 calls for
a "fast" that creates justice rather than merely the appearance of piety,
and Isa 59 calls the people to repent; analogously, Ezra reads the Torah
to the people at the feast of Sukkot and calls for their repentance in
Neh 8–10. Finally, both texts express concern about economic abuses:
Isa 58:6–9 exhorts freeing the oppressed and feeding the homeless poor,
and Neh 5 describes Nehemiah's efforts to free Jewish kindred enslaved
because of debt, and emphasizes that Nehemiah and his brothers did
not demand the governor's food allowance – which amounted to a tax –
nor did they claim land for themselves land as most governors did, in
order to avoid further burdening the people.

Along with these similarities, however, there are profound
differences in outlook and theology among these books. Perhaps the
most striking example is the conflicting view of foreigners. Ezra and
Nehemiah lament and decry the ethnic impurity of the "people of
the land" and exhort the men to send away foreign wives (Ezra 9–10;
Neh 13).[12] By contrast, Isaiah takes an expansive view of ethnic identity to be based primarily on "observance of Judean ethnic markers"
(such as sabbath observance), rather than one based primarily on geography, national identity, and ancestry. Isa 56 proclaims, "Do not let
the foreigner joined to Yhwh say, 'Yhwh will surely separate me from
his people,'" and culminates in the hope that "my house [i.e. Temple]
shall be called a house of prayer for all peoples." This inclusive stance
may be Trito-Isaiah's argument against the Zadokite priesthood excluding non-Judeans and perhaps even some Judeans from the Temple. The
possibility of international proselytes is emphasized by the nations
streaming to Jerusalem to offer gifts in the Temple (see especially Isa
56:1–8, Isa 60, and the nations bringing back the exiles such as the grain

---

[11]   Marvin A. Sweeney, *TANAK: A Theological and Critical Introduction to the Jewish
        Bible* (Minneapolis, MN: Fortress, 2012), 466–467.
[12]   Nehemiah 13:24 indicates the problem of the foreign wives was not just their for-
        eign origin *per se* but more specifically their causing the loss of the Judean language.
        Would Nehemiah have objected if the foreign wives and the children of their union
        with Judean men had "observed the Judean ethnic marker" of the Hebrew language?
        Perhaps not. Ezra, on the other hand, seems to object to the foreignness of the wives.

offerings brought by Israelites in Isa 66:18–23) (LIPSCHITS ET AL. 2011: 92, 122–123). It is possible that even Ezra and Nehemiah would have accepted foreign wives who assimilated fully to Yahwistic Judean culture and language. Such a universalistic perspective makes good sense within the cosmopolitan, international rule of the Persian Empire. If Isa 40–55 could present the foreign king Cyrus as Yhwh's anointed one to manifest Yhwh's universal reign, then the expanded Isa 40–66 could look at Cyrus as an international proselyte par excellence, thereby opening the way for other international proselytes.

There is ample evidence in Isa 40–66, then, of sectarian conflicts in Persian-Period Judah. This is attested in various ways. First, there are recurring references a "servant" in 40–53; and to "servants" in 54–66. This is a complex and heavily studied phenomenon, in that the term "servant" seems to have different referents in different places. It refers at times to the whole nation of Israel (e.g., 41:8; 44:21); but it also refers in some cases to an individual who is cast as a leader of the people (e.g., 49:5) and perhaps a prophetic figure (44:26 says that Yhwh "confirms the word of his servant"). In later chapters, the servant is increasingly portrayed as exhausted and suffering; in 49:4, he says, "I have labored in vain,/ I have spent my strength for nothing and vanity," and in Isa 53:7–9 he is killed and buried, although the text says "he had done no violence,/ and there was no deceit in his mouth." Immediately after the death of this righteous but unsuccessful figure, the first reference to plural servants appears, in 54:17, which announces divine vindication of the "servants." The fact that these servants are a sectarian group opposed to other Persian Period leadership is attested by later proclamations, such as 65:13–16, which announces that the servants will eat drink and be merry, while their opponents will suffer, cry out, and indeed be put to death. And 66:14 is similar: "it shall be known that the hand of Yhwh is with his servants, and his indignation is against his enemies." Joseph Blenkinsopp has very cogently argued that we have here the narrative of a postexilic prophetic leader whose group lost out in a struggle for authority, but whose followers preserved his words and story and augmented them with their own ongoing witnesses (BLENKINSOPP).[13]

Another specific term for the group of pious Judeans in Trito-Isaiah is "those who tremble/shake" at the word of YHWH (*Haredim* in

---

[13] For the later Christian interpretation of the Servant Songs, see PAO, "Isaiah in the New Testament," Chapter 18 in this volume. For the composition of the servant texts, see SWEENEY, "The Formation of the Book of Isaiah," Chapter 7 in this volume.

Isa 66:2, 5). This same rare expression is also found in Ezra 9:4 and suggests a connection between Trito-Isaiah's vision of a faithful community committed to Yhwh and the reform efforts of Ezra and Nehemiah. (The same appellation is used by modern "Haredi" [a.k.a. Ultraorthodox] Jews, and is alluded to in Christian denominations such as the Quakers and Shakers.)

In Isa 66:5, those who tremble are mocked by their opponents, who say: "Let Yhwh be glorified, so that we may see your joy!"[14] But the prophet proclaims: "it is they who shall be put to shame." The contrast between glory and punishment is another of the major themes found toward the end of the book. Isa 66:15–24 describes Yhwh administering judgment against those who practice non-Yahwistic religious practices seen as abominable. Though the description of the wicked in verse 66:17 seems quite specific, the text is difficult, and the references are somewhat obscure. The images of purification, gardens, and the eating of swine resonate with Isa. 65:3–5, as well as 1:29–31.[15] The verse continues by listing a variety of abominable foods that the self-purifiers consume, and concludes with the announcement of their punishment as an oracle of Yhwh. Clearly, the religious practices of the figures of 66:17–18 are not considered orthodox by the author, and therefore the followers of such cults will be punished by Yhwh. And again, this is about practices rather than inherent identity: Neither the cults nor their followers are equated with foreigners. But the extreme violence of the imagery in 66:15–16, 24 seems to reflect the depth of the author's anger over the sectarian strife.

Yhwh's glory is the counterpoint to the theme of judgment, and presumably alludes to the Divine Presence found in the Temple (1 Kgs 8) and Tabernacle (Exod 40). Yhwh's glory is on display for the nations, even the distant coastlands who heretofore have not heard of Yhwh's reputation, by returning the Judean exiles to Jerusalem (Isa 66:18–20). The survivors of the nations will announce the glory of Yhwh to the ends of the earth (66:19), so that all flesh may worship Yhwh and abide by his calendar (66:23). Presumably Yhwh also manifests his glory by creating and sustaining the new heavens and the new earth, as well as sustaining the name and seed of Israel (66:22). The idea that Yhwh gains glory by preserving his people is one that goes back to the Exodus (Exod 14:4, 17–18).

---

[14] Note the echo of the scoffers in 5:19: "let the plan of the Holy One of Israel hasten to fulfillment,/ that we may know it!"

[15] For discussion, see Susan Ackerman, *Under Every Green Tree*, HSM 46 (Atlanta, GA: Scholars Press, 1992), 101–212.

The glory of Yhwh is described by the redactor in terms of Yahwistic religious practices of the Jerusalem Temple. Isa 66:20 describes the return of the exiles by the nations as a cultic offering in Jerusalem like the offerings made by the Judeans. Verse 21 specifies that priests and Levites – the leaders of the Yahwistic cult at Jerusalem – will be chosen from these returned exiles. Even the arrival of all flesh to worship Yhwh in 66:23 is described in terms of the sacred Temple calendar, with its sabbaths and new moons.

CONCLUSION: THE PERSIAN CONTEXT OF ISAIAH AS A WHOLE

The majority of this discussion has focused on the parts of Isaiah composed during the Persian Period (Isa 40–66), but much of Isa 1–39 was also edited and reshaped during this time. The example of the heterodox cultic practices in 1:29–31, mentioned in the preceding section, was a bookending device added in the Persian Period to frame the book as a whole. Furthermore, Isa 35 introduces the new exodus by the exiles to Jerusalem that will feature prominently throughout Isa 40–55, and thus it forms a bridge to chapter 40, marked by the similar terms for the highway for the returnees (35:8; 40:3; and see also 62:10).

Even texts that seem to have been composed in earlier periods were now reframed and reinterpreted for the Persian Period community. Isa 14 provides one such example: The taunt song of Isa 14:4b–21 is widely thought to have been composed upon the death of the Assyrian king Sargon II in battle (in the eighth century), but verses 1–4a and 22–23 reframe it as addressing the King of Babylon (in the sixth century). This testifies to the enduring rhetorical power of the Hebrew prophets since their words continued to be read and reread as relevant to later periods.

Isaiah's oracles against the nations in 14–27 were in fact reinterpreted as a whole with the addition of chapter 13, which describes the Lord summoning an international army from "a distant land" to destroy Babylonia. The same phrase is used to describe the Persians in 46:11, so the sixth-century political situation is now in view. Much of Isa 14–23 otherwise makes more sense in an eighth- and seventh-century context, but with this change it is reappropriated to assert the degradation of Babylon and the supremacy of Yhwh and Persia.

Finally, Isa 2's message of all nations streaming to the Temple in Jerusalem and nation no longer raising the sword against nation takes on additional context when read alongside the universalistic texts of the Persian Period found in Isa 40–66. The Persian Empire emphasized bringing together diverse peoples who (ideally) lived together with various gods, religions, and customs while all under one king and empire. Reciprocally, the Persian king honored, supported, and occasionally participated in the dynasties and religious ceremonies of his subjects from Babylonia to Egypt. Isa 40–66 reorients the universalistic elements of the Persian Period to the prophets' understanding of Yhwh's reign and the Jerusalem Temple as the true center of this unifying world.

During this period, Isaianic authors sought to shift Judean identity from an emphasis on Judean ancestry to an emphasis of Judean practices and other ethnic markers. The early Persian-period portions of Isa 40–55 expand upon this message of Isa 2 from the prophetic writer's experiences within this period, emphasizing Yhwh's creation and reign over the whole world through anointing the Persian king whose empire spanned the known world. Isa 56–66 further builds upon the concept of the nations streaming to Jerusalem from Isa 2. Isa 56 describes how foreigners who have joined themselves to Yhwh will be brought to pray and sacrifice at the Temple in Jerusalem, and Isa 60 describes the wealth the nations will bring to Jerusalem and the homage given to Judah by the descendants of their oppressors. This theme also helps bookend Isaiah in chapter 66, in which the offerings given as acceptable sacrifices to YHWH are the descendants of the exiles brought home to Jerusalem. In essence, the return of the exiles will serve as the very means by which all nations will worship Yhwh: By bringing the exiles home, the nations are bringing sacred offering for the glory of Yhwh.

These ongoing processes of reinterpretation reflect that the book of Isaiah is one of the most treasured writings for Judaism and Christianity – and indeed for Western civilization as a whole. Much of its rhetorical power transcends time, space, and translation. Yet the context of the Persian Period holds particular significance. Reading Isaiah in the context of the Persian Period allows a greater appreciation and understanding of this powerful book.

FURTHER READING

Alstola, Tero. *Judeans in Babylonia: A Study of Deportees in the Sixth and Fifth Centuries*, Culture and History of the Ancient Near East 109. Leiden: Brill, 2020.

Blenkinsopp, Joseph, 'The Servant and the Servants in Isaiah and the Formation of the Book'. Pages 155–175 in *Writing and Reading the Scroll of Isaiah, Volume 1*. Edited by Craig C. Broyles and Craig A. Evans. Leiden: Brill, 1997.

Briant, Pierre. *From Cyrus to Alexander: A History of the Persian Empire*. Winona Lake, IN: Eisenbrauns, 2002.

Fried, Lisbeth S. *The Priest and the Great King: Temple-Palace Relations in the Persian Empire.* Biblical and Judaic Studies from the University of California, San Diego 10. Winona Lake, IN: Eisenbrauns, 2004.

Fried, Lisbeth S. "Cyrus the Messiah? The Historical Background to Isaiah 45:1." *HTR* 95 (2002): 373–393.

Grabbe, Lester L. *A History of the Jews and Judaism in the Second Temple Period Vol. 1: Yehud: A History of the Persian Province of Judah.* Library of Second Temple Studies 47. London: T&T Clark International, 2004.

Kuhrt, Amélie. *The Persian Empire: A Corpus of Sources from the Achaemenid Period.* London: Routledge, 2007.

Lipschits, Oded. *The Fall and Rise of Jerusalem: Judah under Babylonian Rule.* Winona Lake, IN: Eisenbrauns, 2005.

Lipschits, Oded, and Manfred Oeming. *Judah and the Judeans in the Persian Period.* Winona Lake, IN: Eisenbrauns, 2006.

Lipschits, Oded, Gary N. Knoppers, and Rainer Albertz. *Judah and the Judeans in the Fourth Century B.C.E.* Winona Lake, IN: Eisenbrauns, 2007.

Lipschits, Oded, Gary N. Knoppers, and Manfred Oeming, eds. *Judah and the Judeans in the Achaemenid Period: Negotiating Identity in an International Context.* Winona Lake, IN: Eisenbrauns, 2011.

Lipschits, Oded, Yuval Gadot, Benjamin Arubas, Manfred Oeming, Efrat Bocher, Boaz Gross, Uri Davidovich, Itamar Taxel, Ran Morin, Roi Porat, Dvori Namdar, Yoav Farhi, Nirit Kedem, and Keren Ras. *What Are the Stones Whispering? Ramat Raḥel: 3000 Years of Forgotten History.* Winona Lake, IN: Eisenbrauns, 2017.

Potts, D. T. *The Oxford Handbook of Ancient Iran.* Oxford: Oxford University Press, 2013.

Rose, Jenny. *Zoroastrianism: An Introduction.* London: I.B. Tauris, 2011.

Schulte, Lucas L. "Good Public Relations: What Persian Propaganda Tells Us About the 'Nehemiah Memoir'" *The Ancient Near East Today* IV 11 (November 2016). www.asor.org/anetoday/2016/11/what-persian-propaganda-tells-us/

Schulte, Lucas L. *My Shepherd, Though You Do Not Know Me: The Persian Royal Propaganda Model in the Nehemiah Memoir.* CBET 78. Leuven: Peeters, 2016.

Silverman, Jason M, and Caroline Waerzeggers. *Political Memory in and After the Persian Empire.* SBLANEM 13. Atlanta, GA: SBL Press, 2015.

Sweeney, Marvin A. *Isaiah 40–66,* FOTL 19. Grand Rapids, MI: Eerdmans, 2016.

Wiesehöfer, Josef. *Ancient Persia: from 550 BC to 650 AD.* Translated by Azizeh Azodi. London: I. B. Tauris, 2001.

Williamson, H. G. M. *Studies in Persian Period History and Historiography,* FAT 38. Tübingen: Mohr Siebeck, 2004.

5 The Book of Isaiah at Qumran

JESPER HØGENHAVEN

The manuscripts discovered between 1947 and 1956 in eleven caves at Qumran (approximately 900 scrolls) cover a wide variety of literary genres. These scrolls contain ancient Jewish texts spanning a period from the third century BCE to the first century CE. "Biblical" manuscripts (meaning in this context writings that eventually ended up as parts of the Hebrew Bible, or Old Testament) comprise roughly 25 percent of the scrolls. Some of the nonbiblical manuscripts testify to the existence and life of a particular Jewish movement, which seems to have regarded itself as the exclusive representative of the true Jewish tradition. These people are often referred to as the "Qumran community," which is sometimes identified with a Jewish sect of the Second Temple Period. It is unclear whether this entire group lived in the buildings at Qumran, or whether some of them, possibly a core group or an elite within the wider movement, did. Many scholars have seen a close connection between this faction and the "Essenes" mentioned in the writings of Philo, Josephus, and Pliny the Elder. A significant number of writings found in the caves, however, were probably not written by the Qumran community, but rather brought from outside. Still, the collection as a whole seems at some point to have been owned and used by the group (LIM AND COLLINS).

THE ISAIAH MANUSCRIPTS

Twenty-one manuscripts of the book of Isaiah have been discovered in the Qumran caves. Two of these were among the first "Dead Sea Scrolls" found in Cave 1 in the spring of 1947, and are quite extensive. Eighteen more fragmentary Isaiah scrolls have come from Cave 4, and some fragments belonging to yet another Isaiah scroll were found in Cave 5 (TOV; ULRICH).

The number of Isaiah copies clearly testifies to the popularity of this prophetic book in the context of the Qumran scrolls. The only biblical writings represented by a greater number of copies are Deuteronomy (26) and Psalms (36) (TOV: 491). The large number of quotations from Isaiah found in the nonbiblical writings (and, in particular, in the writings associated directly with the Qumran community) confirms the impression that the book was well known and held in high esteem (BROOKE 1997: 609–12).

THE ISAIAH TEXT AT QUMRAN AND THE SHAPE OF THE BOOK

The text represented by the various Qumran manuscripts shows, generally speaking, only minor differences from the standard "Masoretic text" that had long been known, before the discovery of the scrolls, from medieval manuscripts and printed editions. In stark contrast to the other two major prophets, Jeremiah and Ezekiel, there are no indications that fundamentally different versions of Isaiah were in circulation in the late Second Temple period. Most scholars agree that the book of Isaiah in its present form is the result of a long and complicated transmission process. The division of the book into First, Second, and (possibly) Third Isaiah represents a well-established achievement of biblical scholarship. Whatever the redaction history of Isaiah may have looked like, though, this process must have been completed by the second century BCE, and none of the earlier stages can be documented in the Qumran scrolls. In other words, the literary framework and contents of the book had reached a fixed form before the earliest of these manuscripts were written.

Textual variants in the Isaiah manuscripts are numerous, but most of them are of relatively minor importance. The best preserved and therefore most extensively studied manuscript is the "First Isaiah Scroll" (or "Great Isaiah Scroll," 1QIsaᵃ) found in Cave 1. This scroll, which apart from a few damaged places contains almost the entire book of Isaiah, is the longest biblical scroll found at Qumran (7.34 m) and can be dated to the second century BCE. When compared with the Masoretic text, the scroll, while following the general textual framework of the Masoretic text and representing the same basic text type, has a significant number of minor variants. The majority of differences are simply variants at the orthographical level. In many cases, the readings of the scroll are clearly secondary when compared with the Masoretic text: The scroll replaces rare words in the text with more commonly used synonyms or simplifies grammatically difficult sentences. The frequency of this type of variants has led some scholars to label the scroll a "vulgar manuscript," that is, one that sought to make the text more accessible to the reader.

There are a number of cases, however, where the scroll may have preserved the more original reading. One example is Isa 53:11. Here the first line, which is a part of the prophecy about the "suffering servant" of the Lord, in the Masoretic text reads:

Out of the anguish of his soul he shall see and be satisfied.

The Isaiah Scroll has one more word, providing an object for the verb "see":

Out of the anguish of his soul he shall see *light* and be satisfied.

The reading of the scroll is supported by two other Qumran manuscripts, as well as by the ancient Greek version, and some modern Bible translations have indeed adopted it as the superior reading (FLINT: 239).

Interestingly, the First Isaiah Scroll divides the text of Isaiah into two large segments, Isa 1–34 and Isa 35–66, each part written by a different scribe. It is at least worth considering whether this division of the book into two main parts was simply a matter of dividing the production of the scroll between two scribes, or whether it reflects a notion of literary structure. Possibly, the universal focus on the nations in Isa 34 was regarded as a proper conclusion for a first part of the book of Isaiah (FLINT: 236). There are a number of scribal signs in this manuscript, some apparently indicating further divisions of the text, while others may have been inserted to mark passages of particular importance. Many, but not all, of these correspond with the Masoretic divisions of the text. The manuscript exhibits a large amount of scribal errors and corrections, some by the original scribes, others inserted later. A similar text-type to that of the First Isaiah Scroll is found in one other, less well-preserved manuscript, 4QIsaᶜ, as well as in the composition 4QTanhumim (4Q176), which quotes extensively from Isa 43–54. The majority of manuscripts from the Qumran caves, however, exhibit a text type closely aligned to the Masoretic text (TOV; FLINT: 233–9).

QUOTATIONS FROM THE BOOK OF ISAIAH

Quotations and allusions to Isaiah are relatively numerous in Qumran scrolls, and, in particular, in those writings commonly associated with the Qumran community. One of these is the Cairo Damascus Document (CD), which includes admonitions and laws for a Jewish community. It is not, strictly speaking, a Qumran writing: The text was preserved in two medieval manuscripts that were discovered in a synagogue in Cairo in the late nineteenth century. However, several fragmentary manuscripts from Cave 4 at Qumran exhibit basically the same text. Thus, there is widespread agreement that this writing belongs among the Qumran scrolls. In this composition the book of Isaiah (Isa 7:17) is quoted explicitly as an authoritative prophetic source, lending support to the notion that God will in the end time pass judgment upon the wicked:

> But all those who despise—when God visits the earth to repay to the wicked their due, when that happens of which is written in the words of Isaiah son of Amoz, the prophet, who said: "There will come upon you and upon your people and upon your father's house such days as have not come since the day when Ephraim departed from Judah" (CD VII, 10–13)
>
> (after BAUMGARTEN AND SCHWARTZ: 25–27.)

Likewise, the Rule of the Community (1QS), one of the well-preserved manuscripts found in Cave 1, and in all appearance a central document in the life of the Qumran community, invokes the authority of the book of Isaiah (Isa 2:22) in support for the separation of community members from outsiders:

> No one should eat of any of their possessions, or drink or accept anything from their hands, unless at its price, for it is written: "Stop regarding man in whose nostrils is breath, for of what account is he?" For all those not accounted within his covenant will be segregated, they and all that belongs to them. No holy man should support himself on any worthless works, for worthless are all who do not know his covenant. (1QS V, 16–19)
>
> (after GARCÍA MARTÍNEZ AND TIGCHELAAR–8: 81;
> cf. QIMRON AND CHARLESWORTH: 23)

The Rule of the Community gives a particularly prominent place to a quotation from the beginning of Second Isaiah (Isa 40:3):

> And when these have become a community in Israel, in compliance with these arrangements, they are to be segregated from within the dwelling of the men of sin to walk to the desert in order to open there his path. As it is written: "In the wilderness prepare the way of ••••,[1] make straight in the desert a highway for our God." This is the study of the law wh[i]ch he commanded through the hand of

---

[1]   The scribe here used dots in place of the divine name, the Tetragrammaton.

Moses, in order to act in compliance with all that has been revealed
from age to age, and according to what the prophets have revealed
through his holy spirit. (1QS VIII, 12–16)

> (after GARCÍA MARTÍNEZ AND TIGCHELAAR–8: 89–91;
> cf. QIMRON AND CHARLESWORTH: 35–37)

The Isaiah passage on preparing a way in the desert is interpreted
here as pertaining to the establishment, or rather to a certain stage in
the development, of the Qumran community, and as the founding text
legitimizing the community's withdrawal into the "desert" in pursuit
of the study of the Mosaic law. Whether this idea in the Rule of the
Community of a withdrawal into the desert should be understood geographically, as a reference to a settling of the community, or some of its
members, in the Qumran area in the Judaean Desert, or metaphorically,
as indicating their separation from their contemporary fellow Jews in a
broader sense, or both, remains unclear.

Another Isaianic passage that appears to have been of particular
importance to the community is Isa 8:11:

> For Yhwh spoke thus to me with his strong hand upon me, and
> warned me not to walk in the way of this people.

This verse, in fact, is one of the cases where the Great Isaiah Scroll
(1QIsaᵃ) has a variant that may be significant with respect to the meaning and interpretation of the text by the Qumran community. Instead
of the verb "warned me" (*wysrny*, from the root *y-s-r*) found in the
Masoretic text, the scroll has the verb "turned me away" (*wysyrny*,
from the root *s-w-r*):

> For Yhwh spoke thus to me with his strong hand upon me, and
> *turned me away from* walking in the way of this people.

In Hebrew, the difference comes down to just one letter. Indeed, the
Masoretic consonants could be vocalized so as to be read as "turned me
away" as in 1QIsaᵃ, and this understanding of the verb form had been
attested long before the discovery of the scrolls in some of the ancient
versions. Many biblical scholars regard "turned me away" as the original reading of the Isaiah text. At any rate, this seems to have been the
way the passage was read by the authors of the Qumran scrolls. In this
understanding, God actively intervenes in the course of events, turning
the prophet (and, by implication, those who follow his example) away
from walking in the corrupt way chosen by "this people." Apparently,
this image held a powerful appeal for the Qumran community, who saw

themselves as those who had been "turned away" from the sinful and destructive way taken by the majority of contemporary Jews.

Isa 8:11 is quoted explicitly in the composition Florilegium, or Midrash on Eschatology[a] (4Q174) in close connection with a citation from and an interpretation of Psalm 1:1:

> Midrash of "Blessed is the man who walks not in the counsel of the wicked." The interpretation of the passa[ge conc]erns those who have turned away from the way ... which is written in the book of Isaiah the prophet concerning the latter days: "And with his strong [hand upon me, he turned me away from walking in the way of] this people." (4Q174 1, 21, 2 14–16)
>
> (after GARCÍA MARTÍNEZ AND TIGCHELAAR–8: 353; cf. MILGROM: 253)

In this text, unfortunately, the crucial verb "turned me away" is no longer preserved, but the reading can be inferred from the reference to "those who have turned away." (The Hebrew has the participle *sārê*, corresponding to the verb read by the Great Isaiah Scroll.)

The passage states that "the book of Isaiah the prophet" was a well-known entity that could be quoted in an authoritative manner, and that the words of that book were interpreted as regarding "the latter days." The very expression "the latter days" (*'aḥărît hayyāmîm*) is found in Isa 2:2 and some more places in the Hebrew Bible. In Qumran writings, it is a frequently used term designating the eschatological end time (BROOKE 1997).

The expression "those who have turned away from walking in the way of the people," directly based on Isa 8:11, apparently became a self-designation for the Qumran community. We find this use of Isaiah in the Damascus Document (CD VIII, 16), and a very similar use of the phrase from Isa 8:11 is found in the Rule of the Congregation, a document closely related to the Rule of the Community: "the men of the covenant who have tu[rned away from walking in the] way of the people" (1QS[a] I, 2–3).

Another passage from Isaiah that must have played an important part for (some of) the authors of Qumran writings is the "Song of the Vineyard" in Isa 5:1–7. A fragmentary poetical text from Cave 4, 4QBenediction (4Q500), contains clear echoes of it:

> ... may your [mulberry tr]ees blossom and ...
> ... your winepress [bu]ilt of stones ...
> ... to the gate of the holy height ...

... your planting and the streams of your glory ...
... your pleasant branches ...
    ... your [vine]yard ... (4Q500 1, 2–7)

> (after BROOKE 1995: 268–94; cf. GARCÍA MARTÍNEZ
> AND TIGCHELAAR: 993)

This text, apparently a benediction addressed to God, seems to have associated the description of the Lord's vineyard in Isa 5:1–7 specifically with the temple of Jerusalem (BROOKE 1995). Several Qumran manuscripts employ the word "planting" as a metaphor for the community, as in Isa 5:7. Thus, the Rule of the Community calls the community "an everlasting planting" (1QS VIII, 4–8).

A special witness to the importance ascribed to Isaiah is presented by another Cave 4 manuscript, 4QTanhumim (4Q176). This text is a liturgical composition, into which at least two entire columns consisting of passages from Isa 43; 44; 49; 51; 52; 54 have been inserted. The text has a literary framework in which a congregation addresses God, imploring on him to act on their behalf. The tone is lamenting, depicting a situation where the holy city and the temple have been devastated, and the priests and worshippers killed or driven away. Against this background, the text explicitly introduces the long chain of Isaianic passages as citations, beginning with Isa 40:1:

> and perform your marvel, and do justice to your people and ... your sanctuary, and strive against the kingdoms over the blood of ... Jerusalem, and see the corpses of your priests ... and there is no one to bury them. And from the Book of Isaiah consolations: ["Comfort, comfort my people,] says your God. Speak tenderly to Jerusalem, and cr[y to her] that her [warfare is end]ed, that ..." (4Q176 I, 12–16)
> (HØGENHAVEN: 156)

This text is an interesting example of how the second part of the book of Isaiah was interpreted in the Second Temple period. The extensive quotations from Isa 40–53 all occur in their expected biblical order. The passages selected for quotation here focus on the theme of God's love and faithfulness, and promises of a future restoration. The quotations are given without any interpretative or explanatory remarks interrupting the chain. The excerpts from Isaiah seem to have been chosen because they support the notion that God will indeed intervene on behalf of his people, as he had been known to do in the past. In this sense, they serve as words of "consolation," as the text states. The theme of the entire composition is a firm belief in a future transition from a state of humiliation for God's righteous people to a new state where God's glory is revealed, and judgment passed on mankind (HØGENHAVEN). This seems to have been consistent with the Qumran community's understanding of its own identity.

INTERPRETATION OF ISAIAH IN QUMRAN COMMENTARIES (PESHARIM)

In Hebrew, *pesher* means "meaning" or "explanation." The so-called pesharim – running commentaries on (parts of) biblical books – are a particular feature of the Qumran collection of texts. A literary genre in their own right, commentaries of this type quoted passages from a biblical book and commented on them passage by passage. Thus, they are rather similar to compositions that occur later in Jewish and Christian tradition. Judging from the extant material, pesharim of this type were composed only in relation to certain biblical books: Isaiah, the Minor Prophets, and Psalms (LIM: 44–53).

Cave 4 has yielded at least five different manuscripts containing running interpretation of various parts of the book of Isaiah, and there is also a small fragment of an Isaiah commentary from Cave 3. The oldest of the Cave 4 manuscripts (4Q163) comprises sixty-one fragments of a papyrus scroll (or possibly two different scrolls, since two scribal hands can be distinguished in this group of fragments).

We cannot know if these pesher manuscripts represent six distinct "literary works" or should be viewed as copies of one composition. There are no instances of overlapping text connecting any of the manuscripts, and since there are also no instances of different manuscripts interpreting exactly the same biblical text, the evidence remains inconclusive (BROOKE 1997: 618–19). In fact, the term "literary composition" may not be accurate for this type of text. The pesharim could be understood as reflecting an ongoing process of interpreting the prophetic books, taking the form of constant rewriting, expansion, and revision, alongside repetition of earlier interpretative elements.

The Isaiah pesharim are fragmentary, and it is difficult to draw a coherent picture of the way they understand the prophetic text. When compared with the better preserved Qumran commentaries on Habakkuk and Nahum, the surviving remnants of Isaiah pesharim appear less preoccupied with specific figures and events belonging to the Qumran community's notion of its own past (such as the "Teacher of Righteousness"). In a sense, these commentaries remain closer to the meaning of the Isaiah text. However, events described in Isaiah are

sometimes explicitly related to the expected end-time, and interpreted
as pertaining to later situations. An example of this is the explanation
of Isa 10:28–32 given in Pesher Isaiah A (4Q161). The Isaianic passage
seems to describe an Assyrian army's campaign to Jerusalem, and parts
of these verses have been preserved in the Qumran pesher manuscript.
Then the exposition follows:

> [The interpretation of the]matter concerns the latter days, when
> [...] comes [...] when he goes up from the valley of Akko to wage
> war against [...] and there is none like it, and in all the cities of [...]
> and up to the boundary of Jerusalem [...] (4Q161, 2–6,7 26–29)
>
> (after García Martínez and Tigchelaar: 315;
> cf. Horgan: 91)

Various interpretations of this pesher passage have been suggested.
Most scholars now agree that the text probably does not allude to the
"coming" of the Messiah, as had been proposed earlier on, but to an
enemy, as indeed the Isaiah passage indicates (Allegro: 181; Flint:
243). The commentary asserts that the Akko on the Mediterranean
coast is the point of departure for the enemy going up against Jerusalem.
This may be understood as a reflection of historical events, in particular the approach of the Romans. The passage can thus be read in conjunction with other parts of the Isaiah pesher, where the eschatological
enemy is identified with the Kittim, a hostile foreign nation coming
into the land of Israel from the West (Jassen). The Kittim are mentioned sporadically in the Hebrew Bible, where the term denotes people from the Mediterranean realm, in particular the Greek islands. In
Qumran writings, the Kittim occur above all in pesharim and in the
War Scroll (1QM). It seems that "Kittim" became a standard designa-
tion for the Romans, reflecting the overwhelming power and importance of the Roman Empire during the last centuries of the Second
Temple period.[2]

Other parts of the pesher to Isaiah clearly do offer messianic interpretations of the book, however. Isa 11:1–20, which depicts a future
king as the "shoot from the stump of Jesse," is commented on in the
following way in the scroll:

> [... the sprout of] David, who shall stand in the lat[ter days ...]
> ... his [ene]my. And God shall sustain him with a [spirit of mi]ght ...
> ... [a th]rone of glory, a [h]oly crown, and many-colored rob[es ...]

---

[2]   The term "Kittim" seems also to refer to Romans in Dan 11:30.

... in his hand, and over all the nat[ion]s he shall rule, and Magog ...
... [al]l the peoples shall his sword judge, and when it says: "He
    shall [not judge by what his eyes see] or decide disputes by what
    his ears hear," its interpretation is that
... and as they teach him, so he shall judge, and upon their
    authority
... with him. One of the priests of renown will go out, and in his
    hand garments of ... (4Q161 8–10 22–9)
(after GARCÍA MARTÍNEZ AND TIGCHELAAR: 317; cf. HORGAN: 97)

The picture drawn here of the messianic figure should be viewed in the
larger context of what is said in other documents from Qumran such as
the War Scroll and the related text Sefer haMilḥamah (4Q285) (JASSEN:
83–9). The Qumran pesher introduces the figure (or perhaps the land)
of Magog, which has its origins in the book of Ezekiel. In Ezek 38–9,
Gog is introduced as the "chief prince" of the land of Magog. Gog is
an enemy of Israel, arising in the future at a time when the people of
Israel have been restored to their land. God pledges to destroy Gog and
to send fire against the land of Magog. In the pesher, Magog seems to
be an archetypal enemy who plays a role in a universal-eschatological
war scenario.[3] It is also notable that the messianic figure, who is
entrusted with a decisive military action against the enemies of God
and his people, is placed under the authority of the priests in the
Qumran text.

THE WIDER RECEPTION OF ISAIAH AT QUMRAN

The reception of Isaiah in writings found at Qumran shows some interesting features when compared with the reception of other biblical
books. Again, judging from the material that has survived, Isaiah and
the Minor Prophets are the only prophetic books for which pesharim
were composed. No such commentaries on Jeremiah or Ezekiel have
been discovered. On the other hand, Jeremiah and Ezekiel were extensively rewritten in the form of "apocryphal" compositions, expanding
on the stories and sayings of the biblical prophets. This seems not to
have been the case with Isaiah or the Minor Prophets.

It is not clear what conclusions, if any, can be drawn from these
data. It is of course possible that some of these findings may be purely

---

[3]   In a similar way, Gog and Magog are invoked as final enemies in the last days in
    Apoc 20:8.

accidental, as only a part of the manuscripts have survived to be discovered in the caves. If not, then the book of Isaiah may have been finalized and gained authority as a fixed literary composition at an earlier stage than the other prophetic writings. Other factors, however, may have been decisive – indeed, it could be argued that Jeremiah and Ezekiel, when compared with Isaiah, provide more narrative material that would lend itself to creative rewriting and expansion.

In any case, the book of Isaiah seems to have served as a major source of inspiration for the language used in the writings of the Qumran community. An example is the expression "smooth things" (hălāqôt), used with clearly negative connotations in Isa 30:10. Here, the prophet addresses those who do not want to hear true prophecy. Instead, they say to the prophets: "Do not prophesy to us what is right! Speak to us smooth things (hălāqôt), prophesy illusions." In one of the Isaiah pesharim (Pesher Isaiah C, 4Q163) we find the phrase "the seekers after smooth things" (dorshê hălāqôt), which could be read as a reference to the kind of people mentioned in Isa 30:10. In the Qumran pesher commentary on Nahum (4Q169), the "seekers after smooth things" seem to have become a fixed term for a particular group, often identified by modern scholars as the Pharisees.

There are more examples in Qumran texts of terminology apparently borrowed from, or directly inspired by, the book of Isaiah. Isa 28:14 is a condemnation of the ruling class of "scoffers" in Jerusalem ('anshê lāṣôn): "Therefore hear the word of Yhwh, you scoffers, who rule this people in Jerusalem." Several Qumran writings use the same Hebrew expression "scoffer" (in the singular, 'îš hallāṣôn) as a standing term for a specific enemy of the community. The "scoffer" appears to be a sobriquet for some person from the community's past, opposed to the "Teacher of Righteousness" and on the same side as the "wicked priest." The historical identifications of these figures remain uncertain.

To sum up, Isaiah was clearly a book of major importance for the Qumran community, and in all probability a book endowed with undisputed authority in various forms of Judaism in that time more generally. In Qumran writings that interpreted Isaiah, special emphasis was placed on eschatology, and specific passages of the book were assigned particular importance, and were read as prophecies pointing directly to the establishment of the Qumran community, and delivering language and imagery that the community used to describe their identity and divine purpose.

FURTHER READING

Allegro, John M. "Further Messianic References in Qumran Literature." *JBL* 75 (1956): 174–87.

Baumgarten, Joseph L., and Daniel R. Schwartz. "Damascus Document (CD)," Pages 4–57 in *The Dead Sea Scrolls: Hebrew, Aramaic, and Greek Texts with English Translations. Vol. 2: Damascus Document, War Scroll, and Related Literature*. Edited by James H. Charlesworth. Tübingen: Mohr Siebeck; Louisville, KY: Westminster John Knox, 1995.

Brooke, George J. "4Q500 1 and the Use of Scripture in the Parable of the Vineyard." *DSD* 2 (1995): 268–94.

Brooke, George J. "Isaiah in the Pesharim and Other Qumran Texts." Pages 609–32 in *Writing and Reading the Scroll of Isaiah: Studies of an Interpretive Tradition. Vol. 2*. Edited by Craig C. Broyles and Craig A. Evans. VTSup 70/2. Leiden: Brill, 1997.

Flint, Peter W. "The Book of Isaiah in the Dead Sea Scrolls." Pages 229–51 in *The Bible as Book: The Hebrew Bible and the Judaean Desert Discoveries*. Edited by Edward D. Herbert and Emanuel Tov. London: The British Library; New Castle, DE: Oak Knoll Press, 2002.

García Martínez, Florentino, and Eibert J. C. Tigchelaar, *The Dead Sea Scrolls Study Edition*. Vol. 1–2. Leiden: Brill, 1997–1998.

Høgenhaven, Jesper. "4QTanhumim between Exegesis and Treatise." Pages 151–67 in *The Mermaid and the Partridge: Essays from the Copenhagen Conference on Revising Texts from Cave Four*. Edited by George J. Brooke and Jesper Høgenhaven. STDJ 96. Leiden: Brill, 2011.

Horgan, Maurya P. "Isaiah Pesher 4 (4Q162 = 4QpIsaᶜ)." Pages 83–97 in *The Dead Sea Scrolls: Hebrew, Aramaic, and Greek Texts with English Translations. Vol. 6B: Pesharim, Other Commentaries, and Related Documents*. Edited by James H. Charlesworth. Tübingen. Mohr Siebeck; Louisville, KY: Westminster John Knox, 2002.

Jassen, Alex P. "Re-Reading 4QPesher Isaiah A (4Q161)." Pages 57–90 in *The Mermaid and the Partridge: Essays from the Copenhagen Conference on Revising Texts from Cave Four*. Edited by George J. Brooke and Jesper Høgenhaven. STDJ 96. Leiden: Brill, 2011.

Lim, Timothy H. *Pesharim. Companion to the Dead Sea Scrolls 3*. London: Sheffield Academic, 2002.

Lim, Timothy H., and John J. Collins. "Introduction: Current Issues in Dead Sea Scrolls Research." Pages 1–18 in *The Oxford Handbook of the Dead Sea Scrolls*. Edited by Timothy H. Lim and John J. Collins. Oxford: Oxford University Press, 2010.

Milgrom, Jacob. "Florilegium: A Midrash on 2 Samuel and Psalms 1–2 (4Q174 = 4QFlor)." Pages 248–65 in *The Dead Sea Scrolls: Hebrew, Aramaic, and Greek Texts with English Translations. Vol. 6B: Pesharim, Other Commentaries, and Related Documents*. Edited by James H. Charlesworth. Tübingen: Mohr Siebeck; Louisville, KY: Westminster John Knox, 2002.

Qimron, Elisha, and James H. Charlesworth. "Rule of the Community." Pages 1–51 in *The Dead Sea Scrolls: Hebrew, Aramaic, and Greek Texts with*

English Translations. Vol. 1: Rule of the Community and Related Literature. Edited by James H. Charlesworth. Tübingen: Mohr Siebeck; Louisville, KY: Westminster John Knox, 1994.

Tov, Emanuel. "The Text of Isaiah at Qumran." Pages 491–511 in *Writing and Reading the Scroll of Isaiah: Studies of an Interpretive Tradition. Vol. 2.* Edited by Craig C. Broyles and Craig A. Evans. VTSup 70/2. Leiden: Brill, 1997.

Ulrich, Eugene. "Isaiah, Book of." Pages 384–88 in *Encyclopedia of the Dead Sea Scrolls. Vol. 1.* Edited by Lawrence H. Schiffman and James C. VanderKam. Oxford: Oxford University Press, 2000.

6 Early Versions of Isaiah as Translations and Interpretations

RONALD L. TROXEL

We take translation for granted. When we read or hear the words of an official from another country translated by a news service, we rarely question whether the translation is accurate. Occasionally we learn of effects from infelicitous translations, such as Nikita Khrushchev's infamous proclamation in 1956, "We will bury you," for which the underlying Russian turns out to have a less provocative tenor of "We will outlast you" (POLIZZOTTI).

Most translation errors are benign, even if they have consequences. When Jerome translated the report of Exodus 34:29 that Moses, descending from the mountain, "did not know that the skin of his face shone because he had been talking with God," he confused the Hebrew verb for "shone" (*qāran*) with "horn" (*qeren*), thereby translating, "he did not know that his face had horns because of his conversation with God." As a consequence, Michelangelo's sculpture of Moses wears two horns, a feature that spread to images of Moses throughout Europe.

Each of these examples has to do with correctly understanding words in the source language (the language in which the work was composed) and identifying appropriate equivalents in the target language (the translation language). However, when the syntax of the target language is significantly different from that of the source language, the problems involve more than choosing the right word. For example, one might translate the Hebrew infinitive absolute joined with a finite verb in various ways: "He will surely save," "He will keep saving," "He will save completely," and so on. Because English has no precise analogue for the infinitive absolute, a translator must choose an equivalent that expresses the effect that seems most likely to fit the rhetorical context.

How such issues are handled often features in how translations are marketed. Those touted as following the Hebrew, Aramaic, and Greek closely often have stilted English. Those claiming to put the Bible into contemporary English, on the other hand, aggressively resolve ambiguities in the source language by settling on one of several equally possible meanings (as when "love of God" could mean "love for God" or "God's love for people").

For many early readers and hearers, the Hebrew scriptures were not only "Greek to them," but they were also better understood when translated into Greek. That was the case for the large Jewish community in Alexandria, for whom the earliest attempt to render the Hebrew into Greek was made in the third century BCE, beginning with the Torah (MARCOS: 40). The Septuagint translation of Isaiah into Greek dates to around 135 BCE (VAN DER KOOIJ),[1] although it is possible that translations of some passages existed prior to becoming part of the completed translation. I. L. Seeligmann pointed to phrases suggesting that "certain passages in the Septuagint of Isaiah have been formulated under the influence of the liturgy in the Jewish-Alexandrian milieu" (SEELIGMANN: 101–2).[2]

If the Greek translation of Isaiah were marketed today, it would fall solidly among those claiming to present the Bible in contemporary language. The Syriac translation (the Peshitta), undertaken in the latter half of the second century CE, also makes some concessions to readability but hews more closely to the Hebrew (WEITZMAN: 258). (This is perhaps not surprising, since Syriac and Hebrew are both Semitic languages, whereas Greek is Indo-European.) Each translation of Isaiah follows tendencies already established in earlier translations of other biblical books, even if the Greek translator's accommodations to his target language are frequently idiosyncratic. Each is guided by perception of what readers wanted or would tolerate.

The discipline of Translation Studies calls this constraint of readers' expectations on translators "norms" (MUNDAY: 72–3), which are not as rigid as "rules" but do shape how a translator proceeds. After all, the ultimate verdict on the usefulness of a translation is its survival, which has much to do with balancing norms of "acceptability" and "adequacy." "Adequacy" means the degree to which a translation conforms to the source language, while "acceptability" means how many adaptations of the source language to the target language are tolerated (MUNDAY: 173). For example, both the Greek and Syriac translators

---

[1]   Arie van der Kooij notes that the translator of Ben Sira reports that the prophets were translated into Greek by the time he reached Alexandria in 132.

[2]   However, it can be difficult to distinguish between liturgical influence on the translation of a passage, on the one hand, from prior translation of a passage for use in the liturgy that only later became part of the larger translation, on the other.

adjust the grammatical number and even the person of pronouns to match those of other nouns or verbs in the context, and on occasion each will insert a pronoun to clarify a subject or object.

In what follows, examples from these translations show that the range of modifications the Greek translator expected to be tolerable among his readers was larger than that which the Syriac translator expected. In order to study translation, citations of the languages will be necessary.

THE SEPTUAGINT AND PESHITTA AS INTERPRETATIONS

Isaiah 28:10, 13: Obscure Speech

These two adjacent verses provide a good window into some of the problems that confronted the translators, and how their solutions differed. The advantage these verses offer is that their shared obscure vocabulary allows us to gauge how each translator sought to meet the norms of adequacy and acceptability.[3]

Hebrew	Greek	Syriac
[10]For mandate upon mandate,	[10]*Accept affliction* upon	[10]For *dung* upon *dung,*
mandate upon mandate;	*affliction,*	and *dung* upon *dung;*
		and *vomit* upon *vomit,*
line upon line,	*hope* upon *hope*	and *vomit* upon *vomit;*
line upon line,		there a little, there a
there a little,	*yet* a little, *yet* a little	little
there a little		
[13]And the word of Yhwh	[13]And the oracle of the Lord	[13]And the word of the Lord
will be for them	*God* will be for them	will be for them
mandate upon mandate,	*affliction* upon *affliction,*	*dung* upon *dung,* and *dung* upon *dung;*
mandate upon mandate;		and *vomit* upon *vomit,*
line upon line,	*hope* upon *hope,*	and *vomit* upon *vomit;*
line upon line,		there a little, there a
there a little,	*yet* a little, *yet* a little	little
there a little		

---

3   Unless otherwise noted, translations of all Hebrew, Greek, and Syriac are my own, owing to a need to show parallels between them as clearly as possible.

The meaning of the enigmatic Hebrew is less important than noting how each translator rendered the phrases. In both verses the Greek
appears to have related the word for "mandate" (ṣw) to a visually similar word (ṣr), meaning "affliction," while it associated the word for
"line" (qw) with a verb that means "to hope" (qwh). Identifying words
by comparing consonants to other Hebrew words – often by focusing
on just two consonants within a word – is a common strategy for both
translators. However, the Greek translator frequently shows more lat-
itude in such comparisons, as in his association of ṣw with ṣr here. At
the same time, he frequently enough omits repeated words, probably
owing to a tendency to condense verbiage. Another of his tendencies is
evident in his prefixing of the imperative "accept" to verse 10, where no
Hebrew verb is present. His expansion of LORD into Lord <u>God</u> is equally
common for him.

The Syriac translator renders both verses the same way, arriving at
equivalents by comparison with verse 8's "All tables are full of filthy
vomit," where the word for "vomit" is qyʾ, whose consonants are reasonably similar to qw, and the word "filthy" is ṣʾh, which often means
"dung" and could likewise be reasonably associated with ṣw. Some
modern interpreters think these bodily substances were indeed con-
noted by the original Hebrew. In any case, whereas the Greek translator
reasons by association with the larger stock of Hebrew vocabulary, the
Syriac translator finds a solution in similar words nearby.

Isaiah 18:2b, 7b: Divergent Views of a Foreign People

Here again we have Hebrew vocabulary shared by two verses in close
proximity. Even though the Greek translator used the same words for
the obscure Hebrew words of 28:10 and 12, here he varies his equivalents, while the Syriac uses the same words in each verse.

Hebrew	Greek	Syriac
²[...he who sends emissaries	²[...he who sends hostages by	²[...he who sends hostages by
by sea, indeed in	sea and	sea and
papyrus vessels on the water's	papyrus letters upon the water.]	papyrus vessels on the water's surface
surface (saying),]	*For* swift messengers	(saying),]
"Go, swift	*shall go*	"Go, swift messengers
messengers,	to a lofty people and a	to a people *plucked*
to a people tall	*people*	and

and sleek, to a people feared from here and beyond, a nation strong and trampling...."	*foreign* and *fierce* – *who is beyond it?* a nation *hopeless* and trampled	*uprooted,* to a people feared from here and beyond, a people *despised* and trampled...."

⁷[At that time shall a
  gift be
brought to Yhwh of
  Hosts,]
[from] a people tall
  and sleek,
and from a people
  feared
from here and
  beyond,
a people strong and
trampling....
	⁷[At that time shall
	  gifts be
	brought to the Lord
	  Sabaoth]
	from a people *afflicted*
	  and
	plucked
	and from a people *great*
	from *now and forever*,
	a people *hoping* and
	  trampled....
		⁷[In that day shall
		  gifts be
		brought to the Lord
		  Almighty]
		a people *plucked* and
		uprooted
		__ a people feared
		  from
		here (it) and beyond,
		a people *despised* and
		  trampled....

There is no reason to suspect that the words in either translator's source text differed between the two verses more than the minor variations between "to a people" and "from a people" evident in the Hebrew Masoretic Text (hereafter MT).

Taking note of the italicized words that mark differences between each version and the MT, it is clear that the Syriac has fewer differences, and its equivalents in verse 2 and verse 7 are nearly identical.[4] The Greek translation, on the other hand, treats verse 2's initial imperative, "Go," as a finite verb in the future tense, even though the translator renders the same form (*lkw*) elsewhere as "go!" (1:18; 2:3, 5; 30:21; 50:11; 55:3). It is unlikely that his source text read a different form (such as *hlkw*), since "he often sacrifices grammatical accuracy to his own stylistic text-formulation" (SEELIGMANN: 56).

The difference between Syriac's "plucked" and Greek's "lofty" seems rooted in different ways of interpreting the Hebrew passive participle (*mmšk*), "drawn out"/ "extended." Syriac's choice of "plucked" might

---

4   This despite its difficulty understanding the Hebrew terms translated into English as "tall and sleek" and even though it lacks "and from" before "a people feared" and "a people despised" in verse 7.

well have determined its selection of "uprooted" as a companion adjective, owing to unfamiliarity with the Hebrew noun translated "sleek."[5]

After that, the Greek diverges from both the MT and the Syriac notably, first by shifting "people" forward and modifying it with "foreign," which has no apparent connection with the Hebrew word translated "sleek." It was likely chosen because "foreignness" is implied by the need to send messengers, as seems implied again in its reformulation of "from here and beyond" with the question "Who is beyond it?," suggesting they are a great distance away.

If we compare the Greek translation of the same phrases in verse 7, the equivalent for "tall" has shifted to "afflicted," followed by the adjective "plucked." The translator might have chosen "plucked" based on the same reasoning the Syriac inferred from "drawn out," while he chose "afflicted" because it fitted semantically with the violence implied by "plucked." Not only has he left behind the adjective 'foreign' that he used in verse 2, but he has also rendered the second instance of "people" in its original slot: "and from a people great." The difference between "fierce" (v. 2) and "great" (v. 7) is likely connected to the most striking difference between the two verses: "hopeless" (v. 2) and "hoping" (v. 7).

The Hebrew word underlying both "hopeless" and "hoping" is qw – the same word translated "hope" in 28:10, 13. The difference between them is an example of a phenomenon found frequently in the Greek of Isaiah that involves the insertion or omission of a negative particle. Sometimes this is as innocuous as translating a verb with a negative connotation, such as "reject," with its antonym and a negative, as in its rendering of "for they rejected the law of Yhwh of hosts" with "for they *did not want* the law of Yhwh Sabaoth" in 5:24.

However, the translator's use of this device can have dramatic effects, such as in 3:10, where he translates "Tell the righteous that he is fortunate" with "Let us bind up the righteous man, because he is detrimental to us." "Detrimental" renders the Hebrew word for "good" (*ṭōb*), translated "fortunate" – a meaning it can bear alongside others, including "useful." In this case, the translator negated the meaning "useful" by using the Greek prefix *dys-* that we know in English from words such as "dysfunctional" and "dystopia." The translator probably felt compelled to make this shift owing to the talk of "binding" the person, arising from a copying error in his Hebrew text that substituted *'srw*, "bind," for *'mrw*, "say" (Tov 2015: 151).

---

5   Syriac's translation of a form of the same Hebrew word in 50:6, using a noun meaning "buffeting," suggests he was likely uncertain of the word's meaning here.

Likely because a plot to bind a "good" man seemed implausible, the translator negated "useful" to arrive at a sensible statement.

Seeligmann described the Greek translator as "forcibly try[ing] to wrench, from passages which he cannot understand, some signification either by adding a negation not occurring in the Hebrew text, or by neglecting a negation which does figure in the Hebrew original" (SEELIGMANN: 57). That diagnosis might apply to 3:10, but in 18:2 the negative prefix "dys-" is more likely an effect of reasoning about meaning from the larger context, a suspicion that additional observations support.

In verse 2, messengers are sent to a people that verse 1 locates "beyond Ethiopia," characterized as tall, hopeless, and oppressed. The Greek translator inserts "for" to link the forecast of emissaries going to this people with the report of someone sending hostages and papyrus letters by sea. This translator inserts "for" more prolifically than all other translators in the Greek Bible, save Proverbs (TROXEL 2008: 92). It is one of many signals of his intent to provide a translation acceptable to those more at home with Greek than Hebrew.

That hopeless and trampled country will be inhabited and become like a "signal raised from a mountain, like the sound of a trumpet" (v. 3). Verse 7's initial phrase, "in that time," refers back not only to the habitation of that country, but also to the divinely promised "safety in my city" (v. 4). The main action forecast for "that day" will be gifts "brought to Yhwh from a people afflicted and plucked, and from *a great* people *from now and forever,* a nation *hoping* and *trampled.*" The description of them as "trampled" both here and in verse 2 reverses the original author's portrayal of the militarily mighty Kushites and envisions another sort of people entirely (the geopolitics of the eighth century BCE will have been forgotten or ignored by this later period). Meanwhile, the switch from "hopeless" to "hoping" also accords with the shift in fortunes the Greek translator found announced in the end of verse 2 into verse 3:

Hebrew	Greek	Syriac
whose rivers divide its land.	Now the rivers of the land	who *plunder* the rivers of its land.
³All the inhabitants of the earth and the dwellers of the world	³will all be *like an inhabited land;* their land *will be inhabited*	³All the inhabitants of the earth, *who dwell* in the world,
like the lifting of a signal (on) the mountains you will see	*just as* a sign *is raised from* a mountain	*when they lift* up a signal (on) the mountains, you will see

The Hebrew underlying "all the inhabitants of the earth and the dwellers of the world" is commonplace, and Syriac renders the phrases straightforwardly, even if it connects them by means of a relative pronoun ('who dwell'), a tactic it uses frequently for juxtaposed phrases.

The Syriac and Greek translators seem to have taken different paths to dealing with "you will see" on the heels of a comparison. Whereas Syriac transforms the comparison into a temporal clause ("when"), while retaining "you will see," Greek keeps the comparison but drops "you will see." The more significant differences between the Syriac and Greek lie in the end of verse 2 and the start of verse 3.

The Hebrew word translated "divide" (bz'w, v. 2) occurs only here, so it is hardly surprising that neither translator seems to have recognized it. Syriac relates the consonants bz'w to the verb bzz, "plunder." Greek might have connected bz'w with bz't, "in this" and construed it as "in this (time)" = "now." However, this translator so frequently inserts "now" without any basis in the Hebrew text that it is more likely his innovation. In fact, just as the translator supplies "now" at the head of a clause to signal a shift to a new topic (2:5) or a new state of affairs (2:10), he likely supplied it here to signal a shift: The hopeless and trampled nation is about to undergo an elevation of its status. This inference is supported by his transformation of language about "the world's inhabitants" into forecasts of a land's habitation so that it becomes "like a signal from a mountain" or "the sound of a trumpet." This elevation of the nation "in that time" (v. 7) becomes the reason gifts are brought to the Lord, correlative with these people becoming "hopeful." Moreover, whereas in verse 2 they were called "fierce," they are now "great," which likely owes to the translator seeking a less bellicose description for this now delivered people.

Whereas the Syriac often allows the reader to intuit the Hebrew underlying it, the relationship between the Greek and the Hebrew is often tenuous. And although both translators faced uncertainties, the Syriac translator sought to stay close to what seems clear in the Hebrew, whereas the Greek translator was more willing to extrapolate to what he intuited as the larger shape of the passage.

Isaiah 1:25; 3:8: Inserting Lawlessness

The tendency to extrapolate is especially apparent in passages where the Greek translator detects one of his favorite themes. For example, he is frequently drawn to themes having to do with the punishment of the wicked and is willing to elevate that theme beyond the Hebrew text. A case in point arises from comparison of renderings in 1:25:

Hebrew	Greek	Syriac
And I will turn my hand against you	And I will bring my hand against you	And I will turn my hand against you
and I will refine your dross	and I will burn you	and I will refine your rebels *so as to cleanse* [you],
as with lye	_____ *until clean*	and I will remove
and I will remove	and will remove *the disobedient,*	
	and I will extract	all your *iniquities.*
all your alloys.	all the *lawless from you,*	
	and all the proud will I humble.	

Both translators interpret Hebrew *kbr* ("as with lye") by relating its consonants to the verb *brr*, which means "be clean." Both also interpret (rather than translate) the words "dross" and "alloys." For "dross," Syriac uses the same word as for "rebels" in verse 23, perhaps because elsewhere it renders verbs akin to the word "dross" (*sygyk*) as "turn back," and thus found "rebel" a suitable equivalent. The Greek translation, on the other hand, lacks a word in that slot, using its pronoun as direct object: "I will burn *you* until clean."

Although "remove" in both translations is a legitimate rendering of the Hebrew verb, Greek's "the disobedient" does not align with the Syriac's "your iniquities," since it lacks "all," which appears, instead, in its next clause – a clause not found in the Syriac or any other textual witness. Because the Greek's verb "extract" in that clause (*aphelō*) is synonymous with "remove" (*apoleso*), "the disobedient" is likely meant as its equivalent for "dross." In other words, the translator broke the clause "and I will refine your dross as with lye" into two stages: "I will burn you until clean" and "I will remove the disobedient." The Greek translator's choice of "the disobedient" is notable for the fact that it, like Syriac's "rebels," is the same word it uses for the Hebrew word "rebels" in verse 23.[6]

Both the Syriac and Greek translators were likely perplexed by the Hebrew word for "alloys" (*bdylyk*), as appears often to have been the case with rarely occurring words. Whereas the Syriac renders it with "all your iniquities," Greek's "all the lawless" renders it is a plural adjective,

---

6   The Greek translator likely based "rebels" on the Hebrew word *sygyk* (compare 50:5), while the Syriac translator seems to have interpreted the word based on *swrrym* in verse 23, for which it uses a word from the same Syriac root.

"all the lawless *people*," parallel to the "disobedient *people*" and coordinate with "all the proud *people*" in the next clause. The Greek translator uses "lawless" and "lawlessness" frequently (45 times), following a pattern throughout the Greek Bible of using *anomos/anomia* – a negated forms of *nomos* (Torah) – for words denoting misdeeds, for which Torah was the benchmark (SEELIGMANN: 105). The final clause in the Greek version, "and all the proud I will humble," is borrowed from 13:11b: "and the haughtiness of the proud will I humble" (KOENIG: 84).

Similar to his use of words for "lawlessness," the translator frequently drew on the notion of the proud being humiliated, as becomes evident again in 3:8:

Hebrew	Greek	Syriac
For Jerusalem has stumbled	For Jerusalem is defunct,	For Jerusalem has stumbled
and Judah has fallen.	and Judah has collapsed,	and Judah has fallen.
For their tongue and their works (deeds)	*and* their tongue<u>s</u> are (imbued) with *lawlessness, being*	For their tongue and the work *of* their *hands*
are against Yhwh, so as to rebel	*disobedient* in matters *having to do with* the Lord.	they *made bitter before* the Lord
against the eyes of his glory.	*Therefore now is their* glory *abased*	and the *cloud* of his glory.

The translations of the first two lines accord with the Hebrew. The Greek translator's rendering of "their tongue" with "their tongue<u>s</u>" reflects his readiness to tailor grammatical number to his taste (TROXEL, 2008: 91–3).[7] He arrives at "lawlessness" by ascribing a negative sense to "their deeds," an effect of his attraction to words of the "lawless" group noted at 1:25. Even though the word it translates (*mʿllyhm*) could be construed as from a lexical stock that denotes bad behavior (*ʿll*), the translator renders *mʿll* with "their works" in verse 10.[8] Equally significant, he prefixes the preposition "with" and omits the pronoun "your." These observations encourage the conclusion that he chose "lawlessness" based on his own predilection for the term, doubtless reflecting his

---

[7] Greek replaces "for" with "and," a freedom in handling conjunctions this translator shows often.

[8] Compare his translation of *hsyrw rʿ mʿllykm* with "remove the evil deeds from your souls" in 1:16, where he analyzes the form as "from upon you."

religious community's belief in Law/Torah as the standard for ethical behavior (SEELIGMANN: 105).

Whereas the Hebrew nouns "their tongue and their deeds" are the subject complement for "against Yhwh," while the following verb "rebel" has as its object "the eyes of his glory," the Greek translation connects its "being disobedient" with what follows (it associates *lmrwt* with *mrh*, "rebel," and uses the same verb as "the disobedient" in 1:25).[9] It expands "against Yhwh" into "the things having to do with the Lord," accusing the people of "disobeying the things having to do with the Lord."

Finally, whereas the Hebrew speaks of rebellion "against the eyes of his glory," the Greek asserts that "their glory is humbled."[10] This shift might be attributable to confusing the consonants of the word "eyes" (*'ny*) by association with a verb meaning "be humble" (*'nh*), as he does also in 14:32; 49:13; 51:21. Because his insertion of "therefore now" (see the discussion of 'now' in 18:2 earlier) teases out the conclusion that the people's disobedience will bring punishment, his selection of "abased" is likely part of his construal of the verse as a whole. The fact that this tallies with his interest in the humiliation of the wicked elsewhere (such as 1:25) justifies concluding that this view guided his choices.

The Syriac version reflects a different sort of wrestling with the Hebrew of 3:8. Its translator renders the noun "work" appropriately but clarifies it by adding "of their hands," transferring the pronoun from "their works" to "their hands." His use of "made bitter" for the verb "rebel" rests on identifying the consonants (*lmrwt*) with a similar Hebrew verb (*mrr*) meaning "be bitter." Like the Greek, he modified the conjugation, rendering it as a past tense finite verb and (again like the Greek) connecting it with the words preceding it. His choice of "before the Lord" for "towards the Lord" is found again in 19:20 and 37:15. The phrase "the *cloud* of his glory" differs from "the *eyes* of his glory" but is based on identifying Hebrew *'ny* with a noun similar to it (*'nn*) that means "cloud." Unlike the Greek, it retains the grammatical number of the suffix: "the cloud of *his* glory." What remains distinctive in the Greek is its association of "lawlessness" and disobeying "things having to do with the Lord" with punishment by humiliation.

Isaiah 9:9: Babel in Isaiah

The Greek translator's willingness to intuit features not clearly present in his source text becomes even more remarkable in 9:9 (v. 10 in Greek):

---

9   "Being disobedient" also shifts the Hebrew infinitive form (*lmrwt*) to a participle.
10   Notable, also, is that "their glory" entails a shift from the third masculine singular pronoun of "his glory" to the grammatical plural.

Hebrew	Greek	Syriac
Bricks have fallen,	Bricks have fallen,	Bricks *let us raise*,
but with hewn stones we will rebuild;	but *come, let us cut stones*	and *let us make decrees*,
sycamores have been cut down, but we will replace them with cedars.	and *cut* sycamores and cedars, and *let us build a tower for ourselves.*	and *cut* sycamores and cedars let us replace.

Perhaps most arresting is Syriac's "let us make decrees," since the Hebrew says nothing of "decrees." At least the Greek understands that the proposal to cut stones stands over against the bricks that have fallen. Nevertheless, "make decrees" is not as far-fetched as it initially seems, since the idiom for making decrees is to "cut/incise" them (a literal translation of the Syriac would be "let us cut decrees"), and the Hebrew word behind "hewn stones" is the adjective "hewn/cut."[11] The substitution of "let us cut" for "we shall build" doubtless owes to the translator's determination that "cut/hewn" refers to decrees. Syriac gives a series of disconnected commands, evidently trying to understand these words as spoken by the arrogant (v. 8), which is likely why it renders "bricks have fallen" with "let us raise bricks." Neither the Syriac nor the Greek seems to grasp that what is "cut" is used for rebuilding.

The Greek uses the verb "let us build" later in the verse, but for a fresh project: "let us build a *tower* for ourselves." But where did he get "tower"? The answer comes with his expansion to 10:9, for which the Hebrew reads, "Is not Calno like Carchemish, Hamath like Arpad, or Samaria like Damascus?" With these rhetorical questions the Assyrian ruler voices confidence about subduing Samaria. The Greek, however, is more interested in the ruler's claims about Calno: "Did I not take *the territory above Babylon* and Calneh, *where the tower was built*? I also took Arabia, Damascus, and Samaria." Even if the translator was unfamiliar with the name Carchemish (SEELIGMANN: 78), he departed from his most frequent way of handling unfamiliar toponyms, which was to transliterate them, not omit them (TROXEL 2008: 190).

The resolution to this puzzle relates to this translator's rendering of Calno as Calneh, which was a city that Gen 10:10 locates "in the land of Shinar," the site of the Tower of Babel, according to Gen 11:2:

---

[11] Syriac correctly perceives this in Exod 20:25; 1 Kgs 6:36; 7:9, 11, 12; Ezek 40:42; Amos 5:11 (compare 1 Chron 22:2), using a Syriac word for "cut stone."

"And when they journeyed from the east, they found a valley in the land of Shinar and dwelt there." According to 11:9, the name of the city where they built the tower is "Babylon." This appears to be the basis upon which the Greek translator of Isaiah associated Babylon with Calneh and the building of the tower, so that the building with stones in 9:9 evoked for him the story of building the Tower, for which bricks were used *as* stone," according to Gen 11:3.[12] An additional mark of this is his addition *"come,* let us build," which echoes the phrasing in Gen 11:4's "come, let us build for ourselves a building and a tower" (ZIEGLER: 63, 109).[13] His translation of 9:9 and 10:9 with reference to Gen 11 is one of several instances where he shows himself influenced by the Torah (ZIEGLER: 125).[14] It may be that the translator was inspired to connect the excessive pride of the northern kingdom in Isa 9 and the Assyrian king in Isa 10 with the hubristic ambition of the inhabitants of Babel in Gen 11.

INTERPRETATIONS FROM OTHER PASSAGES IN ISAIAH

Isaiah 14:2: Multiplying in the Land
In addition to his reliance on the Torah, the Greek translator was influenced by language from elsewhere in Isaiah, as in 14:2:

Hebrew	Greek	Syriac
And the people will take them and bring them to their place,	And the nations will take them and bring them to their place, and _____ _____ they	And the peoples will take them and bring them to *their land.*
and the house of Israel will inherit them on the land of Yhwh as servants and maidservants	will inherit *and multiply* on the land of God as servants and maidservants	And those of the house of Israel will inherit them in the land of the Lord as servants and maidservants

---

[12] Equally notable is his translation of 'Shinar' with "from the rising sun" in 11:11, reminiscent of Gen 11:2's association of Shinar with the east.

[13] Although Syriac's "bricks let us raise" is similar to its "let us raise bricks" in Gen 11:3, nothing else in 9:9 suggests that the translator patterned his translation of the verse after the story of the tower the way the Greek did.

[14] Compare his translation of 42:13's "Yhwh like a warrior will go forth" with, "the Lord, the God of the mighty men, shall go forth and crush war," under the influence of the Greek translation of Exod 15:3 with "the Lord will crush war."

The Syriac reasonably interprets "their place" as "their land," but otherwise follows the Hebrew precisely. The Greek largely accords with the Hebrew but omits the pronominal object with "inherit" and carries the additional verb "and multiply."

It is clear that "and multiply" was imported from 6:12, where "and great is the abandonment in the midst of the land" is rendered "and those who are left *shall multiply* upon the land" (ZIEGLER: 139; SEELIGMANN: 116).[15] This perception gains validity by comparing 24:14, where the Hebrew says, "These will raise their voice, they will shout; in the majesty of Yhwh they will cry aloud," but the Greek reads, "These shall cry out with a voice, *and those who are left upon the land* shall rejoice together in the glory of the Lord." Besides collapsing "raising their voice" and "will shout" into a single phrase, the translator uses a phrase from 6:12 to identify whose voices are raised. Borrowing from 6:12 in 14:2 is thus quite likely.

Isaiah 6:9–10: Rewriting Divine Wrath

There are places where both translators seem to have found the Hebrew resistant to their assumption of what it should say. The most prominent example is 6:9–10, in which Isaiah receives a counterintuitive and painful prophetic commission:

Hebrew	Greek	Syriac
[9]And he said, "Go and say to this people: 'Listen attentively, but do not understand; look intently, but do not gain knowledge.'	[9]And he said, "Go and say to this people: 'You *shall hear* clearly and *will not* understand, and *despite observing* acutely, you *will not see*.'	[9]And he said *to me*, "Go, say to this people: 'Listen carefully, but you *will not* understand; look intently, but *you will* gain no knowledge.'
[10]Make the heart of this people thick, and make its ears heavy,	[10]*For* the heart of this people *grew thick*, and with *their* ears they *listened* heavily,	[10]*For* the heart of this people *has grown thick*, and its ears *are* heavy, and it closed its eyes,

---

[15]   "Multiply" is based on the Hebrew word "great," *rbh*.

and close its eyes,	and they closed *their*	lest it see with its
lest it look with	eyes, lest *they*	eyes, and hear with
its eyes, and listen	should see with	its ears, and
with	the eyes and hear	understand *with its*
its ears, and its heart	with	*heart*, and return,
comprehend, and	the ears, and	and *be forgiven*."
it turn and be	*with the heart*	
healed."	understand and	
	turn, and *I would*	
	heal them."	

Distinguishing the Greek from the Syriac are the latter's addition of "to me" after "he said" and its rendering of the primary verbs in verse 9 as imperatives, while the Greek translates three of the verbs of verse 9 in the future tense, while relegating the command to "look intently" to a participial clause subordinate to "you will not see." Greek adjusts the grammatical number of the verbs in verse 10 to accord with the pronouns in verse 9, whereas the Syriac hews to the Hebrew with *"its* ears," *"its* eyes," "lest *it* see," and yet interprets "be healed" with "be forgiven."

Despite these differences, both Greek and Syriac supply the conjunction "for" at the outset of verse 10 in order to turn the whole verse into an explanation of *why* verse 9 says that the people will gain no understanding, despite listening and looking.[16] In order to do so, however, each takes advantage of the ambiguous forms of "make thick," "make heavy," and "shut" to render them in the past tense (rather than as imperatives). Additionally, while the Syriac retains the imperatives "hear" and "see" of verse 9, its equivalents for "do not understand" and "do not gain knowledge" are ambiguous forms in Syriac, since they can be analyzed as perfect conjugations. The Greek translator, on the other hand, overrode the imperative forms of "hear," "do not understand," and "see" to render them in the future tense.

The Hebrew text's depiction of the prophet as the means of imposing obduracy on the people is a long-standing problem in the interpretation of the book. Neither the Greek nor the Syriac translator was comfortable with the idea that God intended to make the people blind and deaf so as to punish them. They resolved the issue by giving explanations for

---

[16] The Greek "will not *see*" instead of "gain knowledge" likely owes to its choice of a verb coordinate with "you will see" rather than a different word in its Hebrew source text.

the people's obduracy, likely because the plain meaning of the Hebrew was inconceivable to them.

USE OF THESE VERSIONS IN TEXTUAL CRITICISM

These comparisons demonstrate that each translation entails interpretation, whether by casting Hebrew into the forms of a different language or by providing a more elaborate decoding of meaning than mere lexical and grammatical equivalents. Tracing backwards from a translation to its Hebrew source entails looking for patterns in word choices and handling of grammatical structures to gauge the type of interpretation applied in rendering a passage. The more consistent a translator's choice of equivalents, the more secure one's conclusions about whether the source text was like the MT or points to a different type of text.

Because the Syriac is more regular in its choice of equivalents for Hebrew words and grammatical structures, it often yields a more certain path to reconstructing its source text than the Greek. This is not, however, to say that it gives us access to the most certain Hebrew text. Consensus holds that the Syriac version was undertaken in the latter half of the second century CE, when the forerunners of the MT were becoming the most prevalent copies in circulation, displacing manuscripts that preserved a greater diversity of readings (Tov 2012: 179–80). In fact, the Syriac version of Isaiah overwhelmingly reflects a source text close to the MT.

Although the Greek's reliance on a source text older than the Syriac does not mean that it preserves a more pristine form of the text (Tov 2012: 274),[17] it more frequently attests important variants from the MT, some of which are corroborated in the Hebrew of one or another of the Dead Sea Scrolls. Many agreements are less significant than might be supposed, however, such as cases where Greek *kai* precedes a word that has a prefixed *waw* in a Qumran manuscript, while the MT lacks a conjunction. For example, the Greek of 2:4 reads "*and* he will not take" and 1QIsa^a reads "*and* he will not lift up," whereas the MT reads simply "he will not lift up." The addition of the prefixed conjunction was so often a matter of scribal whim as to make this agreement more likely coincidental than significant.

Other agreements between the Greek and manuscripts from Qumran are more substantive. For instance, 8:1 reports a divine

---

[17]   As Tov 2012 notes, the more important consideration is the line of manuscripts from which a copy descends.

command to write words on a tablet. In the MT, Isaiah says in verse 2, "And I appointed for myself faithful witnesses." In the Greek, however, God continues speaking: "...and appoint as witnesses for me faithful men." This agrees with 1Qisaᵃ, which also contains an imperative form "appoint," suggesting that Greek's use of the imperative form was not simply the translator's whim.

Despite the greater number of agreements in variant readings between the Greek and the Dead Sea Scrolls, Syriac shows occasional distinctive agreements, as in 7:22, where the MT reads "for *everyone* (*kol*) who is left in the midst of the land will eat curds and honey," but Syriac has "because *the one* who is left in the midst of the land will eat honey and curds." Remarkably, whereas 1QIsaᵃ originally read "*everyone*" (*kol*), a corrector crossed it out, so that it read "the one who is left," like the Syriac. Because *kol* is frequently added reflexively by scribes, the lack of its representation in the Syriac and its excision from 1QIsaᵃ suggest that it was a late addition to the Hebrew.

Isaiah 14:2: The House of Israel

Although sometimes variants attested in a version are corroborated by a Hebrew variant in one of the Dead Sea Scrolls, even variants detected only by inference from the character of the translation can be compelling. For example, an additional facet in 14:2, discussed earlier, concerns the absence of a phrase:

Hebrew	Greek
And the people will take them and bring them to their place, and *the house of Israel* will inherit them on the land of Yhwh as servants and maidservants	And the nations will take them and bring them to their place, and *they* will inherit and multiply on the land of God as servants and maidservants.

The difference between Greek's "they" and the MT's "the house of Israel" runs deeper than it might appear, inasmuch as "they" is encoded in the conjugation of the verb rather than representing an independent pronoun (in either Hebrew or Greek). But neither does the Greek have a direct object for "inherit" as does the MT. The probable explanation is that "the house of Israel" is a late scribal addition (later than the source text used by the Greek translator) meant to clarify the subject of "will inherit them," while the Greek resolves the ambiguity of who is inheriting whom by suppressing the object "them" and adding "and they shall multiply" to clarify that it is not foreign people inheriting Israel as slaves but "that the foreign people *themselves* would become slaves of Israel" (VORM-CROUGHS: 338, her italics).

Isaiah 2:9b–10, 22: Later Additions

Chapter 2 holds a more significant contribution by the Greek to understanding how the Hebrew text grew over time. The MT, Syriac, Latin, and 1QIsaᵃ all read 2:22's "Do not rely on [lit. withdraw yourself from] man, whose breath is in his nostrils. For what worth is he?" This caps a section that speaks of the humiliation of people by Yhwh (vv. 6–17) and concludes with the demise of idols and the flight of humans into caves before Yhwh's terror (vv. 18–21). Curiously, verse 22 is absent from the Greek translation. And yet, despite the fact that the verse is attested in all the other extant witnesses, the verdict of most recent commentators is that it is an addition that entered later than the Greek's source text (BEUKEN: 101; BLENKINSOPP: 194; WILLIAMSON: 207).

In fact, there is widespread agreement that 2:6–22 contain evidence of having been assembled in bits and pieces rather than constructed from whole cloth. Not only do verses 18–21 contain repetitive phrases about the fate of idols and humans taking shelter in caves, but another textual witness raises questions about 2:9b–10, which read, "And so people are humbled, and everyone is brought low – do not forgive them! Enter into the rock, and hide in the dust from the terror of Yhwh, and from the glory of his majesty" (NRSV). Although the Greek, Syriac, Latin, and Aramaic translations read these two verses, as do two Qumran scrolls (4QIsaᵃ&ᵇ), 1QIsaᵃ reads "And so people are humbled" at the start of verse 9 but lacks the remainder of verse 9 and all of verse 10. Although scholars are more divided on this instance than the absence of verse 22 from the Greek, a strong case can be made that verses 9b–10 are a late expansion of the passage (TROXEL 2021). Furthermore, although the Greek version attests verses 9b–10, it adds to the end of verse 10, "when he rises up to shatter the earth," a clause not found in any other witness but likely stood in the translator's source text, where it had been added to complete the parallel between verse 10 and verse 19.

Although verses 9b–10 and verse 22 may reasonably be excluded from an attempt to recover the earliest text of Isaiah, the absent words represent more than just evidence of what is not "original," they preserve concrete evidence of the varied processes of expansion and editing of chapter 2 as it was copied by scribes.

CONCLUSION

There never has been a single authoritative translation of Isaiah, and even the first attempt we know (Greek) would hardly satisfy a modern reader's desire to know what the Hebrew says. Nevertheless, the Greek version shows us that the earliest community at least tolerated (and likely wanted) a version that gave them a sense of the overarching themes of the book. Even if the Syriac translation aligns better with our expectations of "fidelity" to the Hebrew, that owes primarily to the expectations and tolerances of the community for whom it was produced. The fact that it accords better with our expectations for a translation does not make it an inherently more authoritative translation.

FURTHER READING

Beuken, W. A. M. *Jesaja 1–12*, HThKAT. Freiburg, Basel, Vienna: Herder, 2003.

Blenkinsopp, J. *Isaiah 1–39*, AB 19. New York: Doubleday, 2000.

Koenig, J. *L'Herméneutique analogique du Judaïsme antique*, VTSup 33. Leiden: Brill, 1982.

Marcos, N. F. *The Septuagint in Context: Introduction to the Greek Versions of the Bible*. Translated by Wilfred G. E. Watson. Leiden: E. J. Brill, 2000.

Munday, J. *Introducing Translation Studies: Theories and Applications*. 3rd ed. Abingdon: Routledge, 2012.

Polizzotti, M. "Why Mistranslation Matters." *New York Times*, July 28, 2018.

Seeligmann, I. L. *The Septuagint Version of Isaiah*. Leuven: Brill, 1948.

Tov, E. *The Text-Critical Use of the Septuagint in Biblical Research*. 3rd ed., Jerusalem Biblical Studies 8. Winona Lake, IN: Eisenbrauns, 2015.

Tov, E. *Textual Criticism of the Hebrew Bible*. 3rd ed. Minneapolis, MN: Fortress, 2012.

Troxel, R. L. *LXX-Isaiah as Translation and Interpretation*, JSJSupp 124. Leiden: Brill, 2008.

Troxel, R. L. "Textual Criticism and Diachronic Study of the Book of Isaiah." In *The History of Isaiah: The Making of the Book and its Presentation of the Past*, ed. J. Todd Hibbard and Jacob Stromberg. Tübingen: Mohr Siebeck, 2021.

van der Kooij, A. "A Short Commentary on Some Verses of the Old Greek of Isaiah 23." *BIOSCS* 15 (1982): 36–50.

Vorm-Croughs, M. v. d. *The Old Greek of Isaiah: An Analysis of Its Pluses and Minuses*, SBLSCS 61. Atlanta, GA: SBL Press, 2014.

Weitzman, M. *The Syriac Version of the Old Testament*. Cambridge, New York, Melbourne: Cambridge University Press, 1999.

Williamson, H. G. M. *Isaiah 1–5*, ICC. London and New York: T&T Clark, 2006.

Ziegler, J. *Untersuchungen zur Septuaginta des Buches Isaias*. Münster: Aschendorffschen Verlagsbuchhandlung, 1934.

7 The Formation of the Book of Isaiah

Foundations and Current Issues

MARVIN A. SWEENEY

Recognition that the book of Isaiah is a composite work appears as early as the Babylonian Talmud and medieval rabbinic commentaries,[1] as well as in critical scholarship during the late-eighteenth and nineteenth centuries.[2] Nevertheless, Bernhard Duhm's 1892 commentary inaugurated modern critical research on the book's composition.[3] Duhm was the first to argue that Isa 56–66 constituted the work of an early post-exilic or Persian-period prophet dubbed Trito-Isaiah that followed upon the work of Proto-Isaiah in Isa 1–39 and Deutero-Isaiah in Isa 40–55. As a student of Julius Wellhausen, Duhm viewed the work of these prophets in source-critical terms as collections and subcollections of short oracles gathered around topical themes that were brought together by later redactors to produce the present form of the book.

Duhm's hypothesis has been extensively modified in subsequent scholarly discussion, particularly by the recognition that the process of the formation of the book of Isaiah was motivated by an intertextual and dialogical process of textual reading, reflection, interpretation, and redaction to enable Isaiah to address the concerns of later times. It remains the foundation for modern critical research on the formation of the book of Isaiah.

Various detailed assessments of research on the formation of the book of Isaiah are available (SWEENEY 1996: 31–62; SWEENEY 2016:

---

[1] See b. Baba Batra 14b–15a, which states that Isaiah was composed by Hezekiah and his colleagues. It also appears in R. Abraham Ibn Ezra's commentary; see M. Friedländer, *The Commentary of Ibn Ezra on Isaiah* (New York: Feldheim, n.d., first published, London, 1873), 1:169–71, 2:106.

[2] Marvin A. Sweeney, "On the Road to Duhm: Isaiah in Nineteenth Century Critical Scholarship," in *"As Those Who are Taught": The Interpretation of Isaiah from the LXX to the SBL*, SBLSym 27, ed. C. Mathews McGinnis and P. K. Tull, (Atlanta, GA: Society of Biblical Literature, 2006), 243–61.

[3] D. Bern. Duhm, *Das Buch Jesaia*, HKAT III/1 (Göttingen: Vandenhoeck & Ruprecht, 1892); see also Bernhard Duhm, *Das Buch Jesaia*, 5th ed. (Göttingen: Vandenhoeck & Ruprecht, 1968).

1–40; STROMBERG 2011b),[4] but it is useful to summarize some points in order to set the context for current issues in the discussion. This chapter therefore focuses on the final form of the book of Isaiah as well as on each segment of Isaiah identified by Duhm in an effort to assess how subsequent research in the late twentieth and early twenty-first centuries has built upon Duhm's work to posit a more developed and nuanced understanding of the formation and compositional history of the book of Isaiah.

THE FORMATION OF THE BOOK AS A WHOLE

Duhm argued that Isa 1–39 constituted a collection of oracular and narrative texts that either derived from Isaiah ben Amoz himself, or from later writers who wrote their own oracles that expressed similar views or narratives that depicted the prophet in historical context.[5] He further posited that Isa 1–39 comprised a number of major collections, which themselves included subcollections, such as the oracles concerning Jerusalem, Judah, and Israel in Isa 1–12, which in turn included subcollections in Isa 1, 2–4, 5, 6:1–9:6, 9:7–11:16, and 12, the oracles concerning the nations in Isa 13–23; additional oracles concerning Jerusalem, Judah, and Israel in Isa 24–35, which included subcollections in 24–27, 28–33, 34, and 35, and the historical narratives derived from 2 Kgs 18–20 in Isa 36–39. Duhm's analysis was based on the regnant methodological viewpoints of the time, namely that oracular texts were originally oral, and that they were normally short, self-contained units that would be easily memorized and repeated by the primitive speakers of the time who were not capable of composing more developed texts. These oracular texts would be gathered by editors into collections, as Assyrian prophetic texts were, for preservation in an archival library; but these editors did not always understand the creative genius of the original prophet. Duhm's hypothesis informed the work of most modern interpreters of Isaiah throughout the twentieth century who generally wrote commentaries and studies on Isa 1–39 as if it was a discrete prophetic book in an effort to reconstruct the original oracles of the eighth century prophet (all dates are BCE unless otherwise noted).

At least three of Duhm's major methodological foundations proved inadequate as research continued through the twentieth century. One

---

4   See also Sweeney, "On the Road to Duhm"; Sweeney, "Isaiah (Book and Person): 1. Hebrew Bible/Old Testament," *EBR* 13:297–305.
5   Duhm, *Das Buch Jesaia* (1892), v–xxi; Duhm, *Das Buch Jesaia* (1968), 1–22.

was the view that oracular texts were necessarily short, self-contained oral units that were simply copied down and archived by collectors. The work of A. B. Lord on Serbo-Croatian oral poets demonstrated that such singers typically developed and performed lengthy, complex oral compositions that resisted literary fixation as each performance drew upon typical phrases and motifs to produce unique texts of any given work of oral poetry and song that would be viewed by their audiences as the same work, even though it varied considerably with each performance.[6] Oral poets were hardly primitive, simple-minded illiterates who could barely remember their texts; rather they were skilled oral poets, performers, and intellectuals, who knew how to develop their texts in complex patterns that would address their audiences and communicate with them.

The second was the advance in the scholarly understanding of redaction criticism that emerged in the latter part of the twentieth century. Redaction criticism is a literary methodology that focuses on the literary collection, editing, arrangement, reformulation, and augmentation of earlier texts by later editors or redactors. Duhm had posited a number of later texts and expansions within his Isaian collections, including Isa 2:2–4, 11:7–16, and even 36–39. But his understanding of redactors was that they were largely collectors and editors who were not creative authors in their own right like the prophets whose works they collected and edited. They often did not understand the oracular material in their hands and, as a result of their misunderstanding of this creative theological material, often corrupted it, prompting modern scholars to recover the original works of the prophetic geniuses from the grasp of their less astute and spiritually deficient handlers. With increasing sophistication in the study of literature and social setting in the twentieth century to came the increasing recognition that editors or redactors had their own creative, theological impulses that guided and informed their redactional work. Focusing especially on the Pentateuch and the Deuteronomistic History, interpreters began to develop tradition-historical and redaction-critical models by which later redactors collected, augmented, and reformed earlier texts in an effort to express their own understandings of earlier works in relation to much later concerns and environments.

Third was the emergence of form criticism. Originally, this was intended as a tool to identify oral genres in biblical literature, and thus

---

[6]   Albert B. Lord, *The Singer of Tales*, 2nd ed. (Cambridge, MA; Harvard University Press, 2000).

to reconstruct the original words of prophets and other figures in the Bible, as Duhm would have postulated. But like redaction criticism, form criticism developed during the course of the twentieth century from a method concerned with oral texts to one concerned with literary compositions.[7] It thereby evolved into a literary methodology that would assess textual structure; the role of typical genres within those larger and more complex literary structures; and the social and historical settings within which complex texts were formulated and functioned.

Such advances in the study of oral poetry, redaction criticism, and form criticism made possible significant advances in the study of the book of Isaiah. Peter Ackroyd's work recognized the role of redaction in the formation of some of Duhm's larger collections, particularly Isa 1–12. He argued that those chapters presented the prophet Isaiah in relation to the later concerns of the Babylonian Exile and beyond in its depiction of judgment against Israel and Jerusalem, followed by restoration.[8] Ackroyd recognized the interplay between the narratives concerning King Ahaz's refusal to trust in Yhwh in Isa 7:1–9:6, which resulted in judgment against Jerusalem and Israel, and Hezekiah's turn to Yhwh in Isa 36–39, which resulted in the deliverance of Jerusalem.[9] But Ackroyd also noted the concluding episode in Isa 39 in which Isaiah condemned Hezekiah for hosting a Babylonian delegation prior to his revolt against Assyria, thereby ensuring that his sons would go into exile and also thereby establishing a literary transition to the work of Deutero-Isaiah in Isa 40. That insight would prove instrumental in explaining the formation of the larger book of Isaiah beyond that posited for only Isa 1–39.[10]

Other scholars also engaged in such work. R. E. Clements demonstrated that Isa 2–4 expressed the concerns of Jerusalem's judgment and restoration in relation to the Babylonian Exile,[11] and his ground-breaking studies on interrelationships between the lexicon and motifs in First and Second Isaiah likewise advanced understanding of the formation

---

[7] Marvin A. Sweeney, "Form Criticism," in *To Each Its Own Meaning: An Introduction to Biblical Criticism and their Application*, Revised and Expanded Edition, ed. S. L. McKenzie and S. R. Haynes (Louisville, KY: Westminster John Knox, 1999), 58–89.

[8] Peter R. Ackroyd, "Isaiah 1–12: Presentation of a Prophet," *Studies in the Religious Tradition of the Old Testament*, ed. Peter R. Ackroyd (London: SCM, 1987), 79–104.

[9] Ackroyd, "Isaiah 36–39: Structure and Function," in *Studies*, 105–20.

[10] Ackroyd, "An Interpretation of the Babylonian Exile: A Study of II Kings 20 and Isaiah 38–39," in *Studies*, 152–71.

[11] Ronald E. Clements, "The Prophecies of Isaiah and the Fall of Jerusalem in 587 B.C.," *VT* 30 (1980): 421–36.

the book of Isaiah as a whole.[12] Jacques Vermeylen examined the interrelationships between Proto-Isaianic texts in Isa 1, 24–27, and 34–35 in
relation to the allegedly apocalyptic outlook of Trito-Isaiah.[13] The present author employed these observations and others in a form-critical
assessment of the whole book of Isaiah, reenvisioning the formal mac-
rostructure of the synchronic form of the Book as a two-part account
of Yhwh's plans to reveal worldwide divine sovereignty in Zion in Isa
1–33 and the realization of Yhwh's plans to reveal worldwide divine
sovereignty in Zion in Isa 34–66 (SWEENEY 1996; SWEENEY 2016).[14]
Other scholars, such as Childs, Blenkinsopp, and Berges, also produced
commentaries and studies that would analyze Isa 1–66 as the final
form of the book of Isaiah that included the presentation of the work
of Isaiah ben Amoz in Isa 1–39 (BERGES 1998; BERGES 2008; BERGES
2015).[15] Nevertheless, the commentaries by Childs and Blenkinsopp
remain indebted to the diachronic conclusions of Duhm insofar as they
both presume the historical divisions into Isa 1–39, Isa 40–55, and Isa
56–66 – whereas Berges has recognized the importance of the differ-
entiation between a diachronic structure for the book as opposed to a
synchronic structure. Diachronic study analyzes the formation of the
book over time, while synchronic study analyzes its literary nature as a
whole. For example, from a diachronic standpoint, he perceives that Isa
55 was composed as the conclusion to Isa 40–55, but it also functions
synchronically as the introduction to Isa 56–66.

There is no doubt among critical scholars that editorial work on
the book took place, but the degree to which one can identify it with
confidence is disputed. For example, the recent commentary on Isa
1–39 by J. J. M. Roberts criticizes the "underlying assumptions" of
redaction critics and their confidence in their reconstructions. Given
the lack of existing manuscripts of Isaiah in other forms, he regards
the editorial process behind a particular book "both private and largely

---

[12]   Ronald E. Clements, "The Unity of the Book of Isaiah," in *Old Testament Prophecy:
       From Oracles to Canon* (Louisville, KY: Westminster John Knox, 1996), 93–104;
       Clements, "Beyond Tradition History: Deutero-Isaianic Development of First Isaiah's
       Themes," in *Old Testament Prophecy*, 78–92.
[13]   Jacques Vermeylen, *Du prophète d'Isaïe à l'apocalyptique: Miroir d'un demi-millènaire
       d'expérience religieuse en Israël* EB (2 vols.; Paris: Gabalda, 1977–78).
[14]   Sweeney, *Isaiah 1–4 and the Post-Exilic Understanding of the Isaianic Tradition*,
       BZAW 171 (Berlin: De Gruyter, 1988).
[15]   Brevard S. Childs, *Isaiah: A Commentary*, OTL (Louisville, KY: Westminster John
       Knox, 2001); Joseph Blenkinsopp, *Isaiah 1–39*, AB 19 (New York: Doubleday, 2000);
       Blenkinsopp, *Isaiah 40–55*, AB 19A (New York: Doubleday, 2002); Blenkinsopp,
       Isaiah 56–66, AB 19B (New York: Doubleday, 2003).

unrecoverable."[16] Because of his familiarity with Assyrian texts and backgrounds, he is aware of the reality of this editorial work, but identifies it only selectively. He admits, however, that his hesitation is based on his focus on Isa 1–39; most critical scholars who have analyzed the book as a whole have perceived more redactional activity in First Isaiah.

THE FORMATION OF ISAIAH 1–39

The discussion concerning the formation of the book of Isaiah as a whole also raises questions specific to Isa 1–39. CHAN ("The Book of Isaiah in the Neo-Assyrian Period," Chapter 2 in this volume) has ably situated the earliest texts in the book in relation to their eighth century context, so I focus here on the much contested issue of the ongoing formation of these chapters.

How and why were Isaianic oracles preserved and read from the time of the prophet (the late eighth century) until the time of Deutero-Isaiah (the late sixth century)? One might suppose that the latter's focus on restoration at the end of the Babylonian Exile and the beginning of Persian rule would provide an appropriate context for reading Isaiah, since King Cyrus of Persia decreed that Jews could return to Jerusalem to restore the Temple. But one major factor does not fit with this scenario: Isaiah's anticipation of a future Davidic monarch as expressed in Isa 9:1–6, 11:1–16, and 32:1–20. Although Deutero-Isaiah is heavily dependent upon Proto-Isaiah, the exilic prophet does not anticipate a new Davidic monarch; rather, the exilic prophet makes it clear in Isa 44:28 and 45:1 that Cyrus is Yhwh's new Messiah and Temple Builder and that the eternal Davidic covenant will not be applied to the House of David, but to the people of Israel instead. This embrace of foreign rule is a striking rejection of Isaiah's earlier positive prophecies about the royal house of David (SWEENEY 2016: 235–48).

A number of scholars, including Hermann Barth, Vermeylen, Clements, and the present author, have called for recognition of an Assyrian or Josianic redaction of Proto-Isaiah that might aid in explaining this shift. Barth was the leading figure in this discussion, but his work was focused more on the anti-Assyrian nature of his proposed redaction rather than upon pro-Davidic elements.[17] Although he was

---

[16] J. J. M. Roberts, *First Isaiah*, Hermeneia (Minneapolis, MN: Fortress, 2015), 2–3.

[17] Hermann Barth, *Die Jesaja-Worte in der Josiazeit*. WMANT 48 (Neukirchen-Vlyun: Neukirchener Verlag, 1977).

willing to concede Isaian interest in Isa 11:1–5, most of his discussion
focused on the anti-Assyrian elements of Isa 10:5–34 and the postexilic
character of Isa 11:6–16. Clements largely followed suit, and likewise
viewed 11:1–16 as postexilic like many scholars at the time.[18]
Vermeylen was willing to see Josian elements in Isa 11:1–5 and postexilic
elaboration in Isa 11:6–16.[19] The present author views Isa 11:1–16 as
entirely Josianic (SWEENEY 1996: 196–211).

H. G. M. Williamson rejects the proposal of a Josianic redaction of Isaiah, largely on grounds put forward by Barth, Clements,
and Vermeylen, for the interpretation of features of Isa 7 and 10
(WILLIAMSON 2006).[20] The present author agrees that Isa 10 is largely
Isaian, but calls for a Josianic reading of the third person narrative in Isa
7:1–25, based especially on its third person form in contrast to the so-
called first person form of the so-called Isaian Memoir in Isa 6:1–9:6 and
in relation to the concerns expressed in Isa 11:1–16 (SWEENEY 1996:
143–64). Williamson contends that this author's argument for reading
Isa 11:1–12:6 as a Josianic text is based on the reference to a small boy in
Isa 11:6–9, but this hardly does justice to the argument.[21] Indeed, there
are five major arguments (SWEENEY 1996: 204–5).

First, Isa 11:1–12:6 presupposes a threat to the House of David that
did not exist in the late eighth century, but such a threat did exist in the
seventh with the assassination of Amon ben Manasseh. When Hezekiah
revolted against the Assyrians, his throne was not under threat. Even as
the Assyrian invasion progressed, Hezekiah was able to retain his throne
owing to Sennacherib's need to move expeditiously against Hezekiah's
ally, Merodach-Baladan of Babylon.

Second, the reference to the monarch as a small boy, which Williamson
does cite, points to the eight-year-old Josiah, who succeeded his father
following his assassination as the result of a failed coup d'état.

Third, the emphasis on the Davidic king's wisdom and justice is a lynchpin of Josiah's reforms. It also contrasts deliberately
with the Assyrian portrayal of the Assyrian king as the ideal human,

[18] Ronald E. Clements, *Isaiah 1–39*, NCeB (Grand Rapids, MI: Eerdmans; London:
      Marshall, Morgan, and Scott, 1980).
[19] Vermeylen, *Du prophète d'Isaïe*, 1:269–80.
[20] See also H. G. M. Williamson, "The Theory of a Josianic Edition of the First Part of
      the Book of Isaiah: A Critical Examination," in *Studies in Isaiah: History, Theology,
      and Reception*, ed. Tommy Wasserman, Greger Andersson, and David Willgren
      (London: Bloomsbury T and T Clark, 2017), 3–21; Williamson, *Isaiah 6–12*, ICC
      (London: Bloomsbury T and T Clark, 2018), 615–704.
[21] Williamson, "The Theory of a Josianic Edition," 15–17.

metaphorically growing from heaven in the form of a tree and displaying the traits of wisdom, justice, beauty, and scent. Such an image would have taken hold in Judah especially during the seventh-century reigns of Esarhaddon, who expanded the Assyrian Empire, and Aššurbanipal, who put down revolt and concentrated on building up Assyrian culture and wisdom, especially by building a state library.

Fourth, the reunification of Ephraim and Judah and their conquest of Philistia, Moab, Edom, and Ammon in Isa 11:10–16 are all portrayed as part of Josiah's program (cf. Zeph 2:4–15 and his strategic marriages to Hamutal of Libnah [2 Kgs 23:31, 24:18] and Zebidah of Rumah [2 Kgs 23:36]) to assert Judean independence and to protect his southern and northern flanks from Egyptian and Assyrian interference. Hezekiah did exert control over Philistia, but there is no indication that he attempted to subjugate the Transjordan, although the small countries there, Ammon, Moab, and Edom, would have acted as his allies out of common interest. Zeph 2:4–15, however, indicates that Josiah would have liked to subjugate the Transjordan in an effort to reinvigorate the older Davidic Empire.

Fifth, the Exodus traditions in Isa 11:1–12:6 and elsewhere were used to portray a new Exodus from Egypt and Assyria, which could only be conceived during the later seventh-century reign of Josiah, when Egypt and Assyria were allied, rather than during the eighth century, when Egypt was an ally of Hezekiah.

A sixth argument might be added: Isa 11:1–12:6 appears to elaborate upon the royal oracle of Isa 9:1–6 in an effort to show what the reign of a Davidic Prince of Peace would entail; that is, a wise king who would eliminate threats and reunite the nation, which Hezekiah failed to do.

Other arguments that support a Josianic redaction of Isaiah include Clements's analysis of Isa 36–39, in which the account of Sennacherib's siege of Jerusalem in Isa 36–37 supports the notion of Yhwh's defense of Jerusalem and the House of David.[22] Such contentions are consistent with those of Isaiah, but they would hardly have stood up to close examination in the aftermath of the Assyrian siege when the country had been devastated by the Assyrian army and Hezekiah survived by the thinnest of margins. Archeological surveys indicate that Judah was devastated, and that the surviving Judean population moved eastward into the Judean hills and southward into the Negeb to escape the presence of the Assyrians, who apparently dominated the western Shephelah and coastal plain in their effort to build up olive oil production to supply

22   R. E. Clements, *Isaiah and the Deliverance of Jerusalem*, JSOTSup 13 (Sheffield: JSOT Press, 1980).

the needs of the Assyrian Empire.[23] It took nearly a century to rebuild the Judean countryside outside Jerusalem; no one would have viewed Hezekiah's survival as a success at the end of the eighth century. By the latter seventh century, however, the House of David could point to indicators of major success in recovering from the Assyrian assault at a time when Assyrian power was waning.

Finally, Christopher B. Hays points to Isa 24–27 as a composition rooted in Josiah's reign, although it has been subsequently reworked as the larger Isaian tradition developed (HAYS). He builds upon this author's view that Isa 27:2–13 was a Josianic text that culminates in an exodus from Egypt and Assyria, like that of Isa 11:10–16. He adds that feasting, overcoming death, and the renewal of creation are characteristic of ancient Near Eastern celebrations from well before Josiah's time and are not limited to a postexilic apocalyptic worldview. He also carefully examines the archeological remains at Ramat Raḥel to the south of Jerusalem that would have functioned as an Assyrian command center that would have been abandoned as Assyrian influence in the region diminished during the reign of Josiah. Earlier arguments for a late dating of Isa 24–27 to the Persian or Hellenistic periods, such as those of Duhm, Rudolph, and Ploeger, are no longer sustainable (HAYS: 24–51).[24]

Altogether, there is ample evidence for a Josianic redaction of Isaiah. Such a redaction would explain the continued relevance of Isaiah's prophecies in the monarchic period. They would have buttressed Josiah's claims to be a just monarch chosen by Yhwh to restore the former glory of Israel, whether real or imagined, and would have paved the way for future restoration following the failure of Josiah's reforms and the subsequent Babylonian Exile. But they would not have fully undergirded Deutero-Isaiah's vision of restoration, insofar as the exilic prophet looked to Cyrus and not the House of David to find Yhwh's Messiah and Temple builder.

THE FORMATION OF ISAIAH 40–55

Duhm argued that Isa 40–55 was the product of an anonymous prophet located in Lebanon (i.e., ancient Phoenicia) at the close of the Babylonian

[23] Baruch Halpern, "Jerusalem and the Lineages in the Seventh Century BCE: Kinship and the Rise of Individual Moral Liability," in *Law and Ideology in Monarchic Israel*, JSOTSup 124, ed. B. Halpern and D. W. Hobson. (Sheffield: JSOT Press, 1991), 11–107.

[24] For example, Duhm, *Das Buch Jesaja*, 172; Wilhelm Rudolph, *Jesaja 24–27*, BWA(N)T 62 (Stuttgart: Kohlhammer, 1933); Otto Ploeger, *Theocracy and Eschatology* (Richmond, VA: John Knox, 1968), 53–78.

Exile, whom he designated simply as Deutero-Isaiah.[25] He defined major subcollections for Isa 40–66 in Isa 40–48, 49–57, and 58–66, although he later defined Isa 56–66 as a collection of materials from Trito-Isaiah.[26] Nevertheless, he viewed the oracles of Deutero-Isaiah as short, self-contained subunits that were collected together by a redactor to form the whole of Isa 40–55. Duhm argued that the work of the redactor was evident in Isa 42:5–7, 44:9–20, 46:6–8, 48, 49:22–50:3, 50:10–11, 52:3–6, 58:13–14, 59:5–8, and 66:23–24. He further argued that the four major "servant songs" which he defined in Isa 42:1–4, 49:1–6, 50:4–9, and 52:13–53:12 were the work of another later poet, and were incorporated by the redactor in Deutero-Isaiah. His conclusion that Deutero-Isaiah was located in Phoenicia is based on his reading of Isa 49:12, which states, "Behold, these [released prisoners/exiles] will come from afar, and behold, they are from north and west, and they are from the land of Sinnim." Duhm read the Hebrew word *sînnîm* as a reference to Phoenicia, based on Gen 10:17. He likewise read Hebrew *miyyām*, "from west," as "from sea," and understood this as a support for his view that *sînnîm* referred to Phoenicia and that the prophet resided there. Later interpreters recognized that *miyyām* refers to the west, that is, west of Babylonia, and the land of Israel, that is, from Egypt and elsewhere in the Mediterranean basin, including Phoenicia, and that the prophet resided in Babylonia (though see TIEMEYER, "The Book of Isaiah and the Neo-Babylonian Period," Chapter 3 in this volume). He defines Isa 56–66 as a later collection by an anonymous prophet of the exilic period that he calls Trito-Isaiah.

Duhm's collection hypothesis for Deutero-Isaiah dominated research on Isa 40–55 for most of the twentieth century prior to World War II, and even beyond. But in the latter half of the twentieth century, interpreters began to experiment with literary and redactional models that could begin to define the form of the book of Isaiah as a whole and its constituent elements. With regard to Isa 40–55, James Muilenberg's 1956 commentary on Isa 40–66 employed his understanding of rhetorical criticism to provide a coherent literary analysis of the work of Second and Third Isaiah.[27] Subsequent work by Claus Westermann extended

[25]   Duhm, *Das Buch Jesaia* (1892) xiii–xiv, xvii–xviii, 345–346; Duhm, *Das Buch Jesaia* (1968) 14–15, 18–19, 373.

[26]   The confusion appears to be based on the appearance of the statement, "there is no peace, says Yhwh, my G-d, for the wicked," in Isa 48:22 and 57:21.

[27]   James Muilenberg, "Isaiah 40–66: Introduction and Exegesis," in *The Interpreters Bible. Volume 5*, ed. G. Buttrick. (Nashville, TN: Abingdon, 1956), 381–773.

the hypothesis of literary coherence to the form-critical analysis of longer generic subunits in Isa 40–66.[28]

A major breakthrough in the field came with the work of Roy Melugin, who read the various genre units that constituted Isa 40–55 as a coherent literary composition that comprised a sequence of genre units that would include Isa 40:12–44:23, 44:24–49:13, and 49:14–55:13 (MELUGIN). This author's own work built upon Melugin's model to posit an arrangement that began with an introduction in Isa 40:1–11, and continued in Isa 40:12–54:17 with a series of arguments concerning Yhwh's actions to maintain covenant and restore Zion, including Isa 40:12–31, which argues that Yhwh is master of creation; Isa 41:1–42:13, which argues that Yhwh is master of human events; Isa 42:14–44:23, which argues that Yhwh is redeemer of Israel; Isa 44:24–48:22, which argues that Yhwh will use Cyrus for the restoration of Zion; and Isa 49:1–54:17, which argues that Yhwh is restoring Zion. Isa 55, although originally written by Deutero-Isaiah, redefined the eternal Davidic covenant to apply to the people of Israel at large and functioned as an introduction to the work of Trito-Isaiah in Isa 56–66, which focused on the observance of Yhwh's covenant. Altogether, Isa 55–66 would function as a prophetic exhortation to Israel to adhere to Yhwh's covenant within the larger formal structure of the book of Isaiah.

Subsequent research would continue to apply holistic literary models to the reading of Isa 40–55, 40–66, and the book of Isaiah as a whole.[29] Rolf Rendtorff posited that Isa 40–55 formed a core of the book of Isaiah around which First Isaiah and Third Isaiah were assembled (RENDTORFF: 146–69). Indeed, he pointed to intertextual elements that linked Trito-Isaiah to Proto-Isaiah, thereby enabling the encasement of Deutero-Isaiah's work (RENDTORFF: 170–80, 181–89). O. H. Steck noted earlier discussion that Isa 35 was associated with Deutero-Isaiah, and he argued that Isa 35 therefore formed a bridge that linked

---

[28]   Claus Westermann, *Isaiah 40–66: A Commentary*, OTL (Philadelphia: Westminster, 1969).

[29]   Edgar W. Conrad, *Reading Isaiah*, OBT (Minneapolis, MN: Fortress, 1991); Katheryn Pfisterer Darr, *Isaiah's Vision and the Family of G-d* (Louisville, KY: Westminster John Knox, 1994); Christopher R. Seitz, "Isaiah 40–66," in *The Interpreters Bible. Volume 6*, ed. L. E. Keck (Nashville, TN: Abingdon, 2001), 309–552; Klaus Baltzer, *Deutero-Isaiah*, Hermeneia (Minneapolis: Fortress, 2001); John Goldingay and David Payne, *Isaiah 40–55*, ICC (2 vols.; London and New York: Bloomsbury T and T Clark, 2006); John Goldingay, *Isaiah 56–66*, ICC (London and New York: Bloomsbury T and T Clark, 2014).

Deutero-Isaiah with Proto-Isaiah.[30] Williamson built on the work of Ackroyd, Clements, Steck, the present author, and others, to argue that Deutero-Isaiah was the redactor who edited Proto-Isaiah so that it could serve as a fitting basis for reading Isa 40–55 (WILLIAMSON 1994). Although there is clear evidence for a sixth-century redaction that would have seen the combination of an early form of Isa 1–39 with Isa 40–55, sixth-century elements within Isa 1–39, such as Isa 2:2–4, 13:1–14:2, 24–27, 35, and 36–39, show insufficient correspondence with Isa 40–55 to make this hypothesis fully tenable.

Despite these advances, there were some, such as Benjamin Sommer and Shalom Paul, who despite important intertextual work on the part of the former and brilliant philological work on the part of the latter, continued to argue that Isa 40–66 was a separate body of literature from Isa 1–39 – largely on historical grounds.[31] A particularly interesting work by Lena-Sofia Tiemeyer attempts to argue that geographical references within Isa 40–55 point to Deutero-Isaiah's location in Jerusalem rather than in Babylon, but in this author's view, the prophet's satirical depiction of the idols burdening those who carry them during the Babylonian Akitu (or Near Year) festival in Isa 46 as well as other references in Isa 40–48 indicate instead that the prophet would have been located in Babylon (TIEMEYER). Nothing, however, precludes the prophet's having been among those who returned from Babylon to Jerusalem. Indeed, the focus in Isa 40–48 on Exodus from Babylon by Jacob and the focus in Isa 49–55 on Daughter Zion in Jerusalem awaiting the return of her husband, Yhwh, and her children, Israel, might well suggest a shift in location of the prophet.

Continental scholarship, such as the work of Reinhard Kratz, points to important motifs, such as the Cyrus layer, within Deutero-Isaiah, although its redaction-critical model for the formation of these chapters is somewhat unwieldly.[32] The insightful commentaries on Isa 40–48 and 49–54 by Ulrich Berges follow a similar line from his earlier overview study of Isaiah, but they also show a capacity to engage with other viewpoints, as illustrated by his decision to read Isa 55 as an introduction to Isa 56–66 (BERGES 2008; BERGES 2015). Other studies, such

[30]   Odil Hannes Steck, *Bereitete Heimkehr. Jesaja 35 als redaktionelle Brück zwischen dem Ersten und dem Zweiten Jesaja*, SBS 121 (Stuttgart: Katholische Bibelwerk, 1985).

[31]   Benjamin D. Sommer, *A Prophet Reads Scripture: Allusions in Isaiah 40–66* (Stanford, CA: Stanford University Press, 1998); Shalom Paul, *Isaiah 40–66* (Grand Rapids, MI, and Cambridge: Eerdmans, 2012).

[32]   Reinhard, G. Kratz, *Kyros im Deuterojesaja-Buch*, FAT 2 (Tübingen: Mohr Siebeck, 1991).

as those by Beuken, Tull (Willey), and Kim, understand the importance of intertextuality for building a network of intertextual references, both within Isa 40–66 and between Isa 1–39 and Isa 40–66, for establishing the literary and conceptual coherence of Isaiah.[33]

Viewed as a whole, scholarship has turned from Duhm's fragmentary approach toward a far more coherent reading of Deutero-Isaiah within the larger form of the book of Isaiah as a whole.

THE FORMATION OF ISAIAH 56–66

Duhm's analysis of Isa 56–66 posited subcollections in Isa 56–60 and 61–66 that were written by a single postexilic writer whom he dubbed Trito-Isaiah.[34] Indeed, Duhm's identification of Trito-Isaiah stands as one of the most enduring contributions of his work. Karl Elliger's attempt to defend Duhm's hypothesis of Trito-Isaiah as a single author, however, has been largely rejected by the field owing to the disparity in the contents and forms of the oracles in Isa 56–66, although his attempt to argue that Trito-Isaiah is the final editor of the book has gained some support in recent study.[35] Westermann's celebrated commentary on Isa 40–66 recognized the diversity of authorship within Trito-Isaiah. Rendtorff argued that Isa 40–55 stands as the core of the book of Isaiah around which the materials from Proto-Isaiah and Trito-Isaiah are redactionally built. Indeed, Rendtorff's model points to the role of Trito-Isaiah as an influential element in the redaction of the book, particularly in relation to the interests in justice (*mišpāṭ*) and righteousness (*ṣĕdāqâ*) that appear in Isa 56:1 and permeate the rest of the book, as well as the interest in these chapters in the questions of divine righteousness posed by Yhwh's commands to the prophet in Isa 6 to render the people blind, deaf, and dumb, so that Yhwh's redemption and worldwide sovereignty might be realized (RENDTORFF: 146–89).

---

33   W. A. M. Beuken, "Jesaja 33 als Spiegeltext im Jesajabuch," *ETL* 67 (1991): 5–35 (see also his commentaries, *Jesaja 1–12*, HThKAT [Freiburg: Herder, 2003]; *Jesaja 13–27*, HThKAT [Freiburg: Herder, 2007]; *Isaiah II: Isaiah 28–39*, HCOT [Leuven: Peeters, 2000]; Patricia Tull Willey, *Remember the Former Things: The Recollection of Previous Texts in Second Isaiah*, SBLDS 161 [Atlanta, GA: Scholars Press, 1997]; see also her commentary, Patricia K. Tull, *Isaiah 1–39* [Macon, GA: Smyth and Helwys, 2010]); Hyun Chul Paul Kim, *Reading Isaiah: A Literary and Theological Commentary*, ROT (Macon, GA: Smyth and Helwys, 2016).

34   Duhm, *Das Buch Jesaia* (1892), xviii–xix; idem, *Das Buch Jesaia* (1968), 19.

35   Karl Elliger, *Die Einheit des Tritojesaia (Jesaia 56–66)*, BWANT III/9 (Stuttgart: W. Kohlhammer, 1928); see also Elliger, *Deuterojesaia in seinem Verhältnis zu Tritojesaia*, BWANT IV/11 (Stuttgart: W. Kohlhammer, 1933).

Seizo Sekine's detailed critique of Elliger's work and his own recon-struction of the compositional reconstruction of Trito-Isaiah stand as the basis for contemporary research, particularly his contention that the late sixth-century material in Isa 60–62 stands as the kernel or core of Trito-Isaiah, and that the early fifth-century material in Isa 56–59 and 63–66 constitutes oracular texts that have been redactionally assem-bled around this core (SEKINE: 242–84). In his estimation, Isa 56:1–8 and 66:18–24 are the redactional "clamps" that hold these chapters together. Steck employs a similar model to recognize the early and cen-tral role of Isa 60–62 while positing a redactional process that forms the surrounding material in Isa 56–59 and 63–66 in the fifth century BCE, although he also points to the role of Trito-Isaiah in redactionally forming the "Great Isaiah Book" as indicated in texts such as Isa 35, which serves as a "bridge" in joining Proto-Isaiah to Trito-Isaiah with Deutero-Isaiah in the middle (STECK).[36] Similar models appear in the work of Koenen, Smith, and Berges.[37]

The present author's own model for the formation of the book of Isaiah is heavily influenced by the work of Sekine, Steck, and Rendtorff, based especially on the contentions that Isa 60–62 forms the core of Trito-Isaiah and that Trito-Isaiah plays a major role in the redaction of the book of Isaiah as whole, particularly in forming Isa 1 and 65–66 as the redactional introduction and conclusion to the book. But previous work needed to recognize the role that the restoration led by Nehemiah and Ezra plays in the formation of book, particularly because Koch points to the modeling of Ezra's return to Jerusalem on the work of Deutero-Isaiah.[38] Trito-Isaiah's interest in the Gentiles is based on the view that Gentile inclusion in the covenant entails a form of conversion to Judaism based on observance of the Sabbath and the other requirements of the covenant. Indeed, such measures would have to be considered in relation to Ezra's prohibition of inter-marriage: Ezra would have been well aware of the requirements of Deuteronomy, which includes some means by which Gentile women could become part of Israel (see Deut 21:10–14; cf. 20:13–14; cf. Ruth) and envisions that at least members of some nations, such as Edom

---

[36] See also Steck, *Bereitete Heihmkehr*; Steck, *The Prophetic Books and their Theological Witness* (St. Louis, MO: Chalice, 2000).

[37] Klaus Koenen, *Ethik und Eschatologie im Tritojesajabuch*, WMANT 62 (Neukirchen-Vluyn: Neukirchener Verlag, 1990); P. A. Smith, *Rhetoric and Redaction in Trito-Isaiah: The Structure, Growth, and Authorship of Isaiah 56–66*, VTSup 62 (Leiden: Brill, 1995).

[38] Klaus Koch, "Ezra and the Origins of Judaism," *JSS* 19 (1974): 173–97.

and Egypt, might become part of Israel,[39] although there are still issues with Moabites, Ammonites, and those who have lost or damaged sexual organs (Deut 23:2–9). It appears that Nehemiah and Ezra are concerned with foreigners who continue to speak their own languages and otherwise show signs of potential apostasy (Neh 13:23–31). They make no mention of those who had assimilated into Judean culture and observed Yhwh's requirements; presumably they would not have been considered foreigners. Like Isa 44:28, 45:1, and 55:1–13, they accept Persian rule.

Finally, Stromberg presents a synthesis of these views to argue that Trito-Isaiah is a reader of the earlier Isaian tradition, particularly in relation to the framework in Isa 56–59 and 65–66, and it thereby serves as a key agent in the interpretation and redaction of the final form of the entire book (STROMBERG 2011a). In his view, the author-redactor of Trito-Isaiah would have written texts in Isa 1–55, such as Isa 1:27–31; 4:3; 6:12–13; 7:15; 11:10; the edited form of 36–39; 48:19b; 54:17b; 55:13 – all of which share views with the work of Trito-Isaiah. He recognizes that his model may not constitute the final form of the text. Hibbard, for example, has employed intertextual reading strategies to argue that the final form of Isa 24–27, for example, is later than the work of Trito-Isaiah.[40] Some of these views may be challenged, but they constitute key elements in refining scholarly understanding of the final redactions that produced the present form of the book of Isaiah.

CONCLUSION

Altogether, this survey points to the key role played by Duhm's 1892 commentary on the book of Isaiah in initiating modern research on the formation of the book. The issues raised here – such as the formation of the final form of the book, the redaction of Isa 1–39, the existence of a late-seventh-century Josianic edition of the book, the formation of Isa 40–55, and the role of Trito-Isaiah in redacting a late or perhaps even a final form of the book of Isaiah – show that scholars are pushing even further in developing models that explain the form, interpretation, and composition of this key prophetic book.

---

[39]   Cf. Brooks Schramm, *The Opponents of Third Isaiah: Reconstructing the Cultic History of the Restoration*, JSOTSup 193 (Sheffield: Sheffield Academic Press, 1995).

[40]   J. Todd Hibbard, *Intertextuality in Isaiah 24–27*, FAT II/16 (Tübingen: Mohr Siebeck, 2006); see also Donald C. Polaski, *Authorizing an End: The Isaiah Apocalypse and Intertextuality*. BibleInt 50 (Leiden: Brill, 2001).

FURTHER READING

Berges, Ulrich, *Das Buch Jesaja: Komposition und Endgestalt*. Freiburg: Herder, 1998.

Berges, Ulrich, *Jesaja 40–48*. HThKAT; Freiburg: Herder, 2008.

Berges, Ulrich, *Jesaja 49–54*. HThKAT; Freiburg: Herder, 2015.

Hauser, Alan J., ed. *Recent Research on the Major Prophets*. Sheffield: Sheffield Phoenix Press, 2008.

Hays, Christopher B., *The Origins of Isaiah 24–27: Isaiah's Festival Scroll for the Fall of Assyria*. Cambridge and New York: Cambridge University Press, 2019.

Kim, Hyun Chul Paul, *Reading Isaiah: A Literary and Theological Commentary*. ROT; Macon, GA: Smyth and Helwys, 2016.

Melugin, Roy F., *The Formation of Isaiah 40–55*. BZAW 141; Berlin and New York: Walter de Gruyter, 1976.

Rendtorff, Rolf, *Canon and Theology: Overtures to an Old Testament Theology*. OBT; Minneapolis, MN: Fortress, 1993.

Sekine, Seizo, *Die tritojesajanische Sammlung (Jes 56–66) redaktionsgeschichtliche untersucht*. BZAW 175; Berlin and New York, 1989.

Steck, Odil Hannes, *Studien zu Tritojesaja*. BZAW 203; Berlin and New York, 1991.

Stromberg, Jacob, *An Introduction to the Study of Isaiah*. London and New York: T and T Clark, 2011a.

Stromberg, Jacob, *Isaiah after Exile: The Author of Third Isaiah as Reader and Redactor of the Book*. Oxford and New York: Oxford University Press, 2011b.

Sweeney, Marvin A., *Isaiah 1–39, with An Introduction to Prophetic Literature*. FOTL 16; Grand Rapids, MI, and Cambridge: Eerdmans, 1996.

Sweeney, Marvin A., *Isaiah 40–66*. FOTL; Grand Rapids, MI: Eerdmans, 2016.

Tiemeyer, Lena-Sofia, *For the Comfort of Zion: The Geographical and Theological Location of Isaiah 40–55* (VTSup 139; Leiden: Brill, 2011).

Williamson, H. G. M., *The Book Called Isaiah: Deutero-Isaiah's Role in Composition and Redaction*. Oxford: Clarendon, 1994.

Williamson, H. G. M., *Isaiah 1–5*. ICC. London: Bloomsbury T and T Clark, 2006; Isaiah 6–12, ICC. London: Bloomsbury T and T Clark, 2018.

Part II

Isaiah in Its Cultural World

8 Ancient Near Eastern Prophecy and the Study of Isaiah

JONATHAN STÖKL

The study of the book of Isaiah has been influenced significantly by the study of ancient Near Eastern prophecy in general and Neo-Assyrian prophecy in particular. This short chapter provides a short introduction to the ancient Near Eastern prophetic texts and shows the significance for selected topics.

Familiarity with nonbiblical Near Eastern prophetic corpora, in particular the Neo-Assyrian corpus, can provide helpful information to understand the wider cultural and religious landscape in which the book of Isaiah acquired its shape, but the literary and historical questions raised by the book cannot be answered by appealing to these corpora. Only Isaianic scholarship itself can do this – in full awareness of the available evidence for prophetic activity and literature during the first millennium BCE. After a brief introduction into the available material, this chapter turns to two interrelated sets of issues: whether Isaiah was a prophet of weal or woe, and the use of gendered imagery in the book.

ANCIENT NEAR EASTERN PROPHECY

General introductions to ancient Near Eastern prophecy are available in other places (STÖKL 2012; NISSINEN 2017; introduction to NISSINEN 2019), so what is offered here is a sketch intended to give the reader a broad sense of the landscape. There are two major corpora from Mesopotamia, supported by more scattered references elsewhere.

Old Babylonian Prophecy

Most of the prophetic texts from the Old Babylonian Period (c. 2000–1500 BCE; all dates are bce unless otherwise noted) are from the city of Mari (Tell Hariri), situated in Syria on a bend of the Euphrates.[1] A small number of texts from other sites, such as ancient Eshnunna, also survive.

[1] The site and the modern city have suffered considerably as a consequence of the occupation of vast areas of Syria by Daesh in the 2010s.

Most of the texts are letters by priests and other officials to the
king, which, among other more mundane matters, also include reports
of oracles by various deities. A few particularly interesting texts have
the appearance of a letter from a deity to the king (e.g., FLP 1674 and
2064 = *66–67).[2] The texts from Mari also include reports of prophetic
oracles delivered outside the kingdom, when the prophet addressed
King Zimri-Lim of Mari (e.g., FM 7 38–39 = *1–2) or where the message
was of relevance for foreign policy decisions (e.g., ARM 26 371 = *47).
This indicates that deities were thought to communicate about political events and across political boundaries.

In addition to the letters containing reports of oracles and dreams,
there are also a great number of administrative texts indicating payments to prophets. Finally, two copies of an end-of-month ritual for
Eštar (the manifestation of Ištar at Mari) contain references to ecstatics
(muḫḫûm).

Neo-Assyrian Prophecy
Simo Parpola's publication of the oracle material encompasses a number
of different genres: two collective tablets, which include several prophetic oracles combined together (SAA 9 1–2 = *68–83); one text (SAA 9
3 = *84–88) likely linked to ritual activity; as well as a number of reports
of prophetic oracles that have been delivered (PARPOLA). In addition to
these, Martti Nissinen has published texts that directly or indirectly
refer to prophetic activity, either because divine speech is referred to, or
because individuals who bear prophetic titles are mentioned (NISSINEN
1998).

Most of the oracle reports contain material linked to the rise to
power of the kings Esarhaddon (c. 681–669) and Aššurbanipal (c. 668–
627). Many have concluded that because Esarhaddon's rise to the
throne was troubled, he was particularly apt to record prophetic oracles
as a means of demonstrating divine support – that is, as propaganda.
However, in the ancient Near East prophecy was a predominantly oral
genre; it was only recorded in writing in specific cases, so it is difficult
to say with certainty to what extent other kings may have relied on
prophetic support. Many have argued that one reason for the continued archiving of prophetic oracles as demonstrated by the oracle collections was to serve as material to be used later in royal inscriptions.
But even when a royal inscription attributes something to a deity, it

---

[2]   In addition to the standard text numbers, I also provide the numbers in NISSINEN
2019.

is impossible for the historian today to determine whether that divine message was received through prophecy or some other divinatory technique.

Hittite, Egyptian, Transjordanian, and Epigraphic Hebrew Material

There are also a number of references to prophets and prophetic activity in Hittite texts, Transjordanian texts, and possibly in Egyptian texts.

From the wider Hittite sphere come references to god-inspired individuals in the Plague Prayers of Muršili II, as well as in a Luwian language inscription from Tell Aḥmar (no. 6 = *143), although the relevant terminology is poorly understood.

There are three Transjordanian inscriptions, the Deir ʿAlla Inscription, the Zakkur Inscription, and the Ammon Citadel Inscription (*136–138), which contain prophetic oracles or reports of prophetic oracles. In particular the Deir ʿAlla Inscription, written with ink on the plaster of a room at Deir ʿAlla, is interesting as it contains an oracle of an impending disaster attributed to a Balaam bar Beʾor, a character also known from the Hebrew Bible (Num 22–24).

There are possible references to prophets in a number of West-Semitic inscriptions. The Hebrew word "prophet" is attested in two ostraca (letters written on potsherds) from early sixth century BCE Lachish (letters 3 and 6 = *139–140). Lachish 3 also contains what appears to be the only surviving oracle spoken by a Hebrew prophet, on an ostracon written at around the time the oracle was delivered. The oracle itself is rather short: "Beware!" (hšmr). Finally, there is a seal from Deir Rifah (UC 51354 = *141a) that belonged to "Qen the seer" (ḥzʾ). Another clay seal impression recently discovered near the Temple Mount has been interpreted as reading "belonging to Isai[ah], proph[et]" (lyšy[hw]/ nby[ʾ]), but the impression is broken and the reading is disputed. Even if the name is correct, there is no certainty that it refers to the prophet of the book.

Most scholars argue that the sociohistorical phenomenon "prophecy" is not attested in Egypt until the Hellenistic period (STÖKL 2012: 14–16; HILBER). Thomas Schneider has, however, suggested that absence of evidence should not be read as evidence of absence, and has shown that there is good reason to believe there were earlier Egyptian precursors (SCHNEIDER). It is undisputed, however, that there are literary predictive texts such as the so-called Prophecy of Neferti and the admonition of Ipu-Wer, in which wise men are represented as predicting the future without divine inspiration. The ancient Egyptian Tale of Wenamun is a travelogue that contains a scene in which the eponymous Egyptian (anti)hero encounters a Semitic prophet (*142 is an excerpt).

WEAL OR WOE, AND THE FUNCTION OF PROPHECY

What kind of oracles did actual Hebrew prophets deliver? It is clear that prophetic books continued to develop beyond the lifetimes of the prophets to whom they are attributed, so the answer to that question would help us to understand both the prophets and the formation of prophetic books. Specifically, is it possible to generalize about whether prophets usually delivered words of judgment or of well-being (Heb. šalôm)? Ancient Near Eastern prophetic texts help the reader think about these questions.

Readers of the Hebrew Bible often consider the archetypal true biblical prophet to be someone such as Jeremiah, predicting the downfall of Israel (or rather Judah) as a consequence of violating the divine will. In the story of the interaction between Jeremiah and Hananiah in Jeremiah 26 (MT; LXX: 33), Hananiah falsely predicts peace while Jeremiah argues that instead of peace, war and destruction are coming to Judah and Jerusalem. Hananiah is portrayed as a state employee falsely toeing the party line. Indeed, in the Septuagint Hananiah is once called a "false prophet" (LXX: Jer 35:1; cf. MT Jer 28:1).

The situation in the book of Isaiah is more complex than this simple dichotomy, repeatedly including oracles of doom and protection side by side and intertwined. This is partly because of the intricacy of the literary character Isaiah across the book and the complex history of growth of the text (see SWEENEY, "The Formation of the Book of Isaiah," Chapter 7 in this volume, as well as WILLIAMSON 1994). If we take as our starting point the figure of Isaiah in First Isaiah, we seem to find a prophet of both doom and peace. In the past, scholars have made rather grand editorial decisions about the alleged genuineness of Isaianic oracles based on whether they predict doom or peace. Based on his literary analysis of the book, Matthijs de Jong has recently argued that the historical Isaiah of Jerusalem was largely a prophet of peace whose oracles foresaw the death of Sennacherib (DE JONG). He then compares this with his analysis of the prophets found in the Neo-Assyrian corpus and finds analogies there: Most Neo-Assyrian prophetic texts suggest that prophets were largely prophets of peace.

However, the origin of the texts in the Neo-Assyrian state archives (that is, the royal archives) suggests that an archival bias toward positive messages is to be expected. Kings would normally seek to preserve oracles that were favorable toward them and their nations. There are, moreover, some surviving prophetic texts that are critical of the rulers. Many of the Old Babylonian prophetic texts suggest criticism of King Zimri-Lim's handling of certain affairs of support for religious institutions. A case in point is ARM 26 215 (*25), in which an ecstatic spoke a message of the god Dagan in which Dagan demanded a better supply of clean water. Another oracle (ARM 26 206 = *16) demands the return of certain materials to a temple, as well as food for the prophet himself. Nissinen rightly concedes that such criticism remains largely at the level of specific points that the king should – and could – easily address.[3] Ancient Near Eastern prophets did, on occasion, point out ethical shortcomings of the king, as exemplified by FM 7 39 (*1): 46–59, which contains an oracle of an *apilum* (spokesperson/prophet) of Adad of Aleppo, in which the prophet demands that the king act as a fair judge for any "man or woman who had been wronged."

In spite of these examples, Nissinen is correct that fundamental criticism of (human) kingship as a concept is not attested. The closest thing to that which we can identify are SAA 16 59–61 (*115–117), which belong to a group of texts related to a case of insurrection in the Neo-Assyrian Empire. In them, a prophet delivers a message supporting an individual called Sasî to become Assyrian king. Sasî never became king of the Assyrian Empire, so this might have been threatening to the actual king; but far from being critical of human kingship, it is comparable to other oracles of divine support for future kings.[4]

Ancient Near Eastern prophets thus criticized their king for not fulfilling their royal function as well as a particular deity expected, but they never criticize them fundamentally. Indeed, any negative outcome with which a king may be threatened is dependent on whether the king would fulfil the divine demand. The king who did was promised rewards such as control of the lands from the sunrise to the sunset (FM 7 39:58–59).

The wall inscription from Deir 'Alla has also been brought to bear on this question. since it contains an oracle of doom. Erhard Blum has suggested that prophecies of doom – even quite extreme doom – were part and parcel of oracles in the wider ancient Near East (WILLIAMSON 2013), so that one should expect them in the preexilic period. For

---

[3]   M. Nissinen, "Das kritische Potential in der altorientalischen Prophetie," in *Propheten in Mari, Assyrien und Israel*, ed. M. Köckert and M. Nissinen (Göttingen: Vandenhoeck & Ruprecht, 2003), 1–33.

[4]   It is likely that Sasî was, in fact, an agent provocateur meant to flush out conspirators against the king. Sasî appears to have fulfilled his mission with success.

Williamson, this leads to the conclusion that an analysis of material in Isaiah needs to rely on internal rather than external evidence. Becker and de Jong, for example, also start their analyses with the internal evidence, but they see the evidence pointing to the direction that oracles of doom are the result of later theological reflection rather than immediate prophetic oracles addressing a specific situation. Their image of what a historical prophet was like rests on the comparative evidence, particularly from Neo-Assyrian texts.

The situation is significantly more complex than either starting point, as the Deir 'Alla text should not be taken as evidence for historical prophetic oracles in the Transjordan. Instead, it is a highly complex and refined theological and literary composition, which is more reminiscent of Egyptian texts such as the 'Prophecy' of Neferti.

Matters are further complicated by the fact that oracles of doom were naturally part of the wider ancient Near Eastern divinatory tradition and repertoire. Mesopotamian compendia contain thousands of omens predicting catastrophic outcomes, all constructed according to the formula of an observation (protasis) with an associated outcome (apodosis), in a structure related to that of casuistic law ("If X happens, then Y will happen"). From omen reports, one can also see that such negative outcomes would at least at times be predicted for kings, armies, and nations. The predicted doom, however, was not necessarily regarded as absolute; it could be averted by asking a slightly different question from the one tested through oracle; by performing a protective ritual (namburbi); or even by ensuring the omen came true for someone else. That was the case of the Neo-Assyrian Substitute King ritual, which was used in cases in which the death of the monarch was predicted. In such cases, rather than risk the death of the actual monarch, someone else was temporarily crowned only to be executed a short while after. That way the Assyrians ensured that the prediction could be fulfilled without any harm to the real monarch.

Thus, although Deut 13:2 and 18:21–22 suggest that true prophecy was determined by whether or not it came true, that may not be absolutely the case, at least for some oracles of doom. Rather, they should be seen as oracles of conditional doom. Read in this light, a prophecy of doom such as Amos's promise that "the end has come" (8:2) predicts that the end will come – *unless* Israel (and later Judah) change the way that they behave. (The book of Jonah dramatizes this same phenomenon.) Indeed, an unconditional oracle of doom makes little theological or pedagogical sense, unless the oracle is the result of theological reflection after the fact and not uttered before the predicted events. There is good comparative evidence for both these things happening historically; that is; conditional oracles of doom *before* the fact (e.g., FM 7 39), as well as unconditional oracles of doom written *afterwards* (e.g., Prophecy of Neferti or the Balaam text from Deir ʿAlla).

Clearly, scholarship on ancient Near Eastern prophets brings texts to the table that help biblical scholars understand how prophecy may have operated as a socioreligious reality in history rather than along the lines of a literary text. Williamson, de Jong, Becker, and Blum all agree on this. They also agree that a literary analysis of the biblical prophetic text, here Isaiah, should not be unduly influenced by such data, that the comparative effort can only provide information once the independent analysis of each text has been completed. It is also noticeable that the literary analysis of an original text of Isaiah by each of these scholars seems to align well with how they understand ancient Near Eastern prophecy to have operated in general.

It seems to me, therefore, that ultimately, two corpora that are different in their genesis are read with the same overarching question, namely what they allow us to say about specific prophets and their oracles as they took place in oral or scribal performance. This question, however, is ultimately an axiomatic and programmatic one: If we believe that we can identify a prophet's own voice in the text of the Hebrew Bible, we are likely to look for it, while those of us who regard the biblical text first and foremost as a complex literary-theological text will want to understand the implications of various text forms.

For one who wants to read Isaiah as a literary and theological text, however complex its origins, it follows that other literary-theological texts, such as Neo-Assyrian royal inscriptions, provide excellent comparative material, as has long been argued. As Peter Machinist demonstrated already in 1983, many expressions in Isaiah are very similar to those found in Assyrian inscriptions. A good example for this is Isa 37:24 ‖ 2 Kgs 19:23, in which the Assyrian king is portrayed as boasting how he cut down the tallest cedars and junipers of Lebanon. A very similar expression can be found in the Kurkh Stele of Shalmaneser III (RIME 3 2: ii 9–10a, as argued in MACHINIST 1983).[5]

Indeed, I would argue that royal inscriptions provide better comparative material than either the contemporary prophetic texts from

---

[5] The argument by ASTER that this necessarily dates the relevant passage to the time of Isaiah does not take into account the use of the historical past to describe the present as can be demonstrated in Daniel. Babylonians use the same technique describing their Persian overlords as Elamites.

Assyria or those a millennium older from Mari. They are our best evidence for ancient Near Eastern (including ancient Israelite and Judean) prophecy. But they do not necessarily help us understand the prophetic texts in the Hebrew Bible. Indeed, such work has been done and continues to be done very profitably (MACHINIST 1991; ASTER). Neo-Assyrian texts are particularly rich for such comparison because of the exploration of theological and political ideas, some of which have counterparts in the Hebrew Bible, and in Second Isaiah in particular.

GENDER

The book of Isaiah is rightly known for treating the question of gender differently from other texts in the Hebrew Bible.[6] Not only is there maternal imagery for Yhwh in Second Isaiah, but there is also the figure of the unnamed female prophet in Isa 8:3. Ancient Near Eastern prophetic material can enhance our understanding of these texts, which also raise their own questions that can in turn meaningfully be asked of the biblical material (NISSINEN 2017: 297–325). The main question raised in the ancient Near Eastern material concerns the construction and understanding of the gender of prophets.

Isa 8:3 refers to a *nĕbîʾāh*, and it remains important to state clearly that the woman must be understood as a prophet in her own right. A woman was not called a prophetess by virtue of being married to a prophet. Titles were not conferred by marriage in ancient Semitic languages, unless the marriage led to a particular role being occupied, as in the case of the queen who oversaw and managed the palace economy – a rather significant role, considering the place of the palace economy in the economic structure of ancient Near Eastern Kingdoms.[7]

The Hebrew Bible only knows of four other named women with the same title (Miriam, Deborah, Huldah, and Noadiah), whereas in the ancient Near Eastern corpus there are many female prophets. Thus, even if the prophet of Isa 8:3 remains nameless in our texts, there is no reason to assume that she was not a prophet – other than perhaps modern cultural bias against women as prophets combined with a

---

[6]   See LØLAND LEVINSON, "Gendered Imagery in Isaiah," Chapter 14 in this volume.
[7]   This point had been demonstrated as early as 1960 by Alfred Jepsen in a short article that is still too often overlooked: A. Jepsen, "Die Nebiah in Jes 8, 3," *ZAW* 72 (1960): 267–268.

nineteenth-century assumption that if Isaiah has sexual intercourse with a woman, that woman must be his wife and that his title is therefore conferred on her, as would have been the case with significant clerical titles in the Western world in the nineteenth (and twentieth) centuries. Such a position is clearly untenable.

There is a vigorous debate among scholars regarding the gender construction of ancient Near Eastern prophets: Among the questions asked are whether the gender of prophets and deities were often the same, whether there were prophets of ambiguous gender, and, indeed, how to understand ancient Near Eastern constructions of gender in the first place.[8]

There are some points on which most scholars agree based on the surviving evidence. For example, female prophets are much more common in Ancient Near Eastern texts than in the Bible: in the Neo-Assyrian corpus, they are in the majority, and the Old Babylonian texts attest a relatively even gender split. (It is unlikely that women prophets were actually as uncommon in Israel and Judah as the Bible makes us think, given that they are mentioned without remark where they do appear.) Furthermore, Esther Hamori has shown that messages by women who prophesy are more often double checked at Mari (HAMORI). Admittedly, establishing such counts of prophetic references depends on how one defines prophecy as well as on identifying the titles used for prophets. The overall counts of prophesying individuals and the deities they speak for vary depending on whether scholars think someone is a professional prophet or not (STÖKL 2013; NISSINEN 2017: 297–304).[9]

In Isa 40–66, Yhwh is repeatedly described in feminine terms. Yhwh "cries out like a woman in labor" (42:14), and is again compared to one in 45:10; Yhwh "formed [Israel] in the womb" (44:2); Yhwh is compared to a mother or nursemaid in 46:3; 49:15; and 66:13 (see further, LØLAND LEVINSON, "Gendered Imagery in Isaiah," Chapter 14 in this volume). The description of a male deity with feminine attributes is not quite as unexpected as it may seem to the modern reader. In several prophetic oracles from Mari, Adad describes himself in maternal terms. Thus, FM 7 39 (*1) contains the following two self-descriptions:

---

[8]   For a discussion of the concept of gender see, for example, LØLAND LEVINSON, "Gendered Imagery in Isaiah," Chapter 14 in this volume.

[9]   The different results to which Nissinen and I have come is caused by that different understanding at the basis of the available corpus.

Am I not Adad, lord of Kallassu, who raised him between my thighs.
(lines 14–16)[10]

Am I not Adad, lord of Aleppo, who raised him in my womb?.
(lines 49–50)[11]

Both these self-descriptions then move onto the claim that it was Adad
who installed King Zimri-Lim on his ancestral throne.

Similarly, keeping with the theme of a deity professing parental
care in terms that go beyond their standard gender role, in SAA 9 2.5:iii
26′–32′ (*82) an unnamed deity promises Esarhaddon that she will be
father and mother to him and keep him between arm and forearm:[12]

26′–28′I am your father and mother! I have raised you between my
wings you! I will see your success!

29′–32′Fear not, Esarhaddon, I will place you between my arm
and forearm. In the midst of pain, I will over[come] the enemies of
my king![13]

It seems that just as in the case of Old Babylonian Mari so also in the
Neo-Assyrian texts, deities claim parental care largely as an expression of protection of the king whom they are promising their ancestral
throne, and the two texts possibly also share the image of the land from
the sunrise to the sunset; but the context in iii 35′–36′ is too uncertain
to draw firm conclusions.

In two Neo-Assyrian prophetic texts, Ištar of Arbela assumes
the image of the nurse or wet nurse who looks after Essarhaddon
(SAA 9 1.6:iii 15′–22′ = *73); a few lines further on (iv 5–6), Ištar of
Arbela describes Esarhaddon as "son of Mullissu." The same division
of labor also carries over to Aššurbanipal (SAA 9 7:r. 6–10 = *92).
Ninurta's lap is used as part of a dynastic promise to Esarhaddon in
SAA 9 1.10: 27–30 (*77), which also appears in a slightly varied form
(before Ninurta, rather than in Ninurta's lap) in SAA 9 2.3: ii 13′14′
(*80).

---

10   14ul anāku 15Addu bēl Kallassu ša ina birīt 16paḫalliya urabbûšuma.

11   49Addu bēl Ḫalab ul anāku 50ša ina suḫātiya urabbûkama. The noun suḫātum denotes
     a body part between the legs and the chest. CAD suggests armpit. On account of the par-
     allel (also noted by Nissinen) with ina birīt paḫalliya, it seems likely that the intended
     body part here is either the lap (so Nissinen) or, tentatively, perhaps even the womb.

12   Likely to be a form of Ištar owing to the special relationship she has with Esarhaddon.

13   26′anāku abuka ummaka 27′birti agappīya urtabbīka 28′nēmalka ammar 29′lā tapallaḫ
     Aššur-aḫu-iddina 30′birti izirîya ammātēya 31′ašakkanka ina libbi ū'a 32′nakarūti ša
     šarriya aka[šša]d.

While the use of (potentially) gender-bending imagery might be expected for Ištar, the same cannot be said for Adad or for Ninurta, but the imagery used there is at least reminiscent of maternal imagery. If my – speculative – translation of *suḫātum* as womb understands what the imagery is trying to evoke, then it seems to me that we have in FM 7 39 (*1) use of language that is similar to the striking images of Yhwh as crying out like a woman in labor (Isa 42:14), following on from a description of the deity as a mighty warrior in the previous verse. This is, indeed, reminiscent of the description and literary gender performance ascribed to Ištar in a wide variety of texts, often side by side, as here in Isa 42. This indicates that far from being unique such a description of a deity with stark images covering a wider gender norm than might have been seen as appropriate for humans was part of the repertoire of religious language, at least in some circles.

In keeping with the way that gender-bending imagery is sometimes used of deities, prophets in the ancient Near East also may have had "ambiguous gender." Evidence for this has been adduced from both the Mari and Neo-Assyrian corpora, although neither is unequivocal. There has been an increasingly entrenched debate in recent years whether these texts reflect nonstandard gender performance.

At Mari, two people called *assinnu*s attested as prophesying, Šelebum (ARM 26 197, 198, 213 = *7, 8, 23) and Ili-ḫaznaya (ARM 26 212 = *22). In a number of other, later texts from the first millennium BCE, the *assinnu* is described as cross-dressing and also as one whose masculinity the goddess had turned into femininity (Erra IV 4:52–59).[14] But no indication is given as to the *assinnu*'s role at Mari, or anywhere else in texts from the Amorite Kingdoms of the first half of the second millennium BCE, other than that they were seen as related to various forms of Ištar. It is therefore not clear whether an early second millennium BCE *assinnu* would also have been expected to portray a gender role that in some shape or form reflected having been changed from masculine to feminine by the titulary deity (ZSOLNAY: 81–99; PELED: 283–297; SVÄRD AND NISSINEN: 373–412). Furthermore, there is no evidence that connects *assinnu*s directly with prophetic activity outside the two *assinnu*s at Mari. It is true that *assinnu*s are attested along with ecstatic prophets in lexical lists and ration lists, but not all such professions in the same context are prophets (for a contrasting view, see NISSINEN 2017: 335–339).

---

[14] According to the Sumerian hymn in-nin ša$_3$-gur$_4$-ra, line 120, Ištar had the power to turn a man into a woman and vice versa.

There are also three instances in the Neo-Assyrian corpus, all in the collection SAA 9 1, in which the grammatical gender and/or the sex of a prophet is unclear. (Although none of the individuals on that tablet receives a prophetic title, they are clearly individuals who prophesy; see NISSINEN 2017: 308–9; STÖKL 2013).

1) Ilussa-amur (SAA 9 1.5 = *72) is spelled with a feminine determinative (a cuneiform sign indicating the gender of a name), but it is also modified by a gentilic adjective *libālā[ya]* (=male from Aššur). Thus Ilussa-amur's name is feminine, but the adjective indicating where she lives is masculine.

2) Baia (SAA 9 1.4 = *71) is also spelled with a feminine determinative, yet is described as a "son" (DUMU=*māru*) of Arbela.

3) The name Issar-la-tašiyaṭ (SAA 9 1.1 = *68) is undoubtedly a masculine name on account of the verb form in the name, and like Baia he is a "son" (DUMU) of Arbela. The determinative before Issar-la-tašiyaṭ's name is peculiar. It has been understood by Simo Parpola as a masculine determinative written over a feminine determinative (PARPOLA: 83; STÖKL 2013: 76). If so, then either Issar-la-tašiyaṭ was first spelled with a feminine determinative, which was later corrected into a masculine determinative, or the double determinative was intentional.

SVÄRD AND NISSINEN (2018) as well as others, point to the unusual combination of female names with grammatically masculine gentilics (indicators of origin) in the case of Ilussa-amur and Baia, while the double gender determinative is itself indication that Issar-la-tašiat performed aspects of both masculine and feminine gender roles. Again, all three examples are on the same tablet, and the scribe of SAA 9 1 is otherwise quite a competent and meticulous scribe; thus, they conclude that he wanted to encode a nonstandard gender performance of these three prophets.

This is, however, not a given; nor is it necessarily the more logical way to understand the text (NISSINEN 2017: 309). SAA 9 1 preserves extraordinarily diverse ways of referring to the prophets and their origins, so that no clear formula can be established from which we would have a divergence in these three cases. The discrepancy between the grammatical genders as indicated by the determinatives and the gentilics in Ilussa-amur's and Baia's case is clear, but the question is what it is intended to indicate. The use of masculine adjectives for feminine nouns is a phenomenon known well enough in Semitic languages. The case is somewhat different for Issar-la-tašiat: This grammatically masculine name contains the name of a female deity, and my own inspection of the tablet suggests that the scribe simply began to write the goddess's name (with a female determinative), and then corrected himself to reflect that the prophet was male.

Since SAA 9 1 is an archival copy collecting nine prophecies probably from individual reports, it seems unlikely that its scribe witnessed the three individuals and then carefully considered how to indicate to a later reader that the gender performance of these three prophets was nonstandard in his/their eyes. Thus, it remains possible that there were ancient Near Eastern prophets who performed nonstandard (from an ancient Near Eastern perspective) gender roles, but the texts adduced so far do not represent sufficient evidence in favor of such a conclusion.

CONCLUSIONS

These pages have briefly introduced the extant ancient Near Eastern prophetic material with a particular attention on how knowledge of these texts and their contexts can help in the interpretation of the book of Isaiah. It is clear that the comparison between the cuneiform and the biblical prophetic texts is not an easy one and that even their generic similarity can be questioned. The cuneiform material is much closer in time and form to the prophetic performance than the biblical books. The cuneiform material gives us glimpses at how prophecy may have operated on the ground as a socioreligious phenomenon. It seems likely that it operated in similar ways also in ancient Judah and Israel.

The book of Isaiah includes texts written over a long period of time, and is thus the result of more and deeper theological reflection than the cuneiform prophetic texts. Adducing the cuneiform evidence, therefore, when trying to delve back into the historical development of the prophetic texts by identifying earlier and later layers, is only helpful insofar as it gives us an indication of the thought-world in which a reconstruction of Isaianic oracles is likely to have originated. The work of careful literary decisions and their theological explanation and interpretation cannot be bypassed. In many places it is, therefore, not the cuneiform prophetic texts that best illuminate text passages in Isaiah but royal inscriptions, treaties, and so on.

One area in which the available cuneiform prophetic texts are helpful in raising our awareness concerns questions of nonmale prophets, of possible cases of nonstandard gender performance as well as gendered imagery for deities. In the latter case, royal inscriptions, prayers, and ritual texts provide further additional material, but the apparent generic

proximity between Isaiah and the Neo-Assyrian oracle collections SAA
9 1 and 9 2 makes the comparison more evident.

Most of the cuneiform prophetic texts are available in an easily
accessible form owing to the efforts of Martti Nissinen as well as the
series editors for the SBL series *Writings from the Ancient World*. The
similarities between some aspects of Isaianic and in particular Neo-
Assyrian prophecy turns studying these texts into a helpful enterprise.

FURTHER READING

Aster, Shawn Zelig. *Reflections of Empire in Isaiah 1–39: Responses to Assyrian
    Ideology*. ANEM 19. Atlanta, GA: SBL, 2017.
Becker, Uwe. *Jesaja – von der Botschaft zum Buch*. FRLANT 178. Göttingen:
    Vandenhoeck & Ruprecht, 1997.
de Jong, Matthijs J. *Isaiah Among the Ancient Near Eastern Prophets: A
    Comparative Study of the Earliest Stages of the Isaiah Tradition and the Neo-
    Assyrian Prophecies*. VTSup 117. Leiden: Brill, 2007.
Hamori, Esther J. "Verification of Prophecy at Mari." *WO* 42 (2012): 1–22.
Hilber, John W. "Prophetic Speech in the Egyptian Royal Cult." Pages 39–53 in
    On Stone and Scroll: Essays in Honour of Prof. Graham Ivor Davies. Edited
    by James Aitken, Katharine Dell and Brian Mastin. BZAW 420. Berlin: de
    Gruyter, 2011.
Machinist, Peter. "Assyria and its Image in the First Isaiah." *JAOS* (1983):
    719–737.
Machinist, Peter. "The Question of Distinctiveness in Ancient Israel: An
    Essay." Pages 196–212 in *Ah Assyria: Studies in Assyrian History and
    Ancient Near Eastern Historiography Presented to Hayim Tadmor*. Edited
    by Mordechai Cogan and Israel Eph'al. ScrHier 33. Jerusalem: Magnes Press
    Hebrew University, 1991.
Mouton, Alice. "Portent Dreams in Hittite Anatolia." Pages 27–41 in *Perchance
    to Dream: Dream Divination in Biblical and Other Ancient Near Eastern and
    Early Jewish Sources*. Edited by Esther J. Hamori and Jonathan Stökl. ANEM
    21. Atlanta, GA: SBL, 2018.
Nissinen, Martti. *References to Prophecy in Neo-Assyrian Sources*. SAAS 7.
    Helsinki: Neo-Assyrian Corpus Project, 1998.
Nissinen, Martti. *Ancient Prophecy: Near Eastern, Biblical, and Greek
    Perspectives*. Oxford: Oxford University Press, 2017.
Nissinen, Martti. *Prophets and Prophecy in the Ancient Near East: With
    Contributions by C.L. Seow, Robert K. Ritner, and H. Craig Melchert*. Edited
    by Peter Machinist. 2nd edition. WAW 12. Atlanta: SBL, 2019.
Parpola, Simo. *Assyrian Prophecies*. SAA 9. Helsinki: Helsinki University Press,
    1997.
Peled, Ilan. "assinnu and kurgarrû Revisited." *JNES* 73 (2014): 283–297.
Schneider, Thomas. "A Land without Prophets? Examining the Presumed Lack
    of Prophecy in Ancient Egypt." Pages 59–86 in *Enemies and Friends of the
    State: Ancient Prophecy in Context*. Edited by Christopher A. Rollston.
    University Park, IN: Eisenbrauns, 2018.

Stökl, Jonathan. *Prophecy in the Ancient Near East: A Philological and Sociological Comparison.* CHANE 56. Leiden: Brill, 2012.

Stökl, Jonathan. "Gender "Ambiguity" in Ancient Near Eastern Prophecy? A Re-Assessment of the Data Behind a Popular Theory." Pages 59–79 in *Prophets Male and Female: Gender and Prophecy in the Hebrew Bible, the Eastern Mediterranean and the Ancient Near East.* Edited by Jonathan Stökl and Corrine L. Carvalho. AIL 15. Atlanta, GA: SBL, 2013.

Svärd, Saana and Martti Nissinen. "(Re)constructing the Image of the Assinnu." Pages 373–412 in *Studying Gender in the Ancient Near East.* Edited by Saana Svärd and Agnès Garcia-Ventura. University Park, IN: Eisenbrauns, 2018.

Williamson, Hugh G. M. *The Book Called Isaiah: Deutero-Isaiah's Role in Composition and Redaction.* Oxford: Clarendon Press, 1994.

Williamson, Hugh G. M. "Isaiah: Prophet of Weal or Woe?" Pages 273–300 in *'Thus Speaks Ishtar of Arbela': Prophecy in Israel, Assyria and Egypt in the Neo-Assyrian Period.* Edited by Robert P. Gordon and Hans M. Barstad. Winona Lake, IN: Eisenbrauns, 2013.

Zsolnay, Ilona. "The Misconstrued Role of the Assinnu in Ancient Near Eastern Prophecy." Pages 81–99 in *Prophets Male and Female: Gender and Prophecy in the Hebrew Bible, the Eastern Mediterranean and the Ancient Near East.* Edited by Jonathan Stökl and Corrine L. Carvalho. AIL 15. Atlanta, GA: SBL, 2013.

9 The Book of Isaiah in the History of Israelite Religion

CHRISTOPHER B. HAYS

The book of Isaiah has been called a "mirror of half a millennium of religious experience."[1] While its formation probably did not span quite that long, it does indeed reflect such a rich array of beliefs and practices that it provides an ideal way to introduce some of the central religious issues in ancient Jerusalem and Judah. The prophet, and his successors who composed the book, simultaneously played a role in shaping that religion over time.

Practically every chapter of Isaiah sheds light on the topic in some way; this chapter can only discuss a certain number of important examples. Other aspects of Isaiah's significance for the history of religion are touched on in other chapters in this volume, such as its relationship to ancient Near Eastern prophecy (STÖKL, "Ancient Near Eastern Prophecy and the Study of Isaiah," Chapter 8) and its contributions to later messianic interpretation (HØGENHAVEN, "The Book of Isaiah at Qumran," Chapter 5; PAO, "Isaiah in the New Testament," Chapter 18).

PROPHETIC MEDIA: WRITING AND ACTION

The origins of the book of Isaiah are connected to the need to verify prophecy. This sheds light on both the book's formation and on ancient attitudes toward prophecy. As Deut 18:21–22 indicates, a true prophet could be recognized only by waiting to see if the prophecies came true. This was surely one of the original motivations for recording prophecies in writing. A *bulla* – a small piece of clay, sometimes stamped with a seal – would have been placed to ensure that the prophecy was not tampered with, so that its accuracy could be assessed later. "Bind up the testimony among my disciples," Isaiah says in 8:16.

---

[1] Jacques Vermeylen, *Du prophète d'Isaïe à l'apocalyptique: Miroir d'un demi-millènaire d'experience religieuse en Israel* EB (2 vols., Paris: Gabalda, 1977–78).

In Isa 8:1, the Lord tells the prophet to write, albeit only a brief phrase in the form of a name. It has even been argued that Isaiah was a court scribe who wrote down his own words, because there is a surviving seal from roughly the right period belonging to "Amoz the scribe,"[2] and scribal training was sometimes passed from father to son. But it is unknown whether this Amoz was Isaiah's father, given that the name was a relatively common one.

Furthermore, in Isa 30:8, Isaiah instructs someone else to write down his words. Then as now, there were levels of literacy, and few expert scribes; it is one thing to be able to write, and another to have literary expertise. In general, it should be assumed that his words were recorded by others, as was the case with other preexilic prophets such as Jeremiah. The eighth-century prophets were essentially speakers, not writers. Once recorded, oracles were occasionally recompiled and edited in order to speak to later events. The recording and compilation of Neo-Assyrian prophecies in the same period supplies an empirical model for the preservation and organization of a substantial corpus of prophecy by a single prophet (see STÖKL, "Ancient Near Eastern Prophecy and the Study of Isaiah," Chapter 8 in this volume).

Words, whether spoken or written, were not the only medium of communication for ancient prophets. Prophets also acted out their message symbolically at times (VIBERG). One fascinating example comes from eighteenth century BCE Mari in Syria, where an ecstatic prophet appeared at a city gate and demanded a lamb, which he proceeded to eat raw. He then announced, "A devouring will take place! Give orders to the cities to return the taboo material!" (ARM 26 206). His act of devouring the lamb symbolized the destruction he foretold if the authorities did not restore what they had taken from a temple.

Among the best-known sign-acts are Jeremiah's putting on a yoke (Jer 27–28) and Hosea's marrying a prostitute (Hos 1–3), but there are numerous other examples.[3] Isaiah also undertook symbolic actions. His naming of children as Shear-Jashub ("a remnant shall return"; 7:3), Immanuel ("God with us"; 7:14; 8:8), and Maher-shalal-hash-baz

---

[2]   Israel Museum, accession no. 71.65.177.
[3]   For example, Jeremiah ruins a loincloth (13:1–11), shatters a jug (19:1–15), buys a field when the nation is on the brink of destruction (32:1–15), buries stones in a clay pavement (43:8–13), and throws a scroll in the Euphrates (51:59–64). Ezekiel lies on his side for more than a year and eats barley-cakes cooked over human dung (4:1–13), shaves his head and beard (5:1–4), drags baggage around and digs through a wall (12:1–16), and writes on sticks (37:15–28); Zechariah collects gold and silver and makes a crown (6:9–15).

("speedy [is the] plunder, swift [is the] prey"; 8:1), each containing a
message for Jerusalem and Judah is reminiscent of Hosea (1:3–9). But
perhaps his most striking sign-act is walking around naked and barefoot for three years (Isa 20). It warned that Egypt and Cush were not to
be relied on as allies. The message was that just as the prophet walks
naked, so would the Egyptians and Cushites be led away naked as captives (see CHAN, "The Book of Isaiah in the Neo-Assyrian Period,"
Chapter 2 in this volume).

ISAIAH'S CALL AND THE DIVINE THRONE-ROOM

For a prophet, the claim to have been sent by God with a message was
an important aspect of authority. The prophets were portrayed as messengers for the divine King, so that the entire enterprise of prophecy
was seen as analogous to the sending and receiving of messages from
a human ruler. Appropriately, this sending takes place in the divine
throne room. The Lord's question to the divine council – "Whom shall
I send?" – is similar to the question in in 1 Kgs 22:20, when the Lord
sending a lying spirit to deceive Ahab.

There has been some debate over whether Isa 6 represented Isaiah's
initial call to prophesy or was merely a calling to a new mission. The
exchange in 6:5–8 suggests that Isaiah was not accustomed to prophesying beforehand, and the story is structurally similar to the standard
form of the call narratives that feature prominently in the accounts of
many other prophets (Exod 3:1–4:17; Jer 1:1–10; Ezek 2:1–3:15, etc.). Up
to a point, Isa 6 follows the normal form of a call narrative: 1) divine
confrontation; 2) introductory word; and 3) commission. However,
these are usually followed by 4) the prophet's objection; and 5) divine
reassurance. Isa 6 turns the form on its head, in that the prophet eagerly
seeks the commission, and the Lord's ensuing words are anything but
reassuring. Indeed, the prognosis gets worse and worse: The prophet is
called to tell the people to fail to understand, leading to the devastation
of the whole land (6:9–13). This emphasizes the gravity of the message:
Even with an eager prophet, the judgment will be severe.

Isa 6 is part of a long tradition of imagery depicting the divine
throne-room that also includes Exod 24; 1 Kgs 22; Ezek 1; Dan 7; 1
Enoch 14; and Rev 4–5. The enduring theological power of these scenes
derives from their claim to reveal insider knowledge of God's purposes,
to which most people are not privy – much like having a friend in the
inner circle of a human king or president. One feature that many of these
throne-room theophanies share is the presence of divine attendants in

a council that mirrors what an ancient king would have had. Similarly, in Ps 82, God stands in the divine council "in the midst of the gods." Sometimes the prophet's mere vision of the divine throne-room functions a statement of his authority, but in some cases the reader is even allowed to glimpse the machinations of God's management of human affairs. In 1 Kgs 22, Micaiah ben Imlah reports that the Lord asked for a volunteer to go and deceive the king of Israel, and a spirit volunteered to inspire the king's prophets to lie. In Isa 6, the prophet also eagerly volunteers, only to receive a similarly troubling commission: to dull the people's comprehension in order to make their punishment more thorough. In sum, then, Isaiah uses the claim of direct commissioning to justify the difficulty of his message and explain the people's failure to accept it.

The Jerusalem Temple where Isaiah's vision took place was a three-room type that was widespread in the Iron Age Levant, and it has often been compared to the temple at 'Ain Dara (in present-day Syria).[4] The fact that it has features in common with other temples in the region is not surprising, since it was built by the enterprising Tyrians, from Phoenicia (1 Kgs 7). Isaiah's vision reflects a number of features of the Temple that are more or less historical, albeit "supernaturalized." For example, the tongs used by the seraphs to pick up a coal are attested as part of the Temple paraphernalia (1 Kgs 7:49; Exod 25:38, etc.); and the "hem of [the Lord's] robe" referred to in 6:1 seems to be an interpretation of the curtain that separated the holy of holies from the outer rooms of the temple (Exod 26:31–35; 2 Chr 3:14, etc.). The prophet imagines the Lord massive in stature and enthroned (Isa 37:16; 2 Kgs 19:15; Ps 99:1, etc.) – presumably upon the cherubim that flank the ark of the covenant, though they are not mentioned.

Another set of supernatural beings that figure prominently are the seraphs – winged serpents that function as servants in the divine throne room. These are attested in Judahite iconography, but even more widely in Egypt as supernatural protectors of the pharaoh, as well as on a Levantine bronze bowl taken as spoil by Tiglath-Pileser III in the eighth century.[5] The term seraph is used elsewhere in the Bible to describe

---

[4] John Monson, "The 'Ain Dara Temple: Closest Solomonic Parallel," *BAR* 26 (2000): 20–35. Tragically, the remains of 'Ain Dara temple were severely damaged by a Turkish air strike in 2018.

[5] See J. J. M. Roberts, *First Isaiah* (Augsburg: Fortress, 2015), 96–98. The Egyptianizing iconography the seal of Hezekiah (an ankh and a winged sun disk) is only one of the indications that Egyptian iconography was widely understood and adopted in eighth century Judah.

poisonous serpents. In Num 21, the Lord sends seraphs to bite the people, then tells Moses, "Make a poisonous serpent, and set it on a pole; and everyone who is bitten shall look at it and live." Later, 2 Kgs 18:4 reports that this item came to be called Nehushtan and was worshiped by the people, so that Hezekiah broke it in pieces. If so, then it would have been in the Temple for a portion of Isaiah's career. Furthermore, Isa 14:29 and 30:6 both describe seraphs as flying, using the same verb as in Isa 6. In sum, it seems that these figures were inspired both by items in the temple, such as the Nehushtan, and by the mythological tradition that they were protectors. Isaiah, however, creatively modifies this tradition: He gives the seraphs six wings, whereas elsewhere they are known to have only two or four, so that they are more impressive than other winged serpents. And in Isaiah's imagery, the seraphs still have to protect *themselves* in the Lord's presence, rather than protecting him; this makes a statement about the Lord's awe-inspiring power.

DEATH, AFTERLIFE, AND RESURRECTION

Israelite and Judahite beliefs about the afterlife have often been represented in partial ways. It is not the case that all expected to go down to forgetfulness in Sheol, nor that being "gathered to one's fathers" in a family tomb was the only form of burial they envisioned. The book of Isaiah reflects and reacts to some of the diversity of ancient Near Eastern beliefs about death and afterlife that were held not only by neighboring nations but among the prophets' own people.

Isaiah particularly inveighed against necromancy, seemingly because the invocation of the dead for supernatural knowledge naturally came into conflict with prophecy. Both were forms of divination that claimed access to supernatural knowledge, but they were bound to differ since they came from different sources and through different mediators. The end of Isa 8 finds Isaiah waiting for the Lord, "who is hiding his face from the house of Jacob." Much like Saul when God refused to answer him by other means (1 Sam 28), Isaiah's contemporaries seem to have sought necromantic consultation; the prophet condemns those who say: "Consult the ghosts and the familiar spirits that chirp and mutter; should not a people consult their gods, the dead on behalf of the living, for teaching and for instruction?" This is creative theological rhetoric, in that the terms for "gods" (*'elohim*) is the same as that for "God"; the term for "teaching" is *torah*, identical to Torah; and the term for "instruction" (*te'udah*) is closely related to terms for "covenant" or "testimony" (it is also used for Isaiah's own teaching in

8:16). In other words, the text portrays the advocates of necromancy as double-talkers who manage to sound inoffensive but are actually advocating dangerous ideas. Isaiah goes on in 8:21–22 to threaten that these advocates will become as the uncared-for dead were thought to be in the ancient Near East: hungry, distressed, and in darkness.

It is not entirely clear whether necromancy and ancestor cult were heterodox in Judah in Isaiah's time – whether he spoke for some sort of authoritative consensus, or was among the first to advocate for what became a normative view (e.g., Deut 18:10–12; for different views, see SONIA; SMITH AND BLOCH-SMITH). Ancestor cult had a long history in the Levant; this is especially clear in the case of royalty, who after death might be summoned to protect and bless the dynasty,[6] and who expected to feast with the gods in the afterlife.[7] The kings of Judah seem to have been buried in or next to the temple (inferring from the condemnation of this practice in Ezek 43:7–9), and probably practiced a mortuary cult akin to those of neighboring kings. Although such beliefs and practices are not as clearly attested in texts for common people, that is partly because they lacked access to writing, not because they had completely different beliefs.[8] It appears to have been eighth-century prophets such as Isaiah who first sought to marginalize and ban necromancy. As Isa 19:3 reflects, the prophet associated it with the Egyptians and Mesopotamians (HAYS 2011: 281–88),[9] and he portrayed it as a foreign practice even though others would have seen it differently. (These condemnations appear to have taken hold in Josiah's time, since he seems not to have been buried in a royal mausoleum [2 Kgs 23:30], and his scribes wrote or compiled the story of Saul's tragic necromantic consultation.)

The condemnation of Shebna's tomb in Isa 22 similarly reflects a rejection of practices that were normal in neighboring countries. It is addressed to a high official in the Jerusalem court who is said to have cut himself "a habitation (*mishkan*) for [him]self in the rock." This "Tomb of the Royal Steward" (Silwan 35), somewhat miraculously, seems to

---

[6] For example, the Ugaritic Royal Funerary Text (RS 34.126/KTU³ 1.161).

[7] For example, the Hadad Inscription (*KAI* 214:15–18; *COS* 2.236).

[8] Analogously, Egyptologists used to speak of the "democratization of the afterlife" between the Old Kingdom and the New Kingdom, but this is now attributed to a growing access to scribal products. See Harold M. Hays, "The Death of the Democratisation of the Afterlife," in *Old Kingdom, New Perspectives: Egyptian Art and Archaeology 2750–2150 BC*, ed. Nigel Strudwick and Helen Strudwick (Oxford: Oxbow, 2011), 115–30.

[9] The passage is addressed to the Egyptians, but uses terms cognate with both Egyptian and Mesopotamian terms for the spirits of the dead.

have been found in the cliffs of Silwan that face the Jerusalem temple, and it includes some features that were elite and not characteristic of Judahite bench tombs of the period.[10] It included individual burial niches without bone pits, rather than benches on which corpses could decompose and then be gathered away with the remains of others in the family. (Other Silwan tombs had stone coffins with lids like sarcophagi.) It also featured the name of the inhabitant carved in stone over the door, as part of an inscription warning grave robbers not to disturb it. The upshot of all this is that Shebna expected to rest in undisturbed glory (with his maidservant) in the afterlife – and perhaps more than that. The term *mishkan* was used for divine dwellings, and the problem for Isaiah was the theological implication that Shebna had built himself a kind of temple in which expected to be divinized.

Isaiah used rhetorical techniques that inverted his opponents' expectations about the afterlife. For example, although the idea of "hell" was not developed in his time as it was later in Western religions, in 5:14 he asserts that the wealthy libertines who ruled Jerusalem unjustly were marching straight into the swallowing maw of the underworld:

> Therefore Sheol has enlarged its appetite
>   and opened its mouth beyond measure;
> the nobility of Jerusalem and her multitude go down,
>   her throng and all who exult in her.

An even more elaborate passage in Isa 14 describes the descent of a Mesopotamian king to Sheol, where he finds himself in a nightmarish version of the afterlife. Rather than being divinized and powerful, he is mocked as powerless by the shades (14:9–10). Rather than resting in solitary splendor, he is told that "maggots are the bed beneath you, and worms are your covering" (14:11), and indeed his tomb and corpse are vandalized: "you are cast out, away from your grave, like loathsome carrion" (14:19).

The book of Isaiah also played a role in the development of later beliefs about resurrection, although this should not be overstated. One much-discussed passage is in Isa 26:19: "Your dead shall live, their corpses shall rise." Much like Hos 6 ("after two days he will revive us; on the third day he will raise us up"), which preceded it historically,

---

[10]   David Ussishkin, *The Village of Silwan: The Necropolis from the Period of the Judean Kingdom* (Jerusalem: Israel Exploration Society, 1993), 188–202; Christopher B. Hays, "Re-Excavating Shebna's Tomb: A New Reading of Isa 22:15–19 in its Ancient Near Eastern Context," *ZAW* 122 (2010): 558–75.

and Ezek 37's revivification of the dry bones, which followed it, Isa 26:19 was originally a promise of national restoration. In the wake of the withdrawal of the Assyrians from the Levant when their empire collapsed, there was a brief time of relative peace and prosperity under Josiah. Thus 26:12–13 reads, "you will ordain peace for us.... Other lords besides you have ruled over us, but we call on your name alone" – classic Deuteronomistic theology characteristic of the Josianic period (cf. Deut 6:4).[11] The optimism of Josiah's reign would have been something of an embarrassment after his premature death (2 Kgs 23:29), so the context of these passages that originally described the restoration of the nation in mythological terms was forgotten. Eventually, some of the same imagery was used to describe the fate of individuals in the afterlife, as in Dan 12:1–3, or Rev 7:15; 21:1–4, and the Isaianic passages were reinterpreted to say the same thing.

Isaiah also includes passages that reflect afterlife judgment. In 33:13–16, sinners fear the Lord's wrath (33:14). The afterlife is certainly in view here; it offers the alternative of "everlasting fire" for the godless, or resting in peace in a rock-cut tomb for the one who acts ethically (33:15–16). For the latter, "his food will be supplied, his water assured" – a straightforward reference to reference to a mortuary cult, the primary goal of which was to provision the dead for the afterlife. Because these verses appear to be an insertion, they are difficult to date, but they are probably postexilic. Also in a late period, the book ends with a final word of warning to "the people who have rebelled against" God: "their worm shall not die, their fire shall not be quenched, and they shall be an abhorrence to all flesh" (66:24). This had an Isaianic precursor of sorts in Isa 30:27–33, which pronounces judgment on the Assyrian king, and it culminates with a "pyre made deep and wide, with fire and wood in abundance; [and] the breath of Yhwh, like a stream of sulfur, kindles it." But that text seems to have been about the king's physical destruction, not the afterlife per se. Later authors elaborated these images with a vengeance (e.g., the "lake of fire" in Rev 19–20), but some of the images that formed Jewish and Christian ideas of eternal damnation are already present in Isaiah.[12]

---

[11]   It must be borne in mind that the theological rhetoric of Deuteronomy was also profoundly political; the two were rarely separable in the ancient Near East. Specifically, Deuteronomy was composed as a reaction against Assyrian hegemony.

[12]   To be more precise, Isaiah in turn may have drawn some of these images from neighboring cultures such as Egypt, whose literature contained very graphic depictions of death as a swallower and the agony of the damned long before the eighth century BCE.

MONOTHEISM

Because of the importance attributed to monotheism in Western religious traditions, from Judaism to Christianity to Islam, the most widely discussed religious innovation of the book of Isaiah is probably the expressions of monotheism found in its latter parts. For example, 45:3–4: "I am Yhwh, and there is no other; besides me there is no god," and related statements in 43:10–13; 44:6–8; 45:18–22; 46:8; 47:8, 10, etc.

There were other totalizing theologies in the Near East: In Egypt, Akhenaten sought to focus worship on the sun disk in the Amarna period, and by priests of Amun-Re to establish a divine theocracy in the New Kingdom and after; and in Babylon there were subtle theologies that could describe nearly all the gods as manifestations of Marduk. Still, actual monotheism, in the sense of the explicit denial of the *existence* of other deities, was almost unheard of.

Even Israelite religion was not originally monotheistic in any strict sense. Earlier statements such as the *Shema* (Deut 6:4–5) do not actually deny the existence of other gods. When it says, "Hear, O Israel: Yhwh is *our* God, Yhwh alone. You shall love Yhwh *your* God with all your heart, and with all your soul, and with all your might" – it demands sole loyalty to the Lord, but it takes for granted that other gods exist. Elsewhere, Deuteronomy warns the people not to follow "any of the gods of the peoples who are all around you" (6:14) lest "the anger of Yhwh … be kindled against you" (7:4). In fact, much of the Hebrew Bible presupposes the existence of other gods; for example, the pervasive condemnations of the people's pursuit of the Baals and Asherahs/Astartes (e.g., Judg 3:7; 1 Sam 7:4), or Mesha of Moab's sacrifice of his firstborn son (presumably to Chemosh) which is effective in 2 Kgs 3:26–27.

Monotheism, properly speaking, entails denying the existence of other gods. But there are other theological views that justify the worship of a single god. Since Deuteronomy generally acknowledges the existence of other gods but forbids worshiping them, it is an example of *monolatry*. Joshua 2:10–19 and Judges 2:11–19 described a more temporary form of monolatry: periods of strict adherence to the worship of one god in an effort to avert a crisis; this is defined as *henotheism* (HAYS 2009: 170).

Although it is true that no earlier Old Testament text enunciates monotheism so clearly as Second Isaiah, already in preexilic texts such as Isa 10:5–15 and 14:24–27, one encounters the claim that the Lord controls history and the workings of the universe. Baruch Levine (LEVINE: 423) takes this as "an explicit statement of Isaiah's monotheism" deriving from a time much earlier than is often thought.

Perhaps it is not surprising to find universalizing claims for God's power in the Neo-Assyrian period. After all, theological rhetoric reflected royal rhetoric (e.g., Ps 10:16: "Yhwh is king!"), and the covenants of the Hebrew Bible are widely compared with ancient treaties dictated by emperors who aspired to far-reaching powers. In Exodus and Deuteronomy, Yhwh is already portrayed as a "suzerain" – a more powerful ruler who has the right to impose terms on his subordinates and demand faithfulness. Biblical authors reacted against the universalizing claims of the Neo-Assyrian kings, who took titles such as "king of the universe" and "ruler of the four corners (of the earth)." Isaiah ben Amoz answered by denying the Assyrian boasts and asserting that the Lord was in control. By the time of Deutero-Isaiah, Yhwh became a universal and imperial ruler, one whose rhetoric of power is unbounded.

IDOL POLEMICS

Isaiah's monotheizing rhetoric came with certain corollaries. On the basis of this controversial worldview, other gods were mocked, demoted, and denigrated as frauds. One example is Isa 46:1–2, in which the two chief deities of the Babylonian pantheon are said to be brought low and exiled: "Bel bows down, Nebo (=Nabu) stoops,/ their idols are on beasts and cattle."[13] The Babylonian gods are mere idols carried by animals, whereas the Lord carries and saves his people (46:3–4).[14]

The most characteristic aspect of Isaiah's anti-idol polemics is a focus on the difference between the Lord, who is the "Maker of all things" (Isa 44:24, and many similar instances), and idols, which are made by human hands. The extended passage in Isa 44 is a prominent example. It begins by asking, "Who would fashion a god or cast an image that can do no good? Look, all its devotees shall be put to shame; the artisans too are merely human. Let them all assemble, let them stand up; they shall be terrified, they shall all be put to shame" (44:10–11). It continues with an extended description of the way a workman cuts down a tree and uses some of it to cook food, while "the rest of it he makes into a god, his idol, bows down to it and worships it; he prays to it and says, 'Save me, for you are my god!'" (44:17). This mockery culminates with the conclusion that "a deluded mind has led

---

[13] Hanspeter Schaudig, "'Bel Bows, Nabu Stoops!': The Prophecy of Isaiah xlvi 1–2 as a Reflection of Babylonian 'Processional Omens,'" *VT* 58 (2008): 557–72.

[14] See further: R. J. Clifford, "The Function of Idol Passages in Second Isaiah," *CBQ* 42 (1980): 450–64.

him astray, and he cannot save himself or say, 'Is not this thing in my right hand a fraud?'" (44:20). Nathanial Levtow has aptly pointed out that these Isaianic texts are part of a discourse of power that seeks to disempower foreign deities while simultaneously championing Yhwh's power; although the polemics emerged from a worldview similar to those of neighboring nations, they wound up also defining Israel/Judah ethnographically (LEVTOW). That is, the rhetoric was so powerful and influential that it shaped the people who embraced it.

It is possible that Israelite religion was aniconic in a de facto sense from early on, as Exod 20:4 might suggest. That would explain why the idea of an anthropomorphic statue for a deity, of the sort that exiles would have encountered in Mesopotamia and other surrounding nations, would have seemed anathema. Yet the situation was more complicated: The Taanach Cult Stand from tenth-century Judah seems to portray the Lord aniconically enthroned in one register, but also as a sun disk with horses in another (cf. 2 Kg 23:11; Ps 104), so multiple views of God seem clearly to have coexisted. There are enough other examples from Israel's environment that this is plausible. The aforementioned temple at 'Ain Dara, a close analogue to the Jerusalem Temple from the same period, included massive footprints carved into its entry steps as an aniconic but visible marker of divine presence. Aniconic worship occurred in the neighboring religion of Phoenicia as well, though alongside iconic worship, so that it was not a programmatic imperative there (DOAK). In the Phoenicians' far-flung trading network, aniconism might have helpfully bridged cultures by not overspecifying the appearance of the gods.

How did aniconism become a defining prohibition in Israelite religion? The Bible itself was formed gradually over a period in which Yahwistic authors seem to have become more careful about avoiding anthropomorphic language for God. Whereas the earlier Pentateuchal sources have God "walking around in the garden" (Gen 3:8) and showing Moses his "back side" (Exod 33:23), and Isaiah speaks regularly of the "outstretched hand" (5:25, etc.) and the mighty arm of the Lord (30:30–32), and even his nose, lips, and tongue (30:27), later authors such as the Priestly editors and Ezekiel tended to avoid anthropomorphisms. Ezekiel couches his divine vision in multiple layers of abstraction: He claims only to have seen "the appearance of the likeness of the glory of Yhwh" (Ezek 1:28).

The anti-idol polemics do not, of course, present the views of statue-makers in an even-handed way. It is true that Mesopotamian texts "can refer to the statue as if it simply were the god him/herself," so that if a statue was taken from the temple, the deity might be said to have gone on a journey. Yet "the Mesopotamians clearly maintained a distinction between the god and his/her statue" (DICK: 42). For example, "the destruction of a cult statue did not entail the destruction of the deity," and "there was no problem with the same god having cult images in two different temples" (DICK: 33–34).[15] Mesopotamian theologians certainly reckoned with this tension, and there were two primary ways in which it was addressed: Workmen ritually swore that they had not made the god; and related rituals acknowledged the earthly origins of the materials, but asserted that they had been reborn as the god. These were referred to as mouth-washing and/or mouth-opening rituals. If these rituals seem self-contradictory or absurd to a modern reader, it is worth considering that most religions have similarly perplexing traditions. Most Christian traditions assert that God is somehow present in the elements of the Eucharist, and Roman Catholicism in particular asserts that the bread and wine are actually "transubstantiated" into the body and blood of Christ (DICK: 57n2).[16] Yet this remains as much a mystery as the rebirth of wood, stone, and metal into a Babylonian cult image.

TEMPLE AND PRIESTHOOD

Isa 56:1–8 reflects controversies of the postexilic period about who could be involved in the Temple cult, and how they could serve; it welcomes in those who had previously been excluded. The passage as a whole shifts the standard of inclusion from ethnic and biological characteristics to ethical behavior and sabbath-keeping.

The first act of inclusion pertains to the eunuch. Leviticus 21:17 had warned: "No one of your offspring throughout their generations who has a blemish may approach to offer the food of his God," and among the disqualifying blemishes were damaged testicles and castration (Lev 21:20; Deut 23:1). But these limitations are set aside in Isa 54:4–5:

> I will give [the eunuch], in my house and within my walls,
> a monument and a name
> better than sons and daughters.
> I will give him an everlasting name
> that shall not be cut off.

[15] Friedrich Delitzsch made this comparison in his second "Babel und Bible" lecture, more than a century ago: "Just as intelligent Catholics see in the images merely the representations of Christ, Mary, and the saints, so did the intelligent Babylonians: no hymn or prayer was addressed to the image as such – they are always appealing to the divinity that dwells beyond the bounds of earth": *Babel und Bibel* (Chicago: Open Court, 1906), 106.

[16] Dick self-identified as a Roman Catholic in making this observation.

In a culture in which procreation was normally a precondition for the preservation of one's property and memory, this is an exceedingly powerful promise. The reference to royal Davidic heirs serving as eunuchs in the Babylonian court in Isa 39:7 points to the possibility that elites returning from exile had been castrated – it was a way for a conqueror to end the threat of a native dynasty without committing murder (compare Isa 14:20b–21) – so it is conceivable that this message was especially intended for them.

The postexilic period was also a time of Judean ethnocentrism, motivated by efforts by returnees from exile to reestablish their communal identity. The books of Ezra and Nehemiah are strongly colored by xenophobia, including sending away foreign wives and condemning what were perceived as foreign cultural influences (Ezra 9–10; Neh 10:30; 13:23–27). This same view has ample support elsewhere in the Bible: Foreigners are also excluded from the assembly and the temple in Deut 23:2–3 and Ezek 44:9, and are forbidden to eat the Passover meal in Exod 12:43.

By contrast, a number of late passages in Isaiah take a broader view of foreign nations, for example 2:3: "Many peoples shall come and say, 'Come, let us go up to the mountain of Yhwh, to the house of the God of Jacob; that he may teach us his ways and that we may walk in his paths'" (cf. Mic 2:15).

The Isaianic authors were not exactly saying, "come as you are"; the passages presuppose that the foreigners will keep the covenant and the sabbath (56:2, 6; and see also 1:13). Sabbath-keeping is, of course, among the Ten Commandments, and excluding business transactions on the Sabbath was a major focal point of Nehemiah's reforms (Neh 10:31; 13:15–22). But in any case, Isa 56:6–7 extends to the foreigner a fairly expansive grace:

> And the foreigners who join themselves to Yhwh
>   to minister to him …
> these I will bring to my holy mountain,
>   and make them joyful in my house of prayer;
> their burnt offerings and their sacrifices
>   will be accepted on my altar;
> for my house shall be called a house of prayer
>   for all peoples. (Isa 56:6–7)

The term "minister" in this passage translates a Hebrew verb (*sharat*) that clearly indicates priestly service, and not just any sort of participation in the Temple. But the priesthood had long been restricted not only to Israelites but also to certain families – for example, Exod 29:9, which limits it to sons of Aaron "by a perpetual ordinance." The phrase "joined to Yhwh" in verses 3 and 6 uses the same Hebrew verb used of the Levites in Num 18:2, 4, so Levitical service may be the specific intention.

From a sociohistorical standpoint, it is clear in the later chapters of the book – especially in the frustration and death of the "servant" (49:4; 52:13–53:12) and the harsh rhetoric against unnamed opponents (e.g., 65:13–15) – that the Isaianic community was part of sectarian conflict with other Judean religious groups (BLENKINSOPP). So it may have been that the call for inclusion of foreigners was partly a statement of solidarity with other excluded groups.

The idea of foreigners serving as priests was so troubling to many of the scribes who copied and transmitted the text that they modified it in various ways over time, as early as the Dead Sea Scrolls and the Septuagint translation.[17] In short, they felt it was important that this text not contradict other scriptural passages (although in fact 66:21 says almost the same thing).

The author of Isa 56 himself, however, seems to have been perfectly clear that he was expanding God's circle of inclusion, in that he closes the passage on this emphatic note:

> Thus says my Lord, Yhwh,
>   who gathers the outcasts of Israel,
> I will gather others to them
>   besides those already gathered. (56:8)

This uses two terms that appeared earlier in the book, in Isa 11:12 – "[Yhwh] will assemble the *outcasts* of Israel, and *gather* the dispersed of Judah from the four corners of the earth." Now, says the author of Isa 56, the Lord will gather more people than before. In the context of the period's religiously motivated debates about Israelite identity, these were forceful and surprising statements from a prophet.

CRITIQUE OF CULT

The Hebrew prophets' invectives against sacrifices have long been a much-discussed aspect of their message (though perhaps disproportionately so among Protestants, who have been only too happy to use them to polemicize

---

[17]   D. W. van Winkle, "An Inclusive Authoritative Text in Exclusive Communities," in *Writing and Reading the Scroll of Isaiah* (Leiden: E. J. Brill, 1997), 423–40.

against Catholics and Jews). Isaiah's polemics in this vein are less widely quoted than, for example, Mic 6:6–8, but insofar as they are prominent in the book's opening and closing chapters, they cannot be overlooked.

Isa 1:10–17 is sometimes taken to have originated with the eighth century prophet. He compares the rulers and people to Sodom and Gomorrah, then says:

> What to me is the multitude of your sacrifices?
>   says Yhwh;
> I have had enough of burnt offerings of rams
>   and the fat of fed beasts;
> I do not delight in the blood of bulls,
>   or of lambs, or of goats.
> When you come to appear before me,
>   who asked this from your hand?
>   Trample my courts no more;
> bringing offerings is futile;
>   incense is an abomination to me.
> New moon and sabbath and the reading of scripture—
>   I cannot endure solemn assemblies with iniquity.

This leads, eventually, to a summons: "cease to do evil, learn to do good; seek justice, rescue the oppressed, defend the orphan, plead for the widow." These quite ancient and widespread social-justice concerns, mentioned in Hammurabi's law code and Ugaritic myths among others, come to be major concerns for the prophet, so it is plausible that they motivated his condemnation of the considerable economic and social energies associated with the Jerusalem temple cult. How, he seems to ask, can you expend such vast resources on sacrifice and festivals while ignoring justice for those most in need?

This is certainly consistent with the critiques of the lack of social justice in, for example, Isa 5 or 4:13–15, although those are never connected with the temple cult. Certain considerations suggest that Isa 1:10–17 may be a late composition: Furthermore, the phrase "reading of scripture" (qr' mqr') seems to me most similar to Neh 8:8: "So they read (qr') from the scroll, from the Torah of God, with interpretation. They gave the sense, so that the people understood the reading (mqr')."[18] Its reference to "Sodom and Gomorrah" suggests that (as with

---

[18] mqr' is the term used for scripture in later Jewish texts. NRSV and NJPS both translate "assemblies with iniquity," but this renders mqr' as "assembly" by comparison with the phrase mqr' qdš in the legal material of Exod–Num. I do not think mqr' is used in the same way here.

the references to Abraham, Sarah, and the Exodus in 40–66), this may have been an author aware of the broad sweep of the Pentateuch. If so, then some of the anticultic language here might also have been drawn from, for example, Amos 5 or Ps 51:18–19 (ET 16–17). While none of this is conclusive, it may point to a postexilic author seeking to connect the book with traditional prophetic themes.

Similar concerns are expressed in Isa 66, which is certainly among the latest texts in the book, probably deriving from the fifth century. The chapter begins with the Lord's statement, "Heaven is my throne, and the earth is my footstool; what is the house that you would build for me?" – expressing the belief that God is not dependent on the Temple, and is indeed too great to be contained by it (compare 2 Sam 7:1–7).

Isa 66 also criticizes the Temple's cultic personnel, but translations often misinterpret the message; 66:3 should be translated:

> The one who slaughters an ox (also) kills a human being;
> the one who sacrifices a lamb (also) breaks a dog's neck;
> the one who presents a grain offering (also) offers swine's blood;
> the one who makes a memorial offering of frankincense (also) blesses an idol.

Interpretations of the condemnations on 66:3 have gone too far in an anticultic direction in arguing that the prophet condemned blood and grain offerings. Many translations create similes that are absent in the Masoretic Text (MT), for example, the NRSV: "Whoever slaughters an ox is like one who kills a human being." The word "like" is not present in the MT. Rather, the accusation is that the ones who are performing orthodox sacrifices are *simultaneously* carrying out forbidden rituals. It would be inconsistent with the rest of the book to condemn sacrifices *as such*; instead, what is envisioned here is the purification of the Temple. The Temple remains important in Third Isaiah (e.g., 56:7; 60:7; 66:20), but has become a locus of hypocrisy (65:5; 66:3). The religious officials who "did what was evil in my sight" (66:4) are contrasted with "the poor/afflicted" (66:2).

Thus, the criticism is not a critique of sacrifice or the temple cult as such, but of larger issues and problems with which it is associated. This is true of prophetic critiques of the cult in general: They should not be generalized, as if the prophets were enemies of ritual or religious law in general. There are various other indications of this in Isaiah. For example, the sign that the Egyptians will know the Lord and become His people in 19:21 is that they "will worship with sacrifice and burnt offering." In Isa 43, the Lord laments that "you have been weary of me, O Israel! You have not brought me your sheep for burnt offerings, or honored me with your sacrifices." The passage comes from a period immediately after the exile when there was no functioning Temple in which to offer proper sacrifices, but it presents God describing this as a temporary hiatus during which "I have not burdened you with offerings." Furthermore, Isa 56 promises to welcome newcomers to the Temple and "make them joyful in my house of prayer ... their burnt offerings and their sacrifices will be accepted on my altar" (56:7).

In sum, offerings and festivals are welcomed by God in Isaiah, but only when they are part of a functioning social fabric that honors the correct divine priorities, especially justice for the poor and disadvantaged.

ONGOING HETERODOXY IN THE PERSIAN PERIOD

One of the enduring images of the prophets is as courageous reformers, changing their societies by castigating apostates and sinners. Yet the prophetic books themselves accurately reflect that their impact was often very limited (e.g., Isa 6:9–10; Amos 7:10–13; Jer 20:1–2; 36:20–25; 42–44, etc.). Another indication of this prophetic frustration is the ongoing descriptions of heterodox religious practices into the very latest strata of Isaiah (ACKERMAN).

There are two substantial catalogues of illicit cultic activities in Third Isaiah: 57:5–10 and 65:3–5; to which one can add other late references in the book's framing chapters: 1:29–30 and 66:3, 17. Among these interesting and complex lists, certain themes emerge. First, all of them make reference to oak trees and gardens as locations of transgression (1:29–30; 57:5; 65:3; 66:17). What does it mean that those condemned "will be ashamed of the oaks (and) gardens" (1:29), or that they will "burn with lust among the oaks, under every green tree" (57:5)? Trees were characteristic of Asherah worship (1 Kgs 15:13; 2 Kgs 23:4–7), but the gardens may have been associated with cults of the dead as well. The "garden of the king" (2 Kgs 25:4; Jer 39:4; 52:7; Neh 3:15) was a site of mortuary rites for the Davidic dynasty, and there are other late Isaianic references to the underworld and cults of the dead: to Sheol and the underworld deity Molech (57:9), who is elsewhere associated with child sacrifice (57:5; cf. Lev 18:21); and to ritual activity in tombs (65:4).

Another common thread in the condemnations is the sacrifice and consumption of pigs, dogs, rodents, and other vermin (65:4; 66:3, 17; see earlier discussion). All of these are unclean animals according to kosher law (Lev 11:7–29). There is evidence for such sacrifices in Persian Period Yehud and its vicinity.[19]

In 57:3–10, these heterodox practices are framed within the metaphor of an adulterous woman, and the "symbol" she sets up just before the overt sexual imagery in 57:8 is sometimes taken to be a phallic symbol or toy of some kind (especially in light of the related term in Ezek 16:17). However, given the strong similarities of the metaphor to Hos 1–3 – both address a "whoring" woman and her children – the sexual aspects here seem primarily a metaphor for the people's pursuit of other divinities.

Overall, the common feature of these lists is that they focus on practices that were carried out apart from the Temple and its traditions. Despite the Isaianic group's sectarian alienation from the Temple's authorities, they still believed that the Temple was important and ought to be purified.

In such overwhelmingly polemical texts, it is valid to ask to what extent any of this reflected reality. Yet there is some material data that reinforces the point that there was very little change in Judean religious practices despite the intermittent attempts at "reform." One much-studied example pertains to the "Judean Pillar Figurines," which were statuettes of nude women that are generally thought to represent goddesses and/or to be related to fertility rituals (DARBY). These are found consistently in Judean tombs before and after the time of Josiah, whom the Bible treats as the agent of a major reform (2 Kgs 23). Readers of the Bible should assume that whatever the dominant theological ideas of a certain period at the center of the religion, they were enunciated against the backdrop of essentially intractable religious realities.

CONCLUSION

For the reader interested in history for its own sake, this chapter has provided a small sampling of the ways that Isaiah sheds light on the history of Israelite religion. The payoff for interpretation (and even mere

---

[19] Meir Edrey, "A Dog Cult in Persian Period Judah," in P. I. Ackerman-Lieberman and R. Zalashik, eds. *A Jew's Best Friend? The Image of the Dog throughout Jewish History* (Brighton: Sussex Academic, 2013), 12–35. But see also the cautions of Helen Dixon, "Late 1st-Millennium b.c.e. Levantine Dog Burials as an Extension of Human Mortuary Behavior," *BASOR* 379 (2018): 19–41.

comprehension) is readily apparent. Readers who are accustomed to the ways in which later religious traditions pick and choose bits of Isaiah and remove them from their contexts may find this contextual reading of the book confusing and disorienting. While some of the ideas later faiths derive from the book, such as its monotheistic emphasis, are richly affirmed, other issues turn out to be far more complicated. The authors of Isaiah were profoundly embedded in the conflicts and social realities of their times, and this means that a deeper awareness of those times allows for more intelligent interpretation and appropriation, regardless of one's purposes.

FURTHER READING

Ackerman, Susan. *Under Every Green Tree: Popular Religion in Sixth-Century Judah*. HSM 46. Winona Lake, IN: Eisenbrauns, 2001.

Albertz, Rainer. *A History of Israelite Religion in the Old Testament Period*. OTL. Louisville, KY: Westminster/John Knox Press, 1994.

Albertz, Rainer, and Rüdiger Schmitt. *Family and Household Religion in Ancient Israel and the Levant*. Winona Lake, IN: Eisenbrauns, 2012.

Blenkinsopp, Joseph. "The 'Servants of the Lord' in Third Isaiah: Profile of a Pietistic Group in the Persian Epoch." Pages 392–412 in *"The Place Is Too Small for Us": The Israelite Prophets in Recent Scholarship*. Ed. Robert P. Gordon. Winona Lake, IN: Eisenbrauns, 1995.

Darby, Erin. *Interpreting Judean Pillar Figurines: Gender and Empire in Judean Apotropaic Ritual*. FAT II/69. Tübingen: Mohr Siebeck, 2014.

Dick, Michael B. *Born in Heaven, Made on Earth: The Making of the Cult Image in the Ancient Near East*. Winona Lake, IN: Eisenbrauns, 1999.

Doak, Brian R. *Phoenician Aniconism in Its Mediterranean and Ancient Near Eastern Contexts*. Archaeology and Biblical Studies 21. Atlanta, GA: SBL Press, 2015.

Hays, Christopher B. "Religio-Historical Approaches: Monotheism, Method, and Mortality." Pages 169–93 in *Method Matters: Essays on the Interpretation of the Hebrew Bible in Honor of David L. Petersen*. Edited by Joel M. LeMon and Kent H. Richards. Atlanta, GA: SBL, 2009.

Hays, Christopher B. *Death in the Iron Age II and in First Isaiah*. FAT 79. Tübingen: Mohr Siebeck, 2011.

Levine, Baruch. "Assyrian Ideology and Biblical Monotheism," *Iraq* 67 (2005): 411–27.

Levtow, Nathaniel B. *Images of Others: Iconic Politics in Ancient Israel*. Biblical and Judaic Studies from UCSD 11. Winona Lake, IN: Eisenbrauns, 2008.

Nissinen, Martti. *Prophets and Prophecy in the Ancient Near East: With Contributions by C.L. Seow, Robert K. Ritner, and H. Craig Melchert*. 2nd edition. WAW 12. Atlanta, GA: SBL, 2019.

Parpola, Simo. *Assyrian Prophecies*. State Archives of Assyria, V. 9. Helsinki: Helsinki University Press, 1997.

Smith, Mark S., and Elizabeth Bloch-Smith. "Death and Afterlife in Ugarit and Israel." *JAOS* 108 (1988): 277–84.

Sonia, Kerry M. *Caring for the Dead in Ancient Israel.* Archaeology and Biblical Studies 27. Atlanta, GA: SBL Press, 2020.

Viberg, Ake. *Prophets in Action: An Analysis of Prophetic Symbolic Acts in the Old Testament.* ConBOTS 55. Stockholm: Almqvist and Wiksell, 2007.

10 Isaiah and Empire

SHAWN ZELIG ASTER

The book of Isaiah's composition spanned the Neo-Assyrian, Neo-Babylonian, and Persian empires, and its different parts are linked by the necessity of responding to empires. Many other texts in the Hebrew Bible also deal with the encounter with empires – the Exodus narrative, for example, much of the books of Kings, and Ps 83 – but Isaiah offers a unique perspective on the theological challenges created by empire. It focuses on the inherent tension between conceiving of God as having unlimited power, and the empire, which portrays itself as invincible and universal.

The actions and policies of empires often diverge from what one would expect of the will of God, and so theological questions emerge about God's nature, intentions, and relationship to empire. Into this breach stepped the authors of Isaiah. They often do not fit the popular image of prophets or seers who predict the future. Instead, they were concerned with explaining to the Judahite elite of the Assyrian periods (740–640; all dates are BCE unless otherwise noted) and to Judahite exiles in the early Persian period (in the years following 538) how the actions of empire fit into the divine plan.

Questions about the disparity between the apparent power of earthly kingdoms and the apparent powerlessness of God appear in biblical narratives about periods long before the Israelites encountered actual empires. For example, the book of Judges recounts Gideon's complaint about the domination of Israel by Midianite nomadic raiders:

> "If Yhwh is with us, why then has all this happened to us? And where are all his wonderful deeds that our ancestors recounted to us, saying, 'Did not Yhwh bring us up from Egypt?' But now Yhwh has cast us off, and given us into the hand of Midian." (Judg 6:13)

But there is a crucial difference between the experience of empire and the domination of Israel by Midian portrayed in the Gideon story. Those experiencing domination by a nomadic culture know it to be transient, its duration influenced by the vagaries of climate and shifting political alliances among nomadic polities. By contrast, empires portray themselves as lasting phenomena, to their elites and to those they dominate. As Hardt and Negri describe it:

> The concept of Empire presents itself not as a historical regime originating in conquest, but rather as an order that effectively suspends history and thereby fixes the existing state of affairs for eternity. From the perspective of Empire, this is the way things will always be, and the way they were always meant to be. In other words. Empire presents its rule not as a transitory moment in the movement of history, but as a regime with no temporal boundaries and in this sense outside of history or at the end of history.[1]

In this emphasis on its enduring nature, empire distinguishes itself from the type of polity portrayed in the Gideon story. The conceptual dissonance between political domination of God's people by imperial forces and Divine Power is even stronger than the conceptual dissonance encapsulated in Gideon's question. Gideon's question "where is God's power?" therefore becomes even stronger for the Israelites or Judahites dominated by empire.

These Israelites or Judahites were acutely aware that empire portrayed itself, to dominated states, as a lasting phenomenon. From the Assyrian empire and on, empires deployed a sophisticated propaganda system in order to portray themselves as invincible and lasting, and thereby convince dominated peoples to submit. Of course, the most fundamental element in convincing dominated states to submit to empire was military force; but deploying military force was costly, so it was a more efficient use of resources to combine it with the written word, speeches, and artistic materials in order to persuade dominated states that the empire was a permanent fixture in their lives.

EMPIRE AND EMISSARIES

Assyria began to dominate the Levant particularly after the rise of Tiglath-pileser III in 744 (ASTER 2007: 10). By approximately 740, the northern kingdom, Israel, had become tributary to Assyria, and Judah became tributary no later than 734 (ASTER 2017: 82–85). As such, they

[1]   Michael Hardt and Antonio Negri, *Empire* (Cambridge, MA: Harvard University Press, 2000), xiv–xv.

were required to participate in the annual ceremony of sending elite emissaries on annual palace visits to the Assyrian capital (ASTER 2017: 42–43). The ostensible purpose of these visits was the delivery of tribute to the Assyrian king. But this tribute could equally well have been delivered to Assyrian officials located closer to the tributary kingdoms; there was another, more insidious purpose to the required annual visit.[2] The visiting officials were exposed to Assyrian palace art and to audiences with Assyrian officials, both of which were carefully orchestrated to impress upon the visitors that the empire was universal, that its ruler was invincible, and that it was therefore in the best interests of the visitors to ally themselves with Assyria.

Accepting the Assyrian empire as a permanent state of affairs was in the best interests not only of the tributary kingdom as a whole, but also of the individual emissary. The Assyrians plied these emissaries with gifts and rewards, including lavish banquets, clothing, and jewelry.[3] These gifts were designed to "turn" the loyalty of the individual emissary, who was usually an influential member of the elite of the tributary kingdom, into an ally of Assyria. This process of coopting local elites, and "turning" them into agents who could advance the interests of the empire, is known from other empires. Stark and Chance, in their anthropological study of local reactions to empire, call it creating "complicity."[4] Assyria's strategy was designed to engender cooperation, and (in something of a vicious circle) perpetuate empire by encouraging local elites to end their resistance to empire, and to accept that empire was a permanent state of affairs. Effectively, complicit local elites helped perpetuate the very state of affairs that they were convinced was permanent.

THEOLOGICAL AND POLITICAL DANGERS OF SUBMISSION TO EMPIRE IN ISA 6–8

The throne-room vision in Isa 6 is an attempt to argue against the tendency of these emissaries to become complicit in perpetuating empire by propagating its ideology (ASTER 2015; cf. COHEN; MACHINIST; LEVINE). It does this by creating an intentional comparison to the

---

[2] John Nicholas Postgate, *Taxation and Conscription in the Assyrian Empire* (Rome: Pontifical Biblical Institute, 1974), 126.

[3] Postgate, *Taxation and Conscription*, 127–28.

[4] B. L. Stark and J. K. Chance, "The Strategies of Provincials in Empires," in M. E. Smith (ed.), *The Comparative Archaeology of Complex Societies* (New York: Cambridge University Press, 2012), pp. 192–237, here 193.

Figure 10.1 Wall panel showing the tree of life, Neo-Assyrian,
c. 865–860 BCE, © The Trustees of the British Museum

throne-room in the Assyrian palace built by Assurnasirpal II at
Calah, which was in use during most of the reign of Tiglath-pileser III
(r. 744–727), the king under whom Judah initially submitted to Assyria.
Emissaries from conquered kingdoms were directed to his throne-room
after viewing many artistic reliefs throughout the palace that depicted
the invincible Assyrian king and his universal empire. A key feature
of this room was the relief known as B-13, which appears twice, once
opposite the entrance and once above the throne (see Figure 10.1).

This relief shows multiwinged creatures flanking the Assyrian king.
They have human heads, though similar creatures depicted elsewhere
in the palace have the heads of birds or snakes. The creatures carry purifying implements, with which they purify the king, who is portrayed
in double, flanking the cosmic tree. The king wears a special hemmed
garment, and salutes the image of the god Assur (the chief national god
of Assyria) in the winged disk. His location above the cosmic tree shows
his role as universal ruler. By saluting Assur and dominating the cosmic
tree, the king ensures order in the universe. The relief thus asserts the
importance of Assyrian imperial rule in maintaining universal order,
and argues that the king is in a close relationship with the god Assur,
the universal ruler.

The relief corresponds to the vision in Isa 6:1–8 in several ways.
First, Isa 6:1–4 describes God seated on a high and mighty throne, with
multiwinged creatures above it:

> Seraphs were in attendance above him; each had six wings: with two they covered their faces, and with two they covered their feet, and with two they flew (6:2)

The vision of "seraphs" suggests the appearance of snakes, since this term is used elsewhere in the Hebrew Bible to refer to snakes (Num 21:6; Isa 14:29). As already noted, snake-headed creatures with multiple wings are found elsewhere in the palace reliefs.

Second, like the Assyrian king in the relief, God is described in 6:1 as wearing a garment with a special hem (Heb. *šūl*). Third, like the multiwinged creatures in the relief, the seraphim in Isaiah's vision have a purifying function:

> Then one of the seraphs flew to me, holding a live coal that had been taken from the altar with a pair of tongs. The seraph touched my mouth with it and said: "Now that this has touched your lips, your guilt has departed and your sin is blotted out." (6:6–7)

But while it evokes the relief, the vision of Isaiah also undermines and attacks the concepts behind the relief by reframing the relationship between the multiwinged creatures and the occupant of the throne in two key ways:

First, the seraphim in Isaiah's vision do not help or assist the figure on the throne (God) in any way. They merely declare (6:3) God's universal rule. By referring to the relief, but depicting a different relationship between the winged creatures and the throne-occupant, Isaiah argues that God does not need the help of the servants.

Second, the seraph in Isaiah's vision purifies the prophet (6:8) – unlike the multiwinged creatures in the Assyrian throne-room, who purify the king. Isaiah here argues that the king in Assyria, like the prophet in Israel, is mortal and therefore needs to be purified. In contrast, God, who occupies the throne in Isa 6, is beyond any possible purity or impurity, and does not need to be purified.

Isa 6:9–13 then moves away from the relationship between the seraphim and God, to describe the relationship between the God and the prophet. God, seated on the throne, seeks representatives: "Whom shall I send, and who will go for us?" (6:8). The prophet volunteers, and is given the contradictory mission to speak to the people, but ensure that they will not understand:

> And he said, "Go and say to this people: 'Keep listening, but do not comprehend; keep looking, but do not understand.' Make the mind of this people dull, and stop their ears, and shut their eyes, so that

they may not look with their eyes, and listen with their ears, and comprehend with their minds, and turn and be healed."

Then I said, "How long, O Lord?"

And he said: "Until cities lie waste, without inhabitant, and houses without people, and the land is utterly desolate; until Yhwh sends everyone far away, and vast is the emptiness in the midst of the land."

This dialogue between God and the prophet echoes and reshapes the relationship between the Assyrian empire and the emissaries sent to represent their kingdoms. The emissaries, initially tasked with representing their kingdoms before Assyria, are turned into emissaries of Assyria to their kingdoms. Exposed to Assyrian images that portray the Assyrian king as invincible and his empire as universal, they are sent to encourage their kingdoms to remain loyal to Assyria. Isa 6:8 satirizes that relationship, by placing the prophet in the guise of the emissaries and God in the guise of the Assyrian king. Like the Assyrian king, God seeks representatives; like the emissaries, Isaiah volunteers. But the insidious nature of the mission becomes clear in 6:9–10: The people are not to understand the real nature of Assyrian kingship. The emissaries hear Assyria's claims of power, but do not understand that this power is temporary and fleeting; they see the trappings of power in the Assyrian palaces, and do not recognize that the Assyrian king is mortal. ("The emperor has no clothes," as a later story puts it.) Their minds and ears (v. 10) are filled with their impressions in the Assyrian palaces. Therefore, they do not understand (v. 11) that reliance on Assyria will cause destruction (and Assyria does not want them to understand this). The prophet asks how long this destruction will last, and God responds with a description (6:11–12) of the devastation that follows from Assyrian destruction.

Translated into political terms, the prophet tells the people that accepting Assyrian ideology, and slavishly becoming vassals to Assyria, will result in the very destruction that Assyria threatens to those who disobey: desolation (6:11), exile (6:12a), and abandonment (6:12b). The political logic behind this prophecy is unimpeachable: Although in the short term, loyalty to Assyria will result in postponing destruction, eventually Judah will lack the resources to pay the heavy annual tribute. At that point, the kingdom will inevitably have to revolt against Assyria (because failure to pay tribute equaled rebellion in the eyes of the Assyrians), and then the threatened destruction will arrive (6:11–12). Judah can save itself from this dire fate only by rejecting Assyrian ideology and recognizing that the Assyrian king is not invincible, nor will the empire last forever.

Of course, the prophet's political views contained a fair measure of theology: His rejection of Assyrian ideology was grounded in his theological assumption that only a single universal ruler exists. But his views did not ignore political realities: He recognized that Judah's submission to Assyria carries dangers for the long term.

This rejection of Judah's submission to Assyria in Isa 6 carries over into Isaiah's discussion with Ahaz in 7:1–17. This passage relates to the Syro-Ephraimitic crisis, which began sometime between 738 and 734. Under pressure to join the anti-Assyrian alliance led by Rezin of Damascus and Pekah of Israel, Ahaz decided to submit to Assyria (2 Kgs 16:7) – apparently in order to obtain its support for his remaining on the throne of Judah. Apparently, Rezin and Pekah sought to replace Ahaz as king (Isa 7:6), and it was this fear that led Ahaz to submit to the Assyrians and send them tribute.

Isaiah castigates Ahaz for submitting to the empire. First, he disparages the danger Ahaz faces from the local actors, Rezin and Pekah, in 7:7–9, and implies that Ahaz' position is no more unstable than that of the "head" of either Damascus or Samaria. Next, he castigates Ahaz for refusing to accept God as reliable protector (7:9b). Finally, he states that as a result of Ahaz's fear of Rezin and his acceptance of Assyrian rule, God will bring the Assyrian king to devastate Judah (7:17) (ASTER 2017: 81–113). The threat of Assyrian invasion is made more explicit in 8:7–8, where Assyria is compared to a raging torrent.

Throughout this rejection, two key points bear highlighting. First, Judah's final destruction is nowhere envisioned. Both in 6:9–13 and in 8:7–8, Judah is to be sorely tried, but its survival is promised: In 6:13, the "trunk" will remain, and in 8:8, the waters will reach Judah's neck, but its head will remain above water. Second, Isaiah disparages and doubts the empire's longevity. He argues that Assyria is hardly the invincible force it portrays itself as, and that submission to Assyria will only create serious political dilemmas in the long term. He instead counsels Judah's leaders to adopt a more neutral and careful position. While he does not explicitly negate the need to submit to Assyria at certain times, as in the case of invasion, he rejects the Assyrian ideology that portrays Assyria as a long-lasting empire.

Effectively, Isa 6–8 seeks to reframe the Assyrian threat within the proportions of the Midianite invasion in the Gideon story. It argues that Assyria is a temporary invader whose ideology must be resisted, even if it is necessary to pay in the short run. His approach can be summarized as: ideological rejection; temporary economic/political accommodation; and an awareness of the long-term dangers of submission to empire.

BATTLE AGAINST EMPIRE: ISA 10:5–19 AND 36–37

A different approach to empire appears in Isa 10:5–19 and in the Sennacherib narrative in Isa 36–37. Instead of the focus on ideological rejection, and a recognition of the need for temporary accommodation of empire, these passages portray empire as an enemy of God that must be defeated. The Assyrian empire has become God's enemy by claiming universal rule and by usurping God's role and privileges as universal ruler.

The most famous passage articulating this view is Isa 10:5–19. In this text, verses 5–11 proclaim God's enmity against Assyria, on the grounds that Assyria has overstepped its divinely-given mandate. Verse 12 describes the impending punishment of Assyria at Jerusalem; verses 13–15 cite Assyrian boasts; and verses 16–19 describe a more general destruction of Assyria.

This last passage was the impetus for Hermann Barth's well-known hypothesis that large sections of Isa 1–39, especially those passages that express enmity toward Assyria, were composed in the reign of Josiah, in the second half of the sixth century, after Assyria had fallen from imperial status.[5] However, a closer look at these verses, as well as at Isa 10:5–15, show that the passage as a whole refers to specific Assyrian claims propagated in the reign of Sargon II (721–705), and to rituals publicly performed during that period (ASTER 2017: 173–218).

The passage begins by describing the clash between God's view of Assyria and Assyria's self-perception:

> Against a godless nation I send him,
>> and against the people of my wrath I command him,
> to take spoil and seize plunder,
>> and to tread them down like the mire of the streets.
> But this is not what he intends, nor does he have this in mind;
>> but it is in his heart to destroy, and to cut off nations, not a few.
>> (10:6–7)

Verse 6 reveals God's plans for Assyria, and his intent in allowing Assyria to dominate the northern kingdom (Israel): taking spoil, and

---

5 Hermann Barth, *Der Jessaja-Worte in der Josiazeit*, WMANT 48 (Neukirchen-Vluyn: Neukirchener, 1977), 249, and see discussion in Peter Machinist, "Ah Assyria .... (Isaiah 10:5ff) Isaiah's Assyrian Polemic Revisited," in *Not Only History: Proceedings of the Conference Held in Honor of Mario Liverani, Sapienza, Universita di Roma, Dipartimento di Scienze dell'Antichità, 20–21 April 2009*, ed. Gilda Bartoloni and Maria Giovanna Biga, with Armando Bramanti (Winona Lake, IN: Eisenbrauns, 2016), 183–218.

reducing Israel's power. Verse 7, in contrast, details Assyria's plans: to eliminate and completely destroy the kingdom of Israel. This reflects the actions of Assyria, which in the early years of Sargon's reign turned the kingdom of Israel into a province, deported significant parts of the population, and left the remnant impoverished.[6] The destruction of Israel is here seen as a sign of Assyria's insubordination to God. Further evidence for this insubordination appears in the Assyrian boasts, cited in verses 8–11 and 13–14. These boasts do not mention Yhwh in any way. This is important because both verses 8–11 and 13–14 are lightly-edited versions of actual Assyrian boasts:

> For he says: "By the strength of my hand I have done it,
>   and by my wisdom, for I have understanding;
> I have removed the boundaries of peoples,
>   and have plundered their treasures;
>   like a bull I have brought down those who sat on thrones.
> My hand has found, like a nest, the wealth of the peoples;
>   and as one gathers eggs that have been forsaken,
>   so I have gathered all the earth;
>   and there was none that moved a wing, or opened its mouth, or
>   chirped." (10:13–14)

Isaiah's representation of the boasting begins with the Assyrian king highlighting his wisdom, and his consequent ability to remove the boundaries of peoples. Sargon II indeed mentioned these things in justifying his invasion of Urartu in 714 (ASTER 2017: 190–206). In a letter to the gods regarding his campaign, he describes himself as "wisest among all kings" (l. 115), and then proceeds to portray himself as defender of other states' borders (l. 124). Furthermore, the boast of finding "the wealth of peoples" in verse 14 corresponds to Sargon's claim that "I laid hands on their accumulated wealth" in the same letter (l. 257).

The concluding statement of Isa 10:14, in which the Assyrian is portrayed as gathering wealth unopposed, while no one even moved a wing or chirped, seems to be drawn from a passage in the same letter that brags about how the Assyrians penetrated into remote mountains that had never been seen by wayfarers, nor had "even a bird of heaven

---

[6]   For a full treatment of the reality in the territory of the kingdom of Israel after its conquest, see Avraham Faust, "Settlement, Economy, and Demography under Assyrian Rule in the West: The Territories of the Former Kingdom of Israel as a Test Case," *JAOS* 135 (2015): 765–89.

in flight passed over, nor built a nest to teach its little ones to spread their wings" (l. 98). The author of Isa 10:5–19, therefore, knew Assyrian boasts, and knew that these boasts do not include polemics against the power of gods of other nations. At most, we find mention of the pillaging of cult-statues, designed to coerce their worshippers to accept Assyrian domination.[7] Assyrians were interested in achieving political power and not in theological discussion. Why then, did he portray Assyria as challenging God, and as God's enemy?

The reason is not because of the specific content of these boasts, but because of the overall ideology they expressed. They were part of a larger ideological project aiming to portray Assyria as the universal ruler, and its king as invincible. It was this ideology that provoked the prophet's ire. In Isaiah's view, Assyria had no right to claim universal or invincible rule; those privileges were God's alone. Such claims were construed by the prophet as a direct attack on God. Rather than seeking some sort of temporary accommodation with Assyria, as he did in the Syro-Ephraimitic crisis, Isaiah progressed in these passages to expecting a divine judgment on Assyria, destroying and eliminating its military threat in order to demonstrate that Assyria's ideological claims are false.

The same attitude toward Assyria is evident in Isa 36–37.[8] In this narrative of Sennacherib's attack on Jerusalem, the prophet (and those who continued to tell stories about him) snatched theological victory from the jaws of military defeat. Aware that Sennacherib devastated the countryside surrounding Lachish (as seen in 1:7–8), Isaiah focuses in chapters 36 and 37 on the salvation of Jerusalem. He sees in its salvation evidence not only for God's military defeat of Assyria, but also for his theological victory over Assyrian claims to sovereignty and universal rule.

While these chapters were edited numerous times before reaching their present state, the mocking song of the "daughter of Zion" in Isa 37:24–32 shows evidence of having been composed with the same

---

[7]   One example of pillaging cult-statues appears in the description of the fall of Samaria in a royal inscription of Sargon II: "27,280 people, together with their chariots and the gods in whom they trust, I counted as spoil" (COGAN: chap. 5, text 19). For a discussion of the goals of this practice, see Karen Radner, *Ancient Assyria: A Very Short Introduction* (Oxford: Oxford University Press, 2015), 15.

[8]   This material parallels 2 Kgs 18:17–19:37. Scholars debate which text is prior, and I have argued that the material originates among the same school that composed much of Isa 1–39, in ASTER 2017: 248–49. In the discussion that follows, only the reference to the Isaiah verses is given; the reader can easily locate the parallel in 2 Kings.

awareness of Assyrian imperial propaganda as Isa 10:13–14.[9] Like the aforementioned passage, Isa 37:24–25 cites and mocks the words of actual Assyrian boasts:

> By your servants you have mocked Yhwh,
> and you have said, 'With my many chariots
> I have gone up the heights of the mountains,
> to the far recesses of Lebanon;
> I felled its tallest cedars,
> its choicest cypresses;
> I came to its remotest height,
> its densest forest.
> I dug wells
> and drank waters,
> I dried up with the sole of my foot
> all the streams of Egypt.'

Each of the claims in these verses echoes motifs in Sennacherib's inscriptions. The claim to have ascended the mountains and drunk water there is paralleled in the following passage, which appears in several of his inscriptions:

> To the highest mountains I ascended against them, in places where my knees became tired, I sat on the side of a mountain-boulder, cold water from the waterskin I drank to my thirst, I chased them to the tops of the mountains.[10]

Similarly, the claim to have cut cedars in lush forests in the mountains appears in several texts in reference to extracting such trees from the Sirara mountains.[11] And in reference to his actions in redirecting canals,

---

9   On the editing of this material, see Amitai Baruchi-Unna, "The Story of Hezekiah's Prayer (2 Kings 19) and Jeremiah's Polemic Regarding the Inviolability of Jerusalem," *JSOT* 39 (2015): 281–97, and Dan'el Kahn, *Sennacherib's Campaign Against Judah: A Source Analysis of Isaiah 36–37*, Society for Old Testament Study Monographs (New York: Cambridge University Press, 2020), which discusses why the division of this material into source B-1 and B-2 is inadequate. On the awareness of Assyrian imperial propaganda, see ASTER 2017: 250–74.
10 Cited from A. Kirk Grayson and Jamie Novotny, *The Royal Inscriptions of Sennacherib King of Assyria (704–689 BC)*, RINAP 3/1 (Winona Lake, IN: Eisenbrauns, 2014), 178 (Sennacherib 22, iv:1–11), paralleled in Sennacherib 222 (RINAP 3/2, 309–10), and Sennacherib 46:38–42 (RINAP 3/2, 81).
11 Sennacherib 17, v:46–47 (RINAP 3/1, 136), and Sennacherib 39:38–41 (RINAP 3/2, 35–36).

Sennacherib claims: "I raised that area out of the water and made it dry land."[12]

Because of the multiple references to actual Assyrian claims in Isa 37:24–25, it is highly unlikely that these verses were composed without knowledge of the Assyrian rhetoric. It is probable that the Jerusalem elite, including the author of this text, heard these claims from emissaries to Assyria, who had in turn heard them in the course of palace visits.

Significantly, Isaiah interprets Assyrian claims of empire as attacks on Yhwh, as in Isa 10:13–14. In Isa 37:24, he makes this interpretation explicit: he prefaces Assyrian claims of empire with the statement "By your servants you have mocked Yhwh," although the claims cited contain no reference to Yhwh. Isaiah understands Assyrian claims to have an invincible king and a right to rule the world as a mockery of and a direct attack on God. For this reason, he envisions an Assyrian defeat at the walls of Jerusalem in 701. Of course, no such unequivocal defeat occurred. After the Assyrian campaign, Judah resumed its status as a vassal kingdom and paid tribute. It lost control of the Shephelah (lowlands) around Lachish, which were handed over to the kings of the Philistine cities. But Jerusalem emerged relatively unscathed, and Hezekiah remained on the throne. But the survival of Hezekiah's kingdom was reinterpreted as a victory of God over empire.

TOWARD A 'REPLACEMENT THEOLOGY': EMPIRE'S FUTURE REPLACEMENT BY GOD

The lack of an actual Assyrian defeat seems to have forced the prophet to shift to yet another approach to empire. This approach is exemplified in the famous passage sometimes called the "End of Days vision," Isa 2:2–4 (paralleled in Micah 5:1–3). This vision is sometimes thought to be late, but instead it too seems to be an adaptation of Assyrian imperial claims (ASTER 2015: 285–90).

In this case, instead of envisioning Assyria as defeated by Yhwh on the battlefield, the prophet imagines a future in which Assyria's claims of empire would be affirmed, but the empire will be headed by God

---

[12] Sennacherib 1:76 (RINAP 3/1, 38); paralleled in Sennacherib 3:49 (RINAP 3/1, 54; cf. 3/2, 35.) Sennacherib 39, lines 25–26. While other kings occasionally mention cutting cedars in the mountains and fashioning dry land out of swamp, the specific motifs found here appear repeatedly in the inscriptions of Sennacherib. Furthermore, the specific boast of drinking water in the mountains while on campaign is found only here. For further discussion, see ASTER 2017: 262–71.

instead of an Assyrian king. God thus replaces the Assyrian king as universal ruler:

> Many peoples shall come and say,
> "Come, let us go up to the mountain of Yhwh,
> to the house of the God of Jacob;
> that he may teach us his ways
> and that we may walk in his paths."
> For out of Zion shall go forth instruction,
> and the word of Yhwh from Jerusalem.

This famous passage describes how the world will seek out "ways" and "paths" identified as belonging to God and emanating from his holy and royal city, Zion. This formulation is based on an Assyrian claim, which we know from an inscription of Sargon II, celebrating the establishment of his capital. Its contents were certainly conveyed orally in the Assyrian palace and by Assyrian officials. In it, Sargon tells how he integrated conquered peoples into a single set of practices, training them in "correct behavior" and Assyrian practices:

> I made the people of the four corners, of foreign tongues and divergent speech.... whom I took captive by my fierce scepter, to be of "one mouth" and settled them therein. I appointed Assyrian natives, experts in crafts, to train them in "correct behavior" and "fear of gods and king."[13]

The opening words of Isa 2:2 ("In days to come...") indicate that immediate fulfilment is not expected. Unlike 10:12, which describes a defeat of Assyria at a clear point in time, Isa 2:2–4 describes a future defeat, at a point whose precise date is unknown. Like many of the other prophecies examined here, it shows a tendency to rework claims of empire, to address the conflict between the notion of an empire ruling the world and a world ruled by God. But by asserting that this conflict will be addressed "in days to come," when God will replace empire, it implicitly recognizes that in the foreseeable future, empire will remain.

ADDRESSING EMPIRE IN ISA 1–39: A SUMMARY

The approach of much of Isa 1–39 to the Assyrian empire has both constant elements and changing ones. The potential for tension between

---

[13]   Author's translation. For the text, see Andreas Fuchs, *Die Inschriften Sargons II aus Khorsabad* (Göttingen: Cuvillier, 1994); it appears both in a cylinder inscription (pp. 43–44, ll. 72–77) and an inscription on bull colossus published (pp. 72–73, ll. 92–97).

imperial rule and God's rule is acknowledged throughout the passages discussed; this tension proceeds from the notion that God is not a local ephemeral potentate, but something much mightier, whose power and lifespan surpass any human experience. Put simply, underlying the tension between God and empire in much of Isa 1–39 is a perception of God as transcendent. This remains constant through all of the passages discussed.

The methods for resolving the contradiction between God and empire change, however, as discussed. In some passages, such as those found in Isa 6–8, the prophet expects empire to be short lived. This expectation is made more active and imminent in the passages cited from Isa 10 and 37. These passages express the expectation that empire will be defeated in the foreseeable future. Isa 2:2–4, in contrast, recognizes the durability of empire, but expects God to replace empire "in days to come."

All of these passages have in common a clear awareness of the language of empire, and a sensitivity to its messages. They reflect an ongoing dialogue with those messages, and are concerned with their influence on the prophet's audience. As we will see, the same is true of Isa 40–66, especially 40–48.

ADDRESSING EMPIRE IN ISA 40–66

Isa 40–66 clearly reflects the context of the Persian empire. The references to Cyrus in 44:28 and 45:1 provide clear evidence of this; in 44:28, he is called God's "shepherd" and in 45:1, his "messiah." These passages are discussed in more detail in SCHULTE, "The Book of Isaiah in the Persian Period," Chapter 4 in this volume, which shows how they are akin to pro-Cyrus texts produced in Babylon and Egypt, especially the Cyrus Cylinder.

Another way to view the Cyrus texts in Isa 40–48 is that they polemicize *against* the theology that Cyrus promulgated in Babylon, according to which he was chosen by Marduk to support worship of Marduk, and was therefore appointed king (KUHRT). The key element in this polemic is to argue against the claim that Marduk appointed Cyrus, and instead to assert that Yhwh himself appointed Cyrus (PAUL 1968; PAUL 2012). The cylinder attributes Cyrus' apparently miraculous rise – from the obscure kingdom of Anshan to the kingship of Babylon – as facilitated by the aid of Marduk. An implicit attack on this theology appears in Isa 41:25:

> I stirred up one from the north, and he has come,
>> from the rising of the sun he was summoned by name.
> He shall trample on rulers as on mortar,
>> as the potter treads clay.
> Thus Yhwh, and not Marduk, is responsible for Cyrus' rise to
>> power.

Similarly, Isa 42:6 argues "I am Yhwh, I have called you in righteous-ness,/ I have taken you by the hand and kept you," polemicizing against Cyrus' claim that Marduk "called out his name … gave him victory…, set him on the road to Babylon, and like a companion and friend, he went at his side."[14] Similarly, in response to Cyrus' claim that Marduk had appointed him to relieve the citizens of Babylon, upon whom his predecessor Nabonidus had "imposed corvée, which was not the god's will and not befitting them, I relieved their weariness and freed them from their service" (COGAN: 277 lines 24–6), Isa 42:7 argues that Cyrus was sent by Yhwh "to bring out the prisoners from the dungeon, from the prison those who sit in darkness."

In these passages, the author of Isa 40–48 walks a very fine line, affirming Cyrus' legitimacy but denying the source Cyrus claims for it. Furthermore, the choice of Cyrus stems not from his actions to restore the cult of Marduk, but from the role Yhwh has assigned to him: "He shall build my city and set my exiles free" (45:13).

Perhaps most significantly, motifs used to describe the gods' choice of Cyrus are deliberately undermined and used to describe Yhwh's choice of Israel. In Mesopotamian royal inscriptions, kings are said to be chosen by the gods for this role before their birth (PAUL 1968). But in Isa 44:24, it is Israel who is said to be chosen in the womb. Thus, Israel replaces Cyrus, while using precisely the same motifs used by Cyrus to affirm his legitimacy.

Like Isa 1–39, Isa 40–48 is acutely attuned to the language of empire, and the need to explain its role in a universe governed by Yhwh. Isa 40–48 accepts the legitimacy of the Persian empire, while simultaneously polem-icizing against the theology that underpins Cyrus' rule over Babylon.

FURTHER READING

Aster, Shawn Zelig. "Transmission of Neo-Assyrian Claims of Empire to Judah in the Late Eighth Century," *HUCA* 78 (2007): 1–44.

---

[14] COGAN, 277, lines 9–19. The Hebrew of Isa 42:6 might better be translated "called you by means of victory" than "called you in righteousness."

Aster, Shawn Zelig. "Images of the Palace of Ashurnasirpal II at Calah in the Throne-Room Vision of Isaiah 6," in *Marbeh Hokma: Studies in the Bible and the Ancient Near East in Loving Memory of Victor Avigdor Hurowitz* ed. Shamir Yona, Edward L. Greenstein, Mayer I. Gruber, Peter Machinist, and Shalom M. Paul, Winona Lake, IN: Eisenbrauns, 2015, 13–42.

Aster, Shawn Zelig. *Reflections of Empire in Isaiah 1–39: Responses to Assyrian Ideology*, SBL Ancient Near Eastern Monographs 19. Atlanta, GA: SBL, 2017.

Cogan, Mordechai. *The Raging Torrent: Historical Inscriptions from Assyria and Babylonia Relating to Ancient Israel*, 2nd updated and expanded edition. Jerusalem: Carta, 2015.

Cohen, Chaim. "Neo-Assyrian Elements in the First Speech of the Biblical Rab-Shaqe." *IOS* 9 (1979): 32–48.

Kuhrt, Amélie. "The Cyrus Cylinder and Achaemenid Imperial Policy," *JSOT* 25 (1983): 83–97.

Levine, Baruch A. "Assyrian Ideology and Israelite Monotheism," *Iraq* 67 (2005): 411–27.

Machinist, Peter. "Assyria and its Image in the First Isaiah," *JAOS* (1983): 719–37.

Paul, Shalom M. "Deutero-Isaiah and Cuneiform Royal Inscriptions," *JAOS* 88 (1968): 180–86.

Paul, Shalom M. *Isaiah 40–66: Translation and Commentary*. Grand Rapids, MI: Eerdmans, 2012.

Roberts, J. J. M. *First Isaiah*. Minneapolis, MN: Fortress Press, 2015.

Sommer, Benjamin D. *A Prophet Reads Scripture: Allusion in Isaiah 40–66*. Stanford, CA: Stanford University Press, 1998.

11   Migration in the Book of Isaiah

C. L. CROUCH

It is often remarked that the Exile is strangely absent from the book of Isaiah: The book transitions from material concerning the preexilic kingdoms of Judah and Israel contained in Isa 1–39 to material concerned with the exiles' departure from Babylonia and the restoration of Jerusalem (Isa 40–66) with no more reference to how the people came to be in Babylonia than a two-verse oracle set in the time of Hezekiah, which warns that

> Days are coming when all that is in your house, and that which your ancestors have stored up until this day, shall be carried to Babylon; nothing shall be left, says Yhwh. Some of your own sons who are born to you shall be taken away; they shall be eunuchs in the palace of the king of Babylon. (Isa 39:6–7)

The shadow of the Exile unquestionably falls over the book, of course; the latter half presupposes its occurrence, as it summons descendants of those taken forcibly to Babylonia to ready themselves to return to Zion, then deals with the disappointed hopes of those who did. Ever since these chapters were recognized as having originated after the catastrophe of Jerusalem's sixth-century BCE destruction, the consequences of the experience in Babylonia, together with the difficulties associated with the eventual return to the homeland, have in some way been acknowledged by interpreters. Most recently, a small but growing body of literature has sought to consider the theological and other implications of these experiences explicitly from the perspective of migration studies, reading the second half of the book in conversation with comparative research from the social sciences (AHN, 159–222; BODA; CROUCH, 91–95, 102–110; CUÉLLAR; HÄGGLUND; SMITH-CHRISTOPHER). Other studies have analyzed the function of "exile" from a literary perspective, recognizing the way that a historical experience came to signify a broader set of ideas and concerns, such as alienation from Yhwh (LANDY) or the need for religious, economic, and social redemption among the community in Yehud (HALVORSON-TAYLOR, 107–149; see also GREGORY; POULSEN; TERBLANCHE).

While understandable in light of the monumental impact of the Babylonian displacements on biblical literature and theology, the focus on the role of "exile" – specifically the Babylonian exile – in Isaiah has overlooked the surprising preponderance of references to other instances of migration in the book. These are the focus of this chapter. It begins by identifying a variety of allusions to migrations by non-Israelites, then turns to analyze references to Judahite and Israelite migration apart from the Babylonian exile, before finally bringing the deportations to Babylonia and the eventual return migrations to Yehud into a richer and more complex picture of migration in the book of Isaiah.

MIGRATION BY FOREIGNERS

Migrations undertaken by Yhwh's people naturally come to the fore in Isaiah, but the book also contains numerous references to migrations undertaken by other peoples. Broadly speaking, these passages are of two sorts: 1) oracles concerned with the migration of non-Israelites to Zion/Jerusalem, which attend especially to religious aspects of their presence in Yhwh's city; and 2) oracles concerned with the migration of non-Israelites in other lands. The latter are more common in the eighth- and seventh-century parts of the book, reflecting the historical and political realities of Assyrian imperial deportation policies, whereas the former are more typical of contributions from the sixth and fifth centuries, under the influence of the people's own experience of deportation and return migration.

Migration of and from Other Nations

The earliest material associated with Isaiah ben Amoz of Jerusalem responds to the efforts of the northern kingdom of Israel and the kingdom of Aram-Damascus to form a coalition of Levantine nations capable of throwing off Assyrian imperial domination. The latter had put great pressure on the region with the campaigns of Tiglath-pileser III in the 740s (unless otherwise stated, all dates are BCE); by the time of Isaiah ben Amoz's prophetic activity, the long-standing Assyrian policy of forced deportations in the wake of successful military campaigns would have been well known among the peoples of the eastern Mediterranean.

The reality of these imperial deportations, as well as other forms of displacement associated with military incursions – such as flight from

advancing armies and the abandonment of destroyed homes and cities –
is reflected in a number of the Isaianic oracles against (or "concerning")
foreign nations and peoples. Thus, when Isaiah ben Amoz is instructed
to undertake a sign-act in which he is to walk naked and barefoot around
Jerusalem for three years (Isa 20:1–5), this bizarre behavior is explained
as anticipating the deportation of Egyptians and Cushites (Ethiopians/
Nubians), following on from the Assyrians' successful conquest of the
Philistine city of Ashdod: "so shall the king of Assyria lead away the
Egyptians as captives (šĕbî) and the Cushites as exiles (gālût), both
the young and the old, naked and barefoot, with buttocks uncovered,
to the shame of Egypt" (Isa 20:4). As part of Isaiah's general antipathy
toward alliances with Egypt, it may be that these deportations are envisioned as involving Egyptian and Cushite soldiers in Ashdod as part of
its failed rebellion against Assyrian authority in the 710s. Or it may be
that Isaiah was anticipating an Assyrian conquest of Egypt and Cush,
which only occurred in the seventh century but had likely been on the
Assyrian agenda earlier.

A number of other polities in the region are also described as displaced, though the cause is not always explicitly identified as Assyria's
deportation policies. The otherwise difficult Arabah desert oracle (Isa
21:13–15), for example, is clear in its vision of "fugitives" (ndd) driven to
flee their homes as a result of military conflict: "they have fled (ndd) from
the swords, from the drawn sword, from the bent bow, and from the stress
of battle" (Isa 21:15). The inhabitants of the coastal cities, especially Tyre
and Sidon, are also depicted as obliged to flee as a result of war: whereas
once the cities' merchants traveled freely for trading purposes (Isa 23:7),
now military conflict spurred on by Yhwh will bring down their defenses
and provoke their inhabitants to seek refuge in Cyprus – though from
there, too, they will be obliged to move on (Isa 23:12).

Ultimately, Yhwh is portrayed as the driving force behind such displacements. This is made explicit elsewhere, in keeping with the book's
theological commitment to Yhwh's global power and authority: The
nations "will flee (nws) far away" from Yhwh's rebuke, "chased like chaff
on the mountains before the wind and whirling dust before the storm"
(Isa 17:13; compare Isa 24:1; 33:2). Analogous to the mass displacement of
foreign peoples as an exhibition of royal social and military might among
human kings, Yhwh's authority as divine king is demonstrated in his
ability to effect the relocation of whole nations away from their native
lands. Thus, in the opening chapter of Second Isaiah's case for the persistence of Yhwh's earthly power, the anonymous prophet declares:

Have you not known? Have you not heard?
Has it not been told you from the beginning?
Have you not understood from the foundations of the earth?
It is he who sits above the circle of the earth,
and its inhabitants are like grasshoppers;
who stretches out the heavens like a curtain,
and spreads them like a tent to live in;
who brings princes to naught,
and makes the rulers of the earth as nothing.
Scarcely are they planted, scarcely sown,
scarcely has their stem taken root in the earth,
when he blows upon them, and they wither,
and the tempest carries them off like stubble. (Isa 40:21–24)

Conversely, the most sustained depiction of non-Israelite migration, a pair of oracles concerning the Moabites, gives little explicit indication that Yhwh is conceived as behind the displacement (Isa 15:1–16:11) – a single anonymous "I" is suggestive of divine intervention (Isa 15:9).[1] Instead, the oracles are focused on the pathos of the migrants themselves. The specific cause of the Moabites' flight is not identified; although commentators often assume that Moab is suffering the effects of military conflict, or perhaps famine, the description of the devastated cities (Isa 15:1) could equally refer to the effects of a major earthquake.[2] The damage, in any case, is extensive, with the population of numerous cities affected negatively.

After a period of lamentation, it seems that a portion of the population concludes that remaining in Moab, at least in the short term, is untenable: Moab's "fugitives (bĕrî᾽ᵃḥ) flee to Zoar, to Eglath-shelishiyah – for at the ascent of Luhith they go up weeping, on the road to Horonaim they raise a cry of destruction" (Isa 15:5). Subsequent verses hint at the secondary consequences of the initial disaster, as the disruption of Moab's normal societal processes impedes agricultural production and the people are forced to rely on the bounty of previous years – a tenuous grip on the resources necessary for their survival (Isa 15:6–7,

---

[1] The Isaianic oracles concerning Moab are related to those in Jeremiah 48, although the nature and direction of the relationship is not agreed.

[2] The cause of the Moabites' flight is described in Isa 16:4 using the same terminology (šdd); the participle is usually translated as a substantive (e.g., NRSV's "the destroyer"), implying a personified and thus probably military persecutor, but it may also be read more generally.

also 16:8–10).[3] These compounding effects of displacement are perhaps also in mind in Isa 15's final declaration, in which the image of a ravening lion stands for societal collapse and the resurgence of the nonhuman (Isa 15:9). Even the remnant (*š^eʾērît*) that has escaped the immediate devastation in Moab (*pĕlêṭâ môʾāb*) will struggle to reestablish themselves in the wake of the disaster.

A second section depicts the Moabite refugees seeking support in Jerusalem (Isa 16:1–5).[4] That a host society may hesitate to welcome refugees, perceiving them as potentially burdensome, is recognized in the suggestion that the migrants send lambs ahead of their arrival, signaling that they come with resources that make them advantageous to the host society to accept (Isa 16:1, compare Jacob sending livestock ahead of him to Esau, Gen 32). The prominence of women in mass displacements is implicitly acknowledged in the comparison of the "daughters of Moab" to a flock of distressed birds, driven away from their homes and obliged to search for safety elsewhere (Isa 16:2).[5]

[3]   Displacement may significantly disrupt agricultural activities; some research suggests that it may take a returning population as long as two years to reestablish itself: D. A. Korn, *Exodus within Borders: An Introduction to the Crisis of Internal Displacement* (Washington, DC: Brookings Institution, 1999), 17–18; L. Hammond, "'Voluntary' Repatriation and Reintegration," in *The Oxford Handbook of Refugee and Forced Migration Studies*, ed. E. Fiddian-Qasmiyeh, G. Loescher, K. Long and N. Sigona (Oxford: Oxford University Press, 2014), 499–511, 505–506, with reference to L. Hammond, *This Place Will Become Home: Refugee Repatriation to Ethiopia* (Ithaca, NY: Cornell University Press, 2004); C. Dolan and J. Large, *Evaluation of UNHCR's Repatriation and Reintegration Programme in East Timor, 1999–2003* (Geneva: UNHCR, 2004). David Korn notes that "child malnutrition rates as high as 70 percent have been recorded in some mass displacements" (*Exodus within Borders*, 16). In the absence of international famine aid, the situation in the ancient world may have been this bad or worse. Cohen and Deng highlight a wide range of consequences on the economic and social lives of the homeland, including major damage to agricultural infrastructure as well as homes and other buildings: R. Cohen and F. M. Deng, *Masses in Flight: The Global Crisis of Internal Displacement* (Washington, DC: Brookings Institution, 1998), 23–26, citing S. Holtzman, "Conflict-Induced Displacement through a Development Lens" (paper prepared for the Brookings Institution, May 1997).

[4]   These verses and thus the whole Moab section are sometimes read ironically, and thus as saying that Jerusalem is *not* obliged to admit the Moabite refugees; for a refutation of this interpretation and discussion of these oracles as an instruction to welcome refugees, in antiquity and today, see ASPRAY.

[5]   Korn notes that "the overwhelming majority of the internally displaced are women and their dependent children," as "men either join or are drafted into the fighting ranks of one side or the other, are killed or disabled, or flee to avoid recruitment": Korn, *Exodus within Borders*, 15; cf. Cohen and Deng, *Masses in Flight*, 42, 51, 60, 66. "Daughter of [place]" can also be used to refer to cities, especially the smaller ones of a region, so there may also here be an emphasis on the rural part of the population. This, too, would be consistent with the demographic realities of most displacements, in which the rural poor are disproportionately represented: Korn, *Exodus within Borders*, 15.

Although later parts of the chapter (Isa 16:6–7, 12–13) begin to blame the Moabites for their own distress – not an unusual strategy, even among the displaced themselves – the initial oracle adjures the Jerusalemites to provide shelter for the displaced Moabites.[6]

"Give counsel (ʿēṣâ),
 grant justice (pĕlîlâ);
make your shade like night
 at the height of noon;
hide the outcasts (niddāhîm),
 do not betray (glh) the fugitive (nōdēd);
let the outcasts of Moab settle (gwr) among you;
 be a refuge to them from the destroyer." (Isa 16:3–4)

Although the language employed is somewhat unusual – ʿēṣâ refers to advice or counsel, while pĕlîlâ is legal terminology – this oracle seems to invoke a legal and moral obligation on the part of the Jerusalemites to receive the outcasts who have been driven out of their homeland and are now arriving in Jerusalem as fugitives (nōdēd). A series of imperatives directed to the Jerusalemites and their city – the de facto equivalence of the former with the latter is apparent from the ambivalent textual tradition, which oscillates between feminine singular and masculine plural imperatives – make clear that among their obligations is not merely passively to allow the refugees to enter the city, but rather an active involvement in their protection and resettlement.

These instructions, especially the use of glh, suggests that the Jerusalemites should not be tempted to push the Moabites onwards to some other place of refuge; rather, they are to allow the Moabites to live alongside them indefinitely, as resident non-Israelites (gwr) – on the model, perhaps, of Zion's function for the Israelites themselves (Isa 14:32).

Elsewhere, Isaiah threatens the displacement of any peoples who displace the Israelites and Judahites – a view of the arc of history toward talionic (retributive) justice that anticipates the suffering wrought upon Israel being experienced in turn by those who inflicted it. Thus, Yhwh assures the audience that Assyria's apparent invincibility will someday end, and describes its eventual defeat as entailing not just death but displacement:

---

[6] On the narration of displacement as the result of collective sin, see Liisa Malkki, *Purity and Exile: Violence, Memory, and National Cosmology among Hutu Refugees in Tanzania* (London: University of Chicago Press, 1995).

'Then the Assyrian shall fall by a sword, not of mortals;
    and a sword, not of humans, shall devour him;
he shall flee from the sword,
    and his young men shall be put to forced labour.
His rock shall pass away in terror,
    and his officers desert the standard in panic,'
says Yhwh, whose fire is in Zion,
    and whose furnace is in Jerusalem. (Isa 31:8–9)

The oracle implies that there will be displacement as a result both of the fighting itself – "he shall flee from the sword ... his officers desert the standard in panic" – and in its aftermath – "his young men shall be put to forced labour."

A turn to the book of Jeremiah unpacks these and other, similar images in Isaiah; Jeremiah depicts conflict-induced displacements ranging from flight away from the path of an advancing army (Jer 6:1; 35:11; 40:11) or from a recently-surrendered city (Jer 39:4) to the forced displacement of survivors to distant lands where they are put to work for the empire (Jer 39:7; 41:17–18; 43:2–7; perhaps Jer 39:7–12 should be viewed in this light) (on Jeremiah see further CROUCH, 115–146).

The hope that the Babylonian perpetrators of those later displacements would in due course also experience the consequences of such policies is expressed obliquely in Second Isaiah's description of Babylonian deities being carried into exile by Babylonian deportees:

Bel bows down, Nebo stoops,
        their idols are on beasts and cattle;
    these things you carry are loaded
        as burdens on weary animals.
They stoop, they bow down together;
        they cannot save the burden,
        but themselves go into captivity. (Isa 46:1–2)

Not all the migrations of the nations are portrayed as punitive, however. There is also the more positive suggestion that a future kingdom of Yhwh will enable the free movement of peoples across traditional boundaries and borders, together with a greater degree of shared religious and cultural activity: "On that day there will be a highway from Egypt to Assyria, and the Assyrian will come into Egypt, and the Egyptian into Assyria, and the Egyptians will worship with the Assyrians" (Isa 19:23).

Migration to Jerusalem

Several passages – in addition to the oracle concerning Moab previously discussed – describe the migration of non-Israelites to Jerusalem, with a particular concern for the religious integration of these immigrants into the worship of Yhwh at Zion. Most of these passages derive from post-exilic parts of the book, reflecting the more international outlook occasioned by the displacements following Jerusalem's destruction. Thus Isa 2, which seems to have served as an introduction to the sixth-century edition of the book, depicts an idealized future in which the kingdom's capital is a welcoming host to foreigners motivated by religious reasons to leave their homes and come to Jerusalem:

> In days to come
>
>   the mountain of Yhwh's house
> shall be established as the highest of the mountains,
>   and shall be raised above the hills;
>   all the nations shall stream to it.
> Many peoples shall come and say,
> "Come, let us go up to the mountain of the LORD,
>   to the house of the God of Jacob;
> that he may teach us his ways
>   and that we may walk in his paths."
> For out of Zion shall go forth instruction,
>   and the word of Yhwh from Jerusalem. (Isa 2:2; cf. 45:14; 55:5)

Even more explicit is the famous passage with which Third Isaiah begins, in which the vision of Yahwistic community is expanded to include foreigners and eunuchs (Isa 56:3–8). Here again, the principal concern appears to be the religious integration of the immigrants: The foreigners in question will not merely be Yahwistic acolytes from afar, but present in Yhwh's temple on Zion, making acceptable offerings there in a sanctuary henceforth to be known as "a house of prayer for all peoples" (Isa 56:7, compare Isa 66:18–21 and perhaps Isa 18:7).

Although parts of Second and Third Isaiah connect the arrival of foreigners in Jerusalem with their role in the return of Yhwh's (traditional) people (Isa 14:1–2; 49:22; 60:3–14; 66:20), the wider picture indicates that this is not the end of the story. Rather, at least some of these envoys are envisioned as remaining in the city and integrating themselves into its culture and religious practice.[7]

---

[7]   On the greater likelihood of integration among migrants to urban destinations, see Malkki, *Purity and Exile*; Elizabeth Colson, "Forced Migration and

MIGRATION BY ISRAELITES AND JUDAHITES

When biblical scholars discuss migration in relation to Israel and Judah, they focus almost exclusively on the Babylonian Exile; indeed, by convention the terms "preexilic" and "postexilic" are taken to reflect a boundary in the year 586. However, not only was the "Babylonian Exile" itself a series of several deportations that occurred over more than a decade, but the threat and reality of such displacements were already familiar to the authors of the Hebrew Bible long before the sixth century, thanks especially to the Assyrian military conquest of Samaria in 721, which triggered the displacement of the inhabitants of the northern kingdom of Israel. From that perspective, it is not surprising that a number of earlier Isaianic passages already envisioned the possibility of Israelite migration.

Deportations Prior to "the Exile"

The oracle that refers to "daughter Zion" as "like a booth in a vineyard, like a shelter in a cucumber field" (Isa 1:8) is often thought to reflect the aftermath of Sennacherib's siege of Jerusalem in 701, when Judah's other major cities had been laid waste and much of the country's hinterland had been stripped from Jerusalem's control and given to Philistine rulers. Although the dating of the passage is sometimes disputed, it appears to allude obliquely to the deportation of a meaningful portion of the population in connection with these events, as it laments the survival in Judah of only "a few survivors (*šārîd*)" (Isa 1:9). Some of those who are no longer in Judah are undoubtedly dead, but others would have been deported by the Assyrian army. Sennacherib's account of the city's siege reports:

> (As for) Hezekiah of the land Judah, I surrounded (and) conquered forty-six of his fortified walled cities and small(er) settlements in their environs ... I brought out of them 200,150 people, young (and) old, male and female ... (Sennacherib 4 49–52)[8]

the Anthropological Response," *Journal of Refugee Studies* 16 (2003): 1–18; Mila Dragojevic, *The Politics of Social Ties: Immigrants in an Ethnic Homeland* (London: Routledge, 2014); Barbara E. Harrell-Bond, *Imposing Aid: Emergency Assistance to Refugees* (Oxford: Oxford University Press, 1986); Julie M. Peteet, *Landscape of Hope and Despair: Palestinian Refugee Camps*, The Ethnography of Political Violence Series (Philadelphia: University of Pennsylvania Press, 2011).

8   This and the following quotation from Sennacherib's inscriptions are from A. Kirk Grayson and Jamie Novotny, *The Royal Inscriptions of Sennacherib, King of Assyria (704–681 BC), Part 1*, RINAP 3/1 (University Park: Pennsylvania State University Press, 2012), here 65–66.

Sennacherib's claim that he deported 200,150 people is placed at this point in the account (here in the version inscribed on the Rassam Cylinder) to highlight Hezekiah's submission, and probably assimilates all deportees from this campaign into a single figure for rhetorical purposes.[9] That a significant number of persons were deported from Judah in connection with Hezekiah's surrender, even if not so many as this, is however quite likely. Indeed, the account goes on to provide a more specific reckoning of the persons who came from Judah to Assyria as a result of Hezekiah's surrender:

> He [Hezekiah] had the auxiliary forces (and) his elite troops ... together with his daughters, his palace women, male singers, (and) female singers brought into Nineveh ... (Sennacherib 4 55, 58)

This displacement is obviously coerced by Sennacherib's military offensive, though the annals present it as a voluntary tribute on the part of Hezekiah. And while the narrative account of the invasion included in the book of Isaiah is shaped from the perspective of a later time, this imperial gloss on the nature of forced displacement is reflected also in the Assyrian Rabshakeh's speech to the people gathered on the walls of Jerusalem, whom he invites in the name of the king of Assyria to

> Make your peace with me and come out to me; then everyone of you will eat from your own vine and your own fig tree and drink water from your own cistern, until I come and take you away to a land like your own land, a land of grain and wine, a land of bread and vineyards. (Isa 36:16–17)

It was typical of Assyrian imperial practice to prefer to induce surrender rather than bearing the costs of battle and siege. In a neat sleight of hand, the Rabshakeh elides the familiarity of home with the inevitability of displacement should the people surrender, as he tempts Jerusalem's defenders to give the city up: He promises that the place to which they would be exiled would be just as good as home. Isaiah ben Amoz's poetic oracles sought to ensure that his hearers would take off these rose-tinted glasses, by casting a spotlight on the harsher reality that awaited those who fell prey to the Assyrians' power.

---

[9]   On the use of numbers in the Assyrian royal inscriptions, see M. De Odorico, *The Use of Numbers and Quantifications in the Assyrian Royal Inscriptions*, SAAS 3 (Helsinki: Neo-Assyrian Text Corpus Project, 1995).

One focus of the Isaianic oracles is the impact of imperial deportation policies on those left behind. The term used in Isa 1 for the "survivors" (šārîd), for example, is suggestive of temporary flight in the face of battle or other life-threatening circumstances; it is a reminder that even those who were ultimately able to remain in their native land might experience temporary or internal displacement as a result of conflict.[10] A poem tracing the Assyrian army's advance on Jerusalem similarly foregrounds the chaos and upheaval triggered by military conflict:

> He has come to Aiath;
> he has passed through Migron,
>   at Michmash he stores his baggage;
> they have crossed over the pass,
>   at Geba they lodge for the night;
> Ramah trembles,
>   Gibeah of Saul has fled.
> Cry aloud, O daughter Gallim!
>   Listen, O Laishah!
>   Answer her, O Anathoth!
> Madmenah is in flight,
>   the inhabitants of Gebim flee for safety.
> This very day he will halt at Nob,
>   he will shake his fist
>   at the mount of daughter Zion,
>   the hill of Jerusalem. (Isa 10:28–32)

The consequences of the Assyrians' arrival for the capital city and its ruling elites are detailed in an extended oracle in Isa 3, which highlights the propensity of the imperial rulers of antiquity to focus their deportation efforts on those in positions of authority and others with the means to threaten to destabilize the imperial hegemon going forward. Among those to be deported from Jerusalem and Judah are

---

[10]   On the prevalence and consequences of internal displacement, see Cohen and Deng, *Masses in Flight*, and Korn, *Exodus within Borders*. On šārîd, see the lexica.
    The appearance of non-Israelites in Judah is also noted in this passage (Isa 1:7), although neither their identity nor the duration of their expected stay is explicit. Thus the "strangers devouring your land" may be Assyrians present to enforce imperial authority, or they may represent the Philistines who now control the Shephelah and who are perceived by the region's former rulers as interlopers. Either way, the comment is a further reminder of the pervasiveness of human mobility and movement in Israelite and Judahite experience.

warrior and soldier,
  judge and prophet,
  diviner and elder,
captain of fifty
  and dignitary,
counsellor and skilful magician
  and expert enchanter. (Isa 3:2)

Those left behind are then depicted as foundering in the absence of effective leaders, as social structures disintegrate – just as the empire intended (Isa 3:4–7). In keeping with Isaianic theology more broadly, the prophetic text identifies Yhwh as the immediate cause of this displacement (Isa 3:1), but the Assyrians lurk behind the scenes.

Ultimately, the Isaianic tradition favors those left behind after Sennacherib's invasion and related forced migrations. Indeed, it comes as something of a shock to those accustomed to the biblical rhetoric favoring those taken into exile in the sixth century to hear words of divine favor pronounced on those left in Judah after the occurrence of Sennacherib's deportations:

> On that day the branch of Yhwh shall be beautiful and glorious, and the fruit of the land shall be the pride and glory of the survivors of Israel. Whoever is left in Zion and remains in Jerusalem will be called holy, everyone who has been recorded for life in Jerusalem, once the Lord has washed away the filth of the daughters of Zion and cleansed the bloodstains of Jerusalem from its midst by a spirit of judgment and by a spirit of burning. (Isa 4:2–4; compare also Isa 37:30–32)

Although the oracle is not clearly tied to a specific historical event – and there has been extensive disagreement about these verses' unity and date – its explicit preference for those remaining in Jerusalem forms a stark contrast to the otherwise all but universal preference for those deported to Babylonia, and suggests that its origins lie in an earlier, monarchic era.

That deportation is viewed as a form of divine judgment already in the material associated with Isaiah ben Amoz is in any case quite clear. The failure of Jerusalem's leaders to prioritize Yhwh and the divine will over their own pleasure is the direct cause of the people's coming exile (*glh*) (Isa 5:11–13). Yhwh's summons to the Assyrian invader, elsewhere described as "the rod of [Yhwh's] anger" (Isa 10:5), depicts the empire as ravening young lions, who carry off the people like raw meat (Isa 5:26–30). Those who seek to elude Yhwh's punishment – for lack of faith and for failures of justice and righteousness – will try but find nowhere to flee (*nws*); their fate is captivity ('*ssîr*) or death (*hrg*) (Isa 10:1–5; 30:15–17; compare Isa 28:13). Beyond Judah's borders but worryingly near to hand, the fate of the Aramean-Israelite coalition threatening Ahaz of Judah will likewise be the desertion and despoliation of their lands, assured by Yhwh and achieved by the Assyrian hand (Isa 7:16–17; 8:3).

Aftereffects of the Babylonian Exile

Although commentators commonly declare that the Babylon Exile is absent from the book of Isaiah, multiple passages clearly refer to the sixth-century deportations initiated by the Babylonian conquest. (The entire latter half of the book, of course, as well as its final form, presupposes Jerusalem's fall and the displacement of much of its population to Babylonia; here our interest is in passages that more explicitly acknowledge these events.)

It is against the theology of deportation developed in the Neo-Assyrian period that the second half of the book grapples with the implications of the destruction of Jerusalem and the exile of its inhabitants by the Babylonians. It is true that these chapters address the realities of displacement less directly than those that originated in the monarchic era; it may be that the difficulty of speaking about traumatic experience is one reason for this reticence. Nevertheless, it would be inaccurate to say that the parts of the book originating after the Babylonian deportations proceed as though they did not happen; indeed, they acknowledge them quite explicitly, just not with great frequency.

Thus Zion, speaking as the mother of the Israelites, describes herself as having been "exiled and sent away" (*gōlâ we-sûrâ*; Isa 49:21). There is no divine denial of this recollection of the Babylonian deportations – unlike a few verses earlier, when Zion's claim that Yhwh had abandoned her is explicitly rejected (Isa 49:14–15). Continuing the tradition of personifying Israel as Yhwh's wife, the next chapter also recalls that she was "sent away," that is divorced (*šlḥ*; cf. Deut 24:1), on account of her sins. This is the same theology of deportation as appears in the older Isaianic traditions: for the people to be sent away from their homes and homeland is a sign of divine judgment. Although it does not spend a great deal of time describing the experience itself, the parts of Isaiah that originate after it do not ultimately contest this interpretation of events; rather, it acknowledges it, then turns to what Yhwh has planned for the future.[11]

---

[11]   Isa 52:3–5 is often translated in a way that suggests that the Israelites were oppressed without cause" (thus NRSV, for *bᵉ'epes* in v. 3 and for *ḥinnām* in v. 5)), that is, that they were unjustly punished; the point is rather that the punishment of Yhwh's people was undertaken for nothing, that is, it was not undertaken for payment.

The oracle concerning Cyrus explicitly acknowledges the deportations when it refers to the Persian king's task as to "set my exiles (*gālûtî*) free" (Isa 45:13). A difficult oracle in Isa 22 may also allude to the Babylonian deportations, or have reinterpreted an earlier oracle in light of them; it laments of Jerusalem that

> Your slain are not slain by the sword,
>   nor are they dead in battle.
> Your rulers have all fled (*ndd*) together;
>   they were captured without the use of a bow.
> All of you who were found were captured,
>   though they had fled (*brḥ*) far away. (Isa 22:2b–3).

This imagery is reminiscent of Jeremiah's description of Zedekiah's attempt to flee the city as it fell to the Babylonians, only to be captured and forcibly deported to Babylonia (Jer 39:4–7).[12]

Return Migrations

The prospect of return migration to Yehud by the descendants of those deported by the Babylonians in the sixth century was of understandably significant interest to Second and Third Isaiah. This theme has been more thoroughly discussed than other cases of migration in the book, and may briefly be summarized.

The famous summons to "Go out from Babylon! Flee (*brḥ*) from Chaldea!" (Isa 48:20) – echoed again in the imperative to "Depart (*swr*)! Depart (*swr*)! Go out from there!" (Isa 52:11) – is perhaps the most explicit call for the community in Babylonia to become return migrants, encouraging them to enter into a new phase in Israel's migrant history. Indeed, Second Isaiah's references to the return migration of Yhwh's people are cast within a network of allusions to Israel's past that foreground its earlier experiences of migration. Abraham and the rest of the ancestral family are described as having begun their relationship with Yhwh when the deity demanded that they leave their homes and migrate to a new land:

---

[12] The reference in Isa 22:6 to Elam and Kir has suggested to some interpreters that this oracle refers to the fall of Jerusalem in the sixth century rather than to events in the late eighth, insofar as the Elamites' involvement in the Babylonians' overpowering of the Assyrian empire is well known; the comment that "he has taken away the curtain (*māsak*) of Judah" (Isa 22:8) may also point to the destruction of the temple by Nebuchadnezzar. Ultimately, the text does not provide sufficient detail to determine definitively whether the oracle – curious also for its appearance among the oracles concerning the nations – refers to the fall of Jerusalem to the Babylonians, although if it does not, then the circumstances of the anonymous leaders' flight are unknown.

You, Israel, my servant,
  Jacob, whom I have chosen,
    the offspring of Abraham, my friend;
  you whom I took from the ends of the earth,
    and called from its farthest corners,
  saying to you, "You are my servant,
    I have chosen you and not cast you off." (Isa 41:8–9)

Later, Yhwh's people "went down into Egypt to reside there as migrants (gwr)" (Isa 52:4). The extent of the exodus allusions in Second Isaiah has been extensively debated, but where they appear they, too, invoke a version of Israelite history that foregrounds mobility and movement (Isa 43:2; 48:21; 51:10; 52:11–12; 63:9–14). Indeed, the Second Isaiah material begins with an image of Yhwh himself as a migrant, making his way through the wilderness in search of home (Isa 40:3; compare Isa 35:8–10, where similar imagery is used for the people's return, and other biblical traditions that depict Yhwh as a migrant, including Exod 13:21–22; 2 Sam 7:6; Ezek 11:22–25). Later, too, Yhwh is depicted as making the return migration to the Levant alongside the people (Isa 40:11; 43:5–6; compare Isa 42:16; 54:7). Elsewhere the servant is charged with bringing the people out of exile – metaphorized as prison and thus foregrounding its limited term – on Yhwh's behalf (Isa 42:6–7, compare Isa 49:5–6; 49:9).

There are, finally, a handful of passages that may be interpreted to refer to the return migrations of those displaced in the sixth century or as referring to the (actual, or simply hoped-for) return of earlier generations of forced migrants from Israel and Judah. Thus, in the midst of promises of divine recompense for Assyrian overreach comes a promise that "the remnant of Israel and the survivors (pělêṭâ) of the house of Jacob … the remnant of Jacob" will return (Isa 10:20–21). Soon after comes a long list of places to which Israelites and Judahites have been driven out (ndḥ) and scattered (pwṣ) and from which Yhwh now intends to gather them back, just as long ago he brought the Israelites out of Egypt:

> On that day the Lord will extend his hand yet a second time to recover the remnant that is left of his people, from Assyria, from Egypt, from Pathros, from Cush, from Elam, from Shinar, from Hamath, and from the coastlands of the sea.

> He will raise a signal for the nations,
>   and will assemble the outcasts of Israel,
> and gather the dispersed of Judah

from the four corners of the earth....
so there shall be a highway from Assyria
  for the remnant that is left of his people,
as there was for Israel
  when they came up from the land of Egypt. (Isa 11:11–12, 16)

CONCLUSIONS

Israel and Judah's long history of displacements lent these and other promises of being gathered back to the home land an enduring significance. From the origins of the Isaianic tradition in the eighth century to its final phases in the fifth or fourth, Yhwh's people were forced to reckon with the reality and persistence of migration. Long before the inhabitants of Jerusalem were forcibly deported to Babylonia – let alone the possibility that some of those deportees' descendants might make a return migration to the ancestral homeland – migration was a part of life.

Neo-Assyrian imperial expansion and policy brought deportation and forced migration well within the experience of the Levantine kingdoms; Hezekiah's rebellion brought their effects deep into the heart of Jerusalem, even into the royal palace. Displacement due to war and conflict was especially common, but could equally be caused by earthquake, famine, and other natural disasters. How to treat refugees from neighboring kingdoms was a live question, and parts of the book explore the possibility of welcoming non-Israelites into Jerusalem and involving them, to greater or lesser degrees, in Yahwistic worship. Throughout, Yhwh is considered the ultimate force behind these mass movements of the earth's human population: Yhwh is the divine king, capable of exercising policies of displacement that human monarchs could only dream of.

FURTHER READING

Ahn, John. *Exile as Forced Migrations: A Sociological, Literary, and Theological Approach on the Displacement and Resettlement of the Southern Kingdom of Judah*. BZAW 47. Berlin: De Gruyter, 2011.

Aspray, Barnabas. "'A Throne Will Be Established in Steadfast Love': Welcoming Refugees and the Davidic Kingdom in Isaiah 16:1–5." *Open Theology* 7 (2021): 426–444.

Berges, Ulrich. "'You Are My Witness and My Servant' (Isa 43:10): Exile and the Identity of the Servant." Pages 33–46 in *The Prophets Speak on Forced Migration*. Edited by Mark J. Boda, Frank R. Ames, John Ahn, and Mark Leuchter. Atlanta, GA: SBL, 2015.

Boda, Mark. "Familial Identity and Conflict through Forced Migration in Isaiah 49:14–66:24." Pages 79–98 in *Women and Exilic Identity in the Hebrew Bible*. Edited by Katherine E. Southwood and Martien A. Halverson-Taylor. LHBOTS 621. London: T&T Clark, 2018.

Crouch, C. L. *Israel and Judah Redefined*. SOTSMS. Cambridge: Cambridge University Press, 2021.

Cuéllar, Gregory. *Voices of Marginality: Exile and Return in Second Isaiah 40–55 and the Mexican Immigrant Experience*. New York: Peter Lang, 2008.

Gregory, Bradley C. "The Postexilic Exile in Third Isaiah: Isaiah 61:1–3 in Light of Second Temple Hermeneutics." *JBL* 126 (2007): 475–496.

Hägglund, Fredrick. *Isaiah 53 in the Light of Homecoming after Exile*. FAT II/31. Tübingen: Mohr Siebeck, 2008.

Halvorson-Taylor, Martien A. *Enduring Exile: The Metaphorization of Exile in the Hebrew Bible*. VTSup 41. Leiden: Brill, 2011.

Landy, Francis. "Exile in the Book of Isaiah." Pages 241–256 in *The Concept of Exile in Ancient Israel and its Historical Contexts*. Edited by Ehud Ben Zvi and Christoph Levin. BZAW 404. Berlin: De Gruyter, 2010.

Poulsen, Frederik. *The Black Hole in Isaiah: A Study of Exile As a Literary Theme*. FAT 125. Tübingen: Mohr Siebeck, 2018.

Rom-Shiloni, Dalit. "Exile in the Book of Isaiah." Pages 293–317 in *The Oxford Handbook of Isaiah*. Edited by Lena-Sofia Tiemeyer. Oxford: Oxford University Press, 2020.

Smith-Christopher, Daniel L. *A Biblical Theology of Exile*. Overtures to Biblical Theology. Minneapolis, MN: Fortress, 2002.

Terblanche, Marius D. "The Theme of the Babylonian Exile as Imprisonment in Isaiah 42:22 and Other Texts in Isaiah 40–55." *OTE* 21 (2008): 482–497.

Part III

Isaiah as Literature

12 Isaiah as Poetry

J. BLAKE COUEY

In most contemporary Bible translations, such as the Common English Bible (CEB) or New Jewish Publication Society (NJPS) or New Revised Standard Version (NRSV), much of the book of Isaiah appears on the page or screen as poetry. Instead of running continuously from margin to margin, the text is graphically broken into discrete lines. This layout usually follows critical editions of the Hebrew Bible such as the *Biblia Hebraica Stuttgartensia* (*BHS*). Although easily taken for granted, it represents a relatively recent development. The first English translation of Isaiah with graphic line breaks did not appear until 1778, in Robert Lowth's *Isaiah: A New Translation; With a Preliminary Dissertation and Notes, Critical, Philological, and Explanatory*. Lowth's lineation was not based on existing biblical manuscripts; rather, he divided lines based on prosodic principles he had outlined in his 1753 *Praelectiones Academicae de Sacra Poesi Hebraeorum* (*Lectures on the Sacred Poetry of the Hebrews*), which set the agenda for modern critical study of biblical poetry. Prophetic texts such as Isaiah do not receive special formatting in the medieval codices on which modern editions of the Hebrew Bible are based. Earlier biblical manuscripts from Qumran employ special formatting for some poetic books such as Psalms, but not Isaiah – with the sole exception of Isa 61:10–62:9 in the Great Isaiah Scroll (1QIsa^a), the rationale for which is unclear. Modern formatting norms for Isaiah reflect scholarly decisions made over the past three centuries, which raises the question of why it makes a difference to present the book in this way.

Poems operate by different conventions than narrative prose. The claim that Isaiah is poetry, even if only made implicitly through textual format, conditions readers to approach these texts in particular ways. It raises the expectation that these texts will share features with other poems, within and outside the Hebrew Bible. And it suggests that appreciating the texts' literary character is a necessary prerequisite to other avenues of inquiry into the book, be they historical, theological, ideological, or otherwise. This chapter works through some of these

implications for identifying Isaiah as poetry, engaging both its similarities to world poetry more broadly and its cultural and historical partic-
ularity as the product of first-millennium BCE Hebrew scribes.

Poetry is notoriously difficult to define, because no single description
adequately captures all of the distinctive features of the diverse body of
texts conventionally deemed poetic. At the same time, two recent definitions by literary critics provide a useful foundation for this discussion.
According to Burton Raffel, "Poetry is a disciplined, compact verbal utterance, in some more or less musical mode, dealing with aspects of internal
or external reality in some meaningful way" (RAFFEL: 1). Similarly, Terry
Eagleton proposes, "A poem is a fictional, verbally inventive moral statement in which it is the author, rather than the printer or word processor,
who decides where the lines should end" (EAGLETON: 25). Both critics
identify qualities of poetry from many times and cultures that also appear
in biblical poems. Building upon their definitions, the following discussion unpacks some important characteristics of Isaiah's poetry under the
broad categories of language, patterning, and imagination.

POETRY AND LANGUAGE

Both definitions include the word "verbal," highlighting the fact that
poems are made of words. Although seemingly obvious, this point offers
a starting point for thinking about Isaianic texts as poems – that is, as
carefully crafted lexical creations that exploit words for more than their
functional communicative value. The expansive vocabulary in Isaiah,
rivaled only by that in Job, reveals a palpable delight with language.
In addition to the synonymous lexical pairs common to much biblical
poetry, one finds word lists spanning multiple poetic lines: anatomi-
cal terms (30:27–30); precious stones (54:11–12); animal names (11:6–8;
13:21–22; 30:6–7; 34:13b–15); and tree names (41:19; 60:13). This item-
izing tendency reaches the limits of exhaustiveness in chapter 3, which
contains lists of sixteen types of political, military, and religious leaders
(vv. 2–3) and twenty-one types of jewelry (vv. 18–23). Contemporary
readers might regard these catalogues as tedious or uncreative, but for
their ancient scribal composers, they demonstrated an erudite mastery
of language. Across the book as a whole, Isaiah's biological lexicon is
particularly impressive, with several terms that appear only once in the
Hebrew Bible: five terms for lions (*ʾărî*, 38:13; *ʾaryēh*, 11:7; 31:4; etc.;
kəpîr, 5:29; 11:6; etc.; *lābî*, 5:29; 30:6; *layîš*, 30:6); six terms for snakes
(*ʾepʿeh*, 30:6, 59:5; *nāḥāš*, 14:29; 65:25; *peten*, 11:8; *ṣepaʿ*, 14:29; *ṣipʿônî*,
11:8; 59:5; *śārāp*, 14:29, 30:6); and at least eight terms for birds (*ʾōḥîm*,

13:21; *bənot ya'ănâ*, 13:21; 34:13; 43:20; *dayyôt*, 34:15; *'ayit*, 18:6; 46:11; *'ôp*, 16:2; 31:5; *'ōrēb*, 34:11; *ṣippôr*, 31:5; *qā'at*, 34:11). Additional rare animal names in the book can no longer be identified confidently, such as *qippôd* in 34:11 (NRSV "hedgehog"; CEB "crow"; NJPS "owl") and *qippôz* in 34:15 (NRSV "owl"; CEB, NJPS "snake"). Such use of rare terms is a hallmark of Isaiah. For instance, three words from the short poem in 5:1–7 appear nowhere else in the Bible: *bə'ūšîm* ("wild grapes," vv. 2, 4), *bātâ* ("waste," v. 6), and *miśpāḥ* ("bloodshed," v. 7). The last word may have been coined for this very poem as an ironic sonic counterpart to *mišpāṭ* ("justice"). In Isa 28:10 and 13, the nonsense words *ṣaw lāṣāw qaw lāqaw* (NRSV "line upon line, precept upon precept") are remarkably polyvalent, evoking the sounds of both infant babbling and foreign speech (compare *qaw-qaw* in 18:2), while also playing on the words *ṣō'â* ("excrement") and *qî'* ("vomit"), which appeared earlier in the poem (v. 8; NRSV "filthy vomit").

Words may be carefully selected to create sonic flourishes, demonstrating the poets' delight in the shape and feel of words beyond their semantic meaning. The first spoken words in Isaiah are alliterative: *šim'û šāmayim* ("Hear, O heavens," 1:2), one of many examples of sibilant (*s*-sound) repetition in the book:

> Do not rejoice (*tiśməḥî*), all you Philistines (*pəlešet*),
> that the rod (*šebeṭ*) that struck you is broken (*nišbar*),
> for from the root of the snake (*miššōreš nāḥāš*) will come forth
>   an adder (*yēṣē' ṣepa'*),
> and its fruit will be a flying fiery serpent (*śārap*). (14:29)

> You conceive chaff (*ḥăšaš*), you bring forth stubble (*qaš*);
> your breath is a fire ('*ēš*). (33:11; compare 5:24)

> They shall obtain joy and gladness (*śāśôn wəśimḥâ yaśśîgu*).
> (35:10; 51:11; compare 22:13, 51:3)

Isaianic soundplay often involves repetition of grammatical forms. A string of *niphal* verbs creates alliteration in 28:13: *wənîšbārû wənôqēšû wənilkādû*, "and be broken, and snared, and taken" (compare 8:15). Isaianic poets have a fondness for repeated syllables, a phenomenon known as reduplication that marks several Hebrew word patterns. Examples include *məṣapṣēp/təṣapṣēp/'ăṣapṣēp* ("chirp," 8:19; 10:14; 29:4; 38:14); *məṭalṭelkā ṭalṭēlâ* ("hurl away violently," 22:17); *pîpîyôt* ("teeth," 41:15); and *yəsaksēk/siksaktî* ("stir up," 9:10; 19:2). In a poem about the Cushites in Isa 18, a triad of reduplicated nouns (*ṣilṣal*, v. 1; *qaw-qaw*, v. 2; *zalzallîm*, v. 5) evokes the sounds of the Egyptian language, which

uses reduplication even more prominently than Hebrew (COUEY 2018).
In some cases, sound repetition calls attention to the content of poetic
lines, such as the use of *m* and *n* sounds to evoke the crashing of waves:

> They will roar (*wəyinhōm*) over it on that day (*bayyôm*)
> like the roaring of the sea (*kənahămat-yām*). (5:30)

> Ah, the thunder of many peoples (*hămôn ʿammîm rabbîm*),
> they thunder like the thundering of the sea (*kahămôt yammîm*
> *yehĕmāyûn*)! (17:12)

In other cases, sonic euphony simply serves the reader's or listener's
pleasure at the textured language and the poet's satisfaction at turning
a pretty phrase.

The use of double entendre throughout Isaiah further demonstrates
linguistic acumen (ROBERTS). Isa 28:14 denounces the "scoffers who
rule (*mōšəlê*) this people." Contextually, *mōšəlê* is most likely a form of
the verb *m-š-l* II "rule." Because these rulers are called "scoffers," however, an alternative derivation from *m-š-l* I "riddle, mock" is also possible. The double meaning underscores how Jerusalem's leaders deceive
their people through political doublespeak. In 19:4, Yhwh threatens to
"deliver (*sikkartî*) Egypt into the hand of a hard master." The NRSV
and other English translations take the verb *s-k-r* as a dialectical variant of *s-g-r* "hand over," which fits nicely with the next poetic line. As
Christopher B. Hays has argued, however, the more common meaning
of *s-g-r* also fits: "I will *stop up* Egypt by the hand of a harsh master."
The following verses, which describe the desiccation of the Nile River
and its environs, pick up on this sense of the word (HAYS). A poignant
example of paronomasia occurs in 46:4, in which God promises to care
for the audience in their old age. The word *śêbâ* "grey hair" is graphically and phonetically similar to *šibyâ* "captivity." (In the medieval
Hebrew manuscript Codex Leningrad, reproduced in *BHS*, the similarity is enhanced by the omission of the pointing that distinguishes the
letters *sin* and *shin*.) This wordplay creates an additional meaning for
the line, that God will also care for the implied audience of Judahite
exiles in their present state of oppression. Making the play more effective, the reader or hearer has already been conditioned for it by the use
of the related noun *šəbî* "captivity" earlier in the poem (v. 2).

Inventive use of language reaches an extreme in Isa 24, where word
choice and morphology combine to create some of the most sophisticated sonic effects in the Hebrew Bible. Consider the following (and
read the transliterated Hebrew aloud if possible):

hibbôq tibbôq hā'āreṣ
wəhibbôz tibbôz

The earth shall be utterly laid waste
and utterly despoiled. (v. 3a)

'ābêlâ nābəlâ hā'āreṣ

The earth dries up and withers. (v. 4a)

*rōaʿ hitrōʿăʿâ 'areṣ
pôr hitpôrərʿâ 'areṣ
môṭ hitmôṭəāâ 'areṣ

The earth is utterly broken,
the earth is torn asunder,
the earth is violently shaken. (v. 19, with slight emendations
   following WILLIAMSON: 5)

The relentless soundplay cannot be captured fully in translation,
although Alonso Schökel nicely proposes "the earth shivers and stag-
gers, stumbles and tumbles, quivers and quavers and quakes, jars and
jerks and jolts" for the last example (Alonso Schökel: 182). In the first
and third examples, the poet uses artificially modified morphology or
syntax to enhance the phonological repetition (WILLIAMSON: 2–3, 5).
These examples also illustrate how *'ereṣ* ("earth") serves as a keyword
in the poem. Root repetition is also prominent, including verbs with
cognate infinitives (vv. 3, 19, 20) and cognate accusatives (vv. 3, 22).
It reaches absurd proportions in verse 16b, a couplet in which all five
words are forms of *b-g-d* ("act treacherously"). Verse 17 threatens the
"inhabitant of the earth" with the alliterative triad *paḥad wāpaḥat
wāpaḥ* (Alter translates as "terror, trench, and trap," ALTER: 192, 274;
NRSV, "terror, and the pit, and the snare"). One of these terms
appears again in each of the next four lines in verse 18a, and the verb
niptāḥû ("opened") in verse 18b contains the same consonants as
"trench" (*paḥat*). In terms of its striking soundplays and likely artifi-
cial sound to native speakers of the language, one might compare the
chapter to the poetry of E. E. Cummings or Gerard Manley Hopkins
in English.

POETRY AND PATTERNING

Another characteristic of poetry, noted in the two definitions given here, is patterning. Poetry takes the everyday, arbitrary rhythms of spoken language and organizes them around perceptible principles that are, according to Raffel, "more or less musical." The most conspicuous feature of this patterning is the arrangement of words into lines. As Eagleton puts it, "The author ... decides where the lines should end." Despite the absence of marked lines in ancient manuscripts, comparisons to other biblical poems and attention to textual features make it possible to determine the lineation of most poems in Isaiah with relative confidence (COUEY 2015: 22–54; DOBBS-ALLSOPP: 29–94). Patterning is most noticeable between contiguous lines, which typically form pairs or couplets (COUEY 2015: 69–95; DOBBS-ALLSOPP: 43–57). Lines in couplets frequently share similar syntactic structures, with noticeable semantic overlap – a phenomenon commonly known as "parallelism," as in the two couplets of the following example:

> He shall judge between nations,
> and shall arbitrate for many peoples;
> they shall beat their swords into plowshares,
> and their spears into pruning hooks. (2:4)

Less commonly, two lines combine to form a single clause, with the second line containing a discrete syntactic element such as a prepositional phrase, vocative, or relative clause. Unlike a couplet with parallel lines, the first line feels incomplete without the second one. The term for such run-on syntax is "enjambment," illustrated by the following couplets:

> How you are fallen from heaven,
> O Day Star, son of Dawn!
> How you are cut down to the ground,
> you who laid the nations low! (14:12)

As in most biblical poetry, a striking feature of Isaiah's poetic lines is their terseness, which serves the oral performance and memorability of the poetry. On average, a line contains about three stresses and eight syllables, although the range goes as low as two stresses and four syllables or as high as six stresses and sixteen syllables. Unfortunately, the effect is seldom evident in English translation, in which more words are necessarily to approximate the content of a line. In Isa 3:13, for example, the NRSV uses thirteen words to translate a pair of three-word Hebrew lines:

niṣṣāb lārîb yhwh
wəʿōmēd lādîn ʿammîm

Yhwh rises to-argue-his-case;
he-stands to-judge the-peoples.

The added hyphens join the English words used to translate single Hebrew words.

Until about 150 years ago, the norm for English-language poetry was metrical verse, in which individual lines consistently contain a predetermined numbers of syllables and pattern of stresses, and lines are usually connected by a predictable rhyme scheme. Biblical poems do not operate within such strict constraints. Although line lengths fall within a narrow range, they vary at least slightly from line to line and across poems. Rhyme appears haphazardly, most often within the line. For these reasons, Isaianic poetry is best thought of as conservative free verse (COUEY 2015: 40–49; DOBBS-ALLSOPP: 99–114). It does not lack patterning, but the patterned features shift from one part of the poem to the next. Repetition with slight variation is the key organizational principle. Any repeatable aspect of the language may be incorporated into the pattern, including syntax, sound, and semantics. As noted earlier, syntactic parallelism is a dominant feature of Isaiah's poetry, but enjambed lines provide variation from this norm. The proportion of parallelism to enjambment can be a determinative characteristic of a particular poem's patterning. In 55:1–13, some 90 percent of the lines (forty-four of forty-seven) are parallel. The only nonparallel lines occur in a single triplet in v. 11a, which contains the poem's central theological claim. By contrast, half of the lines in 15:1–16:11 (forty-four of eighty-eight) are enjambed. Similarly, single lines and triplets offer periodic relief from the ubiquity of the couplet. In particular, triplets provide an effective form of terminal modification to mark the conclusions of poems (2:22; 14:32; 22:14; 63:6) (COUEY 2015: 67; compare ALTER: 40, and DOBBS-ALLSOPP: 128).

Verbal and syntactic repetition are frequent forms of patterning in Isaiah. Entire poems may be held together by keywords, such as the prophecy against Egypt in 19:1–15 ("Egypt"/"Egyptians" in vv. 1–4, 11–15; "Nile" in vv. 5–10). In smaller units of a poem, repetition can occur noticeably at the beginnings of lines, a device known as "anaphora." Runs of lines begin with the words "(and) against" in 2:12–16 or "spirit" in 11:2. Anaphora may alternate between the first and second lines of consecutive couplets, as in 2:7–8 ("their land is filled..." / "and

there is no end to…") or 65:13–15 ("my servants…" / "but you…"). In
other cases, repetition is more diffuse. In 46:1–7, a network of verbal rep-
etitions overlap across a short poem polemicizing Babylonian deities.
The root n-ś-ʾ ("lift," "bear") is the most important keyword, occurring in
verses 1, 3, 4, and 7. Other recurring roots, appearing in a variety of forms,
include k–r–ʿ ("bow down") in verses 1–2; m–l–ṭ ("save") in verses 2, 4;
s–b–l ("carry") in verses 4, 7; ʿ–m–s ("carry" or "bear") in verses 1, 3; ʿ–ś–h
("make") in verses 4, 6; and q–r–s ("stoop") in verses 1, 2. Reinforcing
the repetition, five of the seven roots have a sibilant consonant (s or ś)
and four have a guttural (ʾ or ʿ). The appearance of four of these terms in
verse 4, all with Yhwh as their subject, marks the poem's thematic cli-
max. Overlapping chains of synonyms are key to the structure of 59:1–15,
which uses six terms for ethical incorrectness in verses 2–13 ("iniquities," "sins," "lies," "wickedness" [translating two different Hebrew
words], "transgressions"); four terms for body parts ("hands," "fingers,"
"lips," "tongue") in v. 3; four terms for roadways ("highways," "way,"
"paths," "roads") in verses 7–8; and four terms for ethical correctness
("justice," "righteousness," "truth," "uprightness") in verses 8–15. The
repeated moral language reinforces the poem's central claim, that the
postexilic community's suffering results in part from its own sins.

In other cases, the repetition is more predictably organized. Terms
within one line group may be split and then repeated across subsequent
groups. An example in 24:17–18 was discussed in the preceding section;
another occurs in 59:5–6a:

> They hatch adders' <u>eggs</u>,
> and weave the spider's <u>web</u>.
> Whoever eats their <u>eggs</u> dies,
> and the crushed <u>egg</u> hatches out a viper.
> Their <u>webs</u> cannot serve as clothing;
> they cannot cover themselves with what they make.

In 28:15–18, an alternating arrangement of keywords or phrases – a pattern known as chiasm – creates an intricate pattern across nineteen
poetic lines:

> A We have made a <u>covenant with death,</u>
> and <u>with Sheol</u> we have an <u>agreement</u>. (v. 15a)
>
> B <u>When the overwhelming scourge passes through</u>
> it will not come to us. (v. 15b)
>
> C We have made <u>lies</u> our <u>refuge</u>,
> and in falsehood we have taken <u>shelter</u>. (v. 15b)

D Therefore thus says the Lord Yhwh,
"See, I am laying in Zion a foundation stone..." (vv. 16–17a)

C' Hail will sweep away the <u>refuge</u> of <u>lies</u>
and waters will overwhelm the <u>shelter</u>. (v. 17b)

A' Your <u>covenant with death</u> will be annulled,
and your <u>agreement with Sheol</u> will not stand. (v. 18a)

B' <u>When the overwhelming scourge passes through</u>
you will be beaten down by it. (v. 18b)

The poet resists total repetition by reversing the B' and A' elements, which allows the pattern to be extended further by the repetition of "pass through" in v. 19a.

These last examples involve semantic patterning, which is observable in translation. Poetic patterns can also be built from morphological or syntactic features, which are only fully perceivable in the Hebrew text. Consider a pair of couplets in 1:6b:

A But <u>bruises and sores</u>
B and bleeding <u>wounds</u>;

A' they have not been <u>drained</u>, or <u>bound up</u>,
B' or <u>softened</u> with oil.

"Bruises and sores" in A is the compound subject of the plural verbs "drained" and "bound up" in A', and the feminine singular form "bleeding wounds" in B is the subject of the feminine singular verb "softened" in B'. This subtle, interlocking syntax exemplifies the kinds of small- to medium-scale structures that appear across Isaiah's poems. In 44:24–28, a run of twenty lines is held together by eleven participles ("who" + verb) with Yhwh as the subject. In the next chapter, four consecutive lines end with first-person singular imperfect verbs, with three of the four in the *piel* stem (45:2). Lines with multiple verbs occur frequently in Second Isaiah, contributing to the corpus's distinctive energy. Clusters of such lines appear in 40:24–26, 28–31; 41:9–16; 46:4–8, 10–13; and 51:15–17. In a few cases, morphological or syntactic patterns run across entire poems. A preponderance of second-person, feminine singular verb forms and pronominal suffixes appears in 57:6–13, which is especially striking because these forms are uncommon in the mostly male-focused literature of the Hebrew Bible. In 52:1–11, six couplets (out of twenty-one line groups) have similar structures: one or more imperative verbs in the first line and a vocative in the second (v. 1a, 1b, 2a, 2b, 9a, 11b; cf. v. 11a).

In many poetic traditions, fixed forms such as the sonnet or villanelle control the shapes of whole poems. By contrast, there are few fixed forms in biblical poetry (DOBBS-ALLSOPP: 74–75). Most poetic genres identified in Isaiah by biblical scholars are content-based and distinctive to prophetic literature (e.g., judgment speeches, salvation oracles, admonitions), but several poems adapt genres from outside the prophetic corpus. Lament is the most common. A communal lament in 63:7–64:12 (Heb. 64:11) may be an independent composition that was later incorporated into Isaiah. Prophecies against Moab (Isa 15–16) and Tyre (Isa 23) feature many elements associated with city laments, although scholars debate whether these expressions of grief are genuine or sarcastic. Taunts against the king and city of Babylon (14:4b–21; 47:1–15) parody the lament genre. Hymnic language and forms appear throughout chapters 40–55. The song of the vineyard in 5:1–7 explicitly presents itself as a "love-song" (*širat dôdî*, v. 1). Beyond such generic conventions, most poems in Isaiah display some degree of thematic unity. Isa 3:1–15 coheres around the theme of failed leadership, even though it likely contains multiple originally separate units. Much of Isa 57 concerns illicit religious rituals, while Isa 58 focuses on approved rituals that are not accompanied by a concern for justice. In a smaller number of cases, formal devices known from other biblical poems create structural coherence. Repetition at the beginning and end of a poem, known as inclusio, occurs in 1:2–20, 1:21–26, and 3:1–15. Some interpreters argue that references to the divine word in 40:8 and 55:11 comprise a larger-scale inclusio bounding Isa 40–55 as a whole (but see the objections by HEFFELFINGER: 136–7). In Isa 2, a quasi-refrain appears at inconsistent intervals (vv. 10, 19, 21), although the precise wording varies and not all textual witnesses include all three occurrences. Isa 9:8 (Heb. 9:7)–10:4 has a more conventional stanzaic structure, with a repeated refrain occurring regularly after units of comparable length:

> For all this his anger has not turned away;
> his hand is stretched out still.

The same couplet appears in 5:25b, suggesting that this verse may have been part of an earlier version of the poem.

POETRY AND IMAGINATION

While awareness of poetic language and form enriches the reading of Isaiah, it is equally important to appreciate how the poetic character of these texts flavors their content. Recall that Eagleton describes poetry

as "a fictional ... moral statement," suggesting both that poems create
their own imaginative worlds and remain somehow true. Raffel similarly claims that poetry "deal[s] with internal or external reality in some
meaningful way," which means a poem need not correspond directly
to anything beyond itself, yet cannot be completely divorced from the
worlds outside it. Isaiah's poetry frequently revels in its historical par-
ticularity, especially in the first half of the book. Consider, for instance,
the lists of specific place names in 10:27–32 or 15:1–8, which form
poetic patterns that may also match the itineraries of historical military
campaigns. Historical-critical interpretation of Isaiah has illuminated
the meanings of many texts by situating them against the external geopolitical context of the ancient Near Eastern world. At the same time,
historical events or persons in Isaiah seldom stay within the bounds of
everyday reality (ALTER: 182–83, 188–89). In chapter 13, the poetry
moves nimbly between depictions of a divine army threatening the very
fabric of the universe (vv. 10–13) and a human army threatening the
historical city of Babylon (vv. 15–19), sometimes even within the same
lines (vv. 4–5). Similarly, references to King Cyrus of Persia appear in
41:2–3; 45:1–4, 13; and 46:11, but the poetic presentation of this figure
is hardly constrained by historical realia. He appears as "a bird of prey
from the east," who "delivers up nations to" the Judahite god Yhwh and
receives "the treasures of darkness" in return. These tensions between
fiction and truth, between imagination and reality, animate the poetry
of Isaiah and demand appreciation on their own terms.

The first poem in Isaiah opens with an apostrophe, a fictional
address to the personified entities "heaven" and "earth" (1:2). Through
this invocation, the very cosmos becomes party to the poetic indictment
of Israel's rebellion against God. Later, these same entities are invited to
rejoice aloud over Yhwh's redemption of the exiles from Babylon (44:23;
45:8; 49:13), along with other natural phenomena including mountains,
forests, and trees (44:23). The poetry brings creation to life and casts
it as a witness to divine speech and action. Literary theorist Jonathan
Culler explains the effects of such address:

> The hyperbolic demand that the universe hear you and act accord-
> ingly is a move by which speakers constitute themselves as sub-
> lime poets or as visionary: someone who can address Nature and
> to whom it might respond.... The impossible, hyperbolic impera-
> tives of apostrophes evoke poetic events, things that will be accom-
> plished, if they are accomplished at all, in the event of the poem.
> (CULLER: 76–77)

Poignantly, the invitation to respond with singing over promised restoration is extended to the "ruins of Jerusalem" in 52:9. By implying that
the rubble possesses some degree of agency, the poetry imaginatively
enacts the beginning of the city's restoration – a historical process that
would last centuries. Apostrophe also appears in oracles against foreign
nations, several of which address architectural, geographic, or commercial features of the nations to which they are targeted. Insofar as the
features stand in for the nation itself, these invocations combine the
poetic devices of apostrophe and metonymy:

> Wail, O gate; cry O city! (14:31)

> Ah, land of whirring wings beyond the rivers of Ethiopia.... (18:1)

> Wail, O ships of Tarshish! (23:1, 14; compare 23:10)

These apostrophes collapse the divide between the human and nonhuman realms, creating a vivid panoply in which inanimate features of
the landscape could come to life and burst into song or plaint at any
moment. This poetic boundary-breaking dramatically extends the
scope of God's action in the world and invites the audience to consider
the interconnectedness of ostensibly disparate realms of life.

Other poems more fully develop the personification implicit in apostrophe. The figure of Daughter Zion occupies an especially prominent
place in the book's second half. This personified woman is not a "character" of the sort one encounters in narrative or drama (HEFFELFINGER:
40, 45–51). She never achieves a full or consistent backstory, instead
shifting from one role to another: prostitute (1:21), divorced wife (49:14;
50:1; 62:4), bereaved mother (49:20–21), barren woman (49:21; 54:1),
enslaved woman (52:2–3), widow (54:4), newlywed bride (54:5; 62:5),
woman in labor (66:7–8), and nursemaid (66: 11). She lives within the
poetic text as a voice or object of address. Other cities come to life as
women as well, including Tyre (23:15–18) and Chaldea/Babylon (47:1–
15). The latter becomes a foil both to Yhwh and to Zion (contrast 47:8
with 44:6; 45:5–6 and 49:21; 54:4). Like 14:4–23, in which the king of
Babylon makes similarly hubristic boasts (vv. 13–14), the poem in 47:1–
15 triumphantly celebrates the humiliation of its addressee. While the
vengeful sentiments of an oppressed group are understandable and even
justifiable, the opposition of Zion and Babylon as personified women
unfortunately depicts liberation as a zero-sum game, with one woman's freedom from abuse seeming to demand another woman's subjec-
tion to it. In this way, although less problematic than those in Hosea
or Ezekiel, Isaiah's female personifications remain open to ideological

critique. Another personification, whose voice frequently alternates with that of Daughter Zion, is the enigmatic "servant of Yhwh" (42:1–4; 49:1–6; 50:4–9; 52:13–53:12). Disagreement over the identification over the figure – several dozen historical persons or biblical characters have been proposed – should encourage readers instead to understand him as a poetic construct, another voice in the book's lyric montage, who exists only within the poem and does not correspond completely to any external figure.

Biblical prophetic poetry uses metaphor extensively, and Isaiah is no exception. Metaphors map constitutive features from one concept onto a different one, although it may sometimes be difficult to determine precisely which elements are in play. Several metaphors recur across the book, although each specific instantiation should be appreciated for its own distinctiveness (COUEY 2015: 147–86). Divine judgment is frequently depicted as an agricultural process. For instance, God will destroy Israel and Judah like a disappointed vintner uproots an unproductive vineyard (5:1–7); the post-deportation population of Israel will be as negligible as scattered fruit left for gleaners in a harvested field or orchard (17:5–6; compare 24:13); and the blood of Edomite war casualties will stain God's robes as juice stains the clothes of grape-treaders (63:1–6). As Patricia K. Tull observes, plant metaphors like these effectively "tie human spiritual and societal health to environmental well-being" (TULL: 27). Some of these texts gesture to another recurring metaphor in the book, that of God as laborer. In addition to vintner, the deity appears as a silversmith (1:25), lumberjack (10:33–34), shepherd (40:11), stonemason (54:11–12), and potter 64:8 (Heb. 64:7). In a sarcastic twist on this metaphor, human defiance of God can be absurdly depicted as the rebellion of tools or products against their craftspersons (10:15; 29:16; 45:9). Yet another recurring metaphor in Isaiah compares people or nations to animals. The battle-cry of an advancing army is as terrifying as a lion's roar (5:29); the Assyrian king plunders subdued nations as easily as one collects eggs from an abandoned nest (10:14); and Israel's own rulers are blind but voracious dogs, lacking knowledge but endlessly exploiting their people's resources (56:10–11). All of these metaphors engage the audience's imagination and create meaning by juxtaposing normally unrelated conceptual domains.

To conclude this account of the imaginativeness of Isaiah's poetry, consider two evocative features of the poetic world created within the book. First, its scope is nearly boundless. Within a few lines, a single poem may soar

above the stars of God ...
to the tops of the clouds (14:13)

and then plummet
— down to Sheol,
to the depths of the pit. (14:15)

Invading armies come from the farthest expanses of earth (5:26) and heaven (13:5), while Israel and Judah's exiles are dispersed to and return from "the four corners of the earth" (11:12; compare 43:5–6; 60:4, 9). This expansiveness is especially on display in the second half of the book, where God creates and saves "the ends of the earth" (40:28; 45:22; 52:10) and God's actions are visible to "all flesh" (40:5). Names of distant locations recur throughout these chapters (43:3; 45:14; 66:19), especially the ubiquitous "coastlands" (41:1, 5; 49:1; 51:5; etc.). To preside over this practically limitless space, the poetry evokes a supersized deity growing ever larger and larger. In Isa 40, the divine hand contains the cosmic waters (v. 12), and the divine throne is "above the circle of the earth," whose "inhabitants are like grasshoppers" (v. 22). By the book's final chapter (66:1), the universe itself cannot contain the divine body:

Heaven is my throne
and the earth is my footstool.

This deity hardly needs a temple, unlike the divine body in the prose narrative of 6:1, which is larger than the first temple ("the hem of his robe filled the temple") but constrained by its architecture and iconography.

Within this boundless space, Isaianic landscapes undergo nearly constant transformation. Topographical variation is leveled in 40:3–4 to create "a highway for our God." In 2:2, by contrast, Zion becomes "established as the highest of the mountains" so that all nations may find their way to the holy city. Lush landscapes dry out and become fruitless (19:5–9; 32:13; 42:15), even as deserts bloom and become lush (29:17; 35:1–2, 7; 41:19–20; 43:19–20). Some poems hauntingly describe once-populous urban spaces that are devoid of humans and overrun by wild and exotic animals (5:17; 13:20–22; 32:14; 34:10–17); others celebrate the domestication of wild predators that now live peacefully with other animals and humans (11:6–9; 65:25); and yet another promises the removal of wild predators (35:9). Not surprisingly, human bodies inhabiting these changing landscapes similarly experience transformation (SCHIPPER: 330–33). In Isa 35:6, for example, lame bodies not only have their disability removed, but also become able to "leap like a deer," while the restored exiles of 40:31 receive the capacity to "mount up with wings like eagles," without the usual human limitations of physical exhaustion. The citizens of New Jerusalem enjoy dramatically length-ened lifespans in 65:20. In 66:7–8, Jerusalem's metaphorical female body gives birth instantly and painlessly. Although not completely discontin-uous with mundane experience, the poetic world of Isaiah is decidedly not the everyday world in which its readers and hearers live. The linguis-tic creation of this imaginative realm challenges its audience to expand their ideas about the meanings and possibilities of their own lives.

CONCLUSION

This discussion has demonstrated the ample presence of definitive fea-tures of poetry in Isaiah, including creative use of language, careful pat-terning of verbal and linguistic features, and sophisticated construction of imaginative discourse. Although recurring devices or motifs appear across the book, each individual poem operates according to its own organic principles, which are discovered in the act of reading or listen-ing and must be appreciated on their own terms. Because Isaiah consists almost entirely of poetry – with the partial exceptions of prose narratives in chapters 6–8 and 36–39 – attentive readers or listeners should adopt appropriate strategies for these texts. Attention to word choice, especially sound, is crucial; for this reason, it is best to read the poems aloud when-ever possible. Nonlinear development and ambiguity should be expected. The poetry demands engagement at both the intellectual and emotional levels. Although full aesthetic appreciation is only possible through close reading of the Hebrew text, careful readers of English translations can still perceive some of the repetition and creativity that characterize these poems. The book of Isaiah creates an imaginative universe that is both an extension of and a radical break with our own experiences. The similari-ties offer new insights into the meanings of our own lives and world, even as they challenge us to consider the possibility of their transformation. In this way, Isaianic poetry serves the quintessentially prophetic task of bringing to life a universe that, in the words of English poet Gerard Manley Hopkins, "is charged with the grandeur of God."

FURTHER READING

Alonso Schökel, Luis. "Isaiah." Pages 165–83 in *The Literary Guide to the Bible*, ed. Robert Alter and Frank Kermode. Cambridge, MA: Belknap Press of Harvard University Press, 1987.
Alter, Robert. *The Art of Biblical Poetry*. Rev. ed. New York: Basic Books, 2011.

Couey, J. Blake. "Poetry, Language, and Statecraft in Isaiah 18." Pages 167–83 in *Biblical Poetry and the Art of Close Reading*. Edited by J. Blake Couey and Elaine T. James. New York: Cambridge University Press, 2018.

Couey, J. Blake. *Reading the Poetry of First Isaiah: The Most Perfect Model of the Prophetic Poetry*. Oxford: Oxford University Press, 2015.

Culler, Jonathan. *Literary Theory: A Very Short Introduction*. Oxford: Oxford University Press, 1997.

Dobbs-Allsopp, F. W. *On Biblical Poetry*. New York: Oxford University Press, 2015.

Eagleton, Terry. *How to Read a Poem*. Oxford: Blackwell, 2007.

Hays, Christopher B. "Damming Egypt/Damning Egypt: The Parnomasia of *skr* and the Unity of Isa 19, 1–10." *ZAW* 120 (2008): 612–17.

Heffelfinger, Katie M. *I Am Large, I Contain Multitudes: Lyric Cohesion and Conflict in Second Isaiah*. BibleInt 105. Leiden: Brill, 2011.

Raffel, Burton. *How to Read a Poem*. New York: Meridian, 1984.

Roberts, J. J. M. "Double Entendre in First Isaiah." *CBQ* 54 (1992): 39–48.

Schipper, Jeremy. "Why Does Imagery of Disability Include Healing in Isaiah?" *JSOT* 39 (2015): 319–33.

Tull, Patricia K. "Persistent Vegetative States: People as Plants and Plants as People in Isaiah." Pages 17–34 in *The Desert Will Bloom: Poetic Visions in Isaiah*. Edited by A. Joseph Everson and Hyun Chul Paul Kim. Society of Biblical Literature Ancient Israel and its Literature 4. Atlanta, GA: Society of Biblical Literature, 2009.

Williamson, H. G. M. "Sound, Sense and Language in Isaiah 24–27." *JJS* 46 (1995): 1–9.

13 Isaiah in Intertextual Perspective

HYUN CHUL PAUL KIM

Arguably, the study of Isaiah has been the leading topic of scholarship on biblical intertextuality during the last decades of the twentieth century. Because intertextuality inspects the intricate interrelations of two or more texts, the book of Isaiah with its so-called "three Isaiahs," or three books, has become a natural place for intertextual studies to flourish. Intertextuality in Isaiah scholarship fits within two broad approaches: diachronic (inner-biblical exegesis) and synchronic (final form). Both approaches commonly start with key catchwords/catchphrases or lengthier passages, from either verbatim quotations or comparable language.

The present study is selective, given the abundance of important works. Primary questions on intertextuality in Isaiah concern the past (how did it all start?), present (what has transpired?), and future (where can it connect next)? Keeping these issues in view, we will explore pertinent studies of intertextuality: 1) within the book of Isaiah, both diachronic and synchronic; 2) between Isaiah and other parts of the Hebrew Bible; 3) between Isaiah and other ancient texts/worlds; and 4) between Isaiah and today's texts/worlds.

DIACHRONIC INTERTEXTUAL APPROACHES TO ISAIAH

Ironically, the study of intertextuality in Isaiah started with the identification of *differences* and disjunctions, as an extension of redaction criticism. While form criticism examines the unique genres and settings of delimited texts, redaction criticism investigates distinct editorial strands and rationales within a composition. Accordingly, scholars aim to discover how compositional differences or shifts reveal historical and thematic changes across different eras. For example, moving beyond the classic concern with the "original/authentic" words of the prophet Isaiah (e.g., the "Isaiah memoir" in Isa 6–8), scholars questioned what might have caused the redactional expansions, who would have been

behind them, and why. The overall outcome has been an awareness that
Isaiah is a collage or tapestry of various adaptations. However, scholarly
attempts to discover different "Isaiahs" and editorial layers often contributed to recognizing *similarities* or interconnections among editorial
hands. Hence the redactional movement gave birth to another one that
emphasized unity and intertextual methods.[1] Brevard Childs helped the
field to consider the validity of reading Isaiah *synchronically* as a whole
in its "final form" as canon, but Odil Hannes Steck was instrumental in
retrieving the redactional place and function of the entirety of the book
when read *diachronically*. Steck's proposal to read Isa 35 as a redactional "bridge" that joins the two halves of Isaiah sparked awareness
of the editorial roles of inner-biblical references or modifications.[2] Put
simply, Isaiah scholars have been persuaded to see lexical and thematic
correlations as different yet connected scribal markers for understanding the mosaic of a composite whole.

Much analysis has been devoted to the likely seams of the redactors
within the book of Isaiah as a connected whole. Marvin A. Sweeney
proposes reading Isa 1–4 as an introduction to the final form of Isaiah.[3]
Sweeney compiles numerous linguistic links between Isa 1 and Isa
65–66 (e.g., call to hear in 1:10//66:5; consuming fire in 1:30–31//66:24;
new moon and sabbath in 1:13–14//66:23; blood in 1:15//66:3; gardens
in 1:29//66:17) that reflect intentional editorial allusions in the fifth-
century BCE postexilic setting. Isa 2–4 similarly shows allusions to Isa
40–55 and 60–62 (as well as Haggai and Zach 1–8), pointing to a sixth-
century exilic setting. Read as a whole, the final form of the book connects the paradigmatic dots with emphasis on the Torah (1:10; 2:3; 5:24;
8:16, 20; 24:5; 30:9; 42:4, 21, 24; 51:4, 7).

W. A. M. Beuken's observations on the literary development
of the servant themes, as well as reading Isa 33 as a "mirror text"
(*Spiegeltext*), for the entire book of Isaiah have been influential.[4]
Advancing these insights, H. G. M. Williamson proposes that Deutero-
Isaiah was influenced by Isa 1–39 (e.g., the motif of blind and deaf in

---

[1]   Roy F. Melugin, "Isaiah 40–66 in Recent Research: The 'Unity' Movement," in
      Recent Research on the Major Prophets, ed. A. J. Hauser (Sheffield: Sheffield Phoenix,
      2008), 142–94.
[2]   Odil Hannes Steck, *Bereitete Heimkehr: Jesaja 35 als redaktionelle Brücke zwischen
      dem Ersten und Zweiten Jesaja*, SBS 121 (Stuttgart: Katholisches Bibelwerk, 1985). See
      also Claire R. Mathews, *Defending Zion: Edom's Desolation and Jacob's Restoration
      (Isaiah 34–35) in Context*, BZAW 236 (Berlin: de Gruyter, 1995).
[3]   Marvin A. Sweeney, *Isaiah 1–4 and the Post-Exilic Understanding of the Isaianic
      Tradition*, BZAW 171 (Berlin; de Gruyter, 1988).
[4]   W. A. M. Beuken, "Jesaja 33 als Spiegeltext im Jesajabuch," *ETL* 67 (1991): 5–35.

6:9–10//42:18–20//43:8; potter in 29:15–16//45:9; signal in 5:26//49:22; sealed tablet and hidden face in 8:16–18//30:8//50:4–9//54:8). He argues that the editor of Deutero-Isaiah glossed and reformulated essential portions of Isa 1–39 toward an overall holistic compilation. Select examples of Deutero-Isaianic interconnecting catchphrases include, for example, "the house of Jacob" (2:5//46:3; 48:11) with "walking in the light" (2:5//50:10–11); "roaring of the sea" (5:30//51:15); "the former" and "the latter" (8:23 [ET 9:1]//41:22; 43:18–19); "highway" from Egypt/Assyria (11:11–16//40:3; 49:11; 52:4); hymn for "comfort" (12:1–6//49:13; 51:3; 52:9); divine "compassion" over hard service (14:1–4a//54:8, 10; 55:7); and pardoning of the "iniquity" (33:24//40:2) together with the motif of "tent" (33:20//54:2).[5]

Williamson's students have developed his thesis of Deutero-Isaiah's redactional role. Jacob Stromberg analyzes the inner-biblical markers that characterize the final compositional role of Trito-Isaiah. Isa 61:1–3 showcases a diachronic intertextuality, in that the literary and thematic kernels of Isa 60–62 are drawn from Deutero-Isaiah. Stromberg lays out key interrelated passages and pertinent themes: the Holy One of Israel glorifying Zion (55:5//60:9); the literary blending of "reward" (40:10) and "eternal covenant" (55:3) in 61:8 (cf. 62:11); the divine spirit upon the servant in the third-person, "I have put my spirit upon *him*" (42:1; cf. 11:1–2), now reported in the first-person, "the spirt of Yhwh God is upon *me*" (62:1); the literary combination of "sending" (6:8//61:1) and "anointing" (45:1//61:1) – thereby the servant takes over the royal role from Cyrus; the rebuilding of Judah's desolate ruins (44:26//61:4); the task of "opening" the "prisoners" (42:6–7//61:1); the task of "proclaiming" the "release" (40:2–6//61:1–2); and the task of "comforting" (40:1) the "faint of spirit" (42:3//61:2–3). In addition, Isa 61:1–3 as a part of the earliest core (Isa 60–62) of Trito-Isaiah demonstrates further later editorial development: "those who mourn over Zion" (61:2–3; cf. 60:20) are redefined as the righteous mourners for Jerusalem, as opposed to the wicked (66:10); the unconditional promise of the arrival of "light" (60:1) is made conditional on the obedience of "light" over the sin of darkness (58:10; 59:9); and the exclusive servitude of "strangers" and "foreigners" (61:5–6) is redeveloped into more inclusive consideration of foreigners (56:1–8).[6]

---

[5] H. G. M. Williamson, *The Book Called Isaiah: Deutero-Isaiah's Role in Composition and Redaction* (Oxford: Clarendon, 1994).

[6] Jacob Stromberg, "An Inner-Isaianic Reading of Isaiah 61:1–3," in *Interpreting Isaiah: Issues and Approaches*, ed. David G. Firth and H. G. M. Williamson (Downers Grove, IL: IVP Academic, 2009), 260–72.

Jongkyung Lee, another student of Williamson's, retrieves the concatenation of catchphrases in Isa 13–23: texts condemning the tyrannical nations (14:16–17; 19:16–17; 23:8–9, 11) and texts with inclusive motifs toward foreign nations (14:1–2, 32b; 18:7; 16:1–4a).[7] Lee considers these interrelated texts to have been edited by the same circle of writers responsible for Isa 40–55 during the late-exilic period. These texts also interconnect with the comparably edited texts with the same universal theology toward foreign nations (2:2–4; 25:6–8; 42:1–4, 6, 7; 45:22–23; 49:5; 51:4–5; 56:3, 6–8; 60:3, 9; 61:6; [62:2]; 66:18–24).

J. Todd Hibbard's intertextual study on Isa 24–27 focuses on the consistent patterns and themes Isa 24–27 employs in its shaping of the later compositional stages of the book overall. Picking up from the previous intertextual analyses of Isa 24–27 by Brian Doyle and Donald Polaski, Hibbard examines the pertinent passages echoed in Isa 24–27 and elucidates the rationales of intertextual reuses in light of different settings. Take the case of 27:2–13. First, 27:2–6 contains explicit intertextual connections, alluding to the vineyard song in 5:1–7. Numerous catchwords and motifs recur in reversal, such as a "pleasant vineyard" (5:7//27:2), "thorns and briers" (5:6//27:4), and the motif of rain/water (5:6//27:3). Whereas in 5:5 Yhwh describes breaking down the vineyard of bad grapes, in 27:3 Yhwh vows to guard it. Whereas Israel and Judah are condemned of bloodshed and outcry (5:7), in future days Jacob-Israel is assured that they will blossom with ample fruit (27:6). In light of these intertextual allusions, Hibbard highlights a theme around divine intentions in Yhwh's changed attitude from judgment (Isa 5) to mercy (Isa 27) toward the vineyard.

Furthermore, 27:7–13 displays intertextual connections to 17:1–11 and 11:10–16. Key catchwords – such as "abandoned," "gather," "(fortified) cities" (17:1–3, 9//27:10), as well as "altars" and "sacred poles" (17:7–8//27:9) – correlate Isa 27 to Isa 17. Borrowing imagery and themes from Isa 17, in reversed fashion, 27:7–13 addresses the reality of destruction (from the language of future salvation in Isa 17) and hope of reconciliation (from the language of judgment in Isa 17). Likewise, Isa 27 adopts the language and imagery from 11:10–16, including the "root" (11:10//27:6), the return of the "outcasts" (11:12//27:13), and the (mythological) entities of the sea, Egypt, and Assyria (11:11, 15–16//27:1, 12–13). These interconnections reclaim the common theme of the

---

[7] Jongkyung Lee, *A Redactional Study of the Book of Isaiah 13–23* (Oxford: Oxford University Press, 2018).

return of the diaspora, but again with contextual reapplication and conceptual modification. Thus, whereas Isa 11 projects the theme of return with the restoration of the Davidic leadership ("root" of Jesse), Isa 27 modifies the "root" with (collective) Jacob instead and emphasizes the kingship of God. Rather than the political, national unity in Isa 11, Isa 27 underscores the cultic aspects of the return, thereby opening the door to include non-Jews – a tendency in tune with the universalizing themes elsewhere in Isa 24–27.[8]

SYNCHRONIC INTERTEXTUAL APPROACHES TO ISAIAH

While works on the *diachronic* inner-biblical exegesis have provided invaluable observations on the compositional stages and relationships in Isaiah, more *synchronic* studies tracing and assessing key linguistic or thematic "threads" have produced equally important insights. Ronald E. Clements' many publications break ground in identifying, tracing, and interpreting key motifs – especially those of "light" and "darkness" – as thematic threads that weave through diverse parts of the book. J. J. M. Roberts likewise has presented the "Zion" tradition and its Davidic ideology as another major theological fulcrum for Isaiah. We should still note that in the works of these scholars, as well as those reviewed later, explications of thematic threads inevitably involve both diachronic and synchronic modes.

The House of David

Among many notable monographs in subsequent generations, Dominique Janthial proposes reading the book of Isaiah through the guiding motif of the "house of David" influenced by the oracle of Nathan (2 Sam 7). Building on redactional and synchronic methods, Janthial employs a reader-oriented approach of the (ancient) implied readers to locate the royal dynasty and temple as a *"fil rouge"* ("red thread") that runs through the book, wrestling with the question of whether Yhwh would remain faithful to the covenant given to the Davidic house. Isa 1:1–2:5 (the "porch" of the book of Isaiah as in a house or temple) presents an "inaugural panorama" concerning the punishment of the once "faithful city" Zion (1:21) in the past tense and the reconstruction of the "faithful city" (1:26) in the future tense. Isa 2:6–12:6 ("narthex" in the house/temple) then presents the prophet's message not only of purging

---

[8] J. Todd Hibbard, *Intertextuality in Isaiah 24–27: The Reuse and Evocation of Earlier Texts and Traditions*, FAT 2/16 (Tübingen: Mohr Siebeck, 2006), 176–209.

or emptying the "house" of Yhwh (Isa 6) and the "house" of Ahaz (Isa 7) that are devoid of justice, but also of hope for the resurgence of the house of Jesse/dynasty and Zion/temple (Isa 9–10). Isa 13–23 ("nave") depicts the threefold themes of imprisonment, emptiness, and rebuilding of the house, culminating in the fall of the Jerusalemite house (Isa 22) as well as the offspring's/implied readers' pilgrimage to the house of Yhwh (Isa 23), concordant with the vision of the nation's pilgrimage to the house of Yhwh (2:2–4). Isa 24–33 further describes the collapse of many houses or palaces (23:1; 24:10; 32:14), as the prophet's "woe" concerning the people of unclean lips (6:5) correlates to the "woe" concerning the treachery from the ends of the earth (24:16). Yet this oracle also pronounces the cornerstone in Zion (28:16) for the reestablished house of Jacob (29:22–23).

Next, in Isa 34–46, the architectural hinge with the report of human frailty in the "house" of Hezekiah (Isa 36–39) opens the door for salvific restoration after the demise of the dynasty through the servant Israel (Isa 40–46). The final compartment (Isa 47–66) reasserts the divine promise of Nathan's oracle but now reconceptualizes the house of David with the house of Jacob-Israel the servant as "democratic dynasty," and daughter Zion as "prophetic temple." This new era will bring about the demolition of Babylon (Isa 46–47), the commissioning of the servant (Isa 48–53), and the reconstruction of Zion as the "house" of prayer for all peoples (Isa 54–56). The concluding passages echo the divine question to the Davidic dynasty, "What is the house that you would build for me?" (66:1; cf. 2 Sam 7:5), while bookending the opening chastisement of the rebellious children (Isa 1–2) with the closing assurance of renewal of the covenant for the righteous offspring of the servant (Isa 65–66).[9]

Hardening

Torsten Uhlig investigates the theme of "hardening" as a central thread for the book of Isaiah. Employing the two lenses of "illocutionary" acts (which the prophet performs) and "perlocutionary" effect (resulting from those acts) via speech-act theory and rhetorical analysis, Uhlig detects the progress and implications of the theme of hardening. This theme is inherently associated with the dual issues of sin and righteousness. These issues unveil the people's deeds and consequences that unfold through the proclamation of hardening (Isa 6), the consequential

---

9   Dominique Janthial, *L'oracle de Nathan et l'unité du livre d'Isaïe*, BZAW 343 (Berlin: de Gruyter, 2004).

judgment (Isa 7–39), and the overcoming of hardening both for the exiles (Isa 40–55) and for those in Judah (Isa 56–66).

In Isa 6, we find the foundational vision for hardening "this people" in the prophet's illocutionary act (6:9b) and its perlocutionary effect (6:10). In the deed–consequence connection, the people's perverted attitude (seeing and hearing) and acts of sin fall back upon them, illustrated through gradual prolongation in Isa 7–39. Accordingly, the editors combined Isa 1–39, the prophetic message of hardening, with Isa 40–66 to imply to readers that this message would still be effective for them. Within Isa 40–66, the first half (Isa 40–55) is addressed to the exiles in Babylon. In 42:14–44:23, despite their call to be Yhwh's servant (42:1–9), these addressees reveal their present conditions of both hardness (42:18–25) and sin (43:16–28), entailing their refinement (43:8–13; 44:6–9). Next, in 44:24–49:13, their obduracy is linked to their being sinners "from the womb" (Isa 48:1–11), the theme that guides the communicative progress of Isa 40–49. Yet after this stage, with "new things" revealed (48:16), the audience is summoned to leave Babylon (48:20–21). Then, in 49:14–55:13, reluctant to leave Babylon (50:1–3), the addressees are admonished to listen to the mediating voice of the servant (51:1–8). The prophet presents solutions for overcoming their hardening (50:4–9) through the vicarious suffering and death of the servant (52:13–53:12). Once the exiles in Babylon are transformed, they can fulfill their role as Yhwh's witnesses and servants (54:17) in their return to Zion (55:1–13).

The second half (Isa 56–66) within Isa 40–66 concerns the people in Judah. In 56:9–59:21, the prophet prescribes the same "dehardening" process, except that whereas the exiles' hardness denotes their sinful relationship to Yhwh in 40–55, the prophet defines the hardness of those in Judah in 56–66 through their wrongdoings to one another within the community (56:9–57:2). By removing the stumbling block, acknowledging their blindness, and confessing their sins, the people in Judah can also reenact righteousness (58:1–59:21). Next, in 63:7–64:11, unlike the common view that the communal lament here describes the later generation's frustration over the unfulfilled prophecies of Isa 40–55, Uhlig contends that this passage portrays the utterance of those who are unaffected by the preceding oracles of Isa 40:1–63:6 and thus still remain hardened. Finally, in 65:1–66:24, Yhwh's reply affirms those who "tremble" at the divine word (65:12; 66:2, 5) but condemns those who refuse to obey (65:13–16). Therefore, the theme of hardening as a complex concept plays a significant role in the entire book of Isaiah, presenting the dehardening process as a reformulation of the identity of

the people as Yhwh's transformed servants (for the themes of "the righteous versus the wicked," see also WEGNER).[10]

Eating and Drinking

Andrew T. Abernethy unearths and tracks the theme of "eating and
drinking" as a seam that interconnects the book of Isaiah.[11] The motif
of food, which has diverse sociocultural backgrounds and hermeneutical ramifications, functions as an interpretive axiom in Abernethy's
sequential–synchronic reading. Accordingly, the theme of meals in Isa
1 serves as a hermeneutical guide for the whole book of Isaiah: Even animals such as oxen know the owner's "feeding-trough" while Israel does
not know (1:3); foreign invaders will "eat" off the conquered land (1:7);
Yhwh is "fed up" with the corrupt sacrificial meals (1:11); and, climac-
tically, there is a call for repentance ("if you consent and obey, you will
eat the good of the land"; 1:19) and Yhwh's sovereignty ("if you reject
and rebel, you will be eaten by the sword"; 1:20).

Isa 2–35 follows through the theme as the messages of "food dep-
rivation and provision aptly introduce the concepts of judgment and
restoration."[12] For example, the prophet castigates the corrupt leaders
for their agricultural abuse (5:8–10), the Assyrian oppressors will fall
by the sword (31:8), and the sinners in Zion must repent before the
devouring fire (33:14). The penitent who return to God are promised
plentiful food (23:18; 33:16). This "imperial-retributive" schema culminates in worldwide vine depletion as punishment for sin (24:7–11) and
the replenishing banquet as reward for the obedient (25:6–8), together
accentuating that Yhwh, not the imperial ruler, is the true sovereign of
the world. This polemical theme continues in Isa 36–39, depicting Yhwh
as the provider of food and safety (Isa 36:12, 16–17; 37:30). Similarly,
in Isa 40–55, over against other idols or gods, Yhwh is announced as
God who will guide the people to waters and grazing places (41:17–20;
43:16–21; 44:3; 48:20–21; 49:8–10). Analogous to the banquet motif in
Isa 25, Deutero-Isaianic oracles culminate in Isa 55 with the imagery of
Yhwh as the street merchant "calling on the audience to eat and drink"
for nothing (55:1–3). Finally, the food motif continues in Isa 56–66,
ensuring Zion's descendants sufficient nursing (60:16) and tender care
(66:11–13). Trito-Isaiah condemns the devious practices of pagan eating

---

[10]   Torsten Uhlig, *The Theme of Hardening in the Book of Isaiah: An Analysis of
       Communicative Action*, FAT 2/39 (Tübingen: Mohr Siebeck, 2009).
[11]   Andrew T. Abernethy, *Eating in Isaiah: Approaching the Role of Food and Drink in
       Isaiah's Structure and Message* (Leiden: Brill, 2014).
[12]   Abernethy, *Eating in Isaiah*, 92–93.

(65:3–4, 11; 66:3, 17), while promising the righteous servants sustaining food and drink (58:11, 14; 62:8–9; 65:8, 13, 21–22).

Agrarianism

Daniel J. Stulac introduces an "agrarian hermeneutic" to assess expressions related to ancient Israel's subsistence culture and to explore the implications for reading Isaiah as a whole. For this purpose, Stulac analyzes Isa 28–35, again on matters of "food and drink" through an agroecological lens, with the overarching thesis that "through the language of agrarian wisdom, Isa 28–35 issues a call to obedience that transports the reader from reflections on historical destruction (chs. 1–27) into a holistic vision of ultimate hope (chs. 36–66)."[13] First, Stulac employs an agrarian-rhetorical analysis on Isa 28 by way of the contrast between the exorbitant consumption of insolent drunkards (28:1–22) and the diligent responsibility of the wise farmer (28:23–29). Opposite the dismissal of the inebriated leaders via their land abuse and overconsumption of agricultural commodities, the farmer's parable (28:23–29) accentuates the validity of the divine "plan" (28:29) intimately associated with responsible land use and food distribution. In fact, Stulac considers this parable as an agrarian-rhetorical "axis" for the transition from Isa 1–27 to Isa 36–66.

Concerning the interrelations with the foregoing passages, Stulac discerns many examples rooted in an agrarian context, for example, "ox and donkey" (1:2–3), eating the good of the "land" (1:19–20), "swords into ploughshares" (2:2–4), the song of the "vineyard" (5:1–7), the "soil" (6:11–13), eating "curds and honey" (7:15, 22–23), "devouring" fire (9:11, 17–19 [ET 9:12, 18–20]; 10:17), failed harvest linked to the demolition of the nations' chaos towns and fields (14:22–26, 30; 15:5–7; 16:8; 17:5–6; 18:5; 19:5–10; 23:3, 10), and the culminating collapse of chaos cities into piles (24:4–7; 25:2; 26:5–6). All in all, connected to Isa 1–27 through agrarian motifs, the recalcitrant drunkards versus the farmer's parable in Isa 28 links the past history to the present admonition for the implied audience to be obedient to Yhwh's Torah, which "goes forth" from Zion (2:3//26:21//28:29). Just as the vineyard song shifts from destruction to protection (5:1–7//27:2–6), so Torah obedience joins the nations that beat their "spears into pruning hooks" (2:2–4) with the trustworthy farmer allocating food and drink (28:23–29).

In the subsequent passages of the woe-oracles (Isa 29–35), the historical trajectory of destruction and renewal continues with emphasis

---

[13] Daniel J. Stulac, *History and Hope: The Agrarian Wisdom of Isaiah 28–35*, Siphrut 24 (University Park, PA: Eisenbrauns, 2018), 53.

on the salvific location of Zion (29:17; 32:15; 33:13–16; 35:8–10) and
the creaturely reliance on Yhwh (30:20–24; 32:9–20; 33:2–6, 17–24).
Likewise, within the second-half of the book (Isa 36–66), the agroecological rhetoric finds intrinsic intertextual flow, from Yhwh's land
protection and sustenance in Isa 36–39 (e.g., 37:30–32) into Yhwh's recre-
ative restoration of land and people together in Isa 40–55 (e.g., 41:17–
19; 43:19; 44:3–5; 51:3; 55:10) and finally toward the farmer-disciples'
obedient communal "feeding" on hope in Isa 56–66 (e.g., 58:7–11, 14;
60:16; 61:6–7; 62:8–9; 65:17–25).

Family and Household

Brittany Kim expounds "household" metaphors as key threads in interpreting Isaiah as a complex yet coherent whole. Employing metaphor
theory and rhetorical criticism, Kim examines five metaphors for the
people of Israel and city – "sons/children, daughter(s), mother, wife, and
servant(s)" – along with Yhwh, with regard to their places and functions
in sequential progress throughout the book.[14] First, the study highlights
the presentation of the people of Israel either as "children of Yhwh" or
as "sons of Zion." The opening and closing portrayals of the people of
Israel as Yhwh's wayward children (1:2–4) and the consoled children
(66:13) bracket the entire book, with the prominent themes of parental chastisement and compassion respectively. Traversing through the
book, Kim observes that the metaphor of the "children of Yhwh" dominates in Isa 1–45, while that of the "children of Zion" occurs more
frequently in Isa 49–66. Whereas the description of the "children of
Yhwh" is more negative, coinciding with their rebellion (1:2–4; 30:1, 9;
45:11), the "children of Zion" is depicted mostly positively, in reference
to their close-knit familial union via divine mercy (49:17–25; 50:1; 54:1,
13; 57:3; 60:4–9; 66:7–12).

Second, the city Zion and its people also receive the expression
"daughter(s)." "Daughter Zion" in the appositive phraseology exposes
her vulnerability as a city destroyed and violated (1:8; 10:32; 37:22),
while also evoking divine compassion for her ultimate revival (49:15;
52:2; 62:11). Similarly, the women of Zion being referred to as "daughters of Zion" depict their defilement (3:16–17; 4:3–6), eventually with
the hope of renewal and return (49:22; 60:4). Third, Zion occurs numer-
ously as "mother" of the people of Israel as well as Yhwh's "wife."

---

14   Brittany Kim, *"Lengthen Your Tent-Cords": The Metaphorical World of Israel's
      Household in the Book of Isaiah*, Siphrut 23 (University Park, PA: Eisenbrauns, 2018),
      1, 180.

Against the backdrop of exile, Zion as "mother" is depicted with the incapacity to give birth (37:3), bereavement (49:21), barrenness (54:1), desertion (50:1), devastation (51:18–20), or adultery (57:3), though she is assured of return (60:4–9) and rebirth (54:2–3; 66:7–9). Parallel to the dramatic progress from loss (49:17–25) to birth of children (66:7–14), the marriage metaphor of Zion as Yhwh's "wife" displays a thematic development from spousal abandonment (54:6–8; 57:7–13) to marital reunion (54:10; 62:5).[15] Finally, as legal household members, the "servant(s)" – in alternating correlations with Zion – connect the thematic development from blindness (42:18–19) to bearing witnesses (43:10–12; 44:8, 21) and eventually to making many/all righteous (53:11; 65:8–9; 66:14, 20–21). Therefore, this approach elucidates how key metaphors function independently and uniquely as well as how they present complicated yet coherent thematic progress through concatenated intertextuality within the book.

Exile

Exile has become a significant topic in recent Isaiah scholarship. Following notable works on the compositional and sociological aspects of exile in Isaiah (e.g., Ulrich Berges, Lena-Sofia Tiemeyer, Martien Halvorson-Taylor), Frederik Poulsen expounds *"exile"* as a "black hole," especially detectable from the "gap" (but literary and thematic "center") between Isa 39 and Isa 40, pulling the book of Isaiah together. Accordingly, Isa 5:11–17 construes exile as death in the image of Sheol. Exile as "empty space" is anticipatorily declared as judgment and destruction in 6:1–13; 22:1–14; 39:1–8, while also the object of nostalgia in the lament in 63:7–64:11. Select characters become emblematic for the fate of the collective people regarding exile: Isaiah (20:1–6), Shebna and Eliakim (22:15–25), Hezekiah (38:1–22), and the suffering servant (52:13–53:12). Other texts further bespeak exile through various images: the images of slavery and captivity (14:4b–21; 49:24–26; 51:13–14; 40:1–2); of scattering and dispersion (11:11–16; 27:7–13; 40:10–11; 43:5–7; 49:9b–12); of blindness and disorientation (42:18–25; 48:1–8); and of abandonment and bereavement (47:1–9; 49:14–21; 54:1–6). Thus, amid expressions of vision and redemption, excavating images of "exile" unveils the motifs and memories of darkness and destruction, evoking the theological complexity concerning divine hiddenness.[16]

[15]   Kim, *"Lengthen Your Tent-Cords,"* 109.
[16]   Frederik Poulsen, *The Black Hole in Isaiah: A Study of Exile as a Literary Theme,* FAT 125 (Tübingen: Mohr Siebeck, 2019).

INTERTEXTUALITY BETWEEN ISAIAH AND THE REST OF THE HEBREW BIBLE

When it comes to the inner-biblical relationships between Isaiah and other books, Shalom Paul's midrashic reading of Jeremiah's confessions with the suffering servant passages in Isaiah is fundamental.[17] On the virtual identity of Isa 36–39 with 2 Kgs 18–20 (cf. 2 Chr 32), Song-Mi Suzie Park attempts a new approach for reading the Hezekiah complex intertextually, both diachronically and synchronically. Analogous to the interrelation between Isa 7 (Ahaz) and Isa 36–37 (Hezekiah), Park observes that in the redactional progress from 2 Kings to Isaiah to 2 Chronicles, Hezekiah's role transfers to become more symbolic for the nation Judah regarding trust and deliverance. Park thus interprets Isa 36–39 as a redactional "counter-response" to 2 Kgs 18–20 out of Isaiah's unique sociohistorical situation and ideology. In the Isaianic counter-response to the unsatisfactory conclusion of 2 Kgs 18–20, the Isaianic adaptation highlights that the two seemingly discrepant accounts of disease (Isa 38) and envoys (Isa 39) culminate with the same tones of survival and hope.[18]

There have been numerous other influential or new proposals for interpreting Isaiah in dialogue with other biblical books.

Isaiah and Deuteronomy

Like most biblical books, in Isaiah we can find allusions to the Deuteronomic law codes. Michael Fishbane rehashes cases of inner-biblical adaptations regarding the definitions of community membership: "entering the house of God" and "becoming God's people." In Deut 23:1–8, certain groups of people are ruled as excluded, including the eunuchs, Ammonites, Moabites (and, in principle, Edomites and Egyptians). Ezra 9:1–2 identifies "the people of the lands" as intermarried groups of many nations, as opposed to the "holy seed" (presumably the returnees from the exile). In Neh 13:1–3, we observe almost verbatim citations excerpted from Deut 23:3–4 describing the separation of foreigners. This Deuteronomic legal tradition recurs in other texts to reinforce ethnic identity markers (cf. Lam 1:10; 4Qflor. Col. I.4). Against the comparable postexilic setting, Isa 56:1–7 presents its

---

[17] Shalom Paul, "Literary and Ideological Echoes of Jeremiah in Deutero-Isaiah," in *Proceedings of the Fifth World Congress of Jewish Studies*, vol. 1, ed. P. Peli (Jerusalem: World Union of Jewish Studies, 1969), 109–21.

[18] Song-Mi Suzie Park, *Hezekiah and the Dialogue of Memory* (Minneapolis, MN: Fortress, 2015).

own inner-biblical "lay exegesis" in which justice and righteousness coincide with the observance of the sabbath, concretely illustrated as the inclusion of the eunuchs and foreigners.[19] This Isaianic oracle may envision a community that accepts the two dissenting groups – both the *golah* returnees in the eunuchs, including the royal sons (cf. Isa 39:7), and the remainees, labeled as the foreign descendants – indeed "all" who repent (Isa 55:1, 7). For an intertextual study of the Song of Moses (Deut 32) with Isaiah, see NILSEN.

Isaiah and other Prophets

Almost verbatim interconnections can be found between Isa 2:2–5 and Mic 4:1–5 (cf. Joel 4:9–13 [ET 3:9–13]). Marvin Sweeney delineates the intertextuality in Micah's dialogic debate with Isaiah, as to how Judah should cope with the nations in the early Persian post-exilic period. While the texts are clearly correlated intertextually, their literary sequence and theology convey the marked uniqueness of each. Both Isaiah and Micah yearn for a future era of peace centered in Zion, but whereas Isaiah regards the renewed Israel as a part of the Persian empire under Yhwh's rule, Micah reconceives the rebuilt Israel as an independent state with a Davidic monarch who will punish ruthless nations.[20]

Children as symbols for the fate of Israel and Judah, in Isa 7–8 and Hos 1–3, have been studied by Kay Weißflog. The names of the children – "Shear-jashub" (7:3), "Immanuel" (7:14; 8:8, 10), and "Maher-shalal-hash-baz" (8:1) – present portents of demise (e.g., northern Israel, Aram, and Judah) as well as hope for rescue (e.g., remnants). The children in Hosea – "Jezreel" (1:4), "Lo-ruhamah" (1:6), and "Lo-ammi" (1:9; cf. 2:25 [ET 2:23]) – likewise depict the people's infidelity and loss as well as future reunification and restoration. Additionally, reading the two books intertextually, Weißflog notes the possibility of authorial/redactional intentionality between the two books, postulating that Hos 1–3 neatly fits into the structure of Isa 7–8. In fact, the names – "Isaiah" and "Hosea" – with the same roots may suggest the possibility of a shared persona, or even authorship/ editorship, inviting more intertextual studies between the three major prophets and the twelve minor prophets.[21]

---

[19] Michael Fishbane, *Biblical Interpretation in Ancient Israel* (Oxford: Clarendon, 1985), 114–29.

[20] Marvin A. Sweeney, "Micah's Debate with Isaiah," *JSOT* 93 (2001): 111–24.

[21] Kay Weißflog, *Zeichen und Sinnbilder: Die Kinder der Propheten Jesaja und Hosea* (Leipzig: Evangelische Verlagsanstalt, 2011).

Jeremiah shares close affinities with Isaiah, not only canonically but also linguistically, thematically, and redactionally. The intertextual connections between Isa 13–14 and Jer 50–51, and between Isa 15–16 and Jer 48 have been heavily studied. Benjamin Sommer categorized types of inner-biblical allusion and exegesis. For example, the address to "Jacob/Israel, my servant" has intertextual connections with the salvation oracle "fear not ... I am with you" (Jer 30:10–11; 46:27–28//Isa 41:8–10). Rather than assuming one prophet influenced the other, Sommer posits that Deutero-Isaiah, like Jeremiah, may have taken stock language from ancient Near Eastern tradition.[22] Another example is the prophetic exhortations for the people to "build houses ... settle ... plant gardens ... eat their fruit" (Jer 29:4–6//Isa 65:18–23), which display how Jeremiah's negative oracle denying the exiles' (golah) instant release is reversed by Deutero-Isaiah's exultation (gilah) of renewal and longevity.[23] As a final example, Jeremiah's call with the divine "words in your mouth" (Jer 1:9–10) coheres with the servant's commissioning (Isa 51:16; cf. Isa 6:7; Ezek 3:1–3). Jeremiah's role as a "prophet to the nations" (Jer 1:5) represents that of his people, which recurs in Deutero-Isaiah, as a "light to the nations" (Isa 42:6; 49:6), through the comparable motif of a "tree" (Jer 11:19–21//Isa 51:12–14). These connections lead Jeremiah's persona for Israel into the portrait of the suffering servant in Deutero-Isaiah (Jer 20:11//Isa 50:6–7; Jer 11:19// Isa 53:7–8; etc.).[24] As a result, "the presence of so many allusions at the outset of the work proclaims that the reuse of older material is central to Deutero-Isaiah's project."[25]

The Oracles against/about the Nations (OAN) section in Isa 13–23 also provides a clear venue for intertextuality, since it shares commonalities with Amos 1–2, Zeph 2–3, Jer 46–51, and Ezek 25–32. W. A. M. Beuken offers a promising example. Considering the unique introductory "Behold, I am..." formula (Isa 13:17; Jer 50:9, 18, 31; 51:1, 25, 36), he identifies two correlated oracles against Babylon (Isa 13–14//Jer 50–51) highlighting corresponding structures that end with subsequent actions by Yhwh. The study discovers that the two interrelated oracles not only share concatenated linguistic patterns, but also signify distinct messages: Isaiah invites readers into the thick of military battle

22   Benjamin D. Sommer, *A Prophet Reads Scripture: Allusion in Isaiah 40–66* (Stanford, CA: Stanford University Press, 1998), 34.
23   Sommer, *A Prophet Reads Scripture*, 42–43.
24   Sommer, *A Prophet Reads Scripture*, 62–66.
25   Sommer, *A Prophet Reads Scripture*, 166.

against Babylon, while Jeremiah shares the news of Babylon's fall and the impacts of its aftermath.[26]

Christopher B. Hays offers an insightful intertextual study of Isa 24–27, noting manifold allusions to eighth-century texts such as Hosea, Amos, and Nahum (as well as Proto-Isaiah). Hays argues that these interconnections show how the texts and traditions, especially about the north, were collected and reapplied by a seventh-century scribe at a time when Josiah was appealing to the former northern kingdom to reunite with Judah.[27] He points out that Isa 24–27 also shared terminology with "contemporary" prophetic texts, especially Zephaniah (e.g., "inhabitants of the seacoast/earth" in Zeph 2:5//Isa 24:17; "drinking wine" in Zeph 1:13//Isa 24:9; "exultant/fortified city" turned to "wilderness" and "pastures" where animals "graze" in Zeph 2:6–7, 13–15// Isa 27:10; etc.), so as to hint that Zeph 1–3 and Isa 24–27 exhibit shared worldviews and terminology, if not the same editorial hands.[28] Hays concludes that the many intertextual allusions to various books in the Hebrew Bible within Isa 24–27 evince scribal adaptations and reapplications during the time of Josiah, "in support of Yhwh's defeat of the Assyrians and Josiah's divine manifest destiny in the north."[29]

It is also worthwhile to discern the linguistic and thematic correlations between Isa 36–39 and Jonah 1–4, with particular attention to the common role Assyria plays in the texts. An intertextual reading can examine various interconnections: For example, both passages deal with the tension between Assyria and Israel/Judah; Rabshakeh from Assyria infiltrates Jerusalem whereas Jonah from Israel penetrates Nineveh; kings in both texts put on sackcloth, fast, and repent (Isa 37:1–2// Jonah 3:6–8); penitence of both kings leads to comparable but contrary results, the destruction of 185,000 Assyrians (Isa 37:36) and the deliverance of 120,000 Ninevites/Assyrians (Jonah 4:11); both texts contain unique prayers, of Hezekiah and Jonah, where similar expressions and motifs can be found (e.g., both petitioners at the point of death; theme of "deliverance" [yš'; Isa 38:20//Jonah 2:10 (ET 2:9)]; motifs of Sheol/pit

[26]   W. A. M. Beuken, "Common and Different Phrases for Babylon's Fall and Its Aftermath in Isaiah 13–14 and Jeremiah 50–51," in *Concerning the Nations: Essays on the Oracles against the Nations in Isaiah, Jeremiah and Ezekiel*, ed. Else K. Holt, Hyun Chul Paul Kim, and Andrew Mein, LHBOTS 612 (London: Bloomsbury T&T Clark, 2014), 53–73.

[27]   Christopher B. Hays, *The Origins of Isaiah 24–27: Josiah's Festival Scroll for the Fall of Assyria* (Cambridge: Cambridge University Press, 2019), 213–59.

[28]   Hays, *The Origins of Isaiah 24–27*, 41–43, 230–32.

[29]   Hays, *The Origins of Isaiah 24–27*, 259.

[Isa 38:18//Jonah 2:3, 7 (ET 2:2, 6)], temple [Isa 38:2, 20, 22//Jonah 2:5, 8 (ET 2:4, 7)], and dove [Isa 38:14//Jonah 1:1 – "Jonah" in Hebrew means "dove"]; abruptness of Hezekiah's asking the sign [Isa 38:22] as well as of Jonah's thanksgiving [Jonah 2:10 (ET 2:9)], etc.). These intertextual clues stimulate follow-up analyses concerning the place and function of each text within the larger corpora, especially with the literary role Assyria plays (e.g., both Isaiah and the Twelve Prophets arrange texts concerning Edom and Assyria in sequential order), as well as the significance of reading the two canonical portions together vis-à-vis the backdrops of various empires (e.g., Assyria as a cipher for later empires such as Babylon, Persia, or more likely Hellenistic kingdoms).[30]

Isaiah, Psalms, and Lamentations

Isaiah's intertextual relationship with the Psalms, and also Lamentations, has been widely recognized. Patricia Tull's work offers pioneering analyses on Deutero-Isaiah's recollections of various texts from Psalms, Lamentations, and so on as well as reappropriations for its own message. Among many cases, we will look at Isa 54:1–17. The catchwords ("reject," "abandon," and "anger") conjoin Isa 54:6–8 to Lam 5:19–22, with a divine nod to the complaint in Lamentations that Yhwh abandoned Zion, though not forever. The people, dispossessed of "water" and "money" (Lam 5:4), are offered sufficient "water" without "money" for nothing, along with plentiful wine and milk (Isa 55:1). The "sacred stones" as treasured children of Zion in hunger and plunder (Lam 4:1–2) are assured that they will be restored (Isa 54:11–13). Deutero-Isaiah reverses the imagery of the tent for Zion's desolation (Jer 4:20; 10:20) into her rejuvenation alongside her numerous progeny (Isa 54:1–2). In addition to the striking citations, thematic allusions connect and redirect the motifs of shame (Jer 2:1–2; 3:24–25; 31:19), destruction such as the deluge (Gen 6–9), and the in/security of Zion (Pss 46:2–3; 72:3–7; 89:4, 34–38, 50) toward dignity (Isa 54:4), grace (Isa 54:9), and faithful stability of Zion (Isa 54:8–10, 13–14) respectively. The intertextual connections thus illuminate that "language once used to describe destruction, destitution, and shame in Lamentations and Jeremiah is restructured to announce healing and restoration."[31]

30　　Hyun Chul Paul Kim, "Is the Book of Jonah an Inner-Biblical Exegesis on Isa 36–39?" in *Isaiah and Intertextuality: Isaiah amid Israel's Scriptures*, ed. Wilson de Angelo Cunha and Andrew T. Abernethy, FAT 2/148 (Tübingen: Mohr Siebeck, 2024), 123–35.

31　　Patricia Tull Willey, *Remember the Former Things: The Recollection of Previous Texts in Second Isaiah*, SBLDS 161 (Atlanta, GA: Scholars Press, 1997), 229–61.

Corinna Körting reads Isa 62:1–7 and Ps 45 intertextually (conjecturing that the psalmist may have been well aware of the Isaianic traditions). Select expressions and motifs connect these two texts, such as the motifs of forgetting Zion's past (Ps 45:11 [ET 45:10]; cf. Isa 54:4), the kings serving and escorting Zion (Ps 45:13–14; cf. Isa 49:23; 60:3–7, 16), the wedding (Ps 45:15–16; cf. Isa 62:4–5), the dresses symbolizing the change of Zion's status (Ps 45:14–15; cf. Isa 52:1–2), and numerous offspring with renown (Ps 45:17–18; cf. Isa 49:20; 54:1–3; 62:2, 5, 7; 66:7–12). These interconnections present two interrelated yet unique ways of Zion's becoming the queen. Ps 45 answers the yearning lament to meet God in Zion in Pss 42–44 and anticipates God's kingship in Zion in Pss 46–48. Isa 62 responds to and interacts with the common motifs in Isa 40–55 and 60–62, while adumbrating the processes Zion undergoes: "suffering, restoration, and exaltation."[32]

Joseph Blenkinsopp champions intertextual study with Psalms: "Isaiah and Psalms, when taken together and read intertextually, coalesce in a religious vision, a way of experiencing and articulating commitment to the fundamentals of the faith of Israel."[33] Assuredly, there are innumerable intertextual correlations: for example, summons to heavens and earth (Ps 50:4–6//Isa 1:1); criticism of wrongful sacrifices (Ps 50:8–15//Isa 1:10–20); call to all creation to worship (Ps 96:1–13//Isa 40:10–13);[34] Zion as the highest abode (Ps 48:2–3 [ET 48:1–2]; Isa 14:12–13); the righteous/devout versus the wicked (Pss 1:1–6; 12:2; 116:15//Isa 57:1–2). Therefore, "the beauty of the psalms resounds throughout the book of Isaiah, and the Isaian vision of the Creator God ... is echoed and joyfully proclaimed by the psalmists."[35]

Isaiah and Job

The intertextuality of Deutero-Isaiah and Job has gained much attention as well. Among many (including Yohan Pyeon and Alan Cooper), Jiseong James Kwon's monograph presents cutting-edge updates of

---

[32] Corinna Körting, "Isaiah 62:1–7 and Psalm 45 – or – Two Ways to Become Queen," in *Continuity and Discontinuity: Chronological and Thematic Development in Isaiah 40–66*, ed. Lena-Sofia Tiemeyer and Hans M. Barstad (Göttingen: Vandenhoeck & Ruprecht, 2014), 103–23.

[33] Joseph Blenkinsopp, *The Beauty of the Holiness: Re-Reading Isaiah in the Light of the Psalms* (London: T&T Clark, 2019), 1.

[34] Blenkinsopp, *The Beauty of the Holiness*, 151: "It is in the book of Psalms and the book of Isaiah that the idea of a religion of all humanity is first clearly enunciated."

[35] Blenkinsopp, *The Beauty of the Holiness*, 161. Consider also Risto Nurmela, *The Mouth of the Lord Has Spoken: Inner-Biblical Allusions in Second and Third Isaiah* (Lanham, MD: University Press of America, 2006).

recent scholarship together with insightful analyses and implications. Amid many thematic correlations, a case study examines unique parallel expressions between Job and Deutero-Isaiah, such as "mighty in power" (Job 9:4//Isa 40:26), "he who alone stretched out the heavens" (Job 9:8//Isa 44:24), "beyond investigation" (Job 9:10//Isa 40:28), "what are you doing?" (Job 9:12//Isa 45:9), "the hand of Yhwh has done this" (Job 12:9//Isa 41:20). While raising cautions against hasty assumptions of literary dependence, let alone historical backgrounds, Kwon observes thematic relations between linked passages concerning Job's acknowledgment of the incomprehensibility of God and Deutero-Isaiah's affirmation of God's power to reassure doubts.[36] Intertextuality between these two books also underscores not only similarity regarding the theology of "God's control and freedom," but also differences in that "the book of Job focuses heavily on the issue of the unjust sufferings and fates of the individual, while Deutero-Isaiah talks widely about the disasters and the destiny of the Israelites in an encouraging way."[37]

INTERTEXTUALITY WITH THE ANCIENT TEXTS/WORLDS AND TODAY'S TEXTS/WORLDS

Reception history is the study of how biblical texts have been used, adapted, and interpreted throughout history. It is an extension of intertextuality, insofar as biblical texts have been expanding into "postbiblical" interpretive texts throughout the last two millennia.

Regarding the contemporary world, on the other hand, we should note the interdisciplinary aspects of intertextuality, akin to Izaak J. de Hulster's assertion concerning iconographic interpretation: "texts and images should both be used."[38] Intertextuality in this sense can encompass the areas of art (e.g., stained glass), film, poetry/literature (akin to ancient folktales), modern history, contemporary issues, and the like. Picking up Shalom Paul's inner-biblical exegesis and J. Severino Croatto's hermeneutics, my recent work starts with the textual links between the legacies of Jeremiah and the Suffering Servant (Jer 10:19//Isa 53:4; Jer 10:21//Isa 53:6; Jer 11:19a//Isa 53:7; Jer 11:19b//Isa 53:8) and then expands to embrace the life stories and poems of two modern-day resistance poets

---

[36]   Jiseong James Kwon, *Scribal Culture and Intertextuality: Literary and Historical Relationships between Job and Deutero-Isaiah*, FAT 2/85 (Tübingen: Mohr Siebeck, 2016), 60–69.

[37]   Kwon, *Scribal Culture and Intertextuality*, 209.

[38]   Izaak J. de Hulster, *Iconographic Exegesis and Third Isaiah*, FAT 2/36 (Tübingen: Mohr Siebeck, 2009), 265.

and martyrs, Dietrich Bonhoeffer and Dongju Yun.[39] The comparative study can thus be cross-cultural and cross-contextual, interweaving connected points of intersectionality between ancient texts and contemporary texts, between ancient worlds and today's worlds, and so on.

CONCLUSION

Intertextuality has been an invaluable mode for reading and interpreting Isaiah. While many biblical books cite, allude to, and echo other texts, it is even more justifiable to apply this methodology to the lengthy scroll of Isaiah, strewn with intertextual codes and clues. Rolf Knierim mused that because ancient people did not have TV or internet, perhaps they memorized, recited, and reconceptualized other texts and concepts for their intellectual entertainment and existential reinforcement. We too may learn and benefit if we, as humble readers, heed the echoing words of this beloved prophet: "Seek and read from the book of Yhwh: Not one of these shall be missing" (Isa 34:16).

FURTHER READING

Boda, Mark J., Carol J. Dempsey, and LeAnn Snow Flesher, eds. *Daughter Zion: Her Portrait, Her Response.* SBLAIL 13. Atlanta, GA: SBL Press, 2012.

Carr, David M. "The Many Uses of Intertextuality in Biblical Studies: Actual and Potential." Pages 505–35 in *Congress Volume Helsinki 2010.* Edited by Martti Nissinen. VTSup 148. Leiden: Brill, 2012.

Charlesworth, James H., ed. *The Unperceived Continuity of Isaiah.* London: T&T Clark, 2019.

De Troyer, Kristin and Barbara Schmitz, eds. *The Early Reception of the Book of Isaiah.* Berlin: de Gruyter, 2019.

Grohmann, Marianne and Hyun Chul Paul Kim, eds. *Second Wave Intertextuality and the Hebrew Bible.* Atlanta, GA: SBL Press, 2019.

Hays, Richard B., Stefan Alkier, and Leroy A. Huizenga, eds. *Reading the Bible Intertextually.* Waco, TX: Baylor University Press, 2009.

Hibbard, J. Todd and Hyun Chul Paul Kim, eds. *Formation and Intertextuality in Isaiah 24–27.* SBLAIL 17. Atlanta, GA: SBL Press, 2013.

Lester, G. Brooke. *Daniel Evokes Isaiah: Allusive Characterization of Foreign Rule in the Hebrew-Aramaic Book of Daniel.* LHBOTS 606. London: T&T Clark, 2015.

McGinnis, Claire Mathews and Patricia K. Tull, eds. *"As Those Who Are Taught": The Interpretation of Isaiah from the LXX to the SBL.* Atlanta, GA: SBL Press, 2006.

---

[39] Hyun Chul Paul Kim, "Dietrich Bonhoeffer, Dongju Yun, and the Legacies of Jeremiah and the Suffering Servant," in Grohmann and Kim, 289–309.

Meek, Russell L. "Intertextuality, Inner-Biblical Exegesis, and Inner-Biblical Allusion: The Ethics of a Methodology." *Bib* 95 (2014): 280–91.

Melugin, Roy F. and Marvin A. Sweeney, eds. *New Visions of Isaiah*. JSOTSup 214. Sheffield: Sheffield Academic, 1996.

Nilsen, Tina Dykesteen. *The Origins of Deuteronomy 32: Intertextuality, Memory, Identity*. New York: Lang, 2018.

Schultz, Richard L. "Qoheleth and Isaiah in Dialogue." Pages 57–70 in *Reading Ecclesiastes Intertextually*. Edited by Katharine Dell and Will Kynes. LHBOTS 587. London: T&T Clark, 2014.

Sweeney, Marvin A. *Reading Prophetic Books: Form, Intertextuality, and Reception in Prophetic and Post-Biblical Literature*. FAT 89. Tübingen: Mohr Siebeck, 2014.

Wegner, Paul D. "Seams in the Book of Isaiah: Looking for Answers." Pages 62–94 in *The Bible as a Human Witness to Divine Revelation: Hearing the Word of God through Historically Dissimilar Traditions*. Edited by Randall Heskett and Brian Irwin. London: T&T Clark, 2010.

14 Gendered Imagery in Isaiah

HANNE LØLAND LEVINSON

We could, and presumably should, inquire about gendered imagery in every single book in the Bible, and it would be relevant to do so in each case. This said, the book of Isaiah has drawn special attention when it comes to gendered imagery (LØLAND),[1] because we find here (primarily in Isa 40–66) a collection of female or feminine images for God with no biblical equivalent. These images led to a focus on the book of Isaiah in the 1970s and onwards when the quest for the feminine side of God made its way into biblical scholarship. The discussion of gendered God images will be my main focus in this chapter as well, owing to the occurrences of feminine images for God in Isaiah and the research situation mentioned, but we need more. The question of gendered imagery is more than a search for feminine images for God, and even if this search were our only interest, we would need to reflect on how we carry out such a task properly. We need to know what we talk about when we talk about *gendered imagery*, what *gender* and *imagery* refer to, and how we go about identifying imagery as gendered. We also need to ask what it means, if anything, when an image is gendered. And whose gender are we talking about?

This chapter will therefore be more about *how to read* gendered imagery than actual readings of texts (though we will of course look at examples as well). The goal is to help readers to read more capably on their own.

FROM LANGUAGE TO IMAGES (OR IMAGES IN LANGUAGE): METAPHORS

I will start out with two images that do not evoke any associations with gender (at least not for me), which is helpful for now, so we can focus on images and how to read them.

---

[1] See also my article, Hanne Løland Levinson, "The Never-Ending Search for God's Feminine Side: Feminine Aspects in the God-Image of the Prophets," in *Prophecy*, ed. L. Juliana, M. Claassens, with the assistance of Funlola O. Olojede, *The Bible and Women 1.2* (Atlanta, GA: SBL Press, 2021), 293–306.

We are the clay, and you [Yhwh] are our potter;
we are the work of your hand. (Isa 64:8 [MT 64:7])

The people's claim that they are clay and Yhwh or God is the potter conjures familiar images. (I use the Tetragrammaton Yhwh instead of the traditional English translation "the Lord" throughout this chapter because "the Lord" is a gendered title while Yhwh was a presumably gender-neutral personal name.) In the Hebrew Bible, God is the maker or the potter, forming people, whether it is the first human formed from the dust from the ground (Gen 2:7) or reshaping the people of Israel as clay on the potter's wheel (Jer 18:1–11). God is the potter, the people are the clay. The image is painted for us through the language used in the text, or, formulated more precisely, the *metaphors* used create the images we are left with. "We are the clay" and "you are our potter" are not literal descriptions, either of the people or of God; rather they are metaphorical utterances. There are many definitions of metaphors out there; for our purpose I find Janet M. Soskice's definition helpful. She writes: "metaphor is that figure of speech whereby we speak about one thing in terms which are seen to be suggestive to another" (SOSKICE: 15). The prophet speaks of God (one "thing") through the lens or image of the potter (another thing), and about the people (one thing) through the lens or image of clay (another thing). It is important to note that the metaphors are not limited to the words "clay" and "potter," rather the whole utterances WE ARE THE CLAY and YOU ARE OUR POTTER are each a metaphor. (In metaphor research it has become commonplace to write out the metaphors in capital letters.) Further, metaphors are usually understood to consist of two elements or thoughts often referred to as "source" and "target" or "source domain" and "target domain." Target is the one talked of, in our case "we" in the first example and "you," Yhwh or God, in the second example. The sources are "clay" and "potter." The addition of "domain" to source and target (i.e. source domain and target domain) is important as it makes it clear that it is not only the concepts "clay" and "potter" that are activated when these metaphors are used, but also the associations and connotations that they evoke. These associations and connotations are often called associated commonplaces. In the case of "potter," the source domain would include notions such as: someone who forms pottery (rather obvious), a human activity, creativity, skills, and mess (as far as I can remember from doing pottery in middle school, my only experience in the field; it is a rather messy business), and so on. As for the clay, we are clearly in the same sphere, but the clay is on the receiving end: Clay is the object that is formed. It can be formless or formed into different shapes; it has potential, it can be discharged of; it is also sticky and, yes, messy, and so on.

The meaning of a metaphor is generally understood to be found in the interaction between the source (domain) and the target (domain) or in the blend that is created, in our cognition, when the source and the target interact. The blend is new, and thus the metaphor creates something that is not limited to either source or target. Moreover, in cognitive metaphor theory (the leading approach to metaphors today) metaphors are not seen as a matter of language but rather as a matter of thinking (DESCAMP AND SWEETSER: 215).

Target		*Source*
WE	ARE	THE CLAY
YOU	ARE	OUR POTTER

In practical terms, when the prophet says "we are the clay," he or she sets in motion the images and ideas the reader has of clay and brings them together with how the reader thinks about the "we" of the text.[2] When the prophet says "You are our potter," the reader brings together her notions of potters and pottery with all their associations and her notions of God. Source and target also bring a notion of directionality to the metaphor. We move from the source to the target. Metaphors are not multidirectional or reversible, saying that GOD IS OUR POTTER is not the same as saying THE POTTER IS GOD. (Both metaphors are possible, but they do not activate the same source-to-target mapping.)

Which of all the associations, connotations, and entailments that a metaphor awakens actually contribute to the meaning of the metaphor is one of the challenges scholars are working hard to understand. Sarah Dille, who studies parental language for God in Second Isaiah, formulates it like this: "In a given text using parental language, any entailment that is part of the network of associations ... of father and mother is implicitly present, but some of these associations are downplayed, while others are highlighted" (DILLE: 18). *Downplaying* and *highlighting* are categories borrowed from Lakoff and Johnson, and they also have a third category: *hiding*. They argue that some aspects of the target can be hidden owing to a metaphorical utterance (LAKOFF AND JOHNSON: 10–13). The theories of downplaying, highlighting, and hiding are all

---

[2]   Presumably the prophet was a he, but there were female prophets in ancient Israel as well, and it has been suggested that Second Isaiah was a woman, so there is no way to know for sure.

attempts to explain which of all the potential associations a metaphor could awaken when used in a certain context actually is awakened, that is, what the metaphor means.

Another approach is to ask for the metaphor's salient feature to explain this, which I did in my book on gendered god-language, *Silent or Salient Gender?* My question there was: Is gender salient in metaphor x and y? (We will return to this question again later.) The notion of salient features was introduced into the metaphor discourse by Robert Fogelin. According to Fogelin, features are salient when they stand out and are prominent or conspicuous. Furthermore, to be salient the feature needs to play a role in classifying or sorting things out. In addition to this, Fogelin emphasized that salience is based on context and indicates a direction (FOGELIN: 66). In other words, a metaphor's salient features are not given once and for all; what is salient in a metaphorical utterance depends on the context it is uttered in. *Blending theory*, formulated first by Fauconnier and Turner, is the newest attempt within cognitive linguistics to shed light on what we do when we use and think in metaphors (FAUCONNIER AND TURNER). Specifically, blending theory describes the new domain, called the *blend*, that the interaction between source and target creates. For more on either of these theories other works should be consulted (see Further Reading section). The takeaway here is that a metaphor can awaken a lot of associations, but not all of them will be awakened. Our question is, then, if gender is one of the associations that come into play (or are awakened), how does it work?

But first, one more note on metaphorical language used for God. Linguistically and cognitively there is no difference in how metaphors function when used for God (god-language) compared with how metaphors function otherwise. God-language is humans' language for God, and it is drawn from human experiences. The authors of the Hebrew Bible talked and wrote about God based on their own experiences. Further, god-language is not only formulated based on experience, but it also creates experiences. When the Hebrew Bible authors used a new metaphor, a new image, for the first time, it could open up for new ideas and a new concept of God. This also means that the readers or listeners of the biblical texts probably experienced God differently from each other owing to how the metaphors connected (or did not connect) to their experiences. Our god-language today does the same thing. One big challenge in all religious (or theological) communication is the relationship between a person's own concepts of God, his or her image of God, and the concept and understanding of God that a rabbi, pastor, or teacher wants to give. What we say about God is not necessarily what people hear, because metaphors create different images for different people. Another challenge is that we often confuse our own images or concept of God with God with a capital G (if we, for a moment, as a working hypothesis presuppose that God exists), and do not reflect on the fact that our concept of God is just one way of imagining God, and not God as such. Finally we also need to remember that no metaphors, not even the biblical metaphors, describe God as God really is (see, for example, Deut 4:15–18; 1 Kings 8:14; Isa 40:18, 25; 46:5.) This said, metaphorical language is especially helpful when we talk about God, since metaphors enable "us to see the unseen, hear the unheard, and grasp the ungraspable" (GILLMAN: 9).

METAPHORS AND GENDER: GENDERED METAPHORS

So where does gender come in, in all this? To me, our example metaphors WE ARE THE CLAY and YOU ARE OUR POTTER do not conjure any notion of gender, but it might for someone who comes from a family with a long tradition of women doing pottery. They would very likely think of pottery as a female activity, and thus they may also infer a notion of femininity to the image in Isaiah. How, then, do we identify imagery or a metaphor as gendered? I define a gendered metaphor as a metaphor that awakens associations to gender and thus constructs ideas of gender for the reader. (And I use "gender" to mean both sex and gender, see further discussion in due course.) Critically, in my view gender must be part of the source domain if metaphorical language is to be identified as gendered language. That does not mean that targets cannot be gendered as well, certainly they often are, and at times the gender of the source and target are inconsistent. Still, the source's gender or lack thereof is what determines whether a metaphor is labeled gendered or not because of the direction of the metaphor: We think of the target through the lens of the source.

Metaphors can be explicitly or implicitly marked for gender, and they can be nongendered or gender ambiguous. A metaphor is explicitly marked for gender when the source domain includes male or female biological sex. Male sex is, for example, part of the source domains "father," "king," and "husband," and thus the metaphorical statements GOD IS FATHER, GOD IS KING, and GOD IS HUSBAND are all marked explicitly for male gender/sex. We find all these gendered metaphors used for God within a few chapters in Isaiah (Father in Isa 64:8 [MT 64:7]; king in Isa 43:15; and husband in Isa 54:5).

A prominent female metaphor in the book of Isaiah is ZION IS A
WOMAN (MAIER). Zion is consistently portrayed as a female person, a
woman, throughout the whole book. This is done through personification, which means we see or describe something nonhuman as a human
(LAKOFF AND JOHNSON: 33–34). Personification is a kind of metaphor.
Zion is portrayed as a daughter in the opening of the book in Isa 1:8:
"And daughter Zion is left like a booth in a vineyard, like a shelter in a
cucumber field, like a besieged city." From there she is portrayed as a
whore (Isa 1:21), mother (Isa 50:1), wife (Isa 54:6), a barren woman (Isa
54:1), and a birthing woman (Isa 66:8), to mention some examples. All
of these source domains are explicitly marked for female biological sex.
Zion, like all cities in the Hebrew Bible, is consistently portrayed as a
woman, never a man. One suggestion is that this is due to the fact that
the Hebrew word for "city" ('îr) is a grammatically feminine word, and
that this invites feminine imagery. Another suggestion is that Zion has
here taken over some of the epithets of the goddesses of the ancient
Near East. The reason for the imagery is not crucial for us here, but
rather which images the metaphor awakens for the readers of Isaiah.

When gender is part of the social constructions of what is masculine or feminine (what in the gender–sex pair is usually referred to
as "gender"), gender is implicit in the source. In ancient Israel, only
women were midwives. This profession is not biologically reserved for
women; men can also perform as midwives, and this is thus an example
of a sociocultural construction. When God is portrayed as a midwife as
in Isa 66:9, it is a role implicitly marked for female gender and therefore an example of feminine gendered god-language. "Shall I open the
womb and not deliver? says Yhwh; shall I, the one who delivers, shut
the womb? says your God" (Isa 66:9). On the other hand, being a soldier is a role limited to men in the Hebrew Bible (again not a profession
that needs to be biologically exclusive to males), and thus when God is
portrayed as a soldier and a warrior as in Isa 42:13, this is an example of
an image implicitly marked for male gender.

A source domain can also be nongendered, which could mean no
associations to gender or the source can be gender-ambiguous, and
thus the markers can indicate either male or female gender. The clay
metaphor WE ARE THE CLAY clearly falls into this category. Clay is
inanimate and has no markers for gender or sex; it is an example of a
nongendered metaphor. The potter metaphor GOD IS OUR POTTER
is more complicated. Potters are humans, and thus this is an anthropomorphic metaphor used for God. (The Hebrew Bible authors use
anthropomorphic, zoomorphic, and physiomorphic source domains for

God. God is spoken of as human, animal, or nature.) Humans in the Hebrew Bible come only in two sex variations, male or female (more on this later), and the potter could thus be either a woman or a man, that is, gender ambiguous. The follow up question would be: Were potters in ancient Israel usually women or men, and is there any comparative material from the ancient Near East that would shed light on this role and gender? Carol Meyers argues that both women and men made pottery in ancient Israel – women made pottery for the needs of the household, men for the market (MEYERS: 134). That would mean that "potter" was a gender-ambiguous source also for the ancient reader of Isaiah and could connote both male and female gender.

It is not enough to document whether gender is part of the source domain of a metaphor or not, though it is a crucial and necessary first step. We also have to ask whether gender is of significance, and whether it contributes to the construction of the images we are left with.

GENDER AND SEX ARE NOT WHAT THEY USED TO BE

The categorizations I have lined up here are not without problems. They are binary, heteronormative, and bordering on essentialism. The gender/sex distinction that has been so important to all feminist discourse is under scrutiny today. Gender as social construct and sex as biological essence were, for decades, the way to assign gender/sex labels, and they are the ones I have used here. I do not do this easily, because like many scholars of gender I see not only gender, but also sex as a social construction. This means that biology, body, and other traditional markers are not as stable as gender/sex indicators as we used to think. Gender is something that we perform, not something given. I still choose to use these categories here because I agree with Tamara Kamionkowski (and many other scholars), who argues that "biblical cultures rest firmly on a binary foundation," and one of these binary structures is gender/sex (KAMIONKOWSKI: 3–4). In the Hebrew Bible and ancient Israel only two sexes were recognized, male and female, and the two corresponding genders were man/masculine and woman/feminine. (This is at least the case for the understanding of people; it might be different for the understanding of God. I will return to this later.) I might not agree with these categories and would wish for more gender fluidity, but for documentation purposes we need categories that are in line with the biblical material. This does not mean that we should not question these binary categories, challenge them for our contemporary use, and also question what concept of gender the metaphors we use construct. Corrine Carvalho does this when she raises the thoughtful question "Whose gendered language of God?" in a recent article of the same title. Her concern is "how this more recent research [on gender fluidity] can or should affect a biblically based theology of gender in contemporary churches" (CARVALHO: 12). I would add: "and in contemporary synagogues and in all religious discourses."

BACK TO THE GENDERED METAPHORS IN ISAIAH

Our opening example of clay and potter has a first line that so far I have left out. We will look at it now to see how gendered metaphors work in texts and readings in Isaiah:

> Yet, Yhwh, you are our Father;
> We are the clay and, and you are our potter;
> we are the work of your hand. (Isa 64:8 [MT 64:7])

This new verse line introduces the metaphor: Yhwh/GOD IS OUR FATHER. Father is the source domain, with all its associations and connotations, while God is the target.

Target		*Source*
GOD	IS	OUR FATHER

GOD IS OUR FATHER, the most conventional metaphor for God in Christianity, and often used in Judaism as well, is actually not a frequent way of talking about God in the Hebrew Bible. There are only a handful of examples of this metaphor in the Hebrew Bible. In the book of Isaiah it is used three times, in our example verse Isa 64:8 (MT 64:7) and twice in Isa 63:16, which reads:

> For you are our father,
>> though Abraham does not know us and Israel does not acknowledge us;
>> you, Yhwh, are our father; our Redeemer from of old is your name.

The source "father" is marked explicitly for male gender/sex, since male biological sex is an associated commonplace of the source domain. Fathers are men, of male sex, even when there is no explicit reference to genitals or other biological markers. Male gender/sex is an unavoidable standard feature of this metaphor and thus also a possible salient feature. Gender in a source domain *can* be salient in a metaphorical utterance, and when it is, it constructs a gendered image of the target. Cynthia Chapman demonstrates convincingly how gendered language plays a vital role in the ideological and rhetorical language of warfare in the Israelite/Assyrian encounter. Through curses such as "May your soldiers become women" and "May your king become a prostitute" the enemy (the target) is feminized (CHAPMAN: 48–59). The metaphors are explicitly marked for female gender, as the sources (women and prostitute) have female sex as one of their associated commonplaces. (Men can of course also sell sex for money, but in the examples here the references are women.)

Target		*Source*
YOUR SOLDIERS	ARE	WOMEN
YOUR KING	IS A	PROSTITUTE

The female gender in the source domains is salient here, as it stands out and is surprising. Men are portrayed with characteristics thought to belong to another gender – to women. Here the whole point is that men are called women. It does not mean, of course, that the men (the target) literally become women, but the metaphor constructs an image of them as feminine. Thus, this is an example of how a gendered metaphor constructs a gendered image of the target. So, what does this mean for the GOD IS OUR FATHER metaphor? We have already seen that this metaphor is gendered male, since the source is explicitly marked for male gender, but is gender salient?

Elizabeth Johnson raises an important question – based on a general assumption, namely that GOD IS OUR FATHER is not intended to say anything about God's gender – when she writes: "If it is not meant that God is male when masculine imagery is used, why the objection when female images are introduced?" (JOHNSON: 34). This is an important question. It corrects the idea that female metaphors *gender* (here seen as a verb) God more than male metaphors do. Many discussions on revising liturgies to include female metaphors for God, as GOD IS OUR MOTHER, have been voted down with the argument that it would add a gendered dimension to the image of God, which (it is claimed) is not there with the metaphor GOD IS OUR FATHER. At this point a few things need to be stated very clearly (they should be obvious, but for some reason they do not seem to be): First, female source domains do not construct a gendered image of the target more (or less) than male source domains do. Second, a gendered metaphor, or even a metaphor where gender is a salient feature, does not necessarily gender (determine the gender of) the target! In other words, we can talk of God as father or mother as much as we like, but it does not actually gender, change the gender, or add gender to God (as such).

What I am asking, and the only thing we can say anything about, is whether and how a gendered metaphor *genders* the image or concept of God that we are left with. To do this, I think we need to start by questioning Johnson's first assumption. She is probably right that male gendered metaphors were not chosen to claim that God is male, but that does not mean that they do not contribute to construct a male image of God. Male or masculine metaphors do construct a male or masculine image of the target when gender is salient in the metaphor. Gender is not salient based on the author's intention, but on whether gender stands out, is conspicuous in the context, and so on. It also depends on the reader and how the reader hears or reads the metaphor. Since many of the metaphors used for God in Isaiah (and in the Hebrew Bible as a whole) are explicitly and implicitly marked for male or masculine gender, the GOD IS OUR FATHER metaphor in Isaiah probably did not draw a lot of attention to the fact that the source is explicitly marked for male gender, and thus gender was probably not salient in the metaphor's original context. Still, it confirmed a long line of male and masculine metaphors and contributed to upholding a male gendered image of God (this image is also at times questioned, as we will see later). The surprising part about the GOD IS OUR FATHER metaphor for the first reader/listener of this prophecy might actually have been the source domain: "father." It was not the first time it was used, but fatherhood is not a frequent source domain for the relationship between God and the people in the Hebrew Bible (a more established use was the image of God as father of the king), and was thus novel.

For today's readers GOD IS OUR FATHER is not a surprising metaphor and neither is the fact that the source is gendered male; both are conventional ways of speaking of God. Still, the gender of the source is salient for many of us, simply because we have become much more aware of the way we speak of God when it comes to gender. GOD IS OUR FATHER is not a gender-neutral way of speaking of God.

Again, Zion (the city of Jerusalem) is consistently portrayed as someone of female gender (sex): as a woman, a whore, a daughter, a widow, a divorced woman. All these metaphors are explicitly marked for female gender because female gender is an associated commonplace in all the source domains. These metaphors leave the reader of the text with an image of a female city. This image also allows for the more extended images of Zion as mother and wife, God as the father and husband, and the people as the children (DARR). Isa 50:1 reads:

Thus says Yhwh:
Where is your mother's bill of divorce with which I put her away?
Or which of my creditors is it to whom I have sold you?
No, because of your sins you were sold,
and for your transgressions your mother was put away.

This text is also an example of what is usually referred to as "the marriage metaphor" (BAUMANN). In this metaphorical language Yhwh is the husband (gendered male), and Zion/Jerusalem/Israel is the wife (gendered female).

Target	*Source*
Yhwh IS	THE HUSBAND
ZION IS	THE WIFE
THE PEOPLE ARE	THE CHILDREN

The roles are never reversed: God is never the wife; Zion or the people are never the husband.

Hosea 1–3 is the starting point of the marriage metaphor in the Hebrew Bible, but we find it in several of the prophetic books. The marriage metaphor highlights yet another aspect of the use of gendered metaphors: It is not only the gender labels as such that are challenging, but also the stereotypical ideas of gender that are constructed. The wife in the marriage metaphor is always the untrustworthy one, the promiscuous one, the whore, and she is also often portrayed as a victim. The husband in the marriage metaphor is the one with power, the one in control, and he is also often portrayed as being violent. (This makes the image doubly problematic, both the representation of the husband as violent without it being criticized and the fact that Yhwh is represented as the violent husband.) The marriage metaphor has to be read in the context of the ancient Israel's marriage institution, which was patriarchal, patrilineal, and patrilocal, and also against the background of the shame and honor culture of ancient Israel – and even then, it does not excuse the violent aspects of the image. The biblical marriage metaphors do not make sense against the background of the modern ideal of an egalitarian and reciprocal marriage.

FEMALE/FEMININE METAPHORS FOR GOD IN ISAIAH

It has long been perceived that Isaiah is different from the rest of the Bible when it comes to its use of female/feminine metaphors for God.

It is here, primarily in Isa 40–66, that we find most of the examples of feminine/female metaphors for God in the Hebrew Bible (though we certainly also find examples of them in other places). Let us take a look at some examples (LØLAND: 100–92).

> I [Yhwh] have been silent for a long time,
> I have kept still and restrained myself.
> Like a woman in labor I will cry out,
> I will gasp and pant at the same time. (Isa 42:14, my translation)

"Like a woman in labor I will cry out," Yhwh says. This is technically a simile and not a metaphor, but figurative similes function cognitively the same way as a metaphor (LØLAND: 47–51).[3] We have a source ("a woman in labor") and a target ("Yhwh"), and the process we carry out as readers is seeing Yhwh through the lens of the woman in labor: Yhwh is in travail; Yhwh is crying out in labor pains.

Target   **Source**
Yhwh IS   A WOMAN IN LABOR

The source is explicitly marked for female gender; a woman in labor is female, doing what only female bodies can do. The source domain of laboring awakens a lot of associations ranging from bringing forth new life, a baby, and hope, to pain, fear, and blood, to mention a few. The continuation of the image in the verse draws attention to the breathing: the gasping and panting of labor.

I have argued elsewhere that the salient feature of the laboring simile in Isa 42 is not the outcome of the birth; it is not the baby but the process of labor with all its implications that is emphasized here (LØLAND: 113–128). Birth is a powerful force, but it also entails pain, struggle, and screaming. The gender of the woman in labor was probably salient for the first readers of this oracle as this is a task only women can do, and the verse probably would have left them with an image of God as female, as it does for me as a modern reader (again this does not mean that Yhwh is female, but Yhwh is seen as such in this text). The gender of the woman-in-labor simile also stands out, and thus makes it salient, in the parallel with the soldier and its implicit male gendered source, in the verse before:

---

[3]   There is currently an extensive scholarly debate going on that we cannot go into here, about whether the ancient Israelites envisioned that God had a body or not. It is clear from my own work that God at least is often seen as having body parts and at times specific female body parts. See discussion in LØLAND: 47–51.

Yhwh goes forth like a soldier,
like a warrior he stirs up his fury; he cries out, he shouts aloud,
he shows himself mighty against his foes. (Isa 42:13)

In these two verses in the book of Isaiah, Yhwh is being described
as a soldier, a warrior, a mighty one, and further Yhwh describes him
or herself as a woman in labor, screaming, gasping, and panting in labor
pains. We are transported from the battlefield to the delivery room. In
one instance Yhwh is imagined as the male warrior, in the next as a
female giving birth.

Female and male metaphors are often juxtaposed in parallels when
used for God in the Hebrew Bible, sometimes for contrast, sometimes
for similarity (see, for example, Isa 42:13–14; 45:10; 49:14–15; Deut
32:18). This might have been a way to drive home a theological point,
that God is neither male nor female – or maybe both?

If Isa 42:13 highlights one aspect of childbirth, then Isa 46:3–4 highlights a different one. Here we read:

> Listen to me, house of Jacob
> and all the remnants of the house of Israel.
> You who have been carried since the time of pregnancy
> you who have been lifted up at birth
> Until old age I am,
> and until gray hair I will bear.
> I have made and I will carry,
> and I will sustain and I will save. (Isa 46:3–4, my translation)

Isa 46:3–4 can be read as a story that goes like this: A child has
been carried since the time it was in its mother's womb, it was carried
during the pregnancy. The baby was lifted out and up at birth (here the
text clearly describes the outcome of the birth process) by the midwife.
As the child grows up, and even when it gets old, it is still carried and
sustained until its hair turns gray. The child in the story is Israel, and
the one who is doing the carrying is Yhwh. In this text, Yhwh is said to
have a womb, the only reference to God's womb in the entire Hebrew
Bible (LØLAND: 71–74). Yhwh is depicted as the pregnant woman, but
as the baby is being born, God is no longer the mother but the midwife
lifting the baby up at birth.

The source domain of the last lines of the verse is harder to pin
down, as no one physically carries grownups and the elderly. Though
the elderly would have been sustained and cared for in ancient Israelite
society, this would have been done by their children, and thus the

source is gender ambiguous. We thus have these sources for the god-language in this text:

Target	Source
Yhwh IS	A PREGNANT WOMAN
Yhwh IS	A MIDWIFE
Yhwh IS	THE SUSTAINER AND CARRIER

This being the only text in the Hebrew Bible that imagines God as a pregnant woman (and having a womb), the female gender of this source domain would certainly have been salient. It leaves the reader with an image of a female God. When that image was first established, the gender could have carried over to the continuation of the text as the midwife is also gendered female, but the image could have continued with less emphasis on gender owing to the gender ambiguity of the carrier of the old.

Our final text example is Isa 49:14–15. Here the personified Zion is the one speaking (v. 14). She speaks up against Yhwh whom she portrays as her husband, and she accuses Yhwh of having abandoned her. Yhwh tries to renounce this accusation by arguing (in v. 15) that *she* cannot forget Zion, the same way as nursing mothers cannot forget their children:

> But Zion said, "Yhwh has abandoned me, my lord has forgotten me."
> "Can a woman forget her suckling child, a compassionate mother, the child of her womb?
> Even if these could forget, I cannot forget you." (Isa 49:14–15, my translation)

In this text Yhwh is both the husband and the mother of Zion! This is again an example where male and female metaphors are used together and here in a rather untraditional way. To convince Zion of Yhwh's incapability of forgetting, Yhwh changes the metaphor's source domain from "husband" to "mother," as if to say: "Yes, you are right, husbands can abandon" – and Yhwh actually later in Isa 54:7 admits that he left Zion: "For a brief moment I abandoned you" – "but in this case I am not a husband to you. I am your mother, and mothers cannot forget their suckling children."

Target	Source
Yhwh IS	A HUSBAND
Yhwh IS	A BREASTFEEDING MOTHER

A mother breastfeeding her child is here seen as the strongest bond between two people, with a connection that cannot be broken. This draws upon the Hebrew Bible's general view of breastfeeding as a strong emotional and bodily connection between mother and child. Yhwh is a woman who cannot forget her suckling child. The change from the husband to the breastfeeding mother metaphor is surprising; it draws attention to the gender of both of the source domains and makes gender salient in both the husband and the mother metaphor.

In the three texts we have looked at here, the female god-language is consistently connected to the process of giving birth: of being pregnant, acting as the midwife, being a mother and more specifically, being a breastfeeding mother. One of the main feminist criticisms of the god-language in Jewish and Christian traditions has been that it is very limited. It is limited to men's realm of experiences; women's experiences are not included. In the book of Isaiah (primarily in Isa 40–66) this is dramatically different: Women's experiences are included in the formulation of the god-language in significant ways, and it opens for a female image of God. This again raises the question, though: Whose gender and gender experiences are these? Yes, there are female experiences, but as critics have pointed out, these experiences are not shared by all women, and the images are essentialist in the way women are represented only through the functions of their bodies. This is true, but on the other hand one cannot forget that motherhood, giving birth, and midwifery were highly valued female roles in ancient Israel and thus construct positive and powerful images of female gender – which the wife, whore, and victim metaphors do not.

DOES IT MATTER?

After all is said and done, I feel it is appropriate to ask, *So what?* Or, formulated in a more sophisticated way: *"Does it matter?"* or, *"Why does gender in the gendered language matter?"* My answer is, to no one's surprise: "Yes, it does matter." It matters for our understanding of the biblical material and its understanding of God, and it still matters today for everyday people and their understanding of God and themselves. Let us start with the biblical material.

I have claimed that the gendered metaphors for God do not gender God. That of course raises the question, *"What does gender God?,"* or, stated alternatively, *"Did God have a gender?"* Theologically speaking, most theologians (Jewish and Christians alike) would say "no." Historically speaking, some scholars will say that God in ancient Israel was imagined as a male deity, others that the God of ancient Israel was imagined as being beyond the sex/gender distinction. This is clearly not a question to be solved here, but from what we have seen we can at least say the following: The findings of feminine/female metaphors for God in the book of Isaiah demonstrate that the god-language in the Hebrew Bible is not consistently male. It was possible and permissible to use female metaphors for God. (If this was possible and permissible in biblical god-language, it is harder to understand the arguments against female god-language today.) Further, when female metaphors were used for God in Isaiah, they seemed to have constructed explicit female and even bodily images of God, while in other cases male metaphors clearly constructed male images of God. In other words, gendered images of God were not seen as problematic. If we look at the metaphors for God in Isaiah as a whole, they are gender-inclusive or even gender-queer. The strict male or female labels for humans do not seem to have been required in the same way for God.

Mary Daly famously wrote: "If God is male, then the male is God" (DALY: 19). This quote expresses the main concern in feminist critique of religious god-language, namely that male god-language means that God is male, and if God is male, then men are closer to God than women are, in one way or another. From what I have argued here, Daly is, linguistically speaking, mistaken. The metaphor GOD IS MALE is not reversible and does not equal THE MALE IS GOD. However, direction and nonreversibility of metaphors does not exclude some spillover both ways; this is a result of the interaction. Thus, metaphors can also, to some extent, say something new about the source. After playing with the metaphor GOD IS OUR POTTER, we might think of ourselves as a bit more like creators (or gods) if we get a chance to work with clay. It is this spillover that justifies Daly's claim, and this brings us to why our discussion matters for everyday people's understanding of God and themselves.

If all the metaphors we hear for God are gendered male, it will establish a male image of God, and it might make us think that men are more godlike than women. This is not just the case on paper. I teach a class on a regular basis, called *Women, Gender and the Hebrew Bible*. A couple of years ago I had my students read and write a book report on an article called: "Rupturing God-Language: The Metaphor of God as Midwife in Psalm 22," by Juliana Claassens (CLAASSENS). In the prompt for the book report, I encouraged my students to include a paragraph about their own responses to the article, anything that they found interesting, surprising, challenging in the reading. The students in this class came from Catholic, Lutheran, and evangelical homes, as well as from different Jewish traditions and from nonreligious backgrounds. What kind of upbringing they had did not seem to make a difference to their responses to the article or to how they envisioned God. The responses I got support what feminist scholars have said for a long time. First of all, that women might have problems, for different reasons, with connecting to an all-male God, and further that female god-language can be important for women to feel valued for who they are. The responses also made it clear that we did not solve this challenge in the 1970s and 1980s, and in some ways very little seems to have changed culturally and religiously over the last fifty years. Decades after women in general and feminist scholars in particular started questioning the dominant male image of God, the prevalent image of God is still that of an old white man. As long as this continues to be the case, the discussion of gendered language in the book of Isaiah, in the Bible, and in our own language remains crucial.

FURTHER READING

Baumann, Gerlinde. *Love and Violence: Marriage as Metaphor for the Relationship between Yhwh and Israel in the Prophetic Books.* Translated by Linda M. Maloney. Collegeville, MN: Liturgical Press, 2003.

Carvalho, Corrine L. "Whose Gendered Language of God?" *CurTM* 43 (2016): 12–16.

Chapman, Cynthia R. *The Gendered Language of Warfare in the Israelite-Assyrian Encounter,* HSM 62. Winona Lake, IN: Eisenbrauns, 2004.

Claassens, L. Juliana M. "Rupturing God-Language: The Metaphor of God as Midwife in Psalm 22." Pages 166–75 in *Engaging the Bible in a Gendered World: An Introduction to Feminist Biblical Interpretation in Honor of Katherine Doob Sakenfeld.* Edited by Linda Day and Carolyn Pressler. Louisville, KY: Westminster John Knox, 2006.

Daly, Mary. *Beyond God the Father: Toward a Philosophy of Women's Liberation.* Boston, MA: Beacon, 1973.

Darr, Kathryn Pfisterer. *Isaiah's Vision and the Family of God.* Literary Currents in Biblical Interpretation. Louisville, KY: Westminster John Knox, 1994.

DesCamp, Mary Therese, and Eve E. Sweetser. "Metaphors for God: Why and How Do Our Choices Matter for Humans? The Application of Contemporary Cognitive Linguistics Research to the Debate on God and Metaphor." *Pastoral Psychology* 53 (2005): 207–38.

Dille, Sarah J. *Mixing Metaphors: God as Mother and Father in Deutero-Isaiah.* JSOTSup 398. London: T&T Clark, 2004.

Fauconnier, Gilles, and Mark Turner. *The Way we Think: Conceptual Blending and the Mind's Hidden Complexities.* New York: Basic Books, 2002.

Fogelin, Robert J. *Figuratively Speaking.* New Haven, CT: Yale University Press, 1988.

Gillman, Neil. *Believing and Its Tensions: A Personal Conversation about God, Torah, Suffering and Death in Jewish Thought*. Woodstock, VT: Jewish Light Publishing, 2013.

Johnson, Elizabeth A. *She Who Is: The Mystery of God in Feminist Theological Discourse*. New York: Crossroad, 1993.

Kamionkowski, Tamar S. *Gender Reversal and Cosmic Chaos: A Study on the Book of Ezekiel*. JSOTSup 368. London: Sheffield Academic Press, 2003.

Lakoff, George, and Mark Johnson. *Metaphors We Live By*. Chicago: University of Chicago Press, 1980.

Levinson, Hanne Løland. "The Never-Ending Search for God's Feminine Side: Feminine Aspects in the God-Image of the Prophets." Pages 293–306 in *Prophecy*. Edited by L. Juliana, M. Claassens, with the assistance of Funlola O. Olojede. The Bible and Women 1.2. Atlanta, GA: SBL Press, 2021.

Løland, Hanne, *Silent or Salient Gender? The Interpretation of Gendered God-Language in the Hebrew Bible, Exemplified in Isaiah 42, 46, and 49*. Forschungen zum Alten Testament 2/32. Tübingen: Mohr Siebeck, 2008.

Maier, Christl M. *Daughter Zion, Mother Zion: Gender, Space, and the Sacred in Ancient Israel*. Minneapolis, MN: Fortress Press, 2008.

Meyers, Carol. *Rediscovering Eve: Ancient Israelite Women in Context*. Oxford: Oxford University Press, 2013.

Soskice, Janet Martin. *Metaphor and Religious Language*. Oxford: Oxford University Press, 1985.

15 Divine and Human Plans in the Book of Isaiah

J. TODD HIBBARD

Over the centuries of the book of Isaiah's formation, its various authors created an inner-Isaian theological world in which they introduce various themes and motifs that develop in different directions. Those include Israel's blindness and deafness, divine election, justice and righteousness, and others (UHLIG).[1] One prominent theme developed throughout the book is Yhwh's sovereignty over Israel and Judah, other nations, and even the cosmos itself (DIETRICH; WILDBERGER). The rhetoric about Yhwh's sovereignty involves diverse elements, but one aspect of the idea that appears consistently, especially in Isa 1–39, revolves around the idea of competing "plans" (FICHTNER; JENSEN).

In its most basic form, this discourse appears in texts using some form of the root y-ʿ-ṣ, including, ʿēṣāh "plan, advise, counsel" (18x); yāʿaṣ, "to plan, advise" (12x); and yôʿēṣ, "counsellor" (5x).[2] These terms occur in Isaiah in total thirty-five times, a density that reveals the idea's importance.[3] Texts using other terminology also touch on the theme, but texts using these lexemes appear central to the idea in the book. The primary question that scholars have asked about the appearance and development of this theme in the book revolves around whether the relevant texts can be attributed to Isaiah himself or, in the alternative, must be seen as redactional additions from later periods (WERNER). To be sure, understanding the historical contexts reflected in the relevant passages – which touches on the question of authorship – constitutes an important line of inquiry, but this chapter seeks to understand the literary presentation of this idea in the final form of the book. While this does not preclude historical observations in what follows, the accent

---

[1] See also Ronald E. Clements, "Beyond Tradition-History: Deutero-Isaianic Development of First Isaiah's Themes," *JSOT* 31 (1985): 95–113.

[2] *BDB*, 419–20.

[3] This is made even clearer when by examining the usage in the rest of the prophetic corpus. The term occurs in Jeremiah nine times, Ezekiel three times, and the Book of the Twelve seven times. See Lothar Ruppert, "יעץ," *TDOT* 6:156–85.

will fall on how the book structures and presents this idea in the relevant texts as a mode of anti-imperial discourse (ABERNETHY; ASTER).

The notion of a "plan," whether Yhwh's, the nations', or Judah's, is originally a political idea in Isaiah. The book mentions *yôʿăṣîm* "counselors," who functioned as advisors to the royal court, and it is conceivable that Isaiah would have considered himself a member of this group (ROBERTS). Isaiah mentions these individuals in 1:26 and 3:3 alongside other bureaucratic functionaries such as judges, military commanders and, unexpectedly, types of diviners. All of these groups played a significant role in identifying what they took to be Yhwh's plan, which was then relayed to the king, a process probably behind the demand in 5:19 that Yhwh's plan should hasten to fulfillment so that people may know it. There is nothing distinctively Isaianic about either the reference to the historical category of counselors or to the idea that Yhwh's plan was made public through the work of these persons (WILLIAMSON: 382). Indeed, Isaiah recognizes such advisors exist in other states as well, such as Egypt (19:11) and Babylon (41:28). Rather, in these cases Isaiah simply references a historical reality, one that is found in other texts in the Hebrew Bible (e.g., Amos 3:7).

Beyond this, however, the *book* of Isaiah develops the notion of a plan as part of a theologically inflected, anti-imperial rhetorical strategy. At the literary level of the book, one detects how Isaiah incorporates texts using some form of *yʿṣ* to create a discourse about Yhwh's plans, the plans of the Judean elite, and the plans of other nations. This theme is especially developed in Isa 1–39 in each of the major sections, chapters 1–12, 13–27, and 28–35. Of particular interest is how the book focuses on distinct categories of usage in each of these three sections. In Isa 1–12 the book emphasizes other polities' plans against Judah; in Isa 13–27 the book emphasizes Yhwh's plans against would-be or actual ancient Near Eastern empires; and in Isa 28–35 the book emphasizes Judah's plans (though it contains a specific reference to Yhwh's plan as well). In this way, the book structures the idea as part of a broader critique of other nations.

In what follows, we examine how each of these sections develops this idea, culminating in a brief reflection on how the idea appears beyond Isa 1–39. The texts discussed will be selective and representative rather than comprehensive because of limitations of space.

THE NATIONS' PLANS AGAINST JUDAH (ISA 1–12)

The idea of a plan, whether Yhwh's or others', appears at pivotal places in this opening section of the book. The first occurrence of the important

terminology previously discussed can be found in the third of the series
of six woe oracles in Isa 5:8–24.

> Ah, you who drag iniquity along with cords of falsehood,
>> who drag sin along as with cart ropes,
> who say, "Let him make haste,
>> let him speed his work
>> that we may see it;
> let the plan of the Holy One of Israel hasten to fulfillment,
>> that we may know it!" (Isa 5:18–19)

The passage identifies an unspecified group (presumably political
elites) whom Isaiah criticizes because they are demanding that Yhwh's
plan materialize more quickly. The statement Isaiah attributes to them
might reflect their mockery of his prophetic message or, alternatively,
an impatience with the failure of Isaiah's message to manifest in concrete outcomes. Either way, their reaction has led them to act in ways
that the prophet characterizes as "sin" and "falsehood." Hence, the
first reference to Yhwh's plan in the book reveals it as a contested idea
within Isaiah's community. However, the reference to it here is suffi-
ciently vague that the reader must continue reading to find out what
the idea entails.

Fortunately, other passages in Isa 1–12 shed some light on Yhwh's
plan. The first two verbs used in 5:19a, *mhr* ("make haste") and *ḥûš*
("speed"), recur in 8:1, 3 as part of the third symbolically named child
in the narratives of Isa 7–8: *mahēr šālāl ḥāš baz*. This passage is associated with the so-called Syro-Ephraimite crisis of the 730s BCE. Like the
Immanuel child in 7:14, this child's name suggests that the crisis induced
by Syria and Israel's misguided plan against Jerusalem will quickly come
to naught, because the Assyrians will plunder and crush them (7:8, 16).

The narrative scene in 7:3–9 also drives home this point using
related language. Yhwh instructs Isaiah to speak with Ahaz in order to
remind him that he should not do anything politically rash out of fear
because Aram and Ephraim "have planned (*y's*) disaster against you"
(7:4–5). Isaiah's oracle to Ahaz makes clear their plan will fail: "It will
not stand (*lō' tāqûm*) nor will it come to fruition" (7:7b). This idea is
further expressed within the same broad literary context and historical
horizon in the statement to the peoples to "plan a plan (*'uṣû 'ēṣāh*) but it
will be frustrated; speak a word but it will not stand (*lō' yāqûm*) because
God is with us (*'immānû 'ēl*; cf. 7:14; 8:8)." Hence, Yhwh's plan in 5:19
is contested by and contrasted with the plans of Syria and Israel against
Jerusalem in Isa 7–8, and Isaiah claims that the nations' plan will fail.

Two other texts in this first section of Isaiah also prove relevant to the development of the idea, both of which anticipate a future king. Part of the coronation oracle in Isa 9:1–5 [Eng. 9:2–6] includes a list of four symbolic names for the new king. The first of these is *pele' yô'ēṣ*, traditionally rendered "wonderful counselor," though in light of this discussion we might also suggest "wonderful planner." The second passage, Isa 11:2, also anticipates a future king, in this case one possessing several spiritual endowments including a *rûaḥ 'ēṣāh*, a "spirit of counsel." In the canonical shape of the book, these passages are likely meant to be read in light of the promise of Immanuel child in 7:10–17.[4] This passage's location in the midst of texts developing the idea of competing plans during the so-called Syro-Ephraimite crisis (Isa 7–8) suggests that the promise of a new royal figure characterized in this way is part of the rhetorical and theological response to the crisis. This royal figure embodies Yhwh's plan and acts as a counter to the plans of others, whether from within Judah or outside it. The demand in Isa 5 that Yhwh's plan hasten to fruition finds its resolution in the promises of divine support manifest in the hopes for the Davidic dynasty's survival and prosperity. The realization of this plan for the Davidic house not only counters Syria and Israel's plan for Jerusalem; it also nullifies the need for Assyrian involvement.

Through the connections between all of these texts in Isa 1–12 one begins to see Isaiah's rhetorical aims in the development of this theme. We turn now to the next major section of the book, Isa 13–27, to see how it develops in light of this first section.

YHWH'S PLANS AGAINST THE NATIONS

In Isa 13–23 (Oracles against the Nations) three texts develop the idea of Yhwh's plan against three world powers or empires with imperially minded ambitions: Assyria, Egypt, and Tyre (and Sidon). Each of these passages argues that Yhwh exercises sovereignty over each of these powers, despite appearances to the contrary. While these passages were undoubtedly motivated by historical circumstances that drew the attention of the author, those circumstances are now blurred by editing and are hard to discern on the basis of the texts themselves. However, that

---

4   For example, Ronald E. Clements, "The Immanuel Prophecy of Isaiah 7:10–17 and Its Messianic Interpretation," in *Die Hebräische Bibel und ihre zweifache Nachgeschichte: Festschrift R. Rendtorff zum 65. Geburtstag*, ed. E. Blum, Christian Macholz, and Ekkehard W. Stegemann. (Neukirchen: Neukirchener Verlag, 1990), 225–40.

is a crucial point: The rhetorical strategy of each oracle is subsumed in the book's foregrounding of Yhwh's control or plan. The meaning of these oracles is no longer limited to one particular historical moment. Their placement in the book now enables their once context-specific argument to have a broader theological application about Yhwh's sovereignty over world powers.

Arguably, the book's strongest anti-imperial rhetoric about Yhwh's plan occurs in 14:24–27. That Isa 14:24–27 originated in the period of Judah's domination by Assyria is clear, but its redactional location has now given its anti-imperial language relevance beyond that historical context.

> Yhwh of hosts has sworn:
> As I have designed,
>   so shall it be;
> and as I have planned,
>   so shall it come to pass:
> I will break the Assyrian in my land,
>   and on my mountains trample him under foot;
> his yoke shall be removed from them,
>   and his burden from their shoulders.
> This is the plan that is planned
>   concerning the whole earth;
> and this is the hand that is stretched out
>   over all the nations.
> For Yhwh of hosts has planned,
>   and who will annul it?
> His hand is stretched out,
>   and who will turn it back?

In this passage Yhwh announces the intention to remove Assyria from Judah or, as verse 26 states, to wipe out Assyria from the earth. Verbal forms of the root $y's$ occur three times in this short passage (vv. 24, 26, 27) and the noun *'ēṣāh* occurs in v. 26. The passage asserts that Yhwh's divine intention to break Assyrian hegemony cannot be thwarted, a claim that Yhwh's sovereignty and power are greater than Assyria's. Yhwh's hand is outstretched and no one, especially Assyria, can retract it. The control over Assyria expressed in this passage conforms to the similar passages in First Isaiah that do not include the "plan" language explored here, but detail how Yhwh uses Assyria for his own purposes (e.g., 10:5–19). Structurally, the passage occupies an important position insofar as it concludes or rounds off the section

depicting judgment against the two imperial powers to which Judah
was subjugated, namely Assyria and Babylon (13:1–14:27).

Two elements of the language in verse 25b point back to Isa 7
and 8. First, the verse uses third-person pronouns: *wəsār mē'ălêhem
'ullô wəsubbŏlô mē'al šikmô yāsûr* ("his [i.e., Assyria's] yoke shall
be removed from them,/ and his burden from their shoulder.").[5] The
pronominal objects ("them," "their shoulder") have no immediate
antecedents, however. The text assumes the reader knows of whom
it speaks. Stromberg has argued convincingly that the phrase here is
linked with similar phraseology in Isa 9:3 and 10:27 (STROMBERG: 87–
91). The latter passage is nearly identical to the phrase in 14:25b and
occurs at the end of a short oracle in which Yhwh announces the imminent end of Assyria's domination of Israel. This suggests that Yhwh's
plan announced in 14:24–27 constitutes the fulfillment of what is
declared in 10:27 as occurring "on that day": "[Assyria's] burden will
be removed from your shoulder, and his yoke will be destroyed from
your neck." The lack of specific antecedents for the pronouns in 14:25c
and the similarity of the two texts suggests strongly that the author
of the line had such a connection in view. In the second passage, Isa
9:4 one also finds language similar to 14:25c. The allusion to the royal
child here (9:6: "a son given to us") suggests that he, too, signals the
assurance that Yhwh will break Assyria (9:4: "the yoke of his burden
... you have broken").

There is a second connection between 14:24 and the texts examined
here. As noted earlier, Isaiah states twice that what has been planned
by others against Jerusalem would not stand, using the negative particle
lō' and a form of *qûm*. So, in 7:7 Rezin and Pekah's plan "will not come
to pass" (*lō' tāqûm*) and in 8:10 what the peoples have planned "will
not come to pass" (*lō' yāqûm*). In contrast, 14:24 notes that what Yhwh
has planned "will come to pass" (*hî' tāqûm*). The language here appears
to be an intentional contrast to these earlier plans against Jerusalem.
Because those earlier plans resulted in Assyria's involvement in Judah's
affairs more directly, the plan here to break Assyria in Judah offers a
corrective to those plans.

The next two verses are often considered to have a later origin than
14:24–25. In 14:26–27 Yhwh's plan for Assyria is extended to the whole
earth. In addition to the "plan" language noted earlier, these two verses
feature Yhwh's outstretched hand. This language appears in Isa 5:25 and

---

5   *BHS* suggests emending *šikmô* to *šikmām*, "their shoulder" based on readings in the
    versions. I follow this suggestion here.

9:11, 16, and 20, passages that all express judgment on Israel and Judah. The first of these, 5:25, comes near the end of a section of woe-oracles, one of which contains contention over Yhwh's plan examined earlier (5:19). The three notices about Yhwh's outstretched hand in chapter 9 follow the oracle announcing the new king (9:1–5), also explored earlier. These common references suggest that the author of Isa 14:26–27 was guided by these earlier texts and likely intended this passage to be read in conjunction with them. If that is correct, then the plan announced for the whole earth in chapter 14 should be understood as arguing that if Yhwh was willing to subject his own people to his outstretched hand of judgment, how much more will he subject Assyria and, indeed, the whole earth to that same judgment. This point is driven home further by the second half of verse 27a, which asks, "who will frustrate" (*mî yāpēr*) Yhwh's plan? The use of *prr* recalls 8:10, where the nations were invited to "plan a plan but it will come to naught" (*tupār*). The nations' plans can be annulled by Yhwh, but they lack the ability to annul Yhwh's. Anti-Assyrian rhetoric here morphs into claims of Yhwh's universal sovereignty.

A second polemic appears in Isa 19, one of several texts in Isa 1–39 dealing with Egypt (see also Isa 30:1–5 and 31:1–3). Judah's flirtations with a pro-Egypt alliance designed to stave off Assyrian aggression in the eighth century BCE is well known. The first fifteen verses of Isa 19 are usually regarded as a three-part oracle in which Yhwh denounces Egypt (vv. 1–4, 5–10, 11–15). The first and last portions of the oracle develop the theme of contrasting plans: Egypt's and Yhwh's. In the first section, Yhwh disrupts Egyptian society and their own "plans:"

> I will stir up Egyptians against Egyptians,
>> and they will fight, one against the other,
>> neighbor against neighbor,
>> city against city, kingdom against kingdom;
> the spirit of the Egyptian within ~~them~~ him will be emptied out,
>> and I will confound his plans (*'ăṣātô*). (19:2–3a)

The contents of the Egyptians' plans are not disclosed, but given that Yhwh's alternative features a "fierce king" ruling over them (19:4), it is likely that they were political and military in nature. Later, in the third section, the prophet lampoons the "princes of Zoan" as utterly foolish and the wise counselors of Pharaoh as those who "give stupid counsel" (*'ēṣāh nib'ārāh*), undoubtedly counsel leading to Pharaoh's potential defeat. Their nonsensical plans result from a "spirit of confusion" with which Yhwh afflicted them (19:14). To highlight how

misguided these fallacious sages are, they are challenged to reveal
Yhwh's plans for Egypt, but to no avail. In the first of a series of "on
that day" passages in the second half of Isa 19, the prophet announces
that Judah will stoke fear in Egypt because of Yhwh's plan (v. 17)
against them. The chapter revolves around these competing plans –
Egypt's and Yhwh's – over who really controls national and international affairs. Egypt's national sovereignty is trumped by Yhwh's
divine sovereignty.

The passages in which the language about competing plans
appears contain several verbal links with passages in Isa 1–12, though
different from those established by Isa 14:24–27. Of particular importance appear to be texts from Isa 3 and 9. These connections contribute to the continuing development of the "plan" idea as anti-imperial
rhetoric in Isaiah. The first oracle, 19:1–4, depicts communal chaos
resulting from Yhwh "confusing" ('ăballē(a)') Egypt's plans (v. 3).
In a similar vein, 19:11–15's skewering of Egypt's sages asserts that
they have misled (hit'û) Egypt. These two verbs are found earlier in
Isaiah in 3:12 and 9:15. Both of these passages depict social and political chaos resulting from Judah's leaders misleading the community in
moments of crisis. A similar note is expressed in chapter 19, with one
important modification: It is Yhwh who creates the Egyptian confusion such that their counselors offer misleading advice. The criticism
of Egypt's intelligentsia is further connected with Isa 9 through the
use of the same two sets of images for leadership: "head and tail, palm
branch and reed." This imagery appears in Isa 9:13, where a glossator
has identified these as elders, dignitaries, and prophets. Isa 19 reuses
this description of Judah's leadership as part of its depiction of Egypt's
inept counsellors.

Finally, Egypt's attempt to determine a proper course of action
through divinatory means of various sorts is mentioned in 19:3b: "they
will consult the worthless idols and the spirits of the dead, and the
ghosts and the familiar spirits." The last two objects in this list appear
earlier in Isa 8:19 in a passage where the prophet condemns those who
engage in necromancy of this sort. By including them here, the book
further explicates the degree to which Yhwh has confounded Egypt's
plans: They utilize divinatory practices doomed to fail. All of these
allusions to earlier texts by the oracle(s) in Isa 19 add further nuance
and clarification about Yhwh's anti-Egyptian plans that situate them
squarely within the Isaian literary and theological world.

Finally, a similar situation can be seen in a third passage describing
Yhwh's plans against another world power: Tyre. Isa 23 constitutes a

maśśāʾ against Tyre in two sections: verses 1b–14 and 15–18. The first section reflects on Tyre's (and Sidon's) downfall:

> Who has planned (*yāʿaṣ*) this
>> against Tyre, the bestower of crowns,
> whose merchants are princes,
>> whose traders are the honored of the earth?
> Yhwh of hosts has planned it (*yāʿaṣāh*),
>> to defile the pride of all glory
> to shame all the honored of the earth. (23:8–9)

Yhwh takes responsibility for orchestrating Tyre's demise, though the text provides no specific details. Hence, this text serves as another assertion of Yhwh's sovereignty over a polity with grand imperial ambitions, even one with no apparent hostility toward Judah or Jerusalem.[6]

Unlike the previous two texts examined in this section, Isa 23:1–15 contains no verbal links with earlier texts in Isaiah where some form of the root *yʿṣ* occurs. However, it does use language from earlier in Isaiah that is relevant to understanding Yhwh's "plan" here. For example, Isa 13 envisions Babylon's destruction in some detail. Near the end of the oracle condemning it, we find language that recurs in Isa 23: "And Babylon, the glory (*ṣəbî*) of the kingdoms, the splendor and pride (*gəʾôn*) of the Chaldeans, will be like Sodom and Gomorrah when God overthrew them" (13:19). The two passages share only *ṣəbî* and *gəʾôn*, but these two are comparatively rare in this section of Isaiah. The attentive reader of Isa 23 is invited to think about Tyre's doom along the lines of the pattern outlined for Babylon and its destruction in Isa 13. Both texts highlight the pride (*gəʾôn*) and glory (*ṣəbî*) of these two polities as part of the rationale for their downfall. This is, broadly, in line with Isaiah's critique of pride and arrogance expressed in Isa 2:5–22, though the target there is Israel itself. Finally, Isa 13:21–22 assert that Babylon will become an abode for wild animals in its postdestruction future, the same future envisioned for Tyre at the hand of the Babylonians (23:13).

Hence, in these three passages the book articulates Yhwh's opposition to polities more powerful than Jerusalem. Further, Yhwh's plan seeks to defeat them whether they pose a specific threat to Judah or not. Their existence as states with imperial aspirations is sufficient to warrant their demise.

---

[6] Hélène Sader, *The History and Archaeology of Phoenicia*, ABS 25 (Atlanta, GA: SBL, 2019), 252–55.

JUDAH'S PLANS

Finally, we come to a series of texts in which Yhwh's plan is detailed. Isa 28–33 is a series of woe-oracles that have been supplemented and expanded in various places.[7]

One of the supplements is an agricultural parable of Isa 28:23–29, which uses activities from farming to craft a theology of judgment (STULAC: 72–77). Just as a farmer must "destroy" the ground and some of what it produces (cumin, wheat, dill) in order to render them usable, so Yhwh uses national calamity as a threshing of the community. However, neither the farmer nor Yhwh destroys completely or for the sake of destruction. Rather, they each do so with the force necessary to produce a positive outcome. The parable affirms at the end that in developing such purposeful action Yhwh "causes a plan to be wonderful [and] sound wisdom to become great" (hipli' 'ēṣāh higdîl tûšîyāh). The specific language is reminiscent of Isa 9:5[6], a text examined earlier. Yhwh's plan there was associated with the persistence of the Davidic monarchy in the royal child, symbolically called pele' yô'ēṣ. Hence, the book of Isaiah associates both Yhwh's royal designee and national calamity properly understood via the language of y'ṣ. Additionally, both the child and disaster are made meaningful as part of Yhwh's plan.

This forms the literary backdrop for understanding the idea as presented in Isa 29:15–16 and 30:1(–5), two of the woe-oracles in this section. These texts address the plans crafted by Judah's own political elites that run counter to Yhwh's own plan for the community.

> Ha! You who hide a plan ('ēṣāh) too deep (hamma'ămîqîm) for
>   Yhwh,
>   whose deeds are in the dark,
>   and who say, "Who sees us? Who knows us?"
> You turn things upside down!
>   Shall the potter be regarded as the clay?
> Shall the thing made say of its maker,
>   "He did not make me";
> or the thing formed say of the one who formed it,
>   "He has no understanding"? (29:15–16)
>
> Oh, rebellious children, says Yhwh,
>   who carry out a plan, but not mine;

---

7   Isa 28:1–6; 29:1–4(8); 29:15–16; 30:1–5; 31:1–3; 33:1.

who make an alliance, but against my will,
    adding sin to sin.[8] (30:1)

The structure of Isaiah encourages the reader to understand the negative evaluation of these plans as flowing from the previous texts highlighting Yhwh's frustration of the plans developed by foreign powers, especially Egypt.

While Isa 29 and 30 have been expanded by later additions, most scholars situate the core of these chapters in the political crisis of the late eighth century. In their origins, both 29:15–16 and 30:1–5 have in view Hezekiah's decision to seek assistance from Egypt in his rebellion against Assyria. As these two passages make clear, Isaiah opposed the plan to arrange Egyptian aid. Isaiah mocks proponents of this effort who claim that Yhwh cannot detect what they are up to in verse 15 (perhaps a reference to the covenant arranged on the sly in 28:14–22). The second oracle goes further and argues that seeking Egypt's protection will become the source of Jerusalem's shame (30:3). Though Egypt possessed superior military resources, it proved to be an unreliable ally. Additionally, involving Egypt was likely to compel Assyria to strive even more to assert its will. As such, Isaiah's denunciation of Jerusalem's flirtations with Egypt demonstrate that Yhwh's plan to control the Assyrian empire was being opposed by his own people. Additionally, in light of 28:29 and the earlier discussion here, the book might also be suggesting that Yhwh's plan for Jerusalem involved defeat, though for Yhwh's purpose, not Assyria's.

Several links with earlier material in the book provide a literary framework for understanding the meaning of the notion of "plan" in these two texts. As we saw earlier, Isa 19 established an anti-Egypt sentiment featuring Yhwh's threat to confound and confuse their plans. The passages' common use of $y'ṣ$ in oracles concerning Egypt suggests that the reader of Isa 29 and 30 should recall the earlier expression of Yhwh's control of and disdain for Egypt. However, important differences exist between Isa 19 on the one hand and Isa 29 and 30 on the other, differences that elucidate the harsh criticism found in the latter texts. In Isa 19, the discussion centered on Yhwh's plan to thwart Egypt's own plans (never specified) and replace it with his own. The negative assessment of Egypt expressed there adds another element to why Judah's plan to seek Egyptian aid receives such harsh condemnation here. Jerusalem's plan

---

[8] The use of *ḥaṭṭ'at*, "sin," here should be understood as having political reference not (simply) religious meaning.

to court Egypt stands opposed to Isaiah's view about Egypt expressed earlier in the book.[9] The reader knows it is doomed to failure.

In Isa 30, two linguistic elements from earlier in the book provide an Isaianic frame of reference for the critique. First, the use of "rebellious sons" in 30:1 reminds the reader of 1:23, where one reads that Jerusalem's "princes are rebels." Though the phrase in 30:1 likely refers to those in 29:15 who "make a plan," the similarity to the language used in Isa 1 provides a characterization that informs the reader about such planners from the book's outset. Second, 30:2–3 take issue with those who seek refuge in Pharaoh's protection (mā'ôz). The oracle against Tyre in chapter 23 uses the same lexeme (vv. 4, 14) and has already informed the reader that foreign refuges can fall. Therefore, making a plan that relies on such ostensibly powerful polities entails risk since they might possess less enduring strength than Jerusalem's leaders assume. Rather, Isa 25 points out that Yhwh is the one who makes "wonderful plans" (pele' 'ēṣôt) that include, among other things, Yhwh himself as a refuge (mā'ôz) and shade (ṣēl; cf. 30:2) for his people. That such language appears in a psalm praising Yhwh for toppling a fortified city and noting that "the cities of ruthless nations will fear you" (25:3b) provides a template guiding the reader of chapters 29–30.

These passages teach the reader of chapters 28–33 how to think about entanglements with foreign polities within the textual world of Isaiah. As in Isa 5, the "plan" in Isa 29 and 30 originates in the context of an internal debate within Jerusalem and Judah over what is the proper course of action. Yhwh's own people create a plan contrary to Yhwh's own advice. However, the section asserts Yhwh's control of matters: Though Jerusalem's leaders create a plan, Yhwh prevails (29:9–10). In addition, Yhwh's ability to confound Egypt in chapter 19 renders the decision to seek assistance from Egypt in Isa 29 and 30 nonsensical. Since Yhwh has already declared an intention to thwart Egypt's own plans (19:12, 17), why should Judah's leaders craft a plan in defiance of Isaiah's advice that relies on Egypt?

'PLAN' IN ISAIAH 40–66

The book of Isaiah develops the idea of competing plans primarily in Isa 1–39, but several later texts also use the terminology. In Deutero-Isaiah eight passages use the specific terminology we have been tracking in

---

9   Of course, this has already been moderated to a degree by Isa 19:18–25, which expresses a much more positive view of Egypt (and Assyria!).

this study, terms derived from the root y‘ṣ.[10] It appears twice as a verb (40:14; 45:21) and six times in a noun form (40:13; 41:28; 44:26; 46:10, 11; 47:13). In the first text the presumed speaker is the anonymous prophet, but in all others we find first-person divine speech. Sweeney has identified the form of all these texts as disputation or, in one case, a trial scene, both of which occasionally utilize taunts.[11] These are all types of prophetic speech that are quite common in Isa 40–55 but less so in 1–39 (though not unheard of). Hence, little rhetorical or formal similarity exists between texts in Isa 1–39 and 40–66 that use this terminology.

Given the literary differences between texts developing the idea of "plan" in chapters 1–39 and 40–66, does a difference in meaning also appear? The short answer is yes. The relevant passages in Deutero-Isaiah use the terminology in texts developing two basic ideas. First, we find passages presenting strong polemics against other deities or their images. For example, 40:13–14a states:

Who has directed the spirit of Yhwh,
    or as his counselor (‘ăṣātô) instructed him?
Whom did he consult (nô‘āṣ) for his enlightenment?

The larger section of which this text is a part, 40:12–31, rebuts claims about the Babylonian deity Marduk and the assertions presented in *Enuma Elish* about his power and superiority. These characteristics were thought to be particularly evidenced in his creation of the cosmos. This lengthy section of Deutero-Isaiah argues to the contrary that Yhwh has, in fact, created the cosmos. He did so without consultation (unlike Marduk who consulted with the assembly of the gods) and according to a plan so superior it cannot be fathomed. The idea of Yhwh's plan thus fits within a larger argument against the supremacy of other deities. Similar polemics are found in 41:28 and 45:21.

A second line of argument that develops the notion of Yhwh's plan occurs in texts designed to confirm past and present prophecy (sometimes also in conjunction with claims about creation). A case in point occurs in Isa 46:9–11:

Remember the former things of old;
    for I am god and there is no other;
    I am god and there is no one like me,
declaring the end from the beginning

---

[10]   40:13, 14; 41:28; 44:26; 45:21; 46:10, 11; 47:13.
[11]   Marvin A. Sweeney, *Isaiah 40–66*, FOTL 19 (Grand Rapids, MI: Eerdmans, 2016), 391, 406.

and from ancient times thing not yet done,
saying, "My purpose (ʿǎṣātî) shall stand
    and I will fulfill my intention,"
calling a bird of prey from the east,
    the man for my purpose (ʿǎṣātô) from a far country.
I have spoken and I will bring it to pass;
    I have planned, and I will do it.

As is relatively frequent in Deutero-Isaiah, this text encourages its readers to remember what has happened in the past – often understood as
the author's invocation of earlier Isaianic prophecies – in order to justify its claims about the present and future. This text combines that
notion with claims about Yhwh's uniqueness. As in many of the texts
we examined in Isa 1–39, the claim here is about Yhwh's sovereignty
over geopolitical history. This is especially evident in Yhwh's claim to
have called a "bird of prey from the east," a transparent reference to
Cyrus of Persia, who conquered Babylon (cf. 44:28; 45:1).

Moreover, this is one of the last texts in Isaiah to use this language
of Yhwh's plan (only 47:13 uses it afterward). It appears as though this
text recalls prophecies in Isa 1–39 and uses that invocation to affirm
the plan laid out here. The passage broadly points back to texts about
Yhwh's plan earlier in the book and, as such, forms something of a conclusion to this idea in Isaiah.[12] Indeed, after Isa 47, no form of the root
yʿṣ appears in Isaiah. We can only speculate about why this might be
so, but one possible reason is that the anti-imperial rhetorical purpose
that drove the development and presentation of this idea throughout
the book comes full circle here. The idea is transformed from one that
primarily expresses resistance to the imperial advances of Assyria and
Babylon to one that takes credit for rise of the new Persian empire.
Yhwh's plan no longer opposes empire; it has become the empire.

FURTHER READING

Abernethy, Andrew, Mark G. Brett, Tim Bulkeley, and Tim Meadowcroft.
    Isaiah and Imperial Context: The Book of Isaiah in the Times of Empire.
    Eugene, OR: Pickwick, 2013.
Aster, Shawn Zelig. *Reflections of Empire in Isaiah 1–39: Responses to Assyrian
    Ideology.* ANEM 19. Atlanta, GA: SBL, 2017.
Dietrich, Walter. *Jesaja und die Politik.* Munich: Chr. Kaiser Verlag, 1976.
Fichtner, Johannes. "Jahves Plan in der Botschaft des Jesaja." *ZAW* 63 (1951):
    16–33.

[12]   Sweeney, *Isaiah 40–66*, 153.

Jensen, Joseph. "Yahweh's Plan in Isaiah and in the Rest of the Old Testament." *CBQ* 48 (1986): 443–55.

Roberts, J. J. M. "Enemies and Friends of the State: First Isaiah and Micah." Pages 329–38 in *Enemies and Friends of the State: Ancient Prophecy in Context.* Edited by Christopher A. Rollston. University Park, PA: Eisenbrauns, 2018.

Stromberg, Jacob. *An Introduction to the Study of Isaiah.* London: T&T Clark, 2011.

Stulac, Daniel J. *History and Hope: The Agrarian Wisdom of Isaiah 28–35.* Siphrut 24. University Park, PA: Eisenbrauns, 2018.

Uhlig, Torsten. *The Theme of Hardening in the Book of Isaiah.* FAT 2/13. Tübingen: Mohr Siebeck, 2009.

Werner, Wolfgang. *Studien zur alttestamentlichen Vorstellung vom Plan Jahwes.* BZAW 173. Berlin: de Gruyter, 1988.

Wildberger, Hans. "Jesajas Verständnis der Geschichte." Pages 83–117 in *Congress Volume Bonn 1962.* VTSup 9. Leiden: Brill, 1962.

Williamson, H. G. M. *A Commentary on Isaiah 1–27. Vol. 1: Isaiah 1–5.* ICC. London: T&T Clark, 2006.

Part IV

Afterlives of the Book of Isaiah

16 Theological Tensions in the Book of Isaiah
MATTHEW R. SCHLIMM

At its heart, biblical theology is the study of how biblical books present God, humanity, and creation.[1] A wide array of methodologies and approaches make this field quite diverse. Of the many possible approaches, this chapter treats the book of Isaiah holistically (ROBERTS; GOLDINGAY; PLEINS). Despite the book's complex history of formation, later authors were influenced by earlier texts, so that conversations emerge around key theological topics.[2]

GOD

The book of Isaiah overflows with creative images of God. This deity is compared to a weaver (38:12), a lumberjack (10:33–34), a woman in labor (42:14), a stonemason (28:16), a beautiful wreath (28:5), a nursing mother (49:15), a whistler (7:18), and a trap (8:14). While the book offers many other ways of thinking about God, some portrayals of God are more dominant than others. Among the more dominant images for God in the book, key tensions exist.

Core Characteristics of God: Morality and Love
One can distinguish between core characteristics of God – which do not change – and dynamic roles of God – which vary depending on humanity and the rest of creation. In Isaiah, two of God's most prominent enduring characteristics are morality and love. The book of Isaiah

---

[1] While this definition of biblical theology is a helpful starting point, its nature is heavily debated. See James Barr, *The Concept of Biblical Theology: An Old Testament Perspective* (Minneapolis, MN: Fortress, 1997). This chapter was written near the time of the death of Terence Fretheim, one of the greatest interpreters and biblical theologians of his generation. His deep influence on the author will hopefully be apparent.

[2] See, for example, H. G. M. Williamson, *The Book Called Isaiah: Deutero-Isaiah's Role in Composition and Redaction* (Oxford: Clarendon, 1994).

frames morality in terms of justice and righteousness. Throughout the
book, God displays a profound concern about the lack of justice (*mišpāṭ*)
and righteousness (**ṣdq*) among humanity. In chapter 5, when the book
explains what distinguishes God from humanity, it is precisely these
twin qualities:

> But Yhwh of heavenly forces will be exalted in *justice*,
> and the holy God will show himself holy in *righteousness*. (5:16)[3]

Over one hundred times, the book returns to these themes of justice
and righteousness, often alongside each other. In Isaiah, justice entails
fairness for all, the absence of oppression, and the promotion of peace
(*šālôm*). Righteousness, meanwhile, is fully compatible with justice and
encompasses innocence, honesty, and blamelessness. It is purity from
wickedness. As a moral deity, Isaiah's God stands opposed to evil of all
types.

If morality marks a core characteristic of Isaiah's God, so does
divine love, which the book characterizes as loyalty, an unwavering
commitment to the people. In Isa 54:10, God assures that this commitment will endure, come what may:

> The mountains may shift,
> and the hills may be shaken,
> but my faithful love won't shift from you,
> and my covenant of peace won't be shaken,
> says Yhwh, the one who pities you. (See also 54:8.)

God's loyalty toward Israel is steadfast and unchanging. A key manifestation of this love is found in how God refers to Israel and Judah as "*my
people*" over two dozen times throughout the book (e.g., 3:12; 40:1;
63:8). Repeatedly, the book stresses that God's anger is temporary,[4]
while insisting that God's salvation, covenant, and redemption – all
expressions of divine love – persist across time.[5]

In Isa 51:8, God describes what endures, and it is precisely divine
morality manifest in righteousness and divine love expressed in the
form of salvation:

---

[3]   Italics mine. Unless otherwise noted, quotations come from the Common English
      Bible, though the divine name has here been rendered "Yhwh."
[4]   Isa 10:25; 12:1; 51:22; 54:7–8; 57:16; 60:10. While the book does make this claim
      repeatedly, its manifold complexities mean that such a claim rests in uneasy tension
      with other parts of the book, such as 66:24.
[5]   Isa 45:17; 51:6, 8; 55:3; 59:21; 61:8; 63:16.

My righteousness is forever,
  and my salvation for all generations.

Throughout Isaiah, God is both concerned with what is right and lovingly attached to the people.

Dynamic Roles of God: Punisher and Comforter

Theoretically, God's morality and love need not come into conflict. As long as justice and righteousness characterize the people, God's love can be directed toward them without surprise, tension, or disruption. The problem on which the book of Isaiah is predicated, however, is that the people cannot be characterized as just and righteous. Instead, the people have offended God, repeatedly embodying immorality, wickedness, and evil. As a result, the very object of divine affection has become repulsive to God.

Consequently, the book employs dynamic divine roles that run contrary to each other. On the one hand, God will *punish* the people, seeking both to refine impurities and to bring an end to wrongdoing. On the other hand, God will *comfort* those facing various threats. These roles of punisher and comforter are mutable. In the face of evil, God takes on the role of punisher. In the face of upright, frightened, traumatized, disciplined, or repentant people, God takes on the role of comforter. While these roles are circumstantial, they are related to God's immutable characteristics: God's actions as punisher derives from God's enduring morality, and God's actions as comforter are expressions of God's enduring love.

Every major part of the book of Isaiah describes God as both a punisher and comforter. However, some parts of the book feature one role more prominently than others:

1. In Isa 1–39, the majority of verses portray God as a punisher (or lay the framework for God to function in such a role, for example, by listing the people's sins). However, a significant number of verses, probably around 30 percent (depending on how texts are interpreted) portray God as a comforter in one way or another.[6]
2. Most of the time, Isa 40–55 portrays God as a comforter. However, a significant number of verses (approximately one-third, depending again on how one interprets texts) relate to God's role as a punisher.

---

6   Scholars have sometimes tried to argue that the historical prophet Isaiah brought only a message of doom or only a message of salvation. Most likely, the prophet brought both messages (H. G. M. Williamson, "Isaiah: Prophet of Weal or Woe?" in *"Thus Speaks Ishtar of Arbela": Prophecy in Israel, Assyria, and Egypt in the Neo-Assyrian Period*, ed. Robert P. Gordon and Hans M. Barstad [Winona Lake, IN: Eisenbrauns, 2013], 273–300).

3. Isa 56–66 likewise emphasizes God's role as comforter, but it gives more attention to God's role as punisher than Isa 40–55 (CLAASSENS: 210; PLEINS: 225; GOWAN: 59–77, 146–62, 170–77).[7]

God's roles as comforter and punisher are naturally sometimes more intense than others. For example, Isa 48:22 says that the wicked lack well-being or peace (šālôm), which is disconcerting, but not as haunting as God's gory slaughtering and trampling of Edom in 34:5–6 and 63:1–6, respectively.

One noteworthy feature of Isaiah is how quickly the book can alternate from portraying God as punishing to portraying God as comforting, as the following examples begin to illustrate:

"Yhwh will strike Egypt, striking and then healing (19:22ab).

So God poured out on [Jacob] the heat of his anger and the fury of
    battle...
But now, says Yhwh...
Don't fear, for I have redeemed you;
I have called you by name; you are mine. (42:25–43:1)

I struck them; in rage I withdrew from them.
Yet they went on wandering wherever they wanted.
I have seen their ways, but I will heal them.
I will guide them and reward them with comfort. (57:17b–18d)

The lines between comfort and punishment can become blurred in other ways. In Isa 43:14, for example, God punishes the Babylonians. However, because the audience had suffered at the hands of the Babylonians, there is a sense in which such punishment would have comforted the audience: It entails the serving of justice and the end of Babylonian oppression.

Faced with human wickedness, Isaiah's God neither ignores wickedness nor ultimately abandons the relationship. Instead, the God of this book continually oscillates between being humanity's greatest threat and its greatest consolation.

Several biblical theologians have noted that Isaiah's depictions of God (and similar depictions of the divine elsewhere in the Bible) present challenges, especially for faith communities who understand the book

---

[7] Space constraints prevent a listing of every verse in Isaiah and whether it relates to God as a comforter or punisher.

to speak authoritatively as God's word today (CLAASSENS: 216–17; TULL: 255–66, esp. 257). When describing God as a punisher, for example, the book of Isaiah claims that God causes both violence and suffering. Additionally, Jerusalem is often portrayed with feminine imagery. In a world where many commit violence against women, where a number of people enact violence in the name of God, and where others not only suffer but additionally feel haunted by the idea that God caused their suffering, Isaianic texts need to be handled with utmost care.

One way to deal with such texts with care is to bring Isaiah's texts about violence and suffering into conversation with other biblical texts that promote nonviolence (e.g., Isa 2:4) and maintain that God is not always responsible for suffering (e.g., Isa 54:15).[8] It is also essential to recognize that the book of Isaiah reflects the concerns of a traumatized people. That recognition both encourages contemporary readers to engage in theological reflection even amid tragedy, and furthermore serves as a safeguard against simplistically and uncritically appropriating all of Isaiah's portrayals of God into very different contexts (CLAASSENS: 216–17).

Divine Sovereignty and Human Freedom

The tension between God's roles as punisher and comforter are hardly the only theological tensions within the book of Isaiah. The book as a whole goes to great lengths to emphasize that God is sovereign, the maker and controller of creation. Indeed, for God to punish and bring genuine comfort, God must be sovereign, capable of orchestrating world events so that people can experience both the agony of punishment and the relief of comfort. At the same time, however, the book qualifies any understanding of divine sovereignty by taking the concept of human freedom with great seriousness.

Divine sovereignty is reflected in a variety of ways.[9] Some passages present God in royal imagery to underscore God's power (ABERNETHY; KIM: 21–22; GOLDINGAY: 131–34).[10] Others talk explicitly about

---

[8]   Matthew R. Schlimm, *This Strange and Sacred Scripture: Wrestling with the Old Testament and Its Oddities* (Grand Rapids, MI: Baker Academic, 2015), 70–76, 139–59.

[9]   On the different ways that God's sovereignty is expressed in different parts of the book, see Tim Bulkeley, "What Purposes Do Assertions of Divine Sovereignty Serve in Isaiah?" in *Isaiah and Imperial Context: The Book of Isaiah in the Times of Empire,* eds. Andrew T. Abernethy, Mark G. Brett, Tim Bulkeley, and Tim Meadowcroft (Eugene, OR: Pickwick, 2013), 71–84; cf. Carolyn J. Sharp, *Old Testament Prophets for Today* (Louisville, KY: Westminster John Knox, 2009), 63–65.

[10]   For example, 6:1, 5; 24:23; 33:21–22; 37:16; 41:21; 43:15; 44:6; 52:7; 62:3.

divine strength.[11] God not only is over nations and their rulers, but God also directs them to do divine bidding (CLAASSENS: 216).[12] Repeatedly, the book emphasizes that unlike human plans, God's plans are sure to come to fruition.[13] The fundamental idea in the oracles against the nations (esp. Isa 13–23) is that God stands in judgment over the nations of the world. The book also underscores divine power by reducing other deities to derisible idols while describing God as opposing and even slaying mythological beings (GOWAN: 151–53).[14] This God has power over the sun, moon, stars, and other facets of creation.[15] After all, who can better manipulate creation than the one responsible for its existence?[16] Texts such as 40:12–26 combine many of these ideas, arguing that neither nations, rulers, idols, nor any human being possesses the supreme power of Israel's God.

The book of Isaiah takes divine sovereignty so seriously that it asserts that not only good events but also calamity occur because of God's will. Thus, in 45:7, God says:

> I form light and create darkness,
> make prosperity and create doom;
> I am Yhwh, who does all these things.

In part because Second Isaiah repeatedly asserts that there is only one God, it says that God is responsible for earthly events, good and bad alike.[17]

At the same time, the book of Isaiah implies that God's power has limits. As mentioned earlier, the book is predicated on the fact that people have rejected God and God's teachings. So, while the book may lack creedal statements about divine powerlessness, it nevertheless makes clear that much that transpires runs contrary to God's will. As

---

[11]   For example, 12:2; 28:2; 33:2; 43:13; 45:24; 49:5; 52:10; 59:1, 16; 63:1.

[12]   For example, 5:26; 7:17–20; 22:15–25; 24:21; 34:2; 37:36–38; 41:25; 43:14; 44:28–45:4, 13–14; 49:23; 55:5; 63:1–6.

[13]   For example, 8:10; 14:24–27; 19:3; 30:1. For more on God's plans in Isaiah, see HIBBARD, "Divine and Human Plans in the Book of Isaiah," Chapter 15 in this volume.

[14]   For example, 2:18–20; 10:5–15 (which may address not only Assyria but also its deity Aššur); 25:8 (alluding to Mot); 27:1; 30:22; 31:7; 37:19; 40:19–20; 41:29; 42:17; 44:9–20; 45:16, 20–21; 46:1–7; 48:5; 51:9; 57:9 (likely referring to Molek), 13; cf. 14:12; 26:14.

[15]   For example, 13:10; 24:23; 34:4; 38:8; 43:20; 44:27; 51:10; 60:19–20; 64:2[3].

[16]   Images of God as creator can be found in all major parts of the book, most prominently in Second Isaiah, For example, 17:7; 27:11; 37:16; 40:26–28; 41:20; 42:5; 43:1, 15; 45:7–12, 18; 48:13; 51:13; 54:16; 57:16; 64:7[8]; 65:17.

[17]   See also 13:11–16, which claims God is responsible for disaster, including infanticide and rape. As noted earlier, many Isaianic texts need to be handled with utmost care, especially by faith communities who affirm the authority of Isaiah as scripture.

will be discussed later, sinfulness dominates Isaiah's characterization of humanity.

A particularly noteworthy example about the interplay of divine sovereignty and human freedom is found in Isa 47:5–15.[18] The text says that the Babylonians functioned as God's agents by punishing the people of Judah for their sins (47:6ab). Yet, while functioning as divine agents, the Babylonians went beyond the divine mandate, working against the divine will by exalting themselves (47:7–8) and enacting too much violence (47:6cd). Consequently, they are subject to divine punishment themselves (47:9–11).

As this example suggests, the book of Isaiah affirms God as being in control of the most momentous events of its day: the rise and fall of kingdoms. At the same time, divine sovereignty never completely overrides human freedom. People can simultaneously accomplish parts of God's will (in this case, punishing Judah) while violating other parts of God's will (self-exaltation and failing to show mercy on the most vulnerable). Isaiah's portrait of God is complex, and it is not surprising that different faith communities today differ considerably in how they understand the interplay of divine sovereignty and human freedom.[19] The complexities and intricacies of the biblical text resist simplistic dogmatic systematization.

A God So Far and So Near

Understanding Isaiah's God involves wrestling with the book's ongoing tension between divine transcendence and immanence. To get at these ideas, the book of Isaiah uses its own native vocabulary, describing how God is both distinct from creation and thoroughly enmeshed in relationship with it.

Key to understanding how the book portrays divine transcendence is the concept of holiness. While other books of the Hebrew Bible refer to God only rarely as "the Holy One" or "the Holy One of Israel," these titles are favorites for Isaiah, appearing more than two dozen times (e.g., 5:19; 41:14; 60:9). Holiness is typically defined in terms of being "set apart" or "wholly other," but such definitions only brush the surface of a core biblical term that entails much more. Divine holiness, at least in Isaiah, involves the overwhelming greatness, mystery, and perfection of God. It encompasses all that is pure and dangerous about God. When

---

18   See also 10:5–19, which features many of the same elements, but involves the Assyrians rather than the Babylonians.

19   Calvinists and Wesleyans, for example, tend to disagree significantly about this topic.

individuals encounter God's holiness, they experience fear, shock, awe, stupor, and feelings of their own insufficiencies, as seen in the story of the prophet's call (6:1–13).

Holiness is not the only way in which the book talks about divine transcendence. At times, it explicitly refers to the vast differences between God and humanity:

My plans aren't your plans,
  nor are your ways my ways, says Yhwh.
Just as the heavens are higher than the earth,
  so are my ways higher than your ways,
  and my plans than your plans. (55:8–9)

Elsewhere, the book denounces those who question God's plans (45:9–13; cf. 10:15). Distance between God and humanity finds dramatic expression in accounts of God punishing the people by hiding from them (e.g., 1:15; 8:17; 54:8; 57:17; 59:2; 64:6[7]). Humanity is "less than nothing and emptiness" compared with God (40:17; cf. 40:15, 22).

At other times, the book insists that God is not only different from humanity, but also utterly different from every other deity of which humanity has conceived. Indeed, while the book's monotheistic claims have attracted a fair amount of scholarly attention, these remarks typically serve the rhetorical purpose within the book of underscoring that God is different from everyone and everything – the only one worthy of worship and allegiance.[20] These remarks come primarily in chapters 40–55, which also stress God's role as creator. This role distinguishes God from creation, underscoring God as unequalled and incomparable.[21]

Although divine transcendence thus receives strong emphasis, the book also goes to great lengths to talk about divine immanence. Isaiah's God does not merely relate to and interact with humanity but does so with remarkable intimacy. Isa 25:8 describes God personally wiping tears from every face. In 30:21, God walks directly behind the people,

---

[20] Joel S. Kaminsky and Anne Stewart, "God of All the World: Universalism and Developing Monotheism in Isaiah 40–66," *HTR* 99 (2006): 139–63, here 144; cf. 156. To assert that God exists and no one else (45:6, 14, 22; 46:9) is to contradict what the Babylonians claim about themselves (per 47:8–10) and what they claim about particular gods in the *Enuma Elish* (II 56, 74, 76; IV 4, 6; VII 14, 88, 98; for translation see W. G. Lambert, *Babylonian Creation Myths* [Winona Lake, IN: Eisenbrauns, 2013], 66–67, 86–87, 124–25, 128–29).

[21] See esp. 45:5–8. The Hebrew word for "create" (*bārā'*) has a unique feature in the Bible: in its most common conjugation (the *qal*), only God serves as the verb's subject; no human is capable of this sort of activity. Isaiah uses this word more than any other book of the Bible.

and a few verses later, God personally bandages the people's wounds (30:26). Rather than remaining aloft, God knows of Hezekiah's sickness, hears his prayers, and responds with healing (38:1–5). Several parts of Isaiah suggest that God suffers and is moved to pity because of the intimate relationship between the deity and people.[22] With poetic imagery, Second and Third Isaiah emphasize the tenderness and affection that God has for the people. The text talks of people in God's hand (41:10; cf. 49:16), eyes (43:4), and womb (46:3). In relation to Israel, God is portrayed as a spouse (54:5; 62:4–5; cf. 50:1), a father (45:10; 63:16; 64:7[8]), and a mother (46:3; 49:15; 66:13). Isaiah's God has a covenant bond with the people (54:8, 10; 55:3; 59:21; 61:8).

Divine immanence finds expression not only in intimate imagery, but also in the ways the book talks about Zion (KIM: 26–28).[23] The book emphasizes that God's home is in Jerusalem itself (2:2; 8:18; 18:7; 56:7; 66:20), a place that will be filled with God's glory and dazzling light (4:5; cf. 11:10; 24:23; 60:1–22). Amid close fellowship with God at Zion, people will learn God's ways (2:3; 11:2; 30:19–21), embodying the divine qualities of justice and righteousness (e.g., 1:27; 11:1–5; 33:5), which lead to peace (2:4; 9:6[7]; 11:6–9; 25:8; 26:1–3, 12; 32:17–18; 60:17–18; 65:18–25; 66:12). There, they will experience great happiness, celebration, and joy (e.g., 12:3–6; 25:6–9; 30:19; 35:10; 51:3, 11; 52:9; 60:14–15; 61:2–3; 65:18–19; 66:10–14) (GOLDINGAY: 110–16; GOWAN: 65–68, 154–55).

As with other theological tensions, immanence and transcendence clash in Isaiah. The book's teachings about divine immanence point to God's desire for fellowship with humanity, and are thus closely related to divine love, but the book's teachings about transcendence, especially holiness, suggest that much about humanity is vastly inferior to God. One way in which the book resolves this tension between immanence and transcendence is that it envisions God as purifying Zion and transforming it into a place that can host the divine presence. Chapter 4 says:

> When Yhwh washes the filth from Zion's daughters, and cleanses Jerusalem's bloodguilt from within it by means of a wind of judgment and a searing wind, then Yhwh will create over the whole site

---

[22] On divine suffering, see 15:5; 16:9, 11; 63:9–10; cf. 1:14; 7:13; 42:14; 43:24. On divine pity and compassion (*rḥm), see 14:1; 30:18; 49:10, 13; 54:8, 10; 55:7; 60:10. For more on these themes, see Abraham J. Heschel, *The Prophets*, 2 vols. (New York: HarperCollins, 1962; repr., Peabody, MA: Prince, 1999), 1:61–97, 145–58.

[23] While I mention Zion and Jerusalem in this section, some texts focus on broader locales such as Judah, Israel, and Jacob.

of Mount Zion and over its assembly a cloud by day and smoke and
the light of a blazing fire by night. (4:4–5b)

This text asserts that Zion will become God's home after God first
cleanses Jerusalem from its violence. Envisioning God's presence in
terms of a cloud and blazing fire (4:5), the text not only uses imagery
from exodus traditions (cf. Exod 13:21–22; Num 9:15–16; Deut 1:33),
but also suggests that even when God is palpably present among the
people, God's presence will still be dangerous (similar language is used
in Num 21:28; Ps 83:15[14]; 106:18). In this way, neither transcendence nor immanence is compromised. God will be intensely present
in Jerusalem, but only on God's terms and via divine transformation
of the human city. Thus, God remains distinct from humanity while
enmeshed in relationship with it. Other parts of Isaiah similarly speak
of cleansing, purification, and refinement to describe how God can be
intensely present among humanity whose wickedness offends God
(1:16–17, 25–26; 31:9; 33:14; 48:10–11).

At the end of the book, divine transcendence takes center stage
with important qualifications. The last chapter begins:

Yhwh says:
Heaven is my throne,
    and earth is my footstool.
So where could you build a house for me,
    and where could my resting place be? (66:1)

In isolation from the rest of the book, this rhetorical question would
suggest that no place built by human hands could ever serve as God's
home or resting place. Yet this statement appears after the book has
sung the praises of Zion.[24] And in the next verse, God talks about being
with the afflicted, the broken in spirit, and those obedient to God's
word (66:2; cf. 57:15). For Isaiah's audiences, Jerusalem certainly knew
its share of afflictions and brokenness. It is precisely among the humble
and obedient that this supreme God will make a home (cf. 14:32).

HUMANITY

When it comes to Isaiah's theological anthropology, the dominant note
sounded by the book is humanity's sinfulness. However, there are other
notes as well, particularly as they pertain to the capacity of humanity

---

[24]   Isa 60:13 even equates God's footstool with Zion.

to act with righteousness, the role of human leaders, and the role of the nations and empires.

Sinfulness

The opening words of Isaiah provide an excellent starting point for describing the book's perspective on humanity. They focus on sin:

> Hear you heavens, and listen earth,
> for Yhwh has spoken:
> I reared children; I raised them,
> and they turned against me!
> An ox knows its owner,
> and a donkey its master's feeding trough.
> But Israel doesn't know;
> my people don't behave intelligently.
> Doom! Sinful nation, people weighed down with crimes,
> evildoing offspring, corrupt children!
> They have abandoned Yhwh,
> despised the holy one of Israel;
> they turned their backs on God. (1:2–4)

As if in a court of law, God calls forth the heavens and earth as witnesses to testify against the people.[25] These witnesses are chosen not only because they are everywhere and thus know all that the people have done, but also because, according to the logic of Isaiah, disobeying God entails a perversion of the created order. Even farm animals have more sense than the people who reject the very God who raised them like a parent (DARR).[26] The people's wickedness is so pervasive that it overwhelms the people.

Other parts of Isaiah speak of humanity as sinful in similar ways. In the parable of the vineyard, the people's sin is portrayed as unnatural, the very opposite of what should have happened, given the farmer's care (5:1–7). The people are so foolish that they cannot tell the difference between good and evil (5:20). They have failed to grasp a very basic but very crucial theological point: As creator, God alone is over all and should be exalted. Misunderstanding this point, they have instead exalted themselves to the place reserved for God alone by embodying

---

[25] Like other pieces of prophetic literature, Isaiah uses courtroom imagery to issue indictments, judgments, and punishments (e.g., 1:18–20; 3:13–15; 41:1–5, 21–29; 43:8–13).

[26] Some elements of Isaiah's moral logic have commonalities with wisdom literature (see, e.g., Prov 6:6).

the sin of pride (GOWAN: 61–62, 68–73).[27] Such behavior is utter foolishness, as if an ax thought it were more powerful than a lumberjack or a staff greater than a shepherd (10:15; cf. 29:16; 45:9–10). When not exalting themselves, the people have exalted objects to the place reserved for God alone through the sin of idolatry. They ironically "worship their handiwork, what their own fingers have made" – oblivious to the awe-inspiring splendor and majesty of God (2:8; see also, e.g., 1:29; 2:20; 30:22; 31:7; 40:18–26; 44:9–20; 57:3–13). Because of their inability to grasp the most basic features of the created order, the book portrays humanity as not only foolish, but also deaf, blind, drunk, confused, asleep, and illiterate.[28] As John Barton puts it in his account of ethics in Isa 1–39, "[W]e have an early example of that way of approaching ethics which begins with a hierarchically ordered universe whose moral pattern ought to be apparent to all whose reason is not hopelessly clouded, and one which derives all particular moral offences from the one great sin, a disregard for natural law" (BARTON: 138–139). In Isaiah, the people have lost their moral bearings and are out of sync with creation.

The Possibility of Human Good

In the book of Isaiah, human sin receives primary attention because it presents the greatest problem. It is an offense to divine righteousness and the cause of divine punishment. Some verses suggest that human sinfulness is all-encompassing and pervasive. As Isa 64:5–6a[6–7a] puts it,

> We have *all* become like the unclean; ...
>   our sins, like the wind, carry us away.
> *No one* calls on your name;
>   *no one* bothers to hold on to you. (emphasis added)

On their own, these words suggest that sinfulness has thoroughly infected all people.

These words, however, are part of a larger literary unit that speaks of righteous people. The preceding verse addresses God, beginning, "You look after those who gladly do right" (64:4[5]). Before concluding

---

[27] Isa 2:11–22; 5:15–16; 14:13–14; 25:10b–12; 26:5; cf. 10:32–11:1; 33:5, 10; 40:12–15.

[28] Isa 6:9–10; 28:7–13; 29:9–12; 42:18–20; 43:8; 48:8; 59:9–10. Parts of the book imagine an unblocking of the people's senses (25:7; 29:18; 32:3–4; 35:5–6; 50:5). Even though such language is found within the Bible, readers need to recognize the harmfulness of ableist language (such as envisioning "disability as an anomaly or deficiency," to quote J. Blake Couey, "Isaiah, Jeremiah, Ezekiel, Daniel, and the Twelve," *Disability and the Bible: A Commentary*, ed. Sarah Melcher, Mikeal C. Parsons, and Amos Yong, Studies in Religion Theology & Disability [Waco, TX: Baylor University Press, 2017], 215–73, here 226).

that the book of Isaiah perfectly aligns with modern ideas about total depravity, therefore, it is important to recognize that book's portrait of humanity, like that of God, is rather complex.

As 64:4[5] begins to indicate, the book of Isaiah is not afraid to talk about some people as doing what is right. Often, the book will set such people in contrast to those who disobey God (e.g., 1:19–20; 3:10–11; 33:14–15; 50:11–51:1; 57:13) (KIM: 17–20).[29] A key sin in the book is the persecution of the righteous – which of course presupposes that righteous people do exist (5:23; 29:21; 51:7; 57:1). Parts of the book suggest that people can repent and turn away from sinfulness (1:27; 31:6; 59:20; cf. 30:15).[30] Many texts envision God playing a key role in humanity finding forgiveness and righteousness (6:5–7; 44:22; 56:1; 60:21; 61:3, 10). Together, these texts about human righteousness add important qualifications to the book's rhetorical emphases on human sinfulness.

Leadership
Among those who have sinned, the book lays particular blame on leaders. Especially in First Isaiah, those with power have failed the broader populace, and so God will remove them from power.[31] As chapter 3 puts it:

> As for my people—oppressors strip them and swindlers rule them.
>   My people—your leaders mislead you and confuse your paths....
> Yhwh will enter into judgment
>   with the elders and princes of his people:
> You yourselves have devoured the vineyard;
>   the goods stolen from the poor are in your houses.
> How dare you crush my people
>   and grind the faces of the poor?
>   says Yhwh God of heavenly forces. (3:12, 14–15)

As these verses suggest, some of the sins that the book focuses on are greed, oppression, violence, and mistreatment of the poor (PLEINS: 253–70).[32] Repeatedly, the book makes clear that leaders have used their power selfishly rather than to help the people as a whole. As a

---

29 Proverbs similarly contrasts the righteous and wicked (e.g., 10:3, 6–7).
30 Other verses suggest that repentance and forgiveness will be elusive (6:10–11; 22:14).
31 For example, 1:23; 3:1–15; 5:22–24; 9:13–16[14–17]; 22:15–25; 26:21; 28:1–15; 32:5–7.
32 Eunny P. Lee, "Isaiah," in *The Old Testament and Ethics: A Book-by-Book Survey*, eds. Joel B. Green and Jacquelyn E. Lapsley (Grand Rapids, MI: Baker Academic, 2013), 109–12, here 110.

result, the chief object of God's wrath is the leadership whose oppressive ways stand as an affront to divine righteousness and justice.

God does not seek to punish these leaders merely for the sake of punishing them. Instead, God longs to make Zion a place that reflects God's own righteousness, justice, and holiness. Consequently, several parts of the book envision new leaders who will come and act to realize God's will in the midst of the people (GOLDINGAY: 139–42).[33] At times, this future leadership is described in such lofty terms that Christians have found connections with Jesus. However, the book of Isaiah actually uses the term "messiah" (Heb. *māšîaḥ;* which means simply "anointed one") only once: In 45:1 it describes the Persian king Cyrus, who conquers Babylon and allows the rebuilding of Jerusalem (44:28). On one other occasion, the book uses the related verb for "anoint" to refer to a person:

> Yhwh God's spirit is upon me, because Yhwh has anointed me. He has sent me to bring good news to the poor, to bind up the brokenhearted, to proclaim release for captives, and liberation for prisoners. (61:1)

The text does not identify the speaker. In its original context, it is likely a prophet, a postexilic heir of the Isaianic tradition.[34] However, in Luke 4:18–19, Jesus reads from this verse (as well as Isa 58:6; 61:2a) at a synagogue in his hometown of Nazareth. Afterwards, he says, "Today, this scripture has been fulfilled just as you heard it" (Luke 4:21). For Luke, this proclamation by Jesus begins his earthly ministry, signaling that Jesus embodies the ideals of leadership envisioned by the book of Isaiah.

While this example is thus an important one, it is only one of hundreds of cases where the New Testament connects Jesus and his followers with the book of Isaiah (see PAO, "Isaiah in the New Testament," Chapter 18 in this volume) (SAWYER: 21–41; CHILDS 2004: 5–21). For example, Isaiah's Servant Songs, especially 52:13–53:12, have informed Christian understandings of Jesus (already in the New Testament, see, e.g., Acts 8:26–38). While history is filled with christological interpretations of Isaiah, many modern exegetes warn against the dangers of supersessionism and stress the importance of understanding the text's connection to its earliest audiences before leaping ahead centuries to

---

[33] Isa 1:26; 9:5–6[6–7]; 11:1–10; 16:5; 32:1–5; 42:1–4; 55:3–4; cf. 16:5.
[34] See the discussion of various possibilities in Joseph Blenkinsopp, *Isaiah 56–66: A New Translation with Introduction and Commentary,* AB19B (New York: Doubleday, 2003), 220–23.

connections with Jesus. In the case of the Servant Songs, readers can miss much if they do not consider the ways in which texts spoke in their original context (GOWAN: 159–61).

Nations and Empires

Leaders are not the only ones elected by God for special duties. God also employs nations and empires to carry out aspects of the divine will. The book speaks repeatedly about God choosing Israel and Judah, the home of Zion.[35] Because of their failures, God elected first the Assyrians and later the Babylonians to serve as agents of punishment (POULSEN; ABERNETHY).[36] Later still, God raised up the Persians to end Babylonian domination and allow a restoration (GOWAN: 147–49).[37]

Isaiah's alternating emphases on doom and hope apply not only to Israel and Judah, but also to the broader kingdoms of the world, including empires. The oracles against the nations in chapters 13–23 denounce one nation after another until the text culminates in a denunciation of the earth as a whole (ch. 24). Yet God is not universally opposed to the nations. God's heart appears to cry out when the Moabites suffer (15:5; see also 16:9, 11).[38] Meanwhile, the Ethiopians are envisioned as bringing gifts to God (18:7). Isa 19:18–25 is a remarkable text, describing Egypt (and to a lesser extent Assyria) as worshipping Israel's God.

The portrayal of the nations in Isa 40–66 has raised a fair amount of scholarly debate (KIM: 23–25; GOWAN: 155–59).[39] On the one hand, these chapters contain some of the Hebrew Bible's most positive portrayals of the nations.[40] Future hope emerges repeatedly in these texts, and a recurrent expectation is that various nations will join in worshipping Israel's God. Some scholars even talk about universalism in Isaiah, because texts such as 49:6 talk of God's salvation going out to "the ends of the earth." On the other hand, the language in some texts is ambiguous.

---

35   See 14:1; 41:8–9; 43:10; 44:1–2; 49:7.
36   See, for example, 7:17–20; 8:4–8; 39:6–7.
37   See esp. 44:24–45:4.
38   Isa 15:5 is open to multiple interpretations. It may mock the Moabites, and the speaker may be the prophet rather than God. However, literature from the ancient Near East repeatedly portrays deities mourning over the destruction of cities or land ("A Neo-Babylonian Lament for Tammuz," trans. William W. Hallo [COS 1.118.419–20]; "Lamentation over the Destruction of Sumer and Ur," trans. Jacob Klein [COS 1.166.535–39]). Such cultural evidence suggests that God very well may be the speaker of 15:5, expressing genuine concern rather than mockery.
39   Another helpful entry-point to this debate is Kaminsky and Stewart, "God of All the World," 139–63.
40   For example, Isa 49:6; 51:5; 60:1–22; 61:11; 66:18–23.

For example, Isa 49:6 does not explicitly state whether the phrase "the ends of the earth" refers to the people of Israel and Judah in exile (see 49:6bc) or to foreigners as well (see 49:7). Additionally, the oracles against the nations found in Isa 13–23 resurface in different ways in Isa 40–66 (e.g., 63:1–6). While some texts have peaceful and inclusive visions of foreign nations, they often presuppose the subordination of these nations to Judah (and thus express the desire for imperial domination), rather than offering egalitarian hope (see 45:14; 49:23; 60:12, 14).[41] The book even closes with a mixed message open to multiple interpretations. The book's second-to-last verse says that "all humanity will come to worship" Israel's God, but its final verse depicts a scene of horror where those who have rebelled against God face death, fire, and decay (66:23–24).

One useful step forward in wrestling with the book's diverse teachings about the nations is to recognize that although the final form of the book displays some inclusiveness toward foreigners, this cannot be easily equated with modern ideas of universalism (see also the qualified way universalism is affirmed in GOWAN: 156–57).[42] That is to say, the latest parts of the book hold out hope for all peoples while simultaneously placing key expectations upon them. Thus, texts such as Isa 56:3–8 describe immigrants participating in the worship of God, but it simultaneously expects that they serve God, love the divine name, become God's servants, keep sabbaths, and hold fast to God's covenant.[43] The book of Isaiah contains no unconditional offers of salvation for everyone, even if it has served as a springboard for later thinkers to move in that direction.

CREATION

Previous parts of this chapter have touched on creation, especially God's role as creator and human disobedience as a perversion of the created order. But creation also functions in other important ways in the poetry of the book.

Creation as an Agent of Divine Justice

In Isaiah, because the natural world is created by God, it has moral-religious qualities. Sin's consequences are woven into the fabric of reality. Those who do what is right can expect to "eat the fruit of their

---

[41]   J. J. M. Roberts, "The End of War in the Zion Tradition: The Imperialist Background of an Old Testament Vision of World Wide Peace," *HBT* 26 (2004), 2–22, here 17.

[42]   Brooks Schramm, *The Opponents of Third Isaiah: Reconstructing the Cultic History of the Restoration*, JSOTSup 193 (Sheffield: Sheffield Academic, 1995), 122–23.

[43]   See similarly the prohibitions on impurity in 35:8; 52:1.

labors" (3:10; cf. 1:19). As righteousness and justice are established in the land, deserts will become farmlands while inhabitants will find peace, calm, and safety (32:15–18). Obeying God's commands leads to peace, prosperity, and multiple offspring – the greatest of blessings for biblical people (48:17–19). Like many prophetic writings, the book of Isaiah has similarities with both Deuteronomistic ideas and wisdom literature that speak of blessings for the obedient and curses for the disobedient (see, e.g., Deut 28:1–69; Prov 10:7; 11:11).

When people fail to obey God's commands, they will suffer (1:20). Especially First Isaiah stresses that creation will work in concert with the divine will to ensure that fitting punishments come to the sinful. It contends that those who revere sacred trees and gardens will become like dying trees and waterless gardens (1:29–30). Those who exalted themselves will attempt to hide in the dust of the ground when God arises to make the earth tremble (2:9–21; see also 25:10–12; 26:5–6; 29:4). Proud women who walk adorned will be afflicted with scabs and laid bare (3:16–17) (TULL: 104–10). Those with ill-gotten gains will have nowhere to leave their wealth (10:2–3). The most exalted will be chopped down like tree branches (10:33–34). Because of haughtiness, which includes an unawareness of the creator's exaltedness, the stars, sun, and moon will grow dark, and the heavens and earth will shake (13:10–14; cf. 24:23). The king of Babylon, who aspired to ascend to heaven and raise his throne above the stars, will instead descend into the depths of Sheol on a bed of maggots (14:9–22). Those who act foolishly will be confused with a spirit of distortion, like a drunkard staggering in vomit (19:11–14). Collectively, these texts portray creation as a moral realm, one that can function as an instrument of the creator's judgment on those who have violated its order. Punishments are often related to the violations committed, as though creation itself is somehow able to approximate *lex talionis*, doling out fitting consequences for sins.

Creation's Distortion Owing to Humanity's Wickedness

A great deal of Isaiah's poetry portrays creation as profoundly affected by God's punishment, such that it moves away from a cosmos marked by order and goodness toward one marked by disorder, desolation, and distortion. Divine judgment adversely affects vegetation (5:6; 7:23–25; 10:18–19, 34; 15:6; 16:8, 10; 24:7–13; 32:12–13; 33:9; 42:15), sources of water (15:6, 9; 19:5–10; 34:9; 50:2–3), and animal life (13:21–22; 14:23; 32:14; 34:11–15).

With a barrage of shocking images, Isaiah also portrays the earth itself as profoundly impacted by sin and its consequences. The book's references to Sodom and Gomorrah in its opening verses are only a foreshadowing of descriptions to come (1:9–10; cf. 13:19). Isa 10:23 and 28:22 describe the complete destruction of the entire land (cf. 17:9; 36:10). Elsewhere, the land is no longer able to have inhabitants (13:20). There is also imagery of God striking the earth (11:4) and it being shaken (13:13, 24:19) and trembling (41:5). Isa 34:3–7 talks of mountains being drenched with blood and the land being soaked in it, while 5:25 describes corpses that cover the streets. On another occasion, the earth is portrayed as wearing out like a garment (51:6). In chapter 24, such language reaches its height, where the language of complete destruction and desolation dominates (24:3). The world is portrayed as fading and withering (24:4), then as being broken, splitting open, spinning recklessly, and falling, never to rise again (24:19–20; cf. Isa 21:9; Amos 5:2). In short, the punishment that results from sin irreparably distorts the world. It no longer gives signs of originating from a benevolent creator (Isa 8:21). While functioning as God's agent of punishment, creation has become increasingly disordered.

God's Desire to Recreate the Universe

Consequently, Isaiah anticipates a new creation. Because of the manifold distortions of the created order, it is necessary for God to create anew. Although language of darkness characterizes sin and its punishment (5:20; 13:10–14; 59:9–10), several passages speak of light coming into darkness (9:1[2]; 29:18; 42:16; 58:10; 60:1–3). Vegetation, which in many passages was destroyed as a result of sin, is envisioned as thriving in its healthiest forms (14:8; 32:15–16; 35:1–2, 6–7; 41:19). Water springs forth in dry lands and in places stricken by drought so that deserts become fertile (29:17; 32:15; 35:1–7; 41:17–18; 43:19–21; 44:3). The text also portrays peace between predators and prey (11:6–9; 35:7, 9). Though 16:10 described the removal of gladness and joy, a number of passages anticipate its return (9:2[3]; 14:7–8; 26:19; 29:19; 55:12). In sharp contrast to the language of corpses filling streets (5:25), Isa 25:8 talks of God swallowing death, while 26:19 envisions the dead living and their corpses rising.[44] Not surprisingly, then, several passages describe newness on God's part (e.g., 42:9–12; 43:16–21). Isa 32:11–20

---

[44]   There are many ways of interpreting this language, as is helpfully described by Christopher B. Hays, *Death in the Iron Age II and in First Isaiah*, FAT 79 (Tübingen: Mohr Siebeck, 2011), 318–36.

describes creation falling into disarray through divine punishment, only to be restored again as justice, righteousness, peace, and prosperity arise. In 65:17–25 and 66:22, the text speaks specifically about new heavens and a new earth, the resolution to the problem of a distorted creation. While some of Isaiah's imagery about creation can be understood as metaphors for divine punishment and restoration, the collective weight of this imagery underscores that creation 1) functions as an agent of the creator in doling out punishments, 2) becomes disordered by human sin, and 3) will be recreated by God.

CONCLUSION

Isaiah is one of the most complicated books of the Bible. It interacts with a host of complex historical events spanning several centuries. Its composition reflects several authors and redactors, its poetry contains elusive imagery and ample ambiguities, and its theology is rife with tensions – but all these turn out to be sources of fascination, pushing the reader beyond simple answers.

Divine morality and love find conflicted expression in punishment and comfort. The book's deity could be ironically described as the sovereign ruler of creation whom people regularly disobey. This God is transcendent and exalted, but also immanent and intimately involved with people. Although human wickedness dominates many parts of the book, sinfulness does not rule out all signs of human righteousness. Creation, meanwhile, not only reflects God's design, but also serves as an agent of divine punishment, becomes distorted in the process, and will ultimately be remade. These theological tensions make the book an incredibly rich source for reflection and engagement. The book's sophisticated accounts of God, humanity, and creation have made it one of the most influential prophetic books in Judaism and Christianity.

FURTHER READING

Abernethy, Andrew T. *The Book of Isaiah and God's Kingdom: A Thematic Theological Approach.* New Studies in Biblical Theology 40. London: Apollos/. Downers Grove, IL: InterVarsity, 2016.
Barton, John. "Ethics in Isaiah of Jerusalem." Pages 130–44 in *Understanding Old Testament Ethics: Approaches and Explorations.* Louisville, KY: Westminster John Knox Press, 2003.
Childs, Brevard. *The Struggle to Understand Isaiah as Christian Scripture.* Grand Rapids, MI: Eerdmans, 2004.

Childs, Brevard. *Isaiah. Old Testament Library.* Louisville, KY: Westminster John Knox, 2001.

Claassens, L. Juliana. "Isaiah." Pages 209–22 in *Theological Bible Commentary.* Edited by Gail R. O'Day and David L. Petersen. Louisville, KY: Westminster John Knox, 2009.

Couey, J. Blake. "The Book of Isaiah." in *Oxford Research Encyclopedia of Religion.* Oxford: Oxford University Press, 2016. doi:10.1093/acref ore/9780199340378.013.153.

Darr, Katheryn Pfisterer. *Isaiah's Vision and the Family of God.* Literary Currents in Biblical Interpretation. Louisville, KY: Westminster John Knox, 1994.

Goldingay, John E. *The Theology of the Book of Isaiah.* Downers Grove, IL: InterVarsity, 2014.

Gowan, Donald E. *Theology of the Prophetic Books: The Death and Resurrection of Israel.* Louisville: Westminster John Knox, 1998.

Kim, Hyun Chul Paul. *Reading Isaiah: A Literary and Theological Commentary.* Reading the Old Testament. Macon, Georgia: Smyth & Helwys, 2016.

Pleins, J. David. "The Ethics of Desolation and Hope: Isaiah." Pages 213–75 in *The Social Visions of the Hebrew Bible: A Theological Introduction.* Louisville: Westminster John Knox, 2001.

Poulsen, Frederik. *The Black Hole in Isaiah: A Study of Exile as a Literary Theme.* FAT 125. Tübingen: Mohr Siebeck, 2019.

Roberts, J. J. M. "Isaiah in Old Testament Theology." *Interpretation* 36 (1982): 130–43.

Sawyer, John F. A. *The Fifth Gospel: Isaiah in the History of Christianity.* Cambridge: Cambridge University Press, 1996.

Tull, Patricia K. *Isaiah 1–39.* Smyth & Helwys Bible Commentary. Macon, GA: Smyth & Helwys, 2010.

17 The Ethical and Political Vision of Isaiah

M. DANIEL CARROLL R.

In the mid-nineteenth century, a number of scholars, including most famously Julius Wellhausen, envisioned the prophets of the eighth century BCE – Amos, Hosea, Isaiah, and Micah – as champions of "ethical monotheism." What defined the essence of that faith, it was said, was the just treatment of the vulnerable (the poor, widows, and orphans). Indeed, the book of Isaiah contains a number of chapters condemning their exploitation (e.g., chs. 1, 2, 3, 9, 11, 32, 51, 56, 58, 61). It also has several of what John Barton calls "ethical digests" that list social values demanded by God (1:16–17; 5:20; 33:15; 56:1; 58:6–9).[1] Study of these books no longer circumscribes prophetic faith and these books so restrictively. To this day, however, in common parlance words spoken or actions performed on behalf of the marginalized are said to be "prophetic."

Current research into the social justice concerns of the book of Isaiah is complex. As is the investigation of prophetic ethics generally, this research is methodologically varied and multidisciplinary.[2] Isaiah's large size, its dense message expressed through diverse genres, and knotty debates about its compositional history and historical referents make a survey of its ethical concerns especially challenging insofar as ethics often is connected to historical context.[3] Also complicated is the analysis of the interrelated dimensions of ancient social injustice: systemic socioeconomic abuses, the pressures of international trade, judicial corruption, political intrigue, and regional armed conflict.

This selective introduction to approaches to the social ethics of Isaiah is divided into two principal parts. The first looks at research of

---

[1] John Barton, *Ethics in Ancient Israel* (Oxford: Oxford University Press, 2014), 227–44.

[2] M. Daniel Carroll R., "Ethics," in *Dictionary of the Old Testament Prophets*, ed. M. J. Boda and J. G. McConville (Downers Grove, IL: IVP Academic; Nottingham: Inter-Varsity Press, 2012), 185–93.

[3] See, for example, Christopher B. Hays, "The Book of Isaiah in Contemporary Research," *RC* 5, no. 10 (2011): 549–66. Because of size limitations, this chapter engages critical issues minimally and reads the text synchronically.

a *descriptive* tenor. That is, it reviews studies of key moral themes in the book and the socioeconomic and political contexts that motivated its diatribes. The second section examines different perspectives on the *prescriptive* potential of Isaiah – that is, the possibility that it can speak to contemporary realities.

ETHICS IN THE BOOK OF ISAIAH

Fundamental Themes of Isaiah's Ethics

Research on prophetic literature in the twentieth century was interested in establishing the central theological tradition (or traditions) that informed the message of the prophets and the books that bear their names. The options were the Sinai covenant (which some correlated with vassal treaties), the Pentateuchal law codes, and wisdom circles. Eryl Davies weighed each prospect for the ethics of the book of Isaiah in three test-case passages (1:2–3; 5:8–10; 1:21–26) and found these alternatives wanting (E. DAVIES). He argued, for example, that a covenantal lens in 1:2–3 is overstated and that it cannot be assumed that the announced judgments find their only source in covenant curses. A limitation of the legal tradition is that citing violations of laws would have been an inadequate basis for Isaiah's accusations. Laws could not effectively control social attitudes nor respond to the changing socio-economic world of the monarchy; in addition, the powerful could manipulate juridical protocols and corrupt judges for their own gain. Finally, the vocabulary and ethical concerns that scholars linked to wisdom were shared by these three theological traditions (covenant, law, wisdom) and were not unique to wisdom. Davies also discounted the hypothesis that Isaiah's ethics was dependent on Amos, another eighth-century prophet. In sum, it is impossible to specify, he claims, any one tradition as the exclusive source of Isaiah's ethics. Instead, it was eclectic in its grounding and responded variously to circumstances at hand.

Barton has proposed setting the sociopolitical and economic concerns of the book within a moral order embedded in creation, a concept widely shared in some fashion in the ancient world (BARTON: 130–44, 145–53).[4] Concentrating initially on passages critically accepted as authentic to the historical prophet, Barton singles out those that he believes reveal the essence of Isaiah's ethical vision and what constitutes its violation

---

[4]   cf. Barton, *Ethics in Ancient Israel, passim*; H. G. M. Williamson, *He Has Shown You What Is Good: Old Testament Justice Here and Now* (Eugene, OR: Wipf & Stock, 2012).

(2:6–22; 3:1–12; 5:8–10, 20; 29:15–16). These presuppose, he argues, something akin to natural law. To sin is to challenge or upend the hierarchical scheme of the world established under God's incomparable sovereignty; to do so reveals destructive, foolish human pride – personal, national, or imperial (3:16; 5:21; 22:15–19; 10:5–19). Extending his study to the rest of the book, Barton did not find the same notion of a universal moral order in the denunciation of injustice, even in passages echoing the prophet's ethical teaching and words (e.g., 59:1–8). Other themes, though, do resurface, such as the call to trust and not fear (e.g., 26:3; 33:21–21; 41:14; 43:1; 54:4). The condemnation of pride also reappears, particularly in relation to idols made by human hands (e.g., 41:5–7; 46:1–3).

While Barton's suggestion for the basis of Isaiah's ethics does not have equal resonance across the entire book, several Hebrew terms of its rich justice lexicon (SICRE: 191–249, 238–42, 408–23, 439–53) span the three classic critical divisions of the book and provide a measure of moral coherence (LECLERC).[5] Recent studies have demonstrated thematic continuity through various phrases and themes (e.g., the Holy One of Israel, fear not, light and darkness) and underscored intertextual connections that yield an amazing literary tapestry. The interest here is to discern a consistent ethical trajectory.

The first term is *mišpāṭ*, usually translated as "justice" or "judgment." It occurs 42 times (22 in chs. 1–39; 11 in chs. 40–55; and 9 in chs. 56–66); forms of the verbal root *špṭ* ("to judge"), including the noun *šōpēṭ* ("judge"), appear in more than a dozen passages. The second constellation of terms are from the root *ṣdq*, of which the nouns *ṣedeq* and *ṣədāqâ* ("righteousness") are of particular significance.[6] Together, these various words appear in over 80 instances (28 in chs. 1–39, 30 in chs. 40–55, and 23 in chs. 56–66). Sometimes *mišpāṭ* and *ṣedeq/ṣədāqâ* appear in tandem, on occasion as the hendiadys *mišpāṭ ûṣədāqâ* – usually translated "justice and righteousness," though some have rendered it as "social justice" (e.g., 9:7 [MT 9:6]; 32:16; 33:5) (LECLERC: 12),[7] or separated but within the same verse (e.g., 1:21, 27; 5:7, 16; 59:14).

---

5   John N. Oswalt, "Righteousness in Isaiah: A Study of the Function of Chapters 56–66 in the Present Structure of the Book" in *Writing and Reading the Scroll of Isaiah*, ed. C. C. Broyles and C. A. Evans (Leiden: Brill, 1997), 1:177–92; Hemchand Gossai, *Justice, Righteousness and the Social Critique of the Eighth Century Prophets* (New York: Peter Lang, 1993).

6   Rolf Rendtorff sees the occurrences of the root *ṣdq* as helpful for understanding the composition of the book. See "The Composition of the Book of Isaiah," in Rendtorff, *Canon and Theology: Overtures to an Old Testament Theology*, OBT (Minneapolis, MN: Fortress, 1993), 146–69.

7   See also Moshe Weinfeld, *Social Justice in Ancient Israel and the Ancient Near East* (Jerusalem: Magnes; Minneapolis, MN: Fortress, 1995), 34, 36.

Throughout Isaiah it is presupposed that Yhwh is the source of
human justice: Justice and righteousness are inherent to God's person
and rule (5:16; 30:18; 33:22). In First Isaiah, Judah has willfully forsaken
God (1:2–4), and consequently injustice permeates the social fabric. The
opening condemnation censures the cult (1:11–20), the target of other
preexilic prophets as well (e.g., Hos. 6:6; Amos 4:4–5; 5:4–6, 21–25; Mic.
6:1–8) (Hrobon). Ritual divorced from ethical commitments is unac-
ceptable. No number of feasts, offerings, and prayers can cleanse the
guilt of moral impurity; they are an abomination. The bifurcation of
religiosity and ethics reflected a gross misunderstanding of God. The
cult, even if performed in the temple precincts, sanctified an idol of the
people's own creation whom they worshipped as Yhwh, and thus legit-
imated the unjust status quo. This text compares the nation to Sodom
and Gomorrah (1:10), lists all kinds of religious activities, and then
stresses Yhwh's visceral rejection through several verbs (1:11–15). The
exhortation is to do good, seek *mišpāṭ*, secure justice for (the verb *špṭ*;
NRSV, "defend") the orphan, and contend on the widow's behalf (1:17).
The worshippers' hands are full of blood (1:15): the blood of sacrifices
(1:11) and, in context, more likely the blood of the victims of oppression. It is this blood that makes their sins red like scarlet (1:18)!

The nation's leadership and elites arrogantly ignore justice and twist
legal processes to acquire property and fund their luxuriant excesses (1:23;
5:23; 10:1–2; cf. 2:11–12; 3:8–9, 16–23; 5:8–12, 18–22; 28:7–8). The vulnerable suffer this social violence, and their groans of despair rise heavenward.
In a poignant pun, the damning parable of the vineyard (5:1–7) ends by saying that Yhwh, the owner of the vineyard, "expected justice (*mišpāṭ*) but
saw bloodshed (*miśpāḥ*), righteousness (*ṣədāqâ*) but heard a cry (*ṣəʿāqâ*)!"
(NRSV). Zion, the chosen city of God, should have been a beacon of ethical righteousness but had devolved into a center of sin (1:21).

Therefore, Yhwh will bring judgment (*mišpāṭ*) on Judah, specifically upon these transgressors (e.g., 3:13–15). Consonant with the wider
cultural world, the responsibility to establish justice rested on the king,
who was to model and enforce divine ideals.[8] Because of the failures of
Judah's monarchy, though, hope turned to a messianic Spirit-filled king,
who would ensure justice in the land and beyond (9:6–7 [MT 9:5–6];
11:1–5; 16:5; 28:5–6; 32:1, 16–17).[9] In that day, Zion will be cleansed and
renewed in righteousness (1:26–27; 4:4; 28:16–17; 33:20–22).

---

[8]   Weinfeld, *Social Justice*, 45–74.
[9]   The idea of a royal messiah (i.e., "anointed one") empowered by the spirit of God was
      exemplified already in Saul (1 Sam 11:6) and David (1 Sam 16:13), but took on addi-
      tional meaning in later periods, when these Isaianic texts were reinterpreted.

The perspective changes in Isa 40–55. This is not surprising, since the setting is different, and the people are portrayed as removed from the land and in another social reality. The focus of divine justice shifts from the nation's social injustice to creation and the international arena. The Creator challenges all to appreciate his sovereign administration of Israel and the nations (40:14; 41:1). There is no explicit mention of widows, orphans, and the poor, nor the close connection between *mišpāṭ* and *ṣədāqâ* that is so prominent in the first 39 chapters; instead, *ṣədāqâ* and *yēša'/yəšû'â* ("salvation") are linked. Objectionable worship is not related to injustice (43:22–28), at least not explicitly (unless the moral dimension is assumed to be an aspect of the "sins," "iniquities," and "transgressions" in vv. 24–25). The rituals reflect the people's weariness with Yhwh, even as sins are wearying to God. In an echo of 1:18, there is a juridical tone in the divine challenge in 43:26: "Accuse me, let us go to trial" (the verb *špt*) in order that "you may be proved right" (the verb *ṣdq*).

God's Spirit-filled Servant, not a future king, will establish Yhwh's justice (ironically, a royal duty) over all peoples (42:1–4; cf. 11:1–5). In the other Servant Songs, however, *mišpāṭ* is related to defending his cause in a legal setting (49:4; 50:8; 53:8), not to the plight of the exploited. The restoration of Zion also is announced in striking fashion. God's future justice is described as light (51:4; cf. 42:6–7). The upright will be encouraged by this righteous act of God, which is their salvation (45:8, 21; 46:13; 51:5, 6, 8; cf. 45:21; 54:11–14).

Isa 56–66 returns to some of the social concerns of First Isaiah and to the grounding of justice in God's character (61:8). This section begins with the pairing of *mišpāṭ* and *ṣədāqâ* and the demand to maintain them because of the coming deliverance (56:1). Of the two terms, *ṣədāqâ* is the more prominent (13 times to 9 for *mišpāṭ*; *ṣedeq* occurs 7 times). The need for the clarion call of 56:1 ("Maintain justice, and do what is right!") is clear: There is no moral compass.

The absence of justice and righteousness contaminates the community's life and separates the people from Yhwh; even the righteous are persecuted (57:1–2, 12; 58:1–2; 59:8–15).[10] The criterion of justice for rituals pleasing to God is evident in three passages: 56:1–8 and 58:13–14 speak to Sabbath observance; 58:1–12 critiques the fast. The exhortation to keep justice and do righteousness in 56:1 introduces the section on the Sabbath, thus incorporating the future inclusion and blessing

---

[10]   Scholars debate the reasons behind the problematic context and the identity of the parties in conflict. That discussion lies beyond the purview of this chapter.

of observant eunuchs and foreigners into the book's ethical vision
(56:3–8). God's nonnegotiable requirements regarding a fast are clear
in 58:1–12. The prophetic denunciation of self-justifying rituals belied
by cruel behavior (58:2–5) is followed by the unequivocal link between
religious observance and liberating, compassionate action on behalf of
the oppressed (58:6–12); censure is wedded with solidarity.

Chapter 59 highlights justice in an emphatic invective against legal
wrongs. Eight times the negative particle *'ayin* ("there is no...") communicates the absolute dearth of righteous deeds and just persons (vv.
4 [2x], 8, 10, 11, 15, 16 [2x]). The indictment is telling: "there is no (*'ên*)
mišpāṭ in their paths" (v. 8); "*mišpāṭ* is far from us, and *ṣədāqâ* does not
reach us" (v. 9); "we wait for *mišpāṭ* and there is none (*'ayin*)" (v. 11);
"*mišpāṭ* is turned back, and *ṣədāqâ* stands at a distance" (v. 14); "there
was no (*'ên*) *mišpāṭ*" (v. 15). The language of abuse is vivid, mentioning,
for instance, the shedding of blood – metaphorically and literally (vv. 3,
7; cf. 1:15).

Like 1–39 and 40–55, Isa 56–66 looks beyond the judgment to a
time of restoration and renewal. God personally will accomplish this in
divine righteousness (59:17; 60:17; 61; 63:11; 65:17–25) – not a human
king or the Servant (chs. 60–66),[11] but rather the divine king who sits
on a heavenly throne (66:1). The ethics of Yhwh are a thread that interconnects the book of Isaiah from beginning to end, even if there are different nuances in the three sections. Justice (*mišpāṭ*) and righteousness
(*ṣədāqâ*) characterize the person and rule of God. For this reason, Yhwh
punishes the violation of justice. Nevertheless, judgment (*mišpāṭ*) is not
God's final word. One day, God will inaugurate a new heaven and new
earth; oppression and armed conflict will cease, and Yhwh's people will
come with the nations in obedience to worship the true God (66:7–24).

Socioeconomic Injustice in Isaiah's Ethics

Words such as "injustice" and "oppression" can be abstractions, but
tangible abuses triggered divine displeasure in Isa 1–39. To better understand what warranted such sharp prophetic invective, scholars utilize
social science approaches to reconstruct the socioeconomic realities
of eighth-century Judah. Their theoretical frameworks are diverse, and
proposals disputed. Disagreement exists, for instance, over the nature of

---

[11]   Some relate the one upon whom the Spirit of God rests in 61:1–3 to the Servant of chs.
       40–55; others see this passage as messianic. See, for example, H. G. M. Williamson,
       Variations on a Theme: King, Messiah and the Servant in the Book of Isaiah (Carlisle:
       Paternoster, 1998), 174–88; as well as *He Has Shown You What Is Good*, 101–03.

dependency of rural areas on urban centers, the levels of socioeconomic stratification in rural and urban settings, and the extent of royal control over the economy. There are methodological debates concerning the proper application of social sciences to ancient Israel and over the interpretation of archaeological data.[12]

Marvin Chaney, for example, argues that a combination of external involvements and internal conditions generated the conditions condemned by Isaiah and other eighth-century prophets (CHANEY).[13] Judah had become increasingly involved in international trade. Judah's exports were limited to agricultural commodities, particularly wheat, olive oil, and wine. To acquire sufficient quantities of metal (especially for weaponry), luxury items for ruling elites, and materials (especially lumber) for governmental construction projects required increasing efficiency in the production of exportable crops and improving market exchange (e.g., with the standardization of weights and measures). Extracting existing surpluses could not meet economic and consumption needs.

Increases in agricultural production were made possible through regional specialization of crops to maximize yields (a key passage for Chaney is 2 Chron. 26:10). Archaeological study has revealed technological innovations, such as the beam press in olive oil production and the proliferation of cisterns and olive and grape processing installations. The *lmlk* seals from Judah (and the Samaria ostraca) are evidence for vineyards of the crown, the nobility, and possibly local leaders. At one level, the transformation was successful. Crop specialization, however, ran counter to the subsistence agriculture of the peasantry and jeopardized traditional ways of hedging against risk in an environment of uneven rainfall and unpredictable harvests. A mixed approach of rotating crops during the year and periodically leaving areas fallow, coupled with family and local herding, provided a safety net in difficult times. These time-honored arrangements were compromised to meet the requisite surpluses for export.

Regional specialization, Chaney claims, led to land acquisition by the crown and elites. This "latifundialization," especially in the lowlands, was at times secured unjustly. In the new command economy, in

---

[12]   For surveys, see Walter J. Houston, *Contending for Justice: Ideologies and Theologies of Social Justice in the Old Testament*, rev ed. (London: T&T Clark, 2008), 18–51; cf. M. Daniel Carroll R., "Social Science Approaches," in Boda and McConville, *Dictionary of the Old Testament: The Prophets*, 734–47.

[13]   Marvin L. Chaney, "Whose Sour Grapes? The Addressees of Isaiah 5:1–7 in the Light of Political Economy," *Semeia* 87 (1999): 105–22; cf. D. N. Premnath, *Eighth Century Prophets: A Social Analysis* (St. Louis, MI: Chalice Press, 2003).

years of unsatisfactory crop yields, stressed peasant families would have
sought survival loans, but increased debt for some meant forfeiture of
property. Land, labor, and other components in agricultural production
(such as seed and tools), were separated and became subject to rent. In
this model, absentee landlordism exacerbated the lack of moral over-
sight, as some who now controlled properties did so from afar, from
urban centers. To these oppressive practices was added unfair taxation
and a fraudulent legal system favoring the elites. Privilege and power
were used to advantage, with the unscrupulous possibly driving hard
bargains with the desperate, extracting more tax than required to pro-
cure land, and manipulating law proceedings under the guise of legality.

Several passages could reflect these systemic abuses. In 5:2, it
appears that the vineyard owner is preparing for bigger grape (hence
wine) yields (cf. 3:14; 16:10). Dispossession of peasant property may
be in view in 5:8–10, while creditors might be the target of 3:12–15.
Isaiah repeatedly points to corruption in the legal process (1:21–26; 5:20;
10:1–4; 29:20–21). Extravagant goods from trade are cited in 2:6–7, while
the unconscionable excessive lifestyle of the wealthy is roundly condemned (2:12–17; 3:16–24; 5:11–13, 22–23; 28:1–4, 7–8).

Debates about the details of eighth-century socioeconomic life and
the systemic issues that precipitated the strident prophetic message
will continue. Models analyze archaeological and textual data from
diverse angles and illumine the justice passages in Isaiah in new ways.
At the very least, this research brings realism into this study by remind-
ing us that injustice arises within concrete circumstances and that the
exploitation of the vulnerable triggers moral outrage.

The Political Dimension of Isaiah's Ethics

A comprehensive understanding of the injustices in the book of Isaiah
must account for the effects of Judah's political maneuvering vis-à-vis
regional military conflict and the toll of war. The presence and threats
of the Assyrian empire reverberate across Isa 1–39. Several historical
settings can be identified: the Syro-Ephraimite War of 735–732 BCE, the
Ashdod-led conspiracy against Assyria in 715–711, and Sennacherib's
campaign into Judah after the death of Sargon II in 705 and his siege of
Jerusalem. These threats prompted preparations, such as the securing
of water sources and reinforcement of fortifications in Jerusalem (Isa
22:9–11; 2 Kgs 20:20; 2 Chron. 32:2–6) and elsewhere, the manufacture
of weapons (Isa 22:8), training of soldiers and other able-bodied men,
and the gathering of food supplies. These efforts would have required
taxation and the use of corvée labor. These militarily forced initiatives,

along with the death and maiming of thousands, the disease and destruction left by war, and the detrimental effects of battles on the arable soil, had drastic ramifications for the broader population, especially its most vulnerable groups. Armed conflicts inescapably impacted spheres of justice.

Isaiah was highly critical of the king and his advisors for entering into war and entertaining support, on different occasions, from Assyria, Egypt, and Philistia.[14] The prophet chastises Ahaz for his lack of faith in the face of Israel's and Aram's threats to force Judah to join the coalition against Assyria in 735–732 (Isa 7:4–9; 8:5–18). In fact, Ahaz already had appealed to the Assyrian empire for help, turning Judah into its vassal (2 Kgs 16:5–18). In contrast, Isaiah was able to convince Hezekiah of the folly of joining Philistia and others against Assyria two decades later (715–711; Isa 14:28–32; 20:1–6). However, Hezekiah did join and took a leading role in another coalition against Assyria after Sargon II's death. At this juncture, he did seek help from Egypt (28:14–19; 29:15–16; 30:1–14; 31:1–4; ch. 39; perhaps 22:8–11).[15] The disastrous result was devastating losses, with only Jerusalem miraculously escaping defeat (Isa 36–38). The key terms in this last case are the verbs *bāṭaḥ* ("trust") and *yāṣâ* ("plan") and their respective noun derivatives *beṭaḥ/biṭḥâ/biṭṭāḥôn* ("security, confidence") and *'ēṣâ* ("plan"): Judah's leaders should have trusted in Yahweh and not political and military expediency (30:1–5), for Assyria's downfall had been decreed long before (25:1; 37:26; cf. 14:24–27). The Rabshakeh's taunts at Jerusalem's walls about irrationally trusting in Hezekiah and his allies (36:4–6, 14) and in Yhwh, who would fail as had other gods who had resisted the empire's armies (36:7, 15, 18–20; 37:10–13), were empty words. The word from Yhwh was consistent: "Do not fear" (7:4; 8:12; 37:6). Some scholars argue that the prophet's goal was to inculcate a faith that rejected power politics based on human wisdom,[16] a faith that realized that national

---

14   J. J. M. Roberts, "Enemies and Friends of the State: First Isaiah and Micah," in *Enemies and Friend of the State: Ancient Prophecy in Context*, ed. C. A. Rollston (University Park, PA: Eisenbrauns, 2018), 329–38; M. Daniel Carroll R. "Impulses Toward Peace in a Country at War: The Book of Isaiah between Realism and Hope," in *War in the Bible and Terrorism in the Twenty-First Century*, ed. R. S. Hess and E. A. Martens, *BBRSup* 2 (Winona Lake, IN: Eisenbrauns, 2008), 59–78.

15   José Luis Sicre says that to not have trusted in Yahweh but in political and military alliances was tantamount to political idolatry. See José Luis Sicre, *Los dioses olvidados: Poder y riqueza en los profetas preexílicos*, Estudios del Antiguo Testamento 1 (Madrid: Cristiandad, 1979), 51–64.

16   Millard C. Lind, "Political Implications of Isaiah 6," in *Writing and Reading the Scroll of Isaiah*, ed. C. C. Broyles and C. A. Evans (Leiden: Brill, 1997), 1: 317–38;

security began with justice at home.[17] In the end, Judah's foreign policy had multiple negative consequences, such as the destruction of towns and cities and the nation's infrastructure, the death of thousands in battle and an increase in widows and orphans, food shortages, the increased fragility of the poor, and disruption in food production.

The prophetic rhetoric to trust Yhwh in the face of Assyrian threats is replete with imperial propaganda. Aster contends that chapters 1–2, 6–8, 10–12, 14, 19, 31, 36–37 contain motifs from propagandistic Assyrian royal inscriptions.[18] Even though passages respond to different historical moments of the eighth century and reflect changing perspectives (from recognizing Assyria as God's agent of judgment to God's arrogant and deluded enemy), Isaiah consistently responds to Assyrian rhetoric and asserts that Yhwh, not Assyria's king, rules history and determines the fate of nations. Abernethy demonstrates that Isa 1–39 usurps Assyrian tactics related to food supply (1:7; 3:7) for theological ends (ABERNETHY: 35–50).[19] Military campaigning began at harvest time to feed the troops, and siege warfare included destroying orchards and spoiling crops. While Yhwh is said to use this devastation in judgment, the promise is of abundance for obedience (1:19–20). Isaiah contrasts the false hope offered by the Rabshakeh (36:16–17) with Yhwh's promise of restoration (37:30; 30:23–26). Others have looked at the Isaianic images of Assyria (and other enemies) (EIDEVALL), such as the fly and bee (7:18–19), a river (8:7–8), a tool in God's hand (10:15), and a decimated forest (10:19, 33–34) to demonstrate the supremacy of Yhwh.[20] Each rhetorical strategy undermines in its own way the Assyrian imperial ideology of their matchless monarch and unstoppable strength.

Scholarly awareness of the central role of the Assyrian empire in Isa 1–39 is growing. A recent monograph by Hays argues that Isa 24–27 should not be seen as late (proto)apocalyptic, as is commonly assumed, but rather as a commemoration text centered around the waning presence of Assyria in Judah during Josiah's reign in the late seventh century

---

[17]   Scott M. Thomas, "Isaiah's Vision of Human Security: Virtue Ethics and International Politics in the Ancient Near East," in COHEN AND WESTBROOK, 169–79.

[18]   Shawn Zelig Aster, *Reflections of Empire in Isaiah 1–39: Responses to Assyrian Ideology*, Ancient Near East Monographs 19 (Atlanta, GA: SBL Press, 2017).

[19]   See also Andrew T. Abernethy, *Eating in Isaiah: Approaching the Role of Food in Isaiah's Structure and Message*, BibleInt 131 (Leiden: Brill, 2014), 45–93. This idea resonates with other passages in the book (e.g., 62:8; 65:21–22).

[20]   Mary Katherine Y. H. Hom, *The Characterization of the Assyrians in Isaiah: Synchronic and Diachronic Perspectives*, LHBOTS 559 (New York: T & T Clark, 2012).

BCE.[21] Olof Bäckersten goes so far as to claim (not convincingly, however) that passages regularly linked to justice matters (5:8–24; 10:1–4; 28:1–4), when reread critically, actually are related to foreign policy decisions concerning Assyria (BÄCKERSTEN).

Deconstruction of imperial pretense, with declarations of Yhwh's superiority, is also pronounced against Babylon (e.g., 13:1, 19; 14:4, 22; 47:1; 48:14) and its gods (41:21–29; 43:8–13; 44:9–20; 45:18–25) and in relationship to Cyrus, the Persian king (44:24–45:7).[22] Brett suggests that the theological-ideological framework of Isa 40–66 reflects conversation between Priestly theologians and other groups in postexilic Yehud. This was a reconciling social imaginary,[23] he says, which incorporated the returned exiles as well as foreigners and resisted the claims of empire with claims of Yahweh's sovereignty, as had earlier parts of Isaiah.[24]

The critique of Judah's kings and of the surrounding nations and menacing empires spans the book of Isaiah. That exposé, along with the hope for an ideal king and an empowered Servant (even the democratization of the Davidic promise, 55:3!) who will bring peace, justice, and prosperity, undergird its political vision. The prophetic rhetoric contests the flawed socioeconomic and political ideologies of the people of God and the nations.[25] It points them beyond any human monarch and reign to the one Cosmic King.

In sum, the ethical vision in Isaiah is extensive and complex. This brief summary of various aspects demonstrates its intricacy and the

---

[21] Christopher B. Hays, *The Origins of Isaiah 24–27: Josiah's Festival Scroll for the Fall of Assyria* (Cambridge: Cambridge University Press, 2019).

[22] For example, Millard C. Lind, "Monotheism, Power and Justice: A Study in Isaiah 40–55," *CBQ* 46, no. 3 (1984): 432–46.

[23] Charles Taylor defines a "social imaginary" as "the ways people imagine their social existence, how they fit together with others, how things go on between them and their fellows, the expectations that are normally met, and the deeper motivations and images that underlie these expectations ... that common understanding that makes possible common practices and a widely shared sense of legitimacy." See Charles Taylor, *Modern Social Imaginaries* (Durham, NC: Duke University Press, 2004), 23.

[24] Mark G. Brett, *Political Trauma and Healing: Biblical Ethics for a Postcolonial World* (Grand Rapids, MI: Eerdmans, 2016), 110–26; *Locations of God: Political Theology in the Hebrew Bible* (New York: Oxford University Press, 2019), 86–97. In contrast, Norman K. Gottwald holds that Isa 40–66 reveal the coopting of social justice ideals by returning elites to justify resuming power in the new political configuration under Persia. See Norman K. Gottwald, "Social Class and Ideology in Isaiah 40–55: An Eagletonian Reading," *Sem* 59 (1992): 43–51.

[25] In addition to earlier resources, see Mark W. Hamilton, *A Kingdom for a Stage: Political and Theological Reflection in the Hebrew Bible* (FAT 116; Tübingen: Mohr Siebeck, 2018), 104–33, 134–51.

ways in which social standing, economics, politics, foreign policy, and
their theological correlations interlock with matters of justice.

THE ONGOING VALUE OF THE ETHICS OF ISAIAH

Isaiah as a Positive Source for Ethics

Throughout the centuries, Isaiah has been a relevant text.[26] Three
aspects of its ethical vision have been most compelling. The first is
its consistent call for interhuman justice and its confidence in divine
justice to right wrongs. Multiple passages continue to resonate within
contexts of systemic oppression (e.g., 1:10–17; 5:8–23; 10:1–4; 56; 58;
59:1–15; 61).[27] Sections debunking imperial pretense and political
machinations in ancient times are also appropriated in the contemporary world, both nationally and internationally. Laypeople, activists,
and scholars from all kinds of backgrounds keep turning to the book for
inspiration. Recent examples can be drawn from all over the globe, for
instance, from Latin America[28] and Africa.[29]

The second component of Isaiah's ethical vision that is embraced
is the hope of peace and prosperity. The picture in Isa 2:1–5 of beating
swords into plowshares for many is symbolic of the human aspiration
of peace. This passage, among others, has stimulated those in pacifist

---

[26] See John F. A. Sawyer, *The Fifth Gospel: Isaiah in the History of Christianity*
(Cambridge: Cambridge University Press, 1996); Walter Brueggemann, "Five Strong
Readings of the Book of Isaiah," in *The Bible in Human Society: Essays in Honour of
John Rogerson*, ed. M. Daniel Carroll R., D. J. A. Clines, and P. R. Davies, JSOTSup
200 (Sheffield: Sheffield Academic Press, 1995), 87–104; M. Daniel Carroll R., *The
Lord Roars: Recovering the Prophetic Voice for Today* (Grand Rapids, MI: Baker
Academic, 2022).

[27] The appeal to Isa. 61 at the beginning of Jesus' public ministry (Lk. 4:16–30) and
the importance of Isaiah for his ethical stances have brought significant attention
to its ethical message. Note, for example, David P. Gushee and Glen H. Stassen,
Kingdom Ethics: Following Jesus in Contemporary Context, 2nd ed. (Grand Rapids,
MI: Eerdmans, 2016), 4–10, 21–36, 128–46, 309–18.

[28] For example, J. Severino Croatto, "Isaiah 40–55," "56–66," and "Fourth Isaiah," in
Global Bible Commentary, ed. D. Patte (Nashville, TN: Abingdon Press, 2004), 195–
211; Mercedes L. García Bachmann, "True Fasting and Unwilling Hunger (Isaiah 58),"
in *The Bible and the Hermeneutics of Liberation*, ed. Alejandro F. Botta and Pablo
R. Adiñach, SemeiaSt 59 (Atlanta, GA: Society of Biblical Literature, 2009), 113–31.
These authors, and those in the next footnote, also point to Isaiah's hope passages, the
second aspect.

[29] For example, Victor Zinkuratire, "Isaiah 1–39," in Patte, *Global Bible Commentary*,
186–94; Makhosaznz K. Nzimande, "Isaiah," in *The Africana Bible: Reading Israel's
Scriptures from Africa and the African Diaspora*, ed. H. R. Page, Jr. (Minneapolis, MN:
Fortress, 2010), 136–46; Christopher B. Hays, "Isaiah as Colonized Poet: His Rhetoric of
Death in Conversation with African Postcolonial Writers," in ABERNETHY ET AL., 51–71.

circles,[30] and generated technical exchanges between biblical scholars and international relations scholars (COHEN AND WESTBROOK). Peace activist Daniel Berrigan perceives analogies between the prophet's critique of the deceptive ideology of war and death and what is propagated in the United States.[31] Today, as then, he argues, people misconstrue God and do not embrace the hope of peace. Turning to Isa 40–66 and the Servant Songs, Berrigan finds inspiration in an identity as an exiled people in a strange land and in the sacrificial work of the Servant. This appeal to an existential exile within one's own country (with its socioeconomic, political, and religious implications) also surfaces in Walter Brueggemann's works. He uses the metaphor of exile to explain the American church's crisis of faith and draws direction for ministry in these times from Second Isaiah (BRUEGGEMANN). The poetry of Isa 40–66 is subversive, because it challenges the governing social construction of reality; and redemptive, as it envisions an alternative future, demonstrating what he calls the practice of poetic imagination. For Lee Cuéllar, however, the corollaries are not metaphorical; they are lived.[32] He compares the Jewish diaspora experiences to those of Mexican immigrants and Second Isaiah's rhetorical strategies to Mexican *corridos*, narrative songs about identity and marginalization in a new land.[33] That connection with the Bible in and of itself is an encouragement. In fact, a diaspora hermeneutic is characteristic of significant Latino and Latina readings of the Bible.[34]

A third area that has garnered attention is ecology. Focusing on Isa 1–39, Hilary Marlow surveys the nature imagery in these chapters to exhibit the "interconnectivity" between creation and humans.[35] On the

---

[30]   Mistakenly so, according to J. J. M. Roberts, "The End of War in the Zion Tradition: The Imperialist Background of an Old Testament Vision of Worldwide Peace," in *Character Ethics and the Old Testament: Moral Dimensions of Scripture*, ed. M. Daniel Carroll R. and J. E. Lapsley (Louisville, KY: Westminster John Knox, 2007), 119–28.

[31]   Daniel Berrigan, *Isaiah: Spirit of Courage, City of Tears* (Minneapolis, MN: Fortress, 1996).

[32]   Gregory Lee Cuéllar, *Voices of Marginality: Exile and Return in Second Isaiah 40–55 and the Mexican Immigrant Experience*. American University Studies VII/ 271 (New York: Peter Lang, 2008).

[33]   A *corrido* is a narrative song in the form of a particular kind of ballad.

[34]   Luis Rivera-Rodríguez, "Toward a Diaspora Hermeneutics (Hispanic North America)," in *Character Ethics and the Old Testament: Moral Dimensions of Scripture*, ed. M. Daniel Carroll R. and Jacqueline E. Lapsley (Louisville, KY: Westminster John Knox, 2007), 169–89.

[35]   Hilary Marlow, *Biblical Prophets and Contemporary Environmental Ethics* (Oxford: Oxford University Press, 2009); cf. Patricia K. Tull, "Persistent Vegetative States: People as Plants and Plants as People in Isaiah," in *The Desert Will Bloom: Poetic*

one hand, divine judgment on sin ravages the earth (e.g., 24:1–13; 34:9–15), while on the other hand, Isaiah's portraits of restoration involve the flowering of the created order (e.g., 30:23–26; 32:15–20; 35; 11:1–10). Although largely anthropocentric in perspective, Isaiah's vision of justice incorporates its impact on the environment.

Ambivalence toward the Value of Isaiah's Ethical Vision

Not all are charitably disposed to Isaiah as an ethical source. This stance usually does not mean total rejection of the book, but some recommend more circumspect use. A consistent reason for disapproval is the complaint that the judgments of God are indiscriminate (affecting the guilty and innocent alike) and overly violent, which is regarded as no longer theologically acceptable.[36] Worrisome metaphors in the book include Yhwh as punishing father (64:8–12; 45:9–11) and divine warrior (e.g., 5:24–25; 10:5) (O'BRIEN). Many find Isa 63:1–6 especially troubling.[37] Of course, these discussions raise the question of the possibility and nature of divine judgment in history.

After surveying the ethical material in Isaiah, Andrew Davies accuses God of double standards: Yhwh does not speak or act according to the ethical principles that he demands of the people and nations, thereby undermining the moral vision of the entire book (A. DAVIES). Even Isaiah would admit, Davies says, that his God is inconsistent. With 58:6–10 and 1:16–17 as his starting point and lens, Mark Gray argues for human striving for justice as over against Isaiah's problematic picture of Yhwh (GRAY). More ambivalent are some feminist perspectives that disapprove of Isaiah's various negative constructions of issues related to female gender (e.g., 3:12, 16–17; 64:6), while appreciating passages that portray Yhwh speaking from a woman's point of view (42:14; 66:7–9) or with kind words to his wife (e.g., 40:2; 52;1–2), and which offer feminine images of God (46:3–4; 49:15; 66:13).[38] From disability studies, J.

Visions in Isaiah, ed. A. J. Everson and H. C. P. Kim, *Ancient Israel and Its Literature* 4 (Atlanta, GA: Society of Biblical Literature, 2009), 17–34.

[36] Carol J. Dempsey, *Hope Amid the Ruins: The Ethics of Israel's Prophets* (St. Louis, MO: Chalice, 2000).

[37] See the wrestling, for example, in Dominic S. Irudayaraj, *Violence, Otherness and Identity in Isaiah 63:1–6: The Trampling One Coming from Edom*, LHSOTS 633 (London: Bloomsbury T&T Clark, 2017).

[38] Irmtraud Fischer, "Isaiah: The Book of Female Metaphors," in *Feminist Biblical Interpretation: A Compendium of Critical Commentary on the Books of the Bible and Related Literature*, ed. L. Schotroff and M.-T. Wacker, trans, L. E. Dahill et al. (Grand Rapids, MI: Eerdmans, 2012), 303–18; Patricia K. Tully, "Isaiah," in *Women's Bible Commentary*, ed. C. A. Newsom, S. H. Ringe, and, J. E. Lapsley, 3rd ed. (Louisville, KY: Westminster John Knox, 2012), 255–66.

Blake Couey asserts that Isaiah has more references to disabilities than any other prophetic book; most are negative comparisons of rebellion to deafness, blindness, and sickness. Nevertheless, the Servant of Isa 52:13–53:12 is pictured as stricken, and eunuchs are explicitly included in the future restoration (56:3–5).[39]

CONCLUSION

It is a daunting task to summarize, briefly and selectively, the ethics of Isaiah. Hopefully, this survey of the book's perspectives on justice and of the scholarly literature can point the reader to ongoing discussions of its relevance. Each area touched on in this chapter – theological foundations and themes, socioeconomic and political backgrounds, ethical importance – invites more research. There is much to explore – and, for many, to appropriate.[40]

FURTHER READING

Abernethy, Andrew T., Mark G. Brett, Tim Bulkeley, and Tim Meadowcroft eds. *Isaiah and Imperial Context: The Book of Isaiah in the Times of Empire.* Eugene, OR: Pickwick, 2013.

Bäckersten, Olof. *Isaiah's Political Message: An Appraisal of His Alleged Social Critique.* FAT 29/2. Tübingen: Mohr Siebeck, 2008.

Barton, John. *Understanding Old Testament Ethics: Approaches and Explorations.* Louisville, KY: Westminster John Knox, 2003.

Brueggemann, Walter. *Hopeful Imagination: Prophetic Voices in Exile.* Minneapolis, MN: Fortress, 1986.

Chaney, Marvin L. "The Political Economy of Peasant Poverty: What the Eighth-Century Prophets Presumed But Did Not State." *Journal of Religion & Society Supplement Series* 10 (2014): 34–60.

Cohen, Raymond and Raymond Westbrook, eds. *Isaiah's Vision of Peace in Biblical and Modern International Relations: Swords Into Plowshares.* New York: Palgrave Macmillan, 2008.

Davies, Andrew. *Double Standards in Isaiah: Re-evaluating Prophetic Ethics and Divine Justice.* BibleInt 46. Leiden: Brill, 2000.

Davies, Eryl W. *Prophecy and Ethics: Isaiah and the Ethical Tradition of Israel.* JSOTSup 16. Sheffield: JSOT Press, 1981.

Eidevall, Göran. *Prophecy and Propaganda: Images of Enemies in the Book of Isaiah.* Winona Lake, IN: Eisenbrauns, 2009.

---

[39] J. Blake Couey, "Isaiah, Jeremiah, Ezekiel, Daniel, and the Twelve," in *The Bible and Disability: A Commentary*, ed. S. J. Melcher, M. C. Parsons, and A. Yong (Waco, TX: Baylor University Press, 2017), 218–41.

[40] I would like to thank Daniel Somboonsiri and Benjamin Smith for their help in this research.

Gray, Mark. *Rhetoric and Social Justice in Isaiah*. LHBOTS 432. New York: T & T Clark, 2006.

Hrobon, Bohdan. *Ethical Dimension of Cult in the Book of Isaiah*. BZAW 418. Berlin: de Gruyter, 2010.

Leclerc, Thomas. *Yahweh is Exalted in Justice: Solidarity and Conflict in Isaiah*. Minneapolis, MN: Fortress, 2001.

Lee Cuéllar, Gregory. *Voices of Marginality: Exile and Return in Second Isaiah 40–55 and the Mexican Immigrant Experience*. American University Studies VII/ 271. New York: Peter Lang, 2008.

O'Brien, Julie M. *Challenging Prophetic Metaphors: Theology and Ideology in the Prophets*. Louisville, KY: Westminster John Knox, 2008.

Sicre, José Luis. *'Con los pobres de la tierra': La justicia social en los profetas de Israel*. Madrid: Cristiandad, 1984.

18 Isaiah in the New Testament

DAVID W. PAO

The significance of Isaiah for New Testament (NT) authors is widely recognized. Not only are there more than a hundred quotations from Isaiah in the NT, forty-five of its sixty-six chapters appear in some form within the text of the NT, thus earning it the title of the "Fifth Gospel" in the early church (SAWYER: 30). Beyond explicit quotations and allusions, Isaiah provides the language through which significant theological themes are developed. Moreover, its wider and deeper influence in a number of NT books can be uncovered by tracing literary structures and patterns back to this prophetic work (PAO).[1]

Without intending to provide an exhaustive catalog of individual quotations and allusions, this chapter will begin by discussing important Isaianic texts that exerted formative influence on NT authors and on the theological categories embedded in their works. Then its wider influence on a number of NT books will be discussed. This discussion assumes the availability of some form of the Isaianic texts to the NT authors, although its physical accessibility would have varied from author to author.[2]

---

[1] See also my briefer treatment in "Isaiah (Book and Person). New Testament," in Christine Helmer, Steven L. McKenzie, Thomas Römer, Jens Schröter, Barry Dov Walfish, and Eric Ziolkowski, eds., *Encyclopedia of the Bible and Its Reception*, vol. 13 (Berlin/New York: Walter de Gruyter, 2016), 305–309, upon which this study builds.

[2] Diachronic concerns cannot be fully addressed here, but the several possibilities exist in regard to the physical accessibility of Isaiah. While quoting from "memory" cannot be ruled out, direct literary influence and dependence remain probable especially in light of the intricate arguments made within substantial sections of the book. Cf. Christopher D. Stanley, *Paul and the Language of Scripture*, SNTSMS 74 (Cambridge: Cambridge University Press, 1992), 65–82. Collections of sections of Isaiah may also be available to specific authors. Cf. Christopher D. Stanley, "The Importance of 4QTanhumim [4Q176]," *RevQ* 15 (1992): 589–592, although the limited texts within such possible collections would not explain the use and interaction with many such texts, even if we assume the existence of one prominent group of *testimonia* in which Isaiah might have played an important part. Cf. Robert A. Kraft, "Barnabas' Isaiah

ISAIAH AND THE THEOLOGICAL CONSTRUCTS OF NT AUTHORS

This section highlights one prominent motif associated with each of a number of Isaianic texts that have exerted notable influence across the NT, though it is important to note that passages from Isaiah were often used in multiple rhetorical and theological ways even within one textual context. Although these texts were used in identical ways, several prominent motifs do emerge.

Isaiah 40 and the Dawn of the Eschatological Era

Isa 40:1–11 ("In the wilderness prepare the way of Yhwh...") is often evoked or directly quoted in the NT, especially in introducing the dawn of the new era in the life and ministry of Jesus (Matt 3:3; Mark 1:3; Luke 3:3–5; John 1:23; cf. 1 Pet 1:24–25).[3] This is consistent with its broader uses in Second Temple Jewish literature (Bar. 5.6–9; Pss. Sol. 11.4–6; T. Mos. 10.1; 1 En. 1.6; 1QS VIII, 13–16; IX, 16–21).

That the "preparation of the way" is not merely a reference to the role of John the Baptist is clear especially in Luke 3:4–6, where a lengthy quotation is used (Isa 40:3–5) that encompasses the wider implications of Jesus' ministry ("all flesh shall see the salvation of God," Luke 3:6 [Isa 40:5]). Moreover, the identification of the church as "the Way" (*hē hodos*, Acts 9:2; 22:4; 24:14, 22) likely also draws from Isa 40:3 as the church seeks to identify herself against competitive claims as the heir of the prophetic tradition of Israel (cf. the use of *derek* in 1QS IX, 9, 16–21; X, 21).

The Old Greek translation of Isaiah proclaims the arrival of the eschatological salvation by the use of words related to *parakaleō* ("to urge, exhort, comfort," e.g., "Comfort, O comfort my people," Isa 40:1; also 40:2, 11), and in the Pauline tradition the same terms are used in reference to the "comfort" provided by this eschatological salvation (cf. 2 Cor 1:3–7; Phil 2:1; Col 2:2).[4] The understanding of "comfort" as

---

Text and the 'Testimony Book' Hypothesis," *JBL* 79 (1960): 336–350. Liturgical uses can explain a number of important texts (e.g., Isa 40, 61), while the presence of scriptural scrolls in first-century synagogues may also provide direct access to such texts (e.g., Luke 4:16–20), even though first-century synagogues may not have had permanent structures for the place of scrolls. Cf. Lee I. Levine, *The Ancient Synagogue*, 2nd ed. (New Haven: Yale University Press, 2005), 352.

3   See, in particular, Klyne R. Snodgrass, "Streams of Tradition Emerging from Isaiah 40:1–5 and their Adaptation in the New Testament," *JSNT* 8 (1980): 24–45.

4   For the understanding of this word-group in reference to both divine acts and human responses, see Klaus Baltzer, "Liberation from Debt Slavery after the Exile in Second Isaiah and Nehemiah," in Patrick D. Miller, Jr., et. al., eds., *Ancient Israelite Religion: Essays in Honor of Frank Moore Cross* (Philadelphia: Fortress, 1987), 477–484.

"salvation" is best illustrated by the hendiadys of "comfort and salvation" in 2 Cor 1:6 as Paul depicts his participation in the implementation of God's eschatological program on behalf of God's renewed people (MOYISE AND MENKEN: 135).[5]

Isaiah 61 and the Eschatological Gospel

Both Luke and Matthew introduce the gospel that Jesus proclaims by using Isa 61. In the Nazareth sermon of Jesus in Luke 4:18–19, Isa 61:1–2 (with Isa 58:6) provides a programmatic statement for the good news of God's exiled people: "The Spirit of Yhwh is upon me, because he has anointed me to bring good news to the poor, etc." The same passage is evoked later in Luke (7:22) and in Acts (10:36) when Jesus is depicted as the bearer of the eschatological Spirit.[6]

Less explicit but equally important is the role of Isa 61:1–3 in Matthew where the first beatitudes contain repeated references to this passage as Jesus proclaims the gospel of eschatological reversal (Matt 5:1–12; cf. Q/Luke 6:20–21), for example, "Blessed are the poor in spirit, for theirs is the kingdom of heaven" (Matt 5:3).[7] Recognizing the evocation of the Isaianic eschatological program argues for reading the Matthean beatitudes not merely as moral teachings but as the proclamation of the power of the eschatological gospel.

Terms related to *euangelizō* ("to bring good news") also appear frequently in Isa 40–66 (e.g., 40:9; 52:7; 60:6; 61:1). The numerous uses of Isa 61:1–2, specifically, suggest its formative influence on the NT authors. It is perhaps not an exaggeration, then, to affirm that "perhaps Isaiah's most important contribution is to early Christianity's understanding of its proclamation, that is, its message of 'good tidings' or 'gospel.'"[8]

---

[5] See also 1 Cor 1:18–2:5 that is "sprinkled with echoes of Isa. 61:1–3" as Paul considers such statement "as an indication of his own apostolate." See Florian Wilk, "Isaiah in 1 and 2 Corinthians," in Steve Moyise and Maarten J. J. Menken, eds., *Isaiah in the New Testament* (London: T&T Clark, 2005), 135. See also Ferdinand Hahn, "Der Apostolat im Urchristentum: Seine Eigenart und seine Voraussetzungen," *KD* 20 (1974): 70–73.

[6] Max Turner, *Power from on High: The Spirit in Israel's Restoration and Witness in Luke–Acts* (Sheffield: Sheffield Academic Press, 1996), 262.

[7] Cf. Robert A. Guelich, "The Matthean Beatitudes: 'Entrance-Requirements' or Eschatological Blessings," *JBL* 95 (1976): 415–434.

[8] Craig A. Evans, "From Gospel to Gospel: The Function of Isaiah in the New Testament," in Craig C. Broyles and Craig A. Evans, eds., *Writing and Reading the Scroll of Isaiah: Studies of An Interpretive Tradition*, VTSup 70.2 (Leiden: Brill, 1997), 653. For a further discussion on the influence of Isaiah on the early Christian use of the *euangelizō* word-group, see Peter Stuhlmacher, *Die paulinische Evangelium, 1: Vorgeschichte*, FRLANT 95 (Göttingen: Vandenhoeck & Ruprecht, 1968), 109–179, 218–225.

Isaiah 53 and Christology

The significance of the Fourth Servant Song of Isaiah (52:13–53:12) for the construction of early Christologies has long been recognized, especially as it is evoked throughout the NT (52:15 [Rom 15:21]; 53:1 [John 12:38; Rom 10:16]; 53:4 [Matt 8:17; 1 Pet 2:24]; 53:5 [1 Pet 2:24]; 53:6 [1 Pet 2:25]; 53:7 [Acts 8:32–33]; 53:9 [1 Pet 2:22; Rev 14:5]; 53:12 [Luke 22:37; 1 Pet 2:24]). Perhaps its most extensive use is in 1 Pet 2:22–25 (cf. Isa 53:4, 5, 6, 7, 9, 12), where Christ's own suffering becomes the model for believers to follow.[9] Beyond explicit quotations, many have detected its presence behind the notable ransom saying in Mark 10:45 (cf. Isa 53:10–11),[10] though whether the suffering of this servant involves a vicarious death remains disputed (HOOKER: 148–150).[11] The mere fact of its relative significance in the NT writings (as compared to Second Temple Jewish literature) is noteworthy.[12]

The christological use of Isa 53 does not, however, exhaust its significance within the NT writings. Acts 8:32–33 uses Isa 53:7 to point to the wider eschatological program of the inclusion of the outcasts within God's people, while Isa 53:1 is used in John 12:38–41 and Rom 10:16 (with Isa 6:9–10) to describe the Jewish rejection of the gospel. In both cases, admittedly, Christology still lies in the background, since Christ himself is an outcast and one who suffers derision and rejection.[13]

---

[9]   See also the importance of this servant song behind the wider structure of Romans (cf. Rom 4:24–25; 5:15–19; 10:16; 15:21). Cf. Richard B. Hays, *Echoes of Scripture in the Letters of Paul* (New Haven: Yale University Press, 1989), 63. See also Jean Charles Bastiaens, *Interpretaties van Jesaja 53: Een intertextueel onderzoek naar de lijdende Knecht in Jes 53 (MT/LXX) een in Lk 22:14–38, Hand 3:12–26, Hand 4:23–31 en Hand 8:6–40*, Theologische Faculteit Tilburg Studies 22 (Tilburg: Tilburg University Press 1993).

[10] See, for example, Rikki E. Watts, "Jesus' Death, Isaiah 53, and Mark 10:45: A Crux Revisited," in William H. Bellinger, Jr., and William R. Farmer, eds., *Jesus and the Suffering Servant: Isaiah 53 and Christian Origins* (Harrisburg, PA: Trinity Press International, 1998), 125–151, who situates Mark 10:45 within the wider influence of Isa 40–55 behind the entire gospel of Mark.

[11] Hooker does see the influence of this Isaianic servant figure in the related saying in Rom 4:25. See "Did the Use of Isaiah 53 to Interpret His Mission Begin with Jesus?" in William H. Bellinger, Jr., and William R. Farmer, eds., *Jesus and the Suffering Servant: Isaiah 53 and Christian Origins* (Harrisburg, PA: Trinity Press International, 1998), 101–102.

[12] Marc Zvi Brettler and Amy-Jill Levine, "Isaiah's Suffering Servant: Before and After Christianity," *Int* 73 (2019): 158–173.

[13] Cf. Richard Bauckham, *God Crucified: Monotheism and Christology in the New Testament* (Grand Rapids, MI: Eerdmans, 1999), 49–51.

Isaiah 6 and Obduracy

A number of passages in Isaiah were used in reference to the idolatrous acts of God's people (Isa 29:13 in Matt 15:8–9; Mark 7:6–7) that led to their hearts being hardened (Isa 29:10; in Rom 11:8; cf. Deut 29:4 [ET]) and the gospel becoming a stumbling block (Isa 8:14 and 28:16 in Mark 12:10; Luke 20:17–18; Rom 9:33; 1 Pet 2:6–8; cf. Ps 118:22).

The most prominent of these, however, is Isa 6:9–10, which was repeatedly evoked in reference to the Jewish rejection of the gospel (Matt 13:14–15; Mark 4:12; Acts 28:26–27; cf. Luke 8:10; John 12:40; Rom 11:8). In the context of Isaiah, this passage depicts God's call to the prophet Isaiah to proclaim a message that would not be accepted. It is a proclamation of judgment on an idolatrous people (cf. Isa 2:5–22) who have turned into the idols that they worshipped, with ears and eyes that do not work, so that they "listen, but do not comprehend … look, but do not understand" (Isa 6:9; cf. Pss 115:4–8; 135:15–18).[14] The NT authors compared Jews who rejected the gospel to God's rebellious people of old with a similar fate.

The most striking use of Isa 6:9–10 can be found in Luke–Acts. As noted earlier, the narrative begins with the proclamation of the eschatological reversal contained in Isa 40:3–5 (Luke 3:4–6), as salvation is now offered to God's people despite their rebellious past. At the end of the narrative, however, this "eschatological reversal" is again dramatically reversed as judgment is proclaimed to this people through the use of Isa 6:9–10 (Acts 28:26–27). The movement from judgment to salvation that is found in two call narratives (Isa 6:1–13; 40:1–11) is reversed in Luke–Acts, and moves from to salvation to judgment – the joyous celebration of God's eschatological salvation turns into a tragic note (Pao: 105–109).[15] Paul tells "the leaders of the Jews" that since they will not hear, "this salvation of God has been sent to the Gentiles; they will listen." It should be noted, however, that this tragic note does not represent the final word concerning the state of God's people, since the Isaianic message of the hardening of God's people is but a call to them to repent.[16]

Isaiah 42 and 49 and Universalism

While the Fourth Servant Song (52:13–53:12) played an important role in the construction of early Christian Christologies, the First and

---

[14] Gregory K. Beale, "Isaiah vi 9–13: A Retributive Taunt Against Idolatry," *VT* 41 (1991): 257–278.

[15] Notably, the use of the older form of *sōtērion* appears in both passages (Luke 3:6; Acts 28:28), but nowhere else in the intervening fifty chapters of the narrative.

[16] Cf. Hans Wildberger, *Isaiah 1–12: A Commentary*, trans. T. H. Trapp (Minneapolis, MN: Fortress, 1991), 271.

Second Servant Songs (42:1–4 and 49:1–6) provided language to describe the universal scope of eschatological salvation. The lengthy quotation of Isa 42:1–4 in Matt 12:18–21 points to the ecclesiological implications of the affirmation of Jesus as the servant in whose name "the Gentiles will hope" (Matt 12:21 [Isa 42:4]) (BEATON: 174–191). The mission of this servant is therefore not limited to ethnic Israel.

The same universal vision lies behind the explicit quotation of Isa 49:6 in Acts 13:47 where Paul is called to be "a light for the Gentiles," a mission in continuation of that of Jesus (cf. "a light for revelation to the Gentiles," Luke 2:32 [Isa 42:6; 49:6; 51:4]).[17] Perhaps more important is the allusion to Isa 49:6 in the programmatic statement in Acts 1:8. The phrase "to the ends of the earth" (*heōs eschatou tēs gēs*), which rarely appears in Greco-Roman literature, appears five times in the LXX, four of which are in Isaiah (Isa 8:9; 48:20; 49:6; 62:11; cf. *Pss. Sol.* 1.4). In light of the explicit quotation of Isa 49:6 in Acts 13:47, it seems likely that Isa 49:6 also lies behind Acts 1:8: "you will be my witnesses in Jerusalem, in all Judea and Samaria, and to the ends of the earth." If so, "to the ends of the earth" could be read in light of the parallel phrase in the source text – "a light to the nations" (Isa 49:6) – and both phrases should be understood as referring to the inclusion of the Gentiles in the eschatological era (PAO: 91–96). Instead of referring to a particular geographical locale, therefore, Acts 1:8 points to the movement from Jerusalem to those outside the old covenanted people of God.

FORMATIVE INFLUENCE OF ISAIAH ON NEW TESTAMENT WRITINGS

Beyond the use of individual passages, the influence of Isaiah can also be felt in the wider literary patterns or structures of individual books. The hermeneutical significance of Isaiah is illustrated in these samples.

Matthew

The wider significance of Isaiah in Matthew is felt in both the opening quotation as well as one at the center of the gospel. The first explicit quotation appears in Matt 1:23 from Isa 7:14: "Look, the virgin shall conceive and bear a son, and they shall name him Emmanuel." This

---

[17]   In light of the use of Isa 49:6 in Acts 13:47, the reference behind Luke 24:47 may also be Isa 49:6. Cf. Jacques Dupont, "La portée christologique de l'evangélisation des nations d'après Lc 24,47," in Joachim Gnilka, ed., *Neues Testament und Kirche* (Freiburg; Herder, 1974), 138.

carries both christological and ecclesiological significance. In terms of the identity of Jesus, it points to him as "Immanuel," with an added editorial comment "which means, 'God is with us'". That this is a programmatic note is indicated by the repeated references to Christ's presence in Matt 18:20 ("I am there among them") and 28:20 ("I am with you always").[18]

The ecclesiological implications of Isa 7:14 also need to be noted. In the context of Isa 7–8, the presence of God is also a sign of judgment as he is rejected by the king of Judah. This pattern is repeated in Matt 1–2, when the God who is able to deliver his people is again rejected by the one who claims to be the "King" of Judah (Matt 2:1).[19] This theme of Jewish rejection of the gospel continues throughout Matthew with uses of other passages from Isaiah (cf. Matt 13:13–15 [Isa 6:9–10]; Matt 15:8–9 [Isa 29:13]).

Both christological and ecclesiological concerns are also present in one of the lengthiest quotations of Isaiah in Matt 12:18–21 (Isa 42:1–4):

> "Here is my servant, whom I have chosen,
>> my beloved, with whom my soul is well pleased.
> I will put my Spirit upon him,
>> and he will proclaim justice to the Gentiles."

Situated at the center of the gospel, this quotation does not merely identify Jesus with the Isaianic Servant (as mentioned earlier), it also identifies the pattern of the Servant who is to suffer because of his conflicts with the political establishment in his proclamation of "justice" (Matt 12:18 [Isa 42:1]) to all (cf. Matt 12:15–17) (BEATON: 196).[20] This paves the way toward the cross, as Jesus becomes the rejected Servant.

Mark

Mark begins his gospel by invoking "the prophet Isaiah" (Mark 1:2), followed by a quotation from Isa 40:3 (with material from Exod 23:20 and Mal 3:1), which is taken to provide the "controlling paradigm" for

---

[18]   For the argument that sees Matt 1:23 and 28:20 forming an *inclusio*, see David R. Bauer, *The Structure of Matthew's Gospel: A Study in Literary Design*, BLS 15 (Sheffield: Almond, 1988), 124–125.

[19]   See, in particular, Rikki E. Watts, "Immanuel: Virgin Birth Proof Text of Programmatic Warning of Things to Come (Isa 7:14 in Matt 1:23)," in Craig A. Evans, ed., *From Prophecy to Testament: The function of the Old Testament in the New* (Peabody, MA: Hendrickson, 2004), 92–113.

[20]   Beaton characterizes the mission of this Servant as both "compassionate" and "polemical."

the entire gospel as the mission of "the Way" (MARCUS: 47). Beyond this one quotation, Mark 1:1–15 has been compared to Isa 40:1–11 in that both are prologues that introduce an eschatological program to be fulfilled among God's people; as such, the author of Mark incorporates the story of Jesus into the redemptive-historical program envisioned by Isa 40–55.[21]

For Rikki Watts, this prologue provides three specific connections with Isaiah: 1) The term *euangelion* (Mark 1:1, 14) evokes the Isaianic proclamation of the dawn of the eschatological era (cf. Isa 40:9; 41:27; 52:7; 60:6; 61:1); 2) the tearing open of the heavens and the descent of the Spirit (Mark 1:10) recall the Isaianic note on the delay of the New Exodus (Isa 63:7–64:12, e.g., 64:1: "O that you would tear open the heavens and come down..."); and 3) the allusion to Isa 42:1 in Mark 1:11 identifies Jesus as the Servant (WATTS: 119–120).

Beyond this prologue, the wider three-part structure of Mark has also been understood as corresponding to the three-part structure of the Isaianic New Exodus scheme: 1) the manifestation of God's mighty acts in the restoration of the exiled (Mark 1:16–8:21), 2) the leading of the "blind" people (Mark 8:22–10:45), and 3) the entry into Jerusalem (Mark 10:46–16:8) (WATTS: 371). Whether or not a strict correspondence between the structure of the two programs can be established, the significance of Isaiah for the wider theology of Mark is beyond dispute.

Luke–Acts

The influence of Isaiah on Luke–Acts is also extensive. Isaiah is repeatedly evoked at critical junctures of the narrative (PAO: 41–110). The first lengthy quotation appears in Luke 3:4–6, which uses Isa 40:3–5 to provide the hermeneutic key for the Lukan program. This longer quotation from Isaiah that ends with a universalistic note ("all flesh shall see the salvation of God," Luke 3:6 [Isa 40:5]) not only provides coherence for both volumes of the Lukan writings, but it also incorporates the ministry of the apostles into the mission of Jesus that is grounded in the Scripture of Israel.

After this general introduction to the Lukan program, the quotation from Isa 61:1–2 and 58:6 in Jesus' Nazareth sermon (Luke 4:18–19) provides clear definition of his mission, and it is immediately followed by the themes of rejection (Luke 4:24) and mission to the Gentiles (Luke 4:25–27). These themes are in turn further reinforced by explicit quotations later in Luke's narrative with references to Gentile inclusion in

---

[21]   Richard Schneck, *Isaiah in the Gospel of Mark, I–VIII* (Berkeley: BIBAL, 1994).

the middle (Acts 13:47 [Isa 49:6]) and Jewish rejection at its end (Acts 28:26–27 [Isa 6:9–10]).

Acts also begins with a statement saturated with Isaianic language and motifs. The programmatic statement in Acts 1:8 contains references to the power of the Holy Spirit, the role of the witnesses, and the plan that involves "Jerusalem," "all Judea and Samaria," and "the ends of the earth." With the reference to the Spirit poured out "on us" (eph' hymas) alluding to Isa 32:15, the role of "witnesses" (martyres) to a common motif in Isa 43:10–12, and the phrase "to the ends of the earth" (heōs eschatou tēs gēs) evoking a phrase familiar (only) in Isa 40–55 in reference to the Gentiles (cf. Isa 8:9; 48:20; 49:6; 62:11; see earlier comments), it becomes apparent that the entire verse needs to be understood in reference to the theopolitical program of Isa 40–66 as contained already in its prologue (Isa 40:1–11): (1) "Jerusalem" points to Zion being the focus of God's eschatological salvation for his people (cf. Isa 40:1, 9); (2) "all Judea and Samaria" serves as a reference to the restoration of Israel (cf. Isa 40:10–11); and (3) "to the ends of the world" signifies yet another stage of the restoration program when salvation reaches the Gentiles (cf. Isa 40:3–5). These three stages provide the outline of Acts: the fulfillment of God's eschatological salvation in Jerusalem (Acts 1–7), restoration of God's people (Acts 8), and mission to the Gentiles (Acts 9–28) (PAO: 111–180).[22]

This dependence on Isaiah not only argues that the author viewed the church as the heir of God's promises to his people, but it also reaffirms the common conception that Jesus is the Servant figure who plays a critical role in the fulfillment of God's promises (MALLEN).[23]

John

Beyond the opening quotation from Isa 40:3–5 in John 1:23, two particular recurrent motifs in Isaiah have been understood as providing coherence for larger sections within this gospel. First, Andrew Lincoln suggests that the Johannine "witnessing" motif introduced in John 5:39 and 6:45 (Isa 54:13; cf. John 2:17, 22; 7:39; 12:16) should be read in light of the lawsuit between God and Israel in Isaiah (42:18–25; 43:22–28; 50:1–3) as well as the disputations against the Gentiles (41:1–5; 41:21–29;

---

[22] The restoration program climaxes in Acts 8, but begins already with the selection of Matthias to fulfill the number "twelve" in Acts 1:15–26.

[23] For another study that focuses on the christological import of Luke's use of Isaiah, see Rebecca I. Denova, *The Things Accomplished Among Us: Prophetic Tradition in the Structural Pattern of Luke–Acts*, JSNTSup 141 (Sheffield: Sheffield Academic Press, 1997).

43:9–13; 44:6–8; 45:18–25).[24] That is, since Israel failed as God's witnesses (John 12:38–41 [Isa 6:10; 53:1]) when they rejected Jesus, who was God's own witness, Jesus' followers now assume this role as witnesses being sent "into the world" (John 17:18, 23 [cf. Isa 42:6; 49:6]). The primary purpose of this within the wider lawsuit framework is not for condemnation but for the salvation of the world (3:17).[25]

Other than this witnessing motif within the lawsuit setting, the influence of Isaiah has also been detected in the structure of John. Noting the use of Isa 6:10 in the conclusion of the Book of Signs (1:19–12:50) – an explicit mention of the name Isaiah as one who "saw (Jesus') glory and spoke about him" (John 12:40–41), Andreas Köstenberger argues for reading the seven signs in the first part of John (2:1–11; 4:46–54; 5:1–15; 6:5–14; 6:16–24; 9:1–7; 11:1–45) in light of the seven signs in the first part of Isaiah (Isa 7:11–14; 8:18; 19:20; 20:3–4; 37:30; 38:7; 38:22).[26] This argument does not rest upon the strict correspondence between these two sets of signs, but they are similar: As the Johannine signs point to Jesus as the Messiah, the Isaianic signs point to Yhwh as the sovereign Creator. As such, "in the face of ample divine revelation, the burden rests squarely on God's people for rejecting such light."[27]

Assuming the validity of these readings, John's use of Isaiah is consistent with that of the synoptic authors in emphasizing both the christological and ecclesiological import of the prophetic traditions of Israel.

Romans

Isaiah plays an important role in Paul's writings, and Romans best exemplifies its formative influence in the structure of its theology. The recent work of Robert Olson demonstrates the programmatic significance of Isaiah in the first three chapters of Romans,[28] while others have situated Romans in light of the use of Isaiah in Second Temple Jewish interpretive traditions, pointing to unique Pauline emphasis on the role of the Messiah (in the person of Jesus himself) (SHUM) and the universalistic emphasis of the eschatological program.[29]

---

[24] Andrew T. Lincoln, *Truth on Trial: The Lawsuit Motif in the Fourth Gospel* (Peabody, MA: Hendrickson, 2000), 36–56.

[25] Lincoln, *Truth on Trial*, 51.

[26] Andreas J. Köstenberger, "John's Appropriation of Isaiah's Signs Theology: Implications for the Structure of John's Gospel," *Them* 43 (2018); 376–386.

[27] Köstenberger, "John's Appropriation," 386

[28] Robert C. Olson, *The Gospel as the Revelation of God's Righteousness: Paul's Use of Isaiah in Romans 1:1–3:26*, WUNT 2.428 (Tübingen: Mohr Siebeck, 2016).

[29] Delio DelRio, *Paul and the Synagogue: Romans and the Isaiah Targum* (Eugene, OR: Pickwick, 2013).

J. Ross Wagner's works provide a detailed argument for the influence of Isaiah throughout Romans (WAGNER).[30] From Israel's rebellion (2:24 [Isa 52:5]; 11:8 [Isa 29:10]) and that of all humanity (3:15–17 [Isa 59:7–8]), to the deliverance of the remnant of Israel (9:27–28 [Isa 10:22–23; 28:22]; 9:29 [Isa 1:9]; 9:33 [Isa 28:16; 8:14]; Rom 10:21 [Isa 65:2]; 11:26–27 [Isa 59:20–21; 27:9]) and the nations (Rom 10:20 [Isa 65:1]; 15:12 [Isa 11:10]) through Jesus the Servant (Rom 10:11 [Isa 28:16]), Paul's story of redemption is told through the lens of Isaiah, in concert with other scriptural traditions. That Paul "does not lean on the isolated testimony of a few verses from Isaiah" (WAGNER: 297) is best illustrated by his use of Isa 52, in particular, throughout Romans (2:24 [Isa 52:5]; 10:15 [52:7]; 15:21 [Isa 52:15]).

Beyond this rehearsal of God's redemptive works through his Servant Messiah, Isaiah is also used in situating Paul's own calling and mission within this wider redemptive plan. In 10:15, for example, he situates himself among those who participate in the propagation of the eschatological program ("How beautiful are the feet of those who bring good news!" [Isa 52:7]; see also 10:16 [Isa 53:1]; 14:11 [Isa 45:23]; 15:21 [Isa 52:15]). Following the footsteps of Isaiah, Paul understands himself to be a herald to a divided Israel; at the end, however, both are proclaiming the good news of God's faithfulness despite human faithlessness.[31]

Revelation

Without any explicit quotation (FEKKES: 130),[32] Isaiah nonetheless provides the language for the depiction of the climactic act of Christ that ushers in the eschatological era. Allusions are used throughout Revelation in the depiction of Christ (see, e.g., 3:7 that depicts Christ as having "the key of David, who opens and no one will shut, who shuts and no one opens," which contains an allusion to Isa 22:22 [I will place on his shoulder the key of the house of David; he shall open, and no one shall shut; he shall shut, and no one shall open]; see also 1:16 [Isa 11:4]; 1:17 [Isa 44:6]; 2:17 [Isa 65:15]; 5:5 [Isa 11:10]; 19:15 [Isa 11:4]; 22:16 [Isa 11:10]) and his salvific acts (2:17 [Isa 62:2; 65:15]; 3:9 [Isa 43:4;

---

30   See also J. Ross Wagner, "Isaiah in Romans and Galatians," in William H. Bellinger, Jr., and William R. Farmer, eds., *Jesus and the Suffering Servant: Isaiah 53 and Christian Origins* (Harrisburg, PA: Trinity Press International, 1998), 117–132.

31   Wagner, "Isaiah in Romans and Galatians," 129. Cf. Richard B. Hays, "'Who Has Believed our Message?' Paul's Reading of Isaiah," in J. M. Court, ed., *New Testament Writers and the Old Testament: An Introduction* (London: SPCK, 2002), 46–70.

32   The use of Isa 22:22 in Rev 3:7 comes to being an explicit quotation especially if the author is drawing from a Hebrew text.

49:23]; 7:16–17 [Isa 25:8; 49:10]; 19:7–8 [Isa 61:10]) (FEKKES: 280–282), and two sections in particular reflect a more intense formative influence of Isaiah.

First, in Revelation 14–19, Isaiah is repeatedly evoked in reference to the judgment of Babylon/Rome (14:8 [Isa 21:9]; 14:10–11 [Isa 34:10]; 17:2 [Isa 23:17]; 18:2 [Isa 21:9; 13:21; 34:11–14]; 18:3 [Isa 23:17]; 18:4 [Isa 52:11]; 18:7–8 [Isa 47:7–9]; 18:9 [Isa 23:17]; 18:23 [Isa 23:8]; 19:3 [Isa 34:10]) in concert with Jeremiah's oracles against Babylon (Jer 50–51) and Ezekiel's against Tyre (Ezek 26–27) (MOYISE AND MENKEN: 198). The merging of these traditions points to the finality of God's judgment against evil. Second, the vision of the new heaven and new earth in Rev 21:1–22:5 is also framed by Isaianic material, especially by the use of Isa 54:11–12 (Rev 21:18–21) and 60:1–19 (Rev 21:23–26) (COMBLIN: 172–174).

CONCLUSION

Early Christian communities considered themselves the fulfillment of Isaiah's eschatological program, and Isaiah provided the language and categories through which their identities as Christ's followers could be articulated. In both christological and ecclesiological terms, Isaiah did indeed become an essential "gospel" for these communities.

FURTHER READING

Beaton, Richard. *Isaiah's Christ in Matthew's Gospel*. SNTSMS 123. Cambridge: Cambridge University Press, 2002.

Comblin, José. *Le Christ dans l'Apocalypse*. Biblique de theologie. Theologie biblique 3.6. Paris: Desclée, 1965.

Evans, Craig A. *To See and Not Perceive Isaiah 6,9–10 in Early Jewish and Christian Interpretation*. JSOTSup 64. Sheffield: JSOT, 1989.

Fekkes, Jan. III. *Isaiah and Prophetic Traditions in the Book of Revelation: Visionary Antecedents and their Development*. JSNTSup 93. Sheffield: Sheffield Academic Press, 1994.

Hooker, Morna D. *Jesus and the Servant: The Influence of the Servant Concept of Deutero-Isaiah in the New Testament*. London: SPCK, 1959.

Janowski, Bernd, and Peter Stuhlmacher, ed. *The Suffering Servant: Isaiah 53 in Jewish and Christian Sources*. Trans. Daniel P. Bailey. Grand Rapids, MI: Eerdmans, 2004.

Lehnert, Volker A. *Die Provokation Israels: Die paradoxe Funktion von Jes 6,9–10 bei Markus und Lukas: Ein textpragmatischer Versuch im Kontext gegenweartiger Rezeptionsèasthetik und Lesetheorie*. NTDH 25. Neukirchen-Vluyn: Neukirchener, 1999.

Mallen, Peter. *The Reading and Transformation of Isaiah in Luke–Acts*. LNTS 367. London: T&T Clark, 2008.

Marcus, Joel. *The Way of the Lord: Christological Exegesis of the Old Testament in the Gospel of Mark*. Louisville, KY: Westminster/John Knox, 1992.

Moyise, Steve, and Maarten J. J. Menken, ed. *Isaiah in the New Testament*. London/New York: T&T Clark, 2005.

Pao, David W. *Acts and the Isaianic New Exodus*. WUNT 2.130. Tübingen: Mohr Siebeck, 2000.

Sawyer, John F. A. *The Fifth Gospel: Isaiah in the History of Christianity*. Cambridge: Cambridge University Press, 1996.

Shum, Shiu-Lun. *Paul's Use of Isaiah in Romans: A Comparative Study of Paul's Letter to the Romans and the Sibylline and Qumran Sectarian Texts*. WUNT 2.156. Tübingen: Mohr Siebeck, 2002.

Wagner, J. Ross. *Heralds of the Good News: Isaiah and Paul "In Concert" in the Letter to the Romans*. NovTSup 101. Leiden: Brill, 2002.

Watts, Rikki E. *Isaiah's New Exodus in Mark*. WUNT 2.88. Tübingen: Mohr Siebeck, 1997.

Wilk, Florian. *Die Bedeutung des Jesajabuches für Paulus*. FRLANT 179. Göttingen: Vandenhoeck & Ruprecht, 1998

19 Impressions of Isaiah in Classical Rabbinic Literature

JOSHUA EZRA BURNS

The classical Jewish exegetical treatise Pesiqta of Rab Kahana presents a curious exchange between two rabbinic sages active in the Land of Israel around the turn of the fourth century CE.[1] Their subject of conversation is Isa 40:1, which reads, "Comfort, O comfort my people, says your God."

> Rabbi Ḥanina bar Pappa said: Israel told Isaiah, "Isaiah, our rabbi, are you saying that you came only to comfort the generation in whose days the Temple was destroyed?" He answered them, "I came to comfort all the generations. It is not written 'God said,' but, rather, 'God says.'"
>
> Rabbi Simon said: Israel told Isaiah, "Isaiah, our rabbi, are you saying that all these words are actually from your own heart?" He answered them, "It is not written 'God said right now,' but, rather, 'God says.'"

The Hebrew term for "says" (yōmar) is in the imperfect tense, indicating continuous or future action. Interrogating the word's verbal form, Ḥanina submits that the nation of Israel asked Isaiah whether God meant to comfort only those who were to endure the Babylonian conquest of Jerusalem and the consequent destruction of the First Temple more than a hundred years later after the prophet's day. So did Isaiah reassure them that God speaks to Israel continually, comforting his people in every generation. Simon offers another, complementary, interpretation inferring that Israel asked Isaiah whether he simply made up the contents of his divine oracles. So did the prophet reassure them that God would vindicate his words in time.

On the surface, it appears as though Ḥanina and Simon take extraordinary liberties with a rather ordinary feature of the scriptural text. Although the author of Isa 40, ostensibly Isaiah himself, addresses the

---

[1] Pesiq. Rab Kah. 16:10. The translation is my own.

people of Israel, the text implies no collective national response to his oracle. Hanina correctly infers that the oracle postdates the destruction of the Temple. But the author does not betray his literary conceit by alluding to that event. Simon's claim that Israel accused Isaiah of falsifying the word of God is a startling indictment of his people's trust in the very institution of prophecy. Yet in the sage's account, Isaiah lets their insult pass without comment. Instead, he defends his prophetic authority quite counterintuitively by appealing to his very own speech or, more precisely, a transcription of his speech. None of this makes sense as elucidation of a verse that appears on its surface to require no explanation at all.

The exegetical sensibilities exhibited in the exchange between Hanina and Simon are typical of the interpretive method the sages knew as *midrash*, a term signifying the pursuit of meaning. What the sages pursued when reading the Hebrew Scriptures was not their superficial significance but the deeper meaning they believed was concealed in their divine verbiage. That is what compelled Hanina and Simon to scrutinize Isaiah's seemingly banal choice of words. God, they reasoned, must have made the prophet speak in the imperfect tense to signify something more than the plain sense of his words suggests. What Isaiah himself meant is incidental to that logic, his voice irrelevant to the object of the exegetical pursuit.

To try to encapsulate classical rabbinic attitudes toward Isaiah is to learn that lesson hundreds of times over. The rabbinic sages made extensive use of Isaiah's book. But they used it principally as an exegetical resource, mining its verses for abstract textual "metadata" to help them understand the will of God. Consequently, what the sages thought of the man through whom they believed God spoke can be difficult to tell. The intermittent commentary on the prophet amid their excursions into his language is too sparse to offer more than mere impressions of who the sages believed Isaiah was, what motivated him, and what the effect was on his prophetic idiom. In what follows, I discuss a few of their more noteworthy areas of interest.

ISAIAH IN RABBINIC LORE

Let us begin by defining some key terms. For the purposes of our investigation, the term "rabbinic sages" signifies the Tannaim, who flourished in the Land of Israel, or Palestine, from the first through early third centuries CE, and the Amoraim, who flourished in the Land of Israel and in Babylonia, or southeastern Mesopotamia, from the early third through

the fifth centuries CE. The traditions of the Tannaim are collected in
the Mishnah and Tosefta, compilations of *halakah* or "the way," a term
signifying their program of ritual law, and the Tannaitic *midrashim*,
compilations of exegetical traditions concerning the Pentateuch and
informing their senses of *halakah*. The Amoraim preserved and augmented the traditions of the Tannaim. The Jerusalem or Palestinian
Talmud and the Babylonian Talmud are nominally halakic works that
incorporate copious nonlegal exegetical content of the variety known as
haggadah or narrative. The Amoraic *midrashim*, largely produced after
the age of the Amoraim, are given exclusively to haggadic traditions.

The generic distinctions *halakah* and *haggadah* are largely incon-
sequential to our investigation. To the sages themselves, all their exegetical endeavors belonged to a common order of knowledge known as
Oral Torah (FRAADE: 31–46). The sages believed that they sustained a
continuous tradition of verbal instruction initiated by God's revelation
to Moses at Mount Sinai. They imagined Oral Torah as a natural continuation of the likewise divinely inspired Written Torah inscribed in
the Pentateuch and later additions to the Hebrew Scriptures. That foundational myth gave the sages license among their adherents to interpret
the sacred texts they shared with all Jews as witnesses to their own
uncommon exegetical sensibilities.

Yet not everything recorded in the literature of the sages was of
their own invention. As the sages sought to influence popular Jewish
religious mores, they often appealed to popular lore. Isaiah, for instance,
entered the rabbinic literary imagination with a formidable reputation.
Unaware of twenty-first-century knowledge concerning the complex
compositional history of his book, ancient Jewish audiences regarded
the prophet as a visionary of astounding ability capable of foreseeing
events that would not transpire until long after his lifetime. The sages
thus had to contend with Isaiah's vaunted name even as they questioned aspects of his character.

The abundance of allusions to Isaiah's book in their writings indicate that the sages knew it well. Those allusions, however, are dispersed
amid an assortment of halakic and haggadic compilations of traditions
spanning more than five centuries (NEUSNER). If the rabbinic collective cultivated a systematic approach to interpreting Isaiah's prophecies, no record of it has survived. Isaiah was not exceptional in that
respect among the prophetic books. The primary objective of the rabbinic exegetical enterprise was to expound *halakah*. As the sages did
not consider prophets other than Moses conduits of *halakah*, they used
the books of the prophets principally as resources for the interpretation

of the Pentateuch and its ritual legislation. Nevertheless, a few recurring themes in their haggadic literature suggest that certain aspects of Isaiah's scriptural biography piqued the curiosities of rabbinic masters and disciples through the ages.

ISAIAH'S PROPHETIC VOCATION

No aspect of Isaiah's prophetic career fascinated the sages more than his call to prophesy. According to one Amoraic tradition, Isaiah's vision of God seated upon his celestial throne (Isa 6) set him on a par with Moses, the only other Israelite luminary said in the Hebrew Scriptures to have seen God's physical form.[2] And much as the sages imagined Moses as a member of their scholarly guild, so did some wish to know Isaiah. Another Amoraic tradition fancifully pictures Isaiah pacing in his *beit midrash* or house of study, a typically rabbinic scholastic setting, when he hears God plead, "Whom shall I send, and who will go for us?" (Isa 6:8).[3] Isaiah's eager acceptance of the call – "Here am I; send me!" – prompts God to ask the would-be chastiser of Israel whether he can withstand the degrading reception likely in store for him. Isaiah's readiness to bear the burden of his perilous commission earns him a double dose of divine inspiration, giving him greater oracular insight than God's other prophetic envoys. The resulting image of the learned Isaiah as a superlative medium of divine instruction resonates with the self-perceptions of the sages as teachers of Torah likewise authorized by God.

But not all were sold on Isaiah's magnanimity. One Amoraic tradition depicts God rebuking Isaiah for characterizing Israel as "a people of unclean lips" (Isa 6:5).[4] Before, therefore, allowing Isaiah to receive his divine speech, God orders his seraphs to punish the would-be prophet by searing his own filthy lips with a burning coal (cf. Isa 6:6–7). The scriptural text presents a subtly different story, whereby the seraphs touch the coal to Isaiah's mouth to disinfect it. Although the exegetical figure actually commends Isaiah for his devotion to God's children, its critical undercurrent suggests a sense of discomfort with Isaiah's seeming readiness to denounce his people before receiving his prophetic credentials.

---

[2] Y. Sanh. 10:2, 28c. Compare Tg. Ps.-J. Isa 6:2, 5, where Isaiah is said to have seen only the radiant glory of God's *shekhinah* or divine presence.

[3] Lev. Rab. 10:2. See also b. 'Erub. 26a for an Amoraic tradition indicating that Isaiah established a *yeshivah* or academy at Hezekiah's palace.

[4] Song Rab. 1:6:1.

The characterization of Isaiah as too eager for his vocation is absent from a later retelling of the tale in Pesiqta of Rab Kahana, which includes only flattering Amoraic traditions amid its unqualified praise for the prophet.[5] The positive and the negative stand side by side in a version recorded in the derivative work Pesiqta Rabbati, which combines the two Amoraic accounts of Isaiah's theophany in a story suggesting that Isaiah's cardinal offense – the source of his uncleanliness – was having gazed upon God and not immediately joined the seraphs in sanctifying him (cf. Isa 6:3). Hence the anticipatory lament, "Woe is me! I am lost," preceding his clumsy response to God's call (Isa 6:5).[6]

The author of this synthetic haggadic tradition evidently noticed that the sages of old did not all see eye to eye on the excellence of Isaiah's character. Some considered him a faultless emissary of God, while others found aspects of his self-representation problematic. Even to the eyes of his admirers, Isaiah's claim that he was granted unparalleled access to God made him accountable to a standard of pedagogical integrity not entirely within the prophet's reach.

ISAIAH'S ROYAL SERVICE

The narrative interlude in Isa 36–39 furnished the sages another occasion to evaluate Isaiah's prophetic *modus operandi* (PORTON: 693–716). The prophet's association with King Hezekiah distinguished him as a confidant of one of Israel's most celebrated leaders. One Amoraic tradition depicts Hezekiah and Isaiah as equals, suggesting that the two possessed joint authority to decide whether to form an alliance with the Assyrian king Sennacherib.[7] In contrast, the scriptural account of the Assyrian siege in Isa 36–37 clearly depicts Isaiah as a subordinate to Hezekiah. If the sages saw in Isaiah an archetypical religious leader, his promotion to the height of political power may reflect their ambitions to exercise influence over a Jewish populace beholden to the more persuasive authority of the Roman emperors.

The sages were no less taken by Isaiah's role in the account of Hezekiah's illness in Isa 38. An Amoraic tradition features a narrative expansion of that episode.[8] Told by the prophet that God has bid him to set his affairs in order in advance of his impending death (Isa 38:1),

---

[5] Pesiq. Rab Kah. 16:4.
[6] Pesiq. Rab. 33:3.
[7] Lev. Rab. 5:5. See also b. Ber. 10a for an unsourced tradition attributing them equal righteousness.
[8] Eccl. Rab. 5:6.

Hezekiah angrily rebuffs Isaiah for his unsympathetic manner. Turning away from his advisor, the king refuses to accept Isaiah's prognosis and begs God for mercy in view of his past merits (Isa 38:2–3). God immediately tells Isaiah that he has heard the king's prayer and intends to heal him (Isa 38:4–5). A flustered Isaiah protests that God's contradictory advice to Hezekiah will diminish his prophetic credibility. God responds that the king's humility will spare Isaiah from embarrassment. Yet when the prophet tells Hezekiah the good news, the king merely asserts that he was correct not to have trusted Isaiah to begin with.

On the surface, this tradition appears to cast Isaiah in a negative light, portraying the prophet as cold and argumentative. That said, the story is not really about Isaiah. It is about Hezekiah and his unwavering faith in God's justice. Yet although Isaiah's role in the story is tangential to its moral lesson, its unflattering depiction of the prophet evidently bothered some sages. Alternative versions of the tradition preserved in the two Talmuds depict Isaiah more sympathetically.[9] In those versions, Hezekiah does not rebuff Isaiah for foretelling his death. Instead, he asks the prophet why he is being punished. Isaiah replies that the king has not fulfilled his obligation to produce a royal successor. Hezekiah relates that he has kept from procreating because he has foreseen that he will bear an evil son, namely Manasseh. In the Jerusalem Talmud, Isaiah offers Hezekiah his daughter as wife in the hope that the union will produce a righteous child. It does not. In the Babylonian Talmud, Hezekiah asks Isaiah for his daughter's hand in marriage. The prophet declines the request, expressing resignation that God has already determined the character of Hezekiah's offspring.

The Talmudic versions of the Amoraic tradition transform it from a demonstration of Hezekiah's faith to a demonstration of Isaiah's wisdom. The scriptural account does not probe the cause of Hezekiah's illness. In its Talmudic retellings, the prophet deduces that God is punishing the king for trying to prevent the birth of Manasseh. In the Palestinian version of the story, Isaiah offers a solution whereby Hezekiah might produce a more worthy heir. But the constraints of the scriptural narrative doomed their attempt at dynastic subterfuge. The account of Manasseh's reign in 2 Kings dictated that he would succeed Hezekiah with or without Isaiah's intervention. The folly of the prophet's scheme evidently compelled the author of the Babylonian version to assign it to Hezekiah only for Isaiah to point out its futility.

---

9   Y. Sanh. 10:2, 28b; b. Ber. 10a.

Isaiah's powerlessness against the wicked whims of Manasseh supplies the setting of another dramatic Amoraic narrative tradition concerning the prophet. The Talmuds preserve two versions of an unsourced narrative telling of the new king's murderous pursuit of his father's former associate.[10] The story's exegetical stimulus is the failure of 2 Kings to account for Isaiah's whereabouts after the death of Hezekiah. The Talmudic accounts of the prophet's persecution have attracted much critical attention for their apparent echoes of an early Christian apocalyptic treatise known as the *Ascension of Isaiah*. That work likewise depicts Manasseh pursuing Isaiah before capturing and ordering him killed in a gruesome fashion. These parallels have been taken to indicate that the Christian text incorporates elements of a lost ancient Hebrew account of Isaiah's martyrdom also known to the rabbinic sages (PORTON: 710–15). Yet while it is possible that the Jewish and Christian tales are indebted to a common literary prototype, the rabbinic accounts of Isaiah's death appear to invoke folkloric motifs typical of the Near Eastern cultural contexts of the Talmuds (KALMIN: 29–52). Moreover, they exhibit no interest in representing Isaiah as a witness to his faith in the hagiographic style of the Christian text (HALPERN-AMARU: 170–74). These discrepancies argue against reading the Talmudic stories as anything but products of the rabbinic literary imagination.

In the Palestinian version of the tale, we find Isaiah, on the run from Manasseh, seeking refuge in a cedar tree.[11] Inexplicably, the tree swallows the prophet. Unfortunately, though, Isaiah's *tzitzit*, the scripturally mandated fringes lining his clothing, are left protruding through the tree's exterior (cf. Num 15:37–40; Deut 22:12). Manasseh's henchmen spot the *tzitzit* and report Isaiah's hiding place to the king. Manasseh orders them to cut down the tree. Isaiah's death is confirmed as their hacking begins to yield blood.

If there is a moral lesson to be learned from Isaiah's behavior in this story, it is not readily apparent. The prophet's observance of the Mosaic laws concerning *tzitzit* recommends his piety. But his piety works against him, betraying his location to Manasseh's men. That inference evidently bothered the author of the Babylonian version of the story.[12] That version opens with Manasseh accusing Isaiah of contradicting the teachings of Moses, his principal charge that prophet could not possibly have seen God and lived to report it (Isa 6:1; Exod 33:20). Realizing

---

[10] Y. Sanh. 10:2, 28c; b. Yebam. 49b.
[11] Y. Sanh. 10:2, 28c.
[12] B. Yebam. 49b (cf. b. Sanh. 103b). Variations appear in Pesiq. Rab. 4:3 and the *tosefta* or additions to Tg. Ps.-J. Isa 66:1.

that the king is intent on killing him, Isaiah flees to the cedar tree. He pronounces the name of God and is swallowed whole. Manasseh's men locate the tree (without the aid of Isaiah's *tzitzit*), cut it down, and bring it to the king. They then begin to saw through the hewn wood, Isaiah dies as the blade reaches his mouth, repaying the prophet for having once maligned Israel as "a people of unclean lips" (Isa 6:5).

The Babylonian version of the story eliminates the puzzling implication of the earlier version concerning Isaiah's adherence to the Mosaic law. It further burnishes his prophetic credentials by having Isaiah commence his astonishing diversion with a magical incantation. But, however effective, his trick does not keep Manasseh's men from locating him. With his death comes a cruel reminder of Isaiah's gratuitous degradation of his people upon his initial call to prophesy. Like many other famous heroes of Israel, Isaiah was not perfect. Even his holiness could not save him from what God had in store for him.

Then again, the story represented in both version of the tradition story is not about Isaiah. It is about Manasseh, about his fanatical zeal to eliminate the last living link to the regime of his righteous father (HENZE: 217–20). Driven by exegetical concerns immaterial to Isaiah's character, the authors found the prophet a convenient foil for demonstrating the depravity of the new king. Why God would sanction Isaiah's murder is not the question driving the narrative.

ISAIAH'S PROPHECIES

Hints of interest in the particulars of Isaiah's prophecies appear at a relatively late stage in the history of the rabbinic movement. Its earliest known expressions appear in Lamentations Rabbah, a fifth-century CE haggadic *midrash* compiling Tannaitic and Amoraic exegetical traditions pertaining to its scriptural namesake. The collection begins with a series of proems or brief exegetical discourses ruminating on the Roman destruction of the Second Temple of Jerusalem. The sages cited in those discourses often invoke Isaiah, whose expressions of hope in the restoration of Zion and redemption of Israel countered the despair of Lamentations over the fall of the First Temple. Although their precise origins are obscure, the proems appear to relate to the custom of reciting Lamentations during the liturgy for Tisha b'Av (the Ninth Day of the Month of Av), an annual fast day commemorating the losses of both Temples. Taken as a whole, they suggest a common rabbinic tendency to interpret Isaiah's book as a testament to God's everlasting compassion for Israel, that is, for the Jewish people.

The association of Isaiah with Tisha b'Av developed with the institutionalization of the weekly synagogue lectionary. Adopting a common liturgical practice of the late Second Temple period, the sages added to every Sabbath's recitation from the Pentateuch a complementary *haftarah* or concluding selection from the prophets. The longest of their prophetic books, Isaiah supplied the sages numerous *haftarot*. Prominent among them was a cycle of readings from the chapters of Isaiah known to contemporary scholars as Deutero- and Trito-Isaiah (Isa 40–66) assigned to the seven Sabbaths between Tisha b'Av and Rosh Hashanah, the Jewish New Year festival. The so-called Sabbaths of consolation evidently provided the sages dates on their liturgical calendar to expound on Isaiah's prophecies for homiletical purposes, that is, for exegetical applications other than the exposition of *halakah* (on the origins of this custom, see BARTH: 503–15).

The earliest known attestation of the Sabbaths of consolation cycle appears in the aforementioned Pesiqta of Rab Kahana, a fifth- or sixth-century CE haggadic *midrash* consisting of exegetical miscellanies relating to the *haftarot* for festivals and other special occasions. The chapters corresponding with the seven *haftarot* of consolation (16–22) feature a dense concentration of allusions to Isaiah edited and arranged to advance the hermeneutical strategy seemingly informing the collection of proems in Lamentations Rabbah (on the hermeneutical strategies of the haftarot of consolation, see STERN: 51–76). Isaiah's accurate prediction of the Babylonian conquest of Jerusalem as well as its restoration under Persian rule recommended his prophecy as timeless, or, as Rabbi Ḥanina put it, as though meant to speak to Jews of every generation seeking reassurance that God's devotion to the nation of Israel will never fail. Isaiah's prophecies were especially well suited to the theological needs of the sages and their target audiences, who continued to suffer the unresolved trauma of Rome's destruction of their holy city for hundreds of years after the fact.

The use of Isaiah as a liturgical bridge between the anguish of Tisha b'Av and the optimistic renewal of Rosh Hashanah acquired an apologetic aspect following the Christianization of the Roman Empire. The ninth-century CE haggadic *midrash* Pesiqta Rabbati includes chapters on the *haftarot* of consolation adapted from Pesiqta of Rab Kahana and other classical rabbinic sources (30–34, 36–37). Though likewise rich with allusions to Isaiah, Pesiqta Rabbati diverges from Pesiqta of Rab Kahana in its application of his prophecies to visions addressing the arrival of the Messiah, the storied eschatological king whom Jews believed God would appoint to restore Israel's sovereignty and exact judgement on the nations (for a comparison of the use of Isaiah in the two collections, see ULMER 2016: 215–39). Where the earlier work includes a few Amoraic passages associating Isaiah's visions of redemption with the Messianic age, Pesiqta Rabbati responds to Christian claims about the Messiah with a novel portrayal of Israel's royal redeemer supplied not by the Amoraim but by later Jewish scribal tradents operating in a religious environment more heterogeneous than that of their rabbinic forebears. I will discuss aspects of that portrait shortly.

Other expressions of interest in Isaiah associated with the sages originated in popular Jewish circles of varying proximity to the rabbinic movement. The Aramaic *targum* to Isaiah traditionally ascribed to the first-century BCE proto-sage Jonathan ben Uzziel likely originated in Palestine before his migration to Babylonia and then back to Palestine sometime during the late ancient period. The *targum*'s highly embellished translation varies in the degree of its alignment with the beliefs of the sages. Several *piyyutim* or liturgical poems of that era incorporate elements of Isaiah's prophecies. Abstract selections of Isaiah appear throughout the *siddur* or common Hebrew prayer book codified in the early Middle Ages. These developments arguably advanced Isaiah to a status of recognition in postclassical Judaism more prominent than his standing among the Tannaim and Amoraim who incubated its religious worldview.

But that development was not unprecedented. The rabbinic sages made extensive and liberal use of Isaiah's book in the multiform exegetical project they knew as Oral Torah. Their designs to read his prophecies as signs of God's everlasting bond with their people prompted their literary executors to compile rabbinic exegetical traditions speaking to that theme. In time, heirs of the religious movement initiated by the Tannaim and Amoraim rewrote and reconfigured those traditions better to address theological concerns of their own times. To understand those concerns is essential to understanding the impressions of Isaiah's prophecies left in the pages of the literature conventionally, if not always accurately, associated with the sages.

ISAIAH'S MESSIAH

Although their stories about Isaiah's life and death were determined by the parameters of the scriptural narrative, the rabbinic sages had no such limitations with respect to his prophecies. The sages typically understood prophecy as a multivalent medium of communication liable to result in any number of outcomes in the near and far terms. As noted, late midrashic texts preserve traditions indicating that the sages often read Isaiah's oracles concerning the restoration of Zion as pledges of God's redemption of Israel in a future yet to be realized. Some read them in eschatological terms, imagining their people's long-awaited liberation from foreign rule as a portent of the Messiah. But the sages generally were not preoccupied by Messianic speculation. They therefore did not consider Isaiah's prophecies especially instructive as to the identity of Israel's redeemer king or the schedule of his arrival (on the infrequency of the messianic motif, see STERN: 56–57).[13]

Yet although the sages did not find fertile eschatological soil in Isaiah's prophecies, their attitudes toward those of the prophet's visions traditionally understood by Christians as Messianic prophecies have been subjected to intense scrutiny. In his notorious *c.* 1278 polemical treatise *Pugio fidei* ('Dagger of Faith'), the Dominican scholar Ramon Martí submitted that the ancient rabbis knew that Israel's prophets foretold the advent of the Messiah, that is, of the Christian Messiah (on Martí and his polemical strategy, see CHAZAN: 112–36). The friar's invidious contention that the Jewish sages suppressed the truth of Christianity to the spiritual injury of their people has compelled generations of scholars both Christian and Jewish to investigate just what the Tannaim and Amoraim saw in Isaiah's visions where their Christian contemporaries discerned sure signs of Jesus (HOROWITZ: 419–36). And although its premise has not withstood critical examination, its shameful persistence in Christian apologetics against Judaism recommends addressing Martí's argument here.

Let us consider the two sections of Isaiah's book most prominent in classical Christian reasoning concerning the identity of the Messiah. The first is Isa 7–12, which presents a series of oracles foretelling the birth of a new Davidic king. The second is Isa 52:13–53:12, the so-called song of the suffering servant, which tells of a servant of God detested and abused for the transgressions of his people but destined for prosperity and exaltation. Early Christians understood these passages as prophecies of the birth and crucifixion of their Messiah. But the passages do not actually use the distinctive Messianic language of royal anointment. Nor do they allude to the eschatological beliefs that would accrue to that language during the late Second Temple period. Consequently, their respective verbiages did not compel the rabbinic sages to interpret Isaiah's visions exclusively as Messianic prophecies.

---

[13]   Messianic intimation appears only twice in the chapters on the *haftarot* of consolation in Pesiq. Rab. Kah. (18:6, 22:5).

The propensity of the sages to infer multiple meanings in the wording of their scriptures is evident in their readings of Isa 7–12. To our knowledge, the sages commonly understood Isaiah's visions of an ideal future king of Israel to refer to Hezekiah, who would succeed the king in power at the time Isaiah delivered those oracles. The sages considered Hezekiah both a great leader in his time and a model for future leaders, including the Messiah.[14] But they did not consider that eschatological king the subject of Isaiah's royal birth announcements.

Isa 52:13–53:12 presented the sages more of an interpretive challenge, as the scriptural text suggests no clear candidate for the identity of its subject. Contemporary scholars tend to agree that the "servant" of the Deutero-Isaiah prophecies is a figurative representation of the nation of Israel or an individual member of that nation, battered and broken by the exile but due for a revitalization upon the Persian defeat of Babylon (BRETTLER AND LEVINE: 159–64; BLENKINSOPP). While the sages probably did not appreciate the rhetorical context of the passage's composition, they recognized its allusive ambiguity. They variously interpreted its servant as Moses, Rabbi Akiva, any Jew enduring suffering, and, sometimes, the Messiah (LAATO: 266–80; BRETTLER AND LEVINE: 169–70).[15] But even where the sages opted to hear the song in an eschatological key, their objectives were not to recall a Messiah who once suffered. Rather, they inferred that the Messiah would be made to suffer in the future. In fact, the only known classical rabbinic tradition suggesting that the suffering of the Messiah had already transpired appears in an otherwise unattested textual extract allegedly of a Tannaitic *midrash* preserved in the *Pugio fidei*. Its authenticity is subject to question (FISHBANE: 67–68).[16]

The question of whether the rabbinic sages understood Isaiah's prophecies as visions of the Messianic age would be easily resolved if not for two treatises often mistaken for products of Oral Torah, namely the Aramaic *targum* to Isaiah and Pesiqta Rabbati. As noted, the *targum* is not, strictly speaking, a rabbinic text. Its text evolved among Jews of various religious persuasions for centuries prior to its adoption

---

14 For example, 'Abot R. Nat. A 25; y. Soṭah 9:16, 24c; y. 'Abod. Zar. 3:1, 42c; b. Ber. 28b; b. Sanh. 94a, 99a.

15 Moses: b. Soṭah 14a; Akiva: y. Šeqal. 5:1, 48c; nonspecific Jew: b. Ber. 5a; Messiah: Ruth Rab. 5:6, b. Sanh. 98b.

16 Although Martí credits the passage to a *libro Siphre*, its closest analog appears in Sifra 10:12, which features no allusion to Isaiah. Per Fishbane, it is possible that Martí recorded an authentic but otherwise lost variant of the Sifra's received text. But his polemical design raises doubt as to the friar's fidelity to his sources.

and further embellishment by adherents to the rabbinic way. Similarly, Pesiqta Rabbati, though often taken for a conventional work of haggadic *midrash*, is in fact a postclassical compilation of varied exegetical traditions both rabbinic and popular in nature. Consequently, the Messianic interpretations of Isaiah's prophecies appearing in those texts are not entirely representative of the Tannaitic and Amoraic literature they may resemble to the casual reader. A few examples will illustrate that point.

The Aramaic *targum* includes passing allusions to the Messiah throughout its rendering of Isaiah's Hebrew text. Its translation of Isa 52:13–53:12 offers an especially striking account of the Messiah as a mighty warrior who will vanquish Israel's gentile oppressors, enslave their survivors, gather God's exiled children to their homeland, and restore his holy sanctuary (on the features and likely late ancient context of the targum's Messianic portrait of the suffering servant, see HIMMELFARB: 91–96; LAATO: 129–63).[17] As though rebuffing Christian exegetical claims, the *targum* alternates between identifying the subject of the song with Messiah and his people, a people accounted as basically righteous but in need of their king's intercession should they hope to win God's forgiveness for their past sins. Although no single element of its scriptural montage would have offended the eschatological sensibilities of the Tannaim or Amoraim, the *targum*'s marriage of the Messiah and Israel in the person of Isaiah's suffering servant is without parallel in their literature.

The militaristic Messiah of the *targum* finds a counterpart in Pesiqta Rabbati 36–37. Amid its exegetical miscellanies concerning the last two *haftarot* of consolation, Isa 60:1–22 and 61:10–63:9, the text presents a series of unsourced allusions to a Messiah called Ephraim (for attempts to parse the complex web of traditions informing the account of a Messiah called Ephraim, see FISHBANE: 86–89; LAATO: 281–305; ULMER 2013: 132–41). Secreted from humanity since the beginning of creation, Ephraim is destined to suffer terrible affliction for the sins of his people for seven years before finally revealing himself to a world at war. Powerful nations awed by his might will submit to the fearsome new king of Israel. Israel's dead will be resurrected and their exiles repatriated. The Temple will rise again. God himself will inaugurate Ephraim's kingdom. He will be exalted, clothed in divine splendor with all the righteous, Torah-observant members of his nation serving as witnesses to his glory.

---

[17]   Tg. Ps.-J. Isa 52:13–53:12.

The Messiah Ephraim has no clear precedent in rabbinic traditions predating Pesiqta Rabbati. Nor does his characterization lend itself to reconciliation with the more tentative conceptions of Israel's eschatological king offered by the Tannaim and Amoraim. The author or authors of the traditions concerning Ephraim believed that the Messiah's arrival was imminent. Enumerated among the belligerent nations who will bow to his rule are Persia, Arabia, and Rome, whose battles for supremacy over the Near East during the seventh century CE evidently inspired hope among some Jews in that region that God would soon intervene on behalf of his long-suffering people. In other words, the Messiah Ephraim is not merely an eschatological figure. He is an apocalyptic figure whose appearance signals the end of days.

The emphasis on Ephraim's suffering suggests that his creators fashioned him in reference to another suffering Messiah. To the informed audience, Ephraim reads as an alternative to Jesus; Ephraim was a new champion of Israel for a world where Christian Rome was to be no more. To the Jews of Byzantine Palestine who witnessed successive waves of invaders from the east and south battering their territorial masters, hope for the Empire's imminent collapse was not unrealistic. But neither was it a fait accompli. Pesiqta Rabbati describes its suffering Messiah without explicit allusion to Isa 52:13–53:12. It thereby does not directly challenge the Christian belief that those verses describe none other than Jesus. If those who cultivated the legend of Ephraim envisioned him as a kind of anti-Christ, they evidently took care to avoid giving credence to the idea that Jesus was Israel's savior. And though their Messiah would suffer too, his suffering would not be vicarious. To their minds, the Jews had suffered enough for their past failings to have earned God's mercy.

The *targum* and Pesiqta Rabbati's interpretations of Isaiah's Messiah speak to the beliefs of scribal tradents knowledgeable of classical rabbinic literature but not exclusively beholden to its wisdom. The authors of those texts did not seek merely to comfort Israel. They sought to embolden their people with visions of a glorious future inconceivable to the sages of old. Their Messianic fantasies respond to certain Christian theological claims. But these authors did not conspire to suppress Christian truths. They rejected those truths. Like the sages before them, they discerned in Isaiah's visions their own truths, convictions conditioned by their understandings of God, by their experiences, and by the collective memory of their people. To infer otherwise would be to distort the very nature of the Jewish religion.

CONCLUSIONS

To the rabbinic sages, Isaiah was a prophet of unrivaled talent. Where other prophets foretold developments already in the offing, Isaiah could see into the distant future. A comforter of Israel, he softened his moral censure with messages of consolation and hope for Jews whose suffering might make them question God's dedication to their causes. A confidant to Israel's kings, Isaiah spoke truth to power even at risk of his own safety. But the sages did not consider Isaiah blameless. Although he did the best he could, even the greatest of Israel's prophets could not always live up to the high expectations of his commission.

Although the impressions of Isaiah left in their literature may not seem to recommend him as an exemplary figure, the sages did not expect perfection of their heroes. They expected sincerity. To their minds, Isaiah was man gifted with divine speech but not lacking for human shortcomings. Isaiah was relatable. He was a renowned teacher of Torah in the broad rabbinic sense of the word, trusted by his people to lead them through the wilderness in his generation and in every generation. In that respect, Isaiah was the prophet every sage yearned to be.

FURTHER READING

Barth, Lewis M. "The 'Three of Rebuke and Seven of Consolation' Sermons in the Pesikta de Rav Kahana." *JJS* 33 (1982): 503–15.

Blenkinsopp, Joseph. *Opening the Sealed Book: Interpretations of the Book of Isaiah in Late Antiquity*. Grand Rapids, MI: Eerdmans, 2006.

Brettler, Marc, and Amy-Jill Levine. "Isaiah's Suffering Servant: Before and after Christianity." *Interpretation* 73 (2019): 158–73.

Chazan, Robert. *Daggers of Faith: Thirteenth-Century Christian Missionizing and Jewish Response*. Berkeley: University of California Press, 1989.

Fishbane, Michael. "Midrash and Messianism: Some Theologies of Suffering and Salvation." Pages 57–71 in *Toward the Millennium: Messianic Expectations from the Bible to Waco*. Edited by Peter Schäfer and Mark R. Cohen. Leiden: Brill, 1998.

Fraade, Steven D. "Concepts of Scripture in Rabbinic Judaism: Oral Torah and Written Torah." Pages 31–46 in *Jewish Concepts of Scripture: A Comparative Introduction*. Edited by Benjamin D. Sommer. New York: New York University Press, 2012.

Halpern-Amaru, Betsy. "The Killing of the Prophets: Unraveling a Midrash." *HUCA* 54 (1983): 153–80.

Henze, Matthias. "King Manasseh of Judah in Early Judaism and Christianity." Pages 183–228 in *On Prophets, Warriors, and Kings: Former Prophets through the Eyes of Their Interpreters*. Edited by George J. Brooke and Ariel Feldman. Berlin: de Gruyter, 2016.

Himmelfarb, Martha. *Jewish Messiahs in a Christian Empire: A History of the Book of Zerubbabel*. Cambridge, MA: Harvard University Press, 2017.

Horowitz, Elliot. "Isaiah's Suffering Servant and the Jews: From the Nineteenth Century to the Ninth." Pages 419–36 in *New Perspectives on Jewish-Christian Relations: In Honor of David Berger*. Edited by Elisheva Carlebach and Jacob J. Schacter. Leiden: Brill, 2012.

Kalmin, Richard. *Migrating Tales: The Talmud's Narratives and Their Historical Context*. Berkeley: University of California Press, 2014.

Laato, Antti. *Who Is the Servant of the Lord? Jewish and Christian Interpretations on Isaiah 53 from Antiquity to the Middle Ages*. Turku: Åbo Akademi University; Winona Lake, IN: Eisenbrauns, 2012.

Neusner, Jacob. *Isaiah in Talmud and Midrash: A Source Book*. 2 vol. Lanham, MD: University Press of America, 2007.

Porton, Gary G. "Isaiah and the Kings: The Rabbis on the Prophet Isaiah." Pages 693–716 in vol. 2 of *Writing and Reading the Scroll of Isaiah: Studies of an Interpretive Tradition*. Edited by Craig C. Broyles and Craig A. Evans. Leiden: Brill, 1997.

Stern, Elsie R. *From Rebuke to Consolation: Exegesis and Theology in the Liturgical Anthology of the Ninth of Av Season*. Providence, RI: Brown Judaic Studies, 2004.

Ulmer, Rivka. "The Contours of the Messiah in Pesiqta Rabbati." *HTR* 106 (2013): 115–44.

Ulmer, Rivka. "Isaiah in Pesiqta de Rav Kahana and Pesiqta Rabbati." Pages 215–39 in *Transmission and Interpretation of the Book of Isaiah in the Context of Intra- and Interreligious Debates*. Edited by Florian Wilk and Peter Gemeinhardt. Leuven: Peeters, 2016.

20 The Reception History of Isaiah

Unsealing the Book

BRENNAN BREED

INTRODUCTION: RECEPTION HISTORY AND THE BOOK OF ISAIAH

Besides Moses, Isaiah has undoubtedly been the most influential Hebrew prophet in Jewish, Christian, and Muslim traditions. In Jewish tradition, Isaiah looms large as a Moses-like figure who spoke directly with God (*Lev. Rab.* 10), reduced the Ten Commandments to six, or even two (*b. Mak.* 24a), and whose eponymous book constitutes the largest portion of the *haftarot* readings from the prophets in Ashkenazi lectionaries.[1] Christians have long considered Isaiah the "fifth gospel," an indispensable repository of predictions of Christ's birth, ministry, death, and resurrection.[2] And among Muslim interpreters, Camilla Adang notes that Isaiah "takes pride of place, as was also the case among Christian apologists collecting testimonies to their Messiah."[3]

Reception history is the field of scholarly study that attends to the development of writings – that is, the use, interpretation, appropriation, translation, and reformation of writings – across time and space. The reception history of the book of Isaiah is so rich and diverse that it is impossible to map its trajectories in a single chapter. Instead of attempting a comprehensive analysis of all of Isaiah's reception history, this chapter traces the journey of three related texts—namely, Isa 8:16, 29:11, and 30:8—to demonstrate the expansiveness of Isaiah's reach, and also to model the specific ways in which readers tend to engage and understand them.

It is important to note at the outset that the book of Isaiah is itself the product of a long history of reception that begins within the

---

[1] John Sawyer, *Isaiah Through the Centuries* (Hoboken, NJ: Wiley Blackwell, 2018), 3.
[2] Sawyer, *Isaiah Through the Centuries*, 11.
[3] Camilla Adang, *Muslim Writers on Judaism and the Hebrew Bible from Ibn Rabban to Ibn Hazm* (Leiden: Brill, 1996), 146.

text itself. It seems likely that Isaiah himself reused and adapted parts of his own prophetic oracles that had once proved effective, updating them for different historical situations. An example of such an adapted oracle is 10:11–12.[4] Moreover, several Isaianic motifs, such as the highway (11:16; 19:23; 35:8; 40:3; 62:10), were reused by the scribes who produced successive portions of what became the book of Isaiah. As Andrew Teeter notes, citing the manifold uses of the names of Isaiah's children, "it is widely recognized that prophetic words originally attached to a specific historical situation are extended and given broader application through repetition in the book of Isaiah."[5] This should not be surprising, as elsewhere in the ancient Near East prophecies that were perceived as effective were updated and reused in new situations a few years later.[6] And once oracles were written and edited together, they were continually "recontextualized and reapplied to timeframes later than their place of origin," and the surplus of meaning produced by the prophecies "transcend[s] their original contexts and meanings."[7]

Writing is often thematized in the ancient Near East as an almost magical technology because of its ability to travel through time and space to deliver words from one context into another, separated from the presence of the speaker. Isaiah emphasizes the temporal and spatial displacement of writing in 30:8: "Now come and write it on a tablet, inscribe it on a scroll before their eyes, that it may be there in future days, a testimony for all time." The displacement of the initial speaker and author are mirrored by the displacement of the audience: From the moment of its inscription, it is possible to read Isa 30:8 in contexts unimaginably distant, even incomprehensible to Isaiah ben Amoz. In that sense, ancient and medieval readers, Jewish, Christian, and Muslim alike, would agree with Jacques Derrida that these written prophetic texts continue to function in the absence of their author, even

---

4   J. J. M. Roberts, *First Isaiah: A Commentary*, Hermeneia (Minneapolis, MN: Fortress, 2015), 166–167.

5   Andrew Teeter, "Isaiah and the King of As/Syria in Daniel's Final Vision: On the Rhetoric of Inner-Scriptural Allusion and the Hermeneutics of 'Mantological Exegesis'," pages 169–199 in *A Teacher for All Generations: Essays in Honor of James C. VanderKam. Volume One*, ed. Eric F. Mason, Samuel I. Thomas, Alison Schofield, and Eugene Ulrich (Leiden: Brill, 2012), 195.

6   Martti Nissinen, *Prophets and Prophecy in the Ancient Near East*, 2nd ed., (Atlanta, GA: SBL Press, 2019), 111.

7   Armin Lange, "Literary Prophecy and Oracle Collection," pages 248–275 in *Prophets, Prophecy and Prophetic Texts in Second Temple Judaism*, ed. M. Floyd and R. D. Haak (London: T&T Clark, 2006), 258.

after the author's death, and even in ways that the author would find unimaginable.[8]

At several points in First Isaiah, the prophet describes the act of writing, either metaphorically or literally, as part of the oracle itself (see 8:1, 16; 10:1, 19; 29:11; 30:8). In three of those instances, the prophet refers to the prophetic communication itself as a written message that is uninterpretable to the prophet's immediate audience, but which will be preserved for a future event of unveiling at a time when the people will be more receptive to the inscription (8:16–17; 29:11–12, 18; 30:8). In all three texts, the current generation is depicted as rebellious and divine judgment as imminent (8:15; 29:9–10; 30:9–11), but unspecified future readers will transform their ethical and religious orientations when they read the preserved words of the prophet in a new day (8:16; 29:18–21; 30:8).

In tracing the reception history of these Isaianic texts, I identified three different tendencies among interpreters. Some focused on the displacement of the written message as thematized in 8:16 and 29:11 in particular, ruminating on the content of the sealed revelation. Others emphasized the audience to whom Isaiah was believed to be communicating, often imagining themselves as the intended future recipients of his symbolic scroll. And a third group of readers displaced the speaker of the message from Isaiah ben Amoz of Jerusalem, the ancient Judahite prophet, and imagined other speakers, from Jesus to Mary to Muhammad to Joseph Smith, to be the prophet referred to in the text.

DISPLACED MEANINGS: THE SEALED MESSAGE

Writing is a technology that displaces language in time and space, separating words from the speaker's physical presence. There is no natural or logical endpoint to this displacement: Readers in vastly different cultural and linguistic settings can decipher messages from the distant past. As Isaiah claims, so long as it remains legibly inscribed, the written text is "a witness forever" (30:8). This definitive feature of writing was well known, and even the subject of intense reflection, throughout the ancient Near East (e.g., Job 19:23–24; Jer 17:1; Dan 9:2). Messages from distant times and places are often difficult to interpret because of differences in language and culture between writers and readers. But in Isaiah, the theme of the scroll that is "sealed" or uninterpretable to the

---

[8]   See Brennan Breed, *Nomadic Text* (Bloomington: Indiana University Press, 2014), 105–111.

immediate audience, but communicates seamlessly to a later audience, reverses the expectations of philologists both ancient and modern.[9] His message was apparently not understood, effective, or adopted in his own day (e.g., Isa 6:9–11). And yet, it has had an incredible impact for thousands of years in diverse cultures. It is striking that Isaiah predicted this, and he understood that writing was the technology that made this displacement of meaning possible.

Isaiah was certainly not the only prophet to encounter resistance to his messages (cf. Jer 36–38; Amos 7:10–17; Micah 2:6–11), but he may have been the first to conceive of this resistance as an inability to read and interpret texts. Isaiah also insists that a later generation, in "that day" (29:18) and "the time to come" (30:8), will be able to read the message. This vague eschatological claim opens up his text to anyone and everyone who imagines that their own time is the "now" in which the prophetic message is activated and the "sealed scroll" suddenly becomes readable. It is understandable that Isaiah's sealed scroll and its mysterious moment of hermeneutical activation became an important motif in the early development of apocalyptic literature, which was also preoccupied with the technology of writing and the role of scribes in transmitting teaching. In the apocalyptic visions of Daniel, written between the years 167 and 164 BCE, two references to sealing visions that make little sense in the narrative present but will make sense in the distant future (Dan 8:26, 9:24) and two descriptions of sealed scrolls that transmit ancient predictions to a much later audience (12:4, 9) draw their imagery from Isa 29:11–12.[10] Likewise, the contemporaneous *Animal Apocalypse* from the anthology *1 Enoch* also describes "sealed scrolls" that are opened as part of God's eschatological judgment (*1 Enoch* 89:68–77; 90:19–20; cf. Dan 12:1, 4, 9).[11] Descriptions of Isaiah writing prophecies and sealing them for an ambiguous future time, along with the vague eschatological mentions of "that day" and "latter days" throughout the book of Isaiah (e.g., 2:2), proved tantalizing to apocalyptic readers. Later Christian apocalypses such as Revelation would develop the motif of the sealed scroll, opened at the end of time (Rev 5:1–5).

Often, Jewish readers understood the content of Isaiah's sealed scroll to be the Torah itself ("teaching," or *tôrāh*, is used in 8:16), which was paired with the rare word *tĕ'ûdāh* ("testimony," also 8:20). The

---

9   See Eva Mrozcek, "Without Torah and Scripture," *Hebrew Studies* 60 (2020): 97–122.
10   Blenkinsopp, *Opening the Sealed Book: Interpretations of the Book of Isaiah in Late Antiquity* (Grand Rapids, MI: Eerdmans, 2006), 1–27.
11   See Antti Laato, *Message and Composition of the Book of Isaiah: An Interpretation in the Light of Jewish Reception History* (Berlin: de Gruyter, 2022), 148.

deuterocanonical book of *Jubilees*, written shortly after Daniel's apocalypses and the *Animal Apocalypse* of Enoch, describes itself as angelic dictation to Moses from "the heavenly tablets," which retell the stories of Genesis and Exodus. Thus, in addition to the written Torah of Moses (called "the Torah and the Commandment," cf. Exod 24:12), *Jubilees* introduces the idea of "heavenly tablets" that contain the "Torah and the Testimony," referring to Isa 8:16 (*Jubilees* 30:19–23). According to James VanderKam, this dual conception of Torah "gives insight into how the author understood his own composition in relation to the Torah."[12]

For the community at Qumran that produced the sectarian Dead Sea Scrolls, both *Jubilees* and apocalyptic material from Danielic and Enochian literature were extremely influential. The Damascus Document (CD), which seems to predate the foundation of the Qumran community, refers to the "book of the Torah that is sealed" (CD 5:2; cf. Isa 8:16; 29:11) as a solution to the interpretive problem of early Israelites practicing polygamy. According to CD, David was not able to read the "sealed scroll of the Torah" because it was inside the ark of the Covenant (cf. Exod 25:16), and was unavailable until Zadok later unsealed the scroll.[13] Among sectarian texts from DSS, 4QFlorilegium describes Isaiah himself as the "prophet for the last days" (line 15), and a fragmentary *pesher* text (4QpIsa^c=4Q163) interprets Isa 29:11–12 as a description of the Teacher of Righteousness' power to read and interpret scripture.[14] In the Great Isaiah Scroll (1QIsa^a), a system of later annotations overlay the book of Isaiah that give us tantalizing clues to how the covenanters read and interpreted the text. As Daniel Falk writes, these marks were "likely made by multiple readers, serving different purposes, and most often seem to mark passages of interest," and some markings are in "an intentionally esoteric script unique to a small number of sectarian scrolls found at Qumran, as well as some marginal markings."[15] Chapters 8–9 of Isaiah received a higher distribution of *paragraphoi* marks than other chapters (8:9, 11, 16, 19; 9:2,

---

[12]   James VanderKam, "Psalm 90 and Isaiah 65 in Jubilees 23," pages 73–86 in *Revealed Wisdom: Studies in Apocalyptic in Honour of Christopher Rowland*, ed. J. VanderKam (Leiden: Brill, 2014), 73.

[13]   Timothy Lim, "The Alleged Reference to the Tripartite Division of the Hebrew Bible," *Revue de Qumrân* 20 (2001): 23–37, 30.

[14]   Latto, *Message and Composition of the Book of Isaiah*, 148–149.

[15]   Daniel K. Falk, "In the Margins of the Dead Sea Scrolls," pages 10–38 in *Bible as Notepad: Tracing Annotations and Annotation Practices in Late Antique and Medieval Biblical Manuscripts*, ed. L. I. Lied and M. Maniaci (Berlin: de Gruyter, 2018), 18, 11.

7), suggesting interpretive interest, and it seems to highlight "material easily read in a sectarian manner.... Moreover, the passage most conducive to a sectarian reading in this context—Isa. 8,16 ('Bind up the testimony...')—is additionally marked by a marginal sign in the Cryptic A script, which is almost certainly a sectarian reader's mark," while 8:16–18 is also lined out as a separate section of the text with 20 mm of space to set it apart.[16] At Qumran, it appears as though, for the covenanters, the time of unsealing had arrived—an eschatological prediction found repeated in the book of Isaiah.

In early and medieval Jewish tradition, the theme of the loss and recovery of scripture was an important trope, in which the "sealing" of *tôrāh* in Isa 8:16 and 29:11 played an important part.[17] A story about the temporary loss of Torah drawing from Isa 8:16–17 and 29:11–12 appears in a number of ancient and medieval sources from the third through the tenth centuries CE, from *Genesis Rabbah* (42:3) to the Talmud (*y. Sanh.* 10:2, *b. Sanh.* 103b) and the medieval midrashic compilation *Tanna Devrei Eliyahu* (compiled in c. 950 CE).[18] According to these stories, King Ahaz suppressed worship of Yhwh in the Jerusalem temple and "sealed the Torah" by forbidding its study, citing Isa 8:16 ("bind up the testimony, seal the Torah," cf. 2 Chron 28:24). According to *Tanna Devei Eliyahu*, "In the reign of Ahaz king of Judah, words of Torah were so accessible that they were like living teachers. Hence, Ahaz set to and sealed up the Torah, having decreed that Israel were not to occupy themselves with it, as Isaiah intimates."[19] This anxiety of passing down written tradition, which both extended the voice of the ancient speaker and yet was vulnerable to displacement, sealing, and destruction, is palpable in both Christian and Jewish discussions of scripture, and Isa 8:16 and 29:11 provided a scriptural space for this reflection to occur.

Other interpreters focused on the possibility that Jews might lose familiarity with Torah of their own volition. In his comments on Isa 8:16, Rashi (1040–1105 CE) focuses on the necessity of commitment to study scripture, interpreting the word *tĕ'ûdāh* as "warning": "Bind my warning and seal the Torah on the heart of my disciples.... And if you claim that

---

[16] Falk, "In the Margins," 13.

[17] See Mroczek, "Without Torah."

[18] Jacob Neusner, *Genesis Rabbah: The Judaic Commentary to the Book of Genesis: A New American Translation, Vol. 2, Parashiyyot Thirty-Four through Sixty-Seven on Genesis 8:15 to 18:9* (Atlanta, GA: Scholars Press, 1985), 102–103; William G. Braude and Israel J. Kapstein, eds., *Tanna Debe Eliyyahu: The Lore of the School of Elijah* (Philadelphia: Jewish Publication Society, 1997), 400.

[19] Braude and Kapstein, *Tanna Debe Eliyyahu*, 400.

the word 'binding' does not apply to the study of the Torah, it definitely applies, as it is said: 'Bind them always upon your heart' (Prov 6:21)."[20] The influential early modern Talmudist Elijah ben Solomon Zalman, known as the Vilna Gaon (1720–1797), interpreted Proverbs 7:19–20 as a warning against the "evil inclination" that tempts people to avoid Torah study and the observance of the commandments, by way of Isa 8:16: "The Torah is now bound up and sealed, says the Evil Inclination; even if you exert yourself and struggle, you will be unable to understand it (see Isa 8:16)."[21] For the seventeenth-century scholar Isaac ben Solomon Gabbai, the warning of Isaiah went beyond the Torah and Tanakh: "those who learn [the Mishnah] in a small volume without commentary is as one who reads in "a book that is sealed," referencing Isa 29:11–12.[22] And the eighteenth-century Rabbi David ben Naphtali Fränkel, one of the first commentators on the entire Jerusalem Talmud, titled his commentary *Korban ha-Edah*, "the communal sacrifice," which was intended "as an allusion to the desire to open up a hitherto more or less inaccessible text to the understanding of the people: to 'bring near' (*korban*) the bound-up testimony (*te'uda*; see Isa. 8:16) to the congregation ('*eda*)."[23]

Early Christian interpreters (*c.* 100–450 CE) who stressed the displacement of meaning in Isa 8:16 and 29:11–12 equated the "sealed book" with Christian scripture, which is not comprehensible unless one is a proper "disciple" (8:16). According to third-century Alexandrian scholar Origen, "What is true of Isaiah [29:11–12] is true of every book of the Bible; it can be opened only by the Word who closed it ... and when he opens it, the meaning will be clear."[24] Like Rashi and the Vilna Gaon, Origen fretted about the possibility of losing what had been only recently opened: "I fear that out of excessive negligence or dullness of heart, the divine books will not only be veiled but also sealed [2 Cor 3:15; Isa 29:11]."[25] Jerome (*c.* 345–420) developed this motif by referencing

[20] See Sawyer, *Isaiah Through the Centuries*, 63.
[21] Eliezer Ginsburg, *Mishlei: Proverbs, Volume 1* (Brooklyn, NY: Menorah Publications, 1998), 139.
[22] Marvin J. Heller, *The Seventeenth Century Hebrew Book: An Abridged Thesaurus, Volume 1* (Leiden: Brill, 2010), 567.
[23] Alexander Altmann, *Moses Mendelssohn: A Biographical Study*, (Oxford: The Littman Library of Jewish Civilization, 1973), 13–14.
[24] Robert Louis Wilken with Angela Russell Christman and Michael J. Hollerich, eds. and trans., *Isaiah: Interpreted by Early Christian Medieval Commentators* (Grand Rapids, MI: Eerdmans, 2007), 246;
Matthew R. Crawford, "Scripture as 'One Book': Origen, Jerome, and Cyril of Alexandria on Isaiah 29:11," *Journal of Theological Studies* 64 (2013): 137–153.
[25] Wilken with Christman and Hollerich, *Isaiah*, 246.

the sealed scrolls of Revelation 5:1–5 and the Ethiopian eunuch in Acts 8:26–40.[26] Theodoret of Cyrus (393–457), Cyril of Alexandria (c. 376–444), and the medieval Byzantine monk Symeon the New Theologian (949–1022) all followed Origen's mode of interpretation, noting that the Holy Spirit enabled the understanding of what had previously been incomprehensible.[27] Martin Luther (1483–1546) and John Calvin (1509–1564) agreed with these interpreters, though they both understood the sealed message to relate to their own recent reforms and what they understood to be the potentially impending end of the world.[28]

Methodist leader Charles Wesley's 1740 hymn "Come Holy Ghost, Our Hearts Inspire" includes a stanza inspired by Isa 29:11 and the tradition of interpretation initiated by Origen: "Come, Holy Ghost, for, moved by thee/ thy prophets wrote and spoke/ unlock the truth, thyself the key/ unseal the sacred book." The English poet Henry Attwell published a collection of poems in 1856, one of which was titled "The Parson."[29] It is spoken by the character of a lonely, isolated pastor who is "the world forgetting" and also "by the world forgot"; he sits alone by the dying firelight at sunset digging through ancient books for "gems and flowers both rich and rare" of spiritual knowledge. The parson proclaims: "Bind up the testimony, seal the law, proclaim the Gospel glorious – without flaw, wrinkle, or spot, or shadow of a stain..."[30] The isolation of the religious devotee in early-modern England was, to Attwell, akin to being bound up and sealed, a relic from a religious world that was quickly disappearing. Other Christians who had experienced the loss of cultural and social dominance interpreted Isaiah in other ways: Abraham Kuyper, Prime Minister of the Netherlands and prominent theologian at the turn of the twentieth century, cautioned European Christians not to protest or fight the secularization of European politics and culture: "[Listen to] this call of Isaiah: 'Bind up the testimony; seal the teaching' (Is 8:16). That is, when a nation as a whole can no longer be the instrument for expressing your confession and life, create your own instrument for your Christian life..."[31]

Minoritized Christian communities have engaged Isa 8:16 and 29:11 in slightly different ways, such as Mozarabic Christians in

---

[26]   Wilken with Christman and Hollerich, *Isaiah*, 247.
[27]   Wilken with Christman and Hollerich, *Isaiah*, 248.
[28]   See Sawyer, *Isaiah Through the Centuries*, 63.
[29]   Henry Attwell, *Poems* (Leiden: P.H. van den Heuvell, 1856), 13–14.
[30]   Attwell, *Poems*, 14.
[31]   Abraham Kuyper, *On the Church*, ed. and trans. H. Van Dyke, N. Kloosterman, T. Rester, and A. Vreugdenhil (Bellingham, WA: Lexham Press, 2016), 227.

Muslim-ruled medieval Spain, who sang these verses between the mid-eighth and late fifteenth centuries in their regional liturgy. A canticle consisting of the words of Isa 8:16–9:8, known as *"Liga testimonium,"* is the second canticle listed in the eleventh-century Mozarabic psalter (Madrid 1001), perhaps reflecting the need to conserve teachings and practices for future generations in the face of political, cultural, and social pressure to assimilate.[32] Similarly, enslaved Christian African Americans in the eighteenth and nineteenth centuries also practiced and transmitted their minoritized religious culture through now famous songs, some cryptic and "sealed" to outsiders, including one spiritual recorded in the autobiography of the self-emancipated woman Harriet Jacobs. As literary scholar R. J. Ellis remarks, "these verses seem to derive from a traditional African American folk song ... drawing extensively upon the Bible, for example, Isaiah: 29:11."[33] Similarly, an early twentieth-century Catholic priest serving in New Orleans, Fr. John E. Burke, employed Isa 29:11 to explain why Black priests would be much more effective than white priests in serving the needs of the Black community: whites "live next door to the negro, and yet he is like a sealed book [Isa 29:11]. His lips are closed to the white man. It is only a colored priest who could know all about him."[34]

New American religious movements that emerged in the modern period often referred to the "sealed book" of revelation described in Isa 8:16 and 29:11 when discussing their novel interpretations and teachings. For example, the founder of the Seventh-day Adventist Church, Ellen Gould White (1827–1915), claimed to have received visions and dreams, which she described in her voluminous prophetic writings. One of the first Seventh-day Adventist preachers, John Norton Loughborough, wrote an influential first-hand account of the beginning of the movement, which he described as "a people engaged in restoring the seal to God's law ... [White's] instructions do not come in to give any new revelation to take the place of Scripture..."[35] In this interpretation, the sealed scriptures emphasize continuity of revelation: are

---

[32] James Mearns, *The Canticles of the Christian Church Eastern and Western in Early and Medieval Times* (Cambridge: Cambridge University Press, 1914), 71.

[33] Harriet Ann Jacobs, *Incidents in the Life of a Slave Girl*, ed. R. J. Ellis (Oxford: Oxford University Press, 2015 [=1861]), 233–234.

[34] Donald E. DeVore, *Defying Jim Crow: African American Community Development and the Struggle for Racial Equality in New Orleans, 1900–1960* (Baton Rouge: Louisiana State University Press, 2015), 69.

[35] John Norton Loughborough, *The Great Second Advent Movement: Its Rise and Progress* (Nashville, TN: Southern Publishing Association, 1905), 301.

exactly the same as the ones White revealed in her prophecies—such as the special holiness of the seventh day, the Sabbath.

DISPLACED JUDGMENT: THE REBELLIOUS PEOPLE

Another potential emphasis of interpreters who read Isa 8:16 and 29:11 concerns the larger literary context, in which God severely criticizes Isaiah's contemporaries, especially privileged residents of Jerusalem who use their power for their own gain and disregard the prophetic witness of Isaiah (cf. 5:1–30). In both Isa 8:16–17 and 29:11–13, the failure to comprehend the prophetic message, symbolized as a scroll, is proof of waywardness.

The Old Greek translation of the book of Isaiah shows that the use of *tôrāh* in 8:16 was understood even in the third century BCE as a reference to Mosaic Law, allowing readers to connect religious observance and obedience with the ability to interpret scripture. The Old Greek of Isa 8:16 reads as follows: "Then the ones who seal up the law in order not to learn will be revealed."[36] While the entire ancient Greek translation of Isaiah demonstrates a concern for the Mosaic Law, Chapter 8 in particular was interpreted as conversation in which Jews argue that gentiles must worship Yhwh and observe the Torah commandments. The translator seems to have misread the Hebrew word for "testimony" (*tw'dh*) as the similar word "to know" (*yd'*) and "among my disciples" (*blmdy*) as the phrase "that they might not learn" (*bly lmd*). Combined with the Old Greek rendering of 8:20 ("He gave the law, however, as a help"), the translation focuses on the consequences of ignoring (or "sealing") the Torah's commandments. Setting aside the probably intentional misreadings, the point of OG Isaiah agrees, at least in part, with Isaiah's emphasis on the misunderstanding of his initial audience (Isa 6:9–10). Likewise, *Targum Pseudo-Jonathan*, an Aramaic translation of Isaiah (*c.* 1100 CE, though incorporating much earlier material), similarly explains that the Torah has been sealed, and thus hidden, from those who do not wish to learn it. In both of these examples, the content of the message is taken to be well known, even obvious, but the obstinacy of the "rebellious people" (30:9) has rendered the written material a "witness forever" against them (30:8). The identity of these symbolically illiterate interlocutors, however, is what is displaced: Isaiah's contemporaries are replaced by a litany of "others" who seemingly refuse to understand.

---

[36] See J. Ross Wagner, "Identifying 'Updated' Prophecies in Old Greek (OG) Isaiah: Isaiah 8:11–16 as a Test Case," *JBL* 126 (2007): 251–269.

Many Jewish and Christian scholars have used Isa 29:11 in particular to criticize their rhetorical opponents hyperbolically as being functionally illiterate. Maimonides (1138–1204), for example, used this text often to rebut interpreters who read scripture differently. After being criticized for his allegorical understanding of Isa 11 in his treatise on resurrection, Maimonides argued that his interpretation is similar to many respected Jewish commentators from the past. Citing Isa 11:9, Maimonides asks if it seems likely that any "intelligent person" would expect "during our own times" to find a lion who "repents and knows what he needs to know of his Creator, and knows that he should not injure, and repent and eat straw?" If you could find this person, Maimonides concludes, then the following Scriptural phrase would be fulfilled: "And the vision of all this is become unto you as the words of a sealed book, etc. [Isa 29:11]."[37] What Maimonides means is that a person with these expectations would not be able to interpret the book—that is, the person who can technically read cannot really understand what they are reading. In conclusion, he writes, "the Messianic era will not differ from the order of creation."[38] Soon after Maimonides' death, the European Jewish community – long considered the preeminent experts in medicine among European Christians – began to reject the study and practice of medicine because of newly strict rabbinical arguments about the usefulness of science and medical research. In response, the Provençal Jewish astronomer and physician Jacob ben Makhir ibn Tibbon (c. 1236–1304) argued that scientific research and the dialectical approach of Scholastic thought were Jewish inventions, but that "exile and oppression" had separated Jews from their own intellectual heritage: Those "learned in the Torah" offered "words concerning the profane sciences [that are] like 'the words of a sealed book'..."[39] And in eighteenth-century England, Jewish leader Abraham ben Naphtali Tang used the same text to excoriate what he thought to be the worthless rabbinical leadership of his day.[40] Likewise, the contemporary poet Robert Harris refashions Isa 29:11–14 as a critique of the

---

[37] Moses Maimonides, *Moses Maimonides' Treatise on Resurrection*, trans. and ed. Fred Rosner (Lanham, MD: Rowman & Littlefield, 1997), 37.

[38] Maimonides, *Treatise on Resurrection*, 38.

[39] Luis Garcia-Ballester, Lola Ferre, and Eduard Feliu, "Jewish Appreciation of Fourteenth-Century Scholastic Medicine," *Osiris* 6 (1990): 85–117, 97–100.

[40] David B. Ruderman, *Jewish Enlightenment in an English Key Anglo-Jewry's Construction of Modern Jewish Thought* (Princeton: Princeton University Press, 2018), 116.

hypocrisy and senselessness of contemporary culture in his poem "Isaiah by Kerosene Lantern Light."[41]

Christian readers have often understood Isa 29:11–12 to refer to the refusal of Jews to accept Jesus as the Messiah, thus participating in a broader anti-Jewish supersessionist theology that sought to displace Jews as the people of God. Many Christians before the early fifth century who read the Septuagint, a Christian revision of the Old Greek version, took the polemical verses about the "law" (Isa 8:16, 20) as a reference to the Jews. Hippolytus of Rome (c. 175–235 CE), for example, claimed that the symbolically illiterate in Isa 29:11–12 referred to the Pharisees in the Gospels, and thus his contemporary Jews by extension (*Comm. Dan.* 4.33), drawing on Paul's use of Isa 8–9 in 2 Cor 3:14–4:8. A vast number of famous Christian interpreters, such as Jerome, Cyril, Eusebius, Isidore of Seville, Thomas Aquinas, Martin Luther, and John Calvin have included this interpretation in their comments on the text.[42] During the period of the Inquisition, Castilian Bishop Alonso de Espina (c. 1412–1464) wrote the apologetic treatise *Fortalitium Fidei*, which focused on arguing with Jews, Muslims, and other "heretics." In *Fortalitium*, Alonso argued that Jewish unbelief was the result of free will, and thus any punishment for disbelief was deserved: "they have passed 1460 years from his birth, and they have paid attention to see how the prophecies are already fulfilled in the curse of the said scripture: *bind the testimony*..."[43]

Other readers who focused on the rebellious and disobedient ones have instead seen the unsealing of the message as the remedy to their situation. The medieval Jewish Iberian poet Shelomo ibn Gabriol (c. 1021–1058), in the poetic prologue to his Hebrew grammar, wrote about those "Lacking all vision, living far from their Law, they couldn't fathom the simplest inscription [Isa 29:11] ... My Lord, who could save the blind in their drowning? Who could bring their ship into port?" The poet finally understands that it is his responsibility to help save his own people who have lost their way because they cannot read and understand their Law—by teaching them Hebrew through writing a grammar, through

---

[41] Robert Atwan and Laurance Weider, eds., *Chapters Into Verse: A Selection of Poetry in English Inspired by the Bible from Genesis Through Revelation* (Oxford: Oxford University Press, 2000), 196–197.

[42] Sawyer, *Isaiah Though the Centuries*, 62,114; Thomas Aquinas, *Commentary on Isaiah*, trans. L. St. Hilaire (Steubenville, OH: Emmaus Academic, 2021), 3.290.

[43] Rosa Vidal Doval, *Misera Hispania Jews and Conversos in Alonso de Espina's Fortalitium Fidei* (Oxford: The Society for the Study of Medieval Languages and Literature, 2013), 99.

which the poet is "yearning to forge through this book of our grammar a zone of repair for the language of Cain..." and thus using poetry and language instruction as a tool to repair the world.[44] Percy Bysshe Shelley, the nineteenth-century English Romantic poet, saw the liberating power of language working in Isa 29:11 in a very different way. Shelley reacted to the Peterloo Massacre of 1819 by working on a volume of "popular songs wholly political, & destined to awaken & direct the imagination of the reformers." As an avowed atheist, Shelley declared in his poem "Sonnet: England in 1819" that the religion of the corrupt, dying king and parasitic royals is merely "a book sealed." This was also a covert response to John Taylor Coleridge's review of Shelley's earlier work, in which Coleridge called the Bible "a sealed book to a proud spirit" such as Shelley; thus Shelley's response was that the true apocalypse is imminent, when the old order breaks apart and state religion crumbles—with the resurrection of liberty to come afterwards.[45]

Some readers of Isa 8:16 and 29:11 have understood themselves, or their own experiences and embodiments of trauma, to be the opponents referenced in Isaiah's diatribes. Isaiah's claim that God is "hiding" the divine presence from "the house of Jacob" (8:17) "is a theological theme much discussed in post-holocaust Jewish literature."[46] One survivor of a concentration camp who escaped in 1944, Don Pagis, wrote several poems that dealt with themes emanating from Isa 29:11–12.[47] Many of Pagis' poems "concern the sealed consciousness of those who have undergone trauma," which "will forever inflict the horrors of the past upon the survivor."[48] Pagis' brief poem "Written in Pencil in the Sealed Railway-Car," a poem written for Holocaust Remembrance Day, evokes the desperate last thoughts of someone on their way to a concentration camp. Tuvia Rübner, Pagis' friend, noted that "the quasi-rhyme *katuv-hatum* [written-sealed] leads to Isaiah 29:11," and Shahar Bram deepens the interpretive connection: "Consciousness is truly a sealed book to one that is learned—its owner ... [Pagis' poetry offers] the testimony of the survivor with a captive consciousness."[49] The poem, a meditation

---

[44]   Peter Cole, *The Dream of the Poem: Hebrew Poetry from Muslim and Christian Spain, 950–1492* (Princeton: Princeton University Press, 2007), 76–77.

[45]   Morton D. Paley, *Apocalypse and Millennium in English Romantic Poetry* (Oxford: Oxford University Press, 1999), 233–234.

[46]   Sawyer, *Isaiah Through the Centuries*, 63.

[47]   See Shahar Bram, "Remembering the Past and the Trap of Consciousness: Dan Pagis and the Photograph," *Prooftexts* 32 (2012): 357–380.

[48]   Bram, "Remembering the Past," 375.

[49]   Bram, "Remembering the Past," 375.

on the brutality that began with Cain and continues unabated, seems to propose a deep understanding of suffering and yet ends in midthought, interrupted by the violence that nearly ended Pagis' own life—and which frustrates any interpretation of humanity, rendering us a "sealed book" incapable of making sense.

DISPLACED IDENTITIES: THE FUTURE DISCIPLES

In Isa 8:16, a cryptic reference to "my disciples" brings into view both the initial audience who preserved Isaiah's unpopular teachings and those later recipients who revisited the preserved writings, understood themselves as living at the time of the fulfillment of the promises of blessing indicated in Isaiah's prophecies (such as 2:1–4), and continued to pass them down to later generations. Throughout history, many readers have sought a new identity for both the speaker and the implied audience for 8:16 and 29:11 in order to make sense of the texts in their own contexts. Many Christian readers, for instance, have simply assumed that the implied speaker of all prophetic texts in the Old Testament is Jesus; this typological hermeneutical strategy can be found even in the pages of the New Testament. Heb 2:10–13, for example, quotes Isa 8:18 and understands it as a declaration from Christ about the creation of a new family out of his followers. Drawing on the overwhelmingly Christological interpretation of Isa 7:14 in Christian tradition, and the reference to "Immanuel" in 8:8, many Christian interpreters understood 8:16 as an expression of the mystery of Christ, such as Nicholas of Lyra (1270–1349) and Marcus Marulus (aka Marko Marulić; 1450–1524).[50]

Other Christians, however, understood the "sealed scroll" in Isa 29:11 to refer to Mary, the mother of Jesus. Jacob of Serugh, a fifth-century Syriac theologian who lived on the Euphrates river, provides an early example of this interpretation: Jacob explains that Mary was the sealed scroll because in her womb was the Word, in which "were hidden mysteries of the Son and his depth," from which "forgiveness was sent out to the whole world."[51] Eastern Orthodox Christians have often referred to Mary as the "sealed book"; Maximos of Simonopetra (b. 1961) writes that Mary's grief at the foot of the cross, watching her son die, held "all the pain of motherhood" in which the "seals of

---

50 Franz Posset, *Marcus Marulus and the Biblia Latina of 1489: An Approach to His Biblical Hermeneutics* (Göttingen: Vandenhoeck & Ruprecht, 2013), 136.

51 James Puthuparampil, *The Mariological Thought of Mar Jacob of Serugh (451–521)* (Piscataway, NJ: Gorgias Press, 2012), 198–199.

her being are torn apart, rent like the veil of the temple."[52] Roman
Catholic Christians have also understood Mary, usually depicted as an
avid reader, as the "sealed book": Richard of Saint-Laurent (c. 1200–
1250), commenting on Matthew 1:1, wrote that Mary herself was the
"book of the generation of Jesus Christ," the great tablet upon which
Isaiah was commanded to write (Isa 8:1), also the sealed scroll that
John saw (Rev 5:1) which contains all knowledge necessary for salvation, and the sealed book (Isa 29:11) that was, according to Richard,
kept by the side of the ark—another symbol for Mary, who held the
presence of God inside her. Richard explains that Mary was "sealed"
because she must be revealed: she is not remarkable to those who
cannot perceive God's presence within.[53] In medieval and early modern Christian Annunciation scenes, Mary is often depicted as holding
or seated in front of a closed book, which is a subtle reference to Isa
29:11.[54]

While Isaiah does not appear in the Qur'an, Muslim interpreters
have been fascinated with the book of Isaiah at least since the time
of Ibn Ishāq (704–767 CE), who understood Muhammad as the prophetic figure described in Isa 42:2–7 and 40:6.[55] Isaiah also featured
prominently in the apologetic discourse of early Islam, in which scholars rebutted Christian criticisms of Muhammad's teachings, because
Isaiah's prophecies were seen to predict Muhammad's activity more
accurately than Jesus'. For example, many Muslim scholars such as Ibn
Qutayba (828–889), Ibn Rabbān al-Ṭabarī (838–870), and Ibn al-Layth
(c. 850–902) understood Isa 21:6–7 to predict the coming of Jesus on a
donkey and Muhammad on a camel, which became "one of the very
first artistic depictions showing Muhammad's face," occurring in "an
illustrated manuscript of al-Bīrūnī's Chronology of Ancient Nations."[56]

Isaiah was also featured in the Muslim tradition of "Stories of the
Prophets" (Qiṣaṣ al-Anbiyāʾ), wherein much of the influential author
Ibn Rabbān al-Ṭabarī's treatment of Isaiah derives from Ben Sira

---

[52]   M. Constas, *The Art of Seeing: Paradox and Perception in Orthodox Iconography*
       (Alhambra, CA: Sebastian Press, 2014), 127–128.
[53]   Rachel Fulton Brown, *Mary and the Art of Prayer: The Hours of the Virgin in Medieval
       Christian Life and Thought* (New York: Columbia University Press, 2017), 255.
[54]   As seen in an early thirteenth-century Annunciation relief from Tuscany in the
       Cloisters collection (60.140), Lisbeth Castelnuovo-Tedesco and Jack Soultanian,
       Italian Medieval Sculpture in the Metropolitan Museum of Art and the Cloisters
       (New York: Metropolitan Museum of Art, 2010).
[55]   Martin Whittingham, *A History of Muslim Views of the Bible: The First Four
       Centuries* (Berlin: de Gruyter, 2021), 63, 79–80.
[56]   Whittingham, *Muslim Views of the Bible*, 92–94.

48:17–25, dealing with the flight of Sennacherib's army from Jerusalem and the healing of King Hezekiah.[57] A description in the Qur'an (7:157–158) of Muhammad as "the Messenger, the unlettered prophet they find described in the Torah," and a *hadith* from al-Bukhari (810–870; *hadith* no. 1814) led many Muslims to understand that Muhammad was illiterate, providing further evidence of the miraculous nature of the written Qur'an.[58] Muhammad's ability to read a "sealed scroll" even when illiterate was understood as a fulfillment of Isa 29:11–12, which positions the inability to read as a positive, rather than a negative, feature of Isaiah's interlocutors. Until the present day, Isa 29:11–12 functions as an important rhetorical touchstone in Muslim dialogue and debate with both Christians and Jews.[59] Muslim interpreters have also understood Isa 8:16 as a prophecy describing how Muhammad "will bind up the testimony and the law ... he took every possible measure to preserve the Quran in its pristine purity and he sealed the law. The Holy Quran bears testimony to this in these verses: 'He is the Apostle of Allah and the seal of the prophets' (S 33:40)."[60]

Another example of the effective displacement of the presumed initial speaking and listening subjects of Isa 8:16 and 29:11 comes from the community of the Church of Latter-day Saints, also known as the Mormons. Joseph Smith himself (1805–1844), the founding prophet of the movement, referenced Isa 8:16 as he offered a prayer of dedication of the first Mormon temple in Kirtland, Ohio, in 1836, which he claimed was revealed to him. One sentence of the prayer reads as follows: "O Lord, deliver thy people from the calamity of the wicked; enable thy servants to seal up the law, and bind up the testimony, that they may be prepared against the day of burning."[61] Smith's Book of Mormon is filled with references to Isaiah, but the book of 2 Nephi in particular engages Isaiah closely.[62] As David Wright explains, 2 Nephi 26–27 is

---

57 Whittingham, *Muslim Views of the Bible*, 100–101.
58 Sebastian Günther, "Muhammad, the Illiterate Prophet: An Islamic Creed in the Qur'an and Qur'anic Exegesis," *Journal of Qur'anic Studies* 4 (2002): 1–26.
59 John Chesworth, "Polemical Revival: Attacking the Other's Texts," pages 355–378 in *Interreligious Hermeneutics in Pluralistic Europe Between Texts and People*, ed. David Cheetham, Judith Gruber, Oddbjørn Leirvik, and Ulrich Winkler (Amsterdam: Adophi, 2011), 372.
60 Ali Musa Raza, *Muhammad in the Quran* (Delhi: Idarah-i Adabiyat-i, 1980), 13.
61 Brigham Henry Roberts, *History of the Church of Jesus Christ of Latter-Day Saints: Period 1, History of Joseph Smith, the Prophet, Volume 2* (Salt Lake City, UT: Deseret News, 1904), 423.
62 David P. Wright, "Joseph Smith's Interpretation of Isaiah in the Book of Mormon," *Dialogue: A Journal of Mormon Thought* 31 (1998): 181–206.

an extended repurposing of Isa 29:11–12 wherein "the major innovation in Smith's interpretation of Isaiah 29 is turning the simile of a sealed book in vv. 11–12 into a prediction of the [Book of Mormon] and relating it to an experience that his aid and supporter had with Charles Anthon, a professor of classical studies and literature at Columbia College."[63] Smith's associate brought copies of the Book of Mormon to New York in 1828, and Prof. Anthon agreed that some of the writing was in ancient Egyptian; Anthon asked him to bring the original tablets, and was informed that some were still sealed, to which Anthon replied, "I cannot read a sealed book," inadvertently quoting Isa 29:12. Second Nephi 27 rewrites Isa 29:11–12 as a predictive prophecy of that very conversation as a means of validating the Book of Mormon itself; as Wright explains, "Smith's reuse of Isaiah is not new, but follows an age-old impulse, found even among many of the religious thinkers of and just prior to Smith's time, as we have seen, to reapply the prophetic works to the reader's own time."[64]

CONCLUSION

This brief overview of just a few verses of the book of Isaiah merely scratches the surface of its rich and variegated reception history. Other studies can offer more information about important aspects that this chapter has overlooked, such as the ancient text and influential medieval traditions that flow from the Martyrdom and Ascension of Isaiah.[65] Nevertheless, the example of Isa 8:16, 29:11, and 30:8 reveals a dense network of interpretation that spans both the globe and the thousands of years between Isaiah ben Amoz and the present day.

Reception history traces different readers' attempts to understand a text in many different circumstances. At times, these readers reveal hermeneutical capacities of ancient texts that are surprising to modern scholars—and at other times, readers simply twist and contort texts to make them say whatever they want. These are both common themes in the interpretation of sacred texts that have been displaced in time, space, and cultural context; they can only be engaged in contexts other than their contexts of production, can only be read by "other" audiences, and can only be rewritten in "other" languages, since no language remains static.

[63] Wright, "Joseph's Smith's Interpretation," 200–01.
[64] Wright, "Joseph's Smith's Interpretation," 203–04.
[65] Sawyer, *Isaiah Through the Centuries*, 3, 14.

Focusing on the divergent uses of Isa 8:16, 29:11, and 30:8 highlights the never-ending struggle to read, "unseal," and reactualize the enigmatic and effective words of the prophet, from the ancient world to the modern. Yet this exercise also reveals sharply polemical uses of scripture: Isa 8:16 and 29:11–12 were both polemical texts from the very beginning, since the prophet employs the metaphor of a "sealed scroll" to accuse his critical interlocutors of misunderstanding God's message and the prophet who bore them. Interpreters over the centuries have followed suit, using these texts to accuse others of metaphorical illiteracy and ignorance of divine matters.

As much as reception history offers the potential for mutual understanding and dialogue, it reveals a radical diversity in deeply held opinions, political commitments, moral imaginations, cultural assumptions, and religious convictions reflecting concrete differences that cannot be ignored. These differences often lead to conflicts, as the reception history of the texts in question demonstrate. Isaiah did not shy away from conflict with his interlocutors, and he often stated his conviction that these differences both mattered and could not be ignored. Yet Isaiah did not resort to force or violence to force his interlocutors to agree with him: Isaiah maintains that judgment, in that sense, is God's alone (Isa 3:13–15). Perhaps the rhetorical judgment of "sealed scrolls" and the hope that future readers may understand us—both encapsulated in the complex reception history of Isa 8:16, 29:11, and 30:8—might remind us of the tensions that result from holding on to the hope for mutual understanding while recognizing the inescapable reality of differences in interpretation.

FURTHER READING

Childs, Brevard S. *The Struggle to Understand Isaiah as Christian Scripture.* Grand Rapids, MI: Eerdmans, 2004.

Holladay, William L. *Unbound by Time, Isaiah Still Speaks.* Cambridge, MA: Cowley, 2002.

Laato, Antii. *Who Is the Servant of the Lord? Jewish and Christian Interpretations on Isaiah 53 from Antiquity to the Middle Ages.* Studies in Rewritten Bible 4. Winona Lake, IN: Eisenbrauns, 2012.

McGinnis, Claire Mathews, and Patricia K. Tull, eds. *"As Those Who Are Taught": The Interpretation of Isaiah from the LXX to the SBL.* SBL Symposium Series 27. Atlanta, GA: Society of Biblical Literature, 2006.

Porton, Gary. "Isaiah and the Kings: The Rabbis on the Prophet Isaiah." Pages 693–716 in *Writing and Reading the Scroll of Isaiah*, volume 2. Edited by C. C. Boyles and C. A. Evans. Leiden: Brill, 1997.

Sawyer, John F. A. *The Fifth Gospel: Isaiah in the History of Christianity*. Cambridge: Cambridge University Press, 1996.

Scherman, Nosson. *Isaiah: The Later Prophets with a Commentary Anthologized from the Rabbinic Writings*. Milstein Edition. New York: Mesorah, 2013.

Tiemeyer, Lena-Sofia, ed. *The Oxford Handbook of Isaiah*. Oxford: Oxford University Press, 2020.

Wilken, Robert L., ed. *Isaiah: Interpreted by Early Christian and Medieval Commentators*. Grand Rapids, MI: Eerdmans, 2007.

Scripture Index

Other Texts Index

Subject Index

For EU product safety concerns, contact us at Calle de José Abascal, 56–1°,
28003 Madrid, Spain or eugpsr@cambridge.org.

www.ingramcontent.com/pod-product-compliance
Ingram Content Group UK Ltd.
Pitfield, Milton Keynes, MK11 3LW, UK
UKHW020455240426
470322UK00016B/360